DIAMONDS

Foremost of all amongst the glittering race
Far India is the *Diamond's* native place;
Produced and found within the crystal mines,
Its native source in its pure lustre shines:
Yet though it flashes with the brilliant's rays
A steely tint the crystal still displays.
Hardness invincible which nought can tame,
Untouched by steel, unconquered by the flame;
But steeped in blood of goats it yields at length,
Yet tries the anvil's and the smiter's strength.

With these keen splinters armed, the artist's skill
Subdues all gems and graves them at his will.

Part of a poem probably composed by the Abbott Marbodus (Marboeuf) when master of the Cathedral School of Anjou from 1067 to 1081.

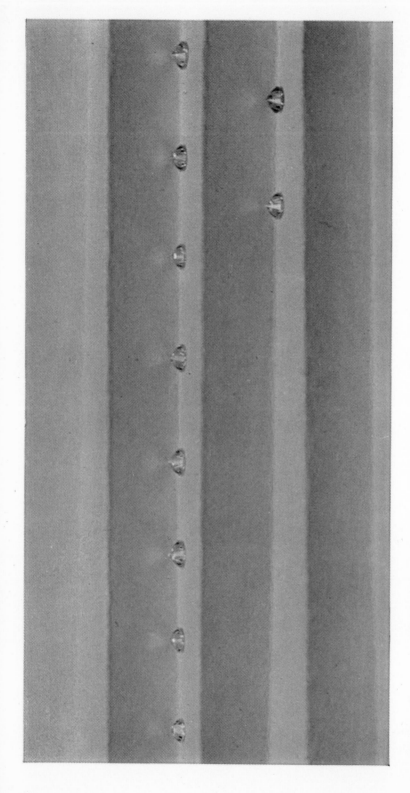

It is impossible to show on the printed page an accurate range of polished diamonds graded for colour and the object of this plate is to give some idea of the narrowness of the range of colour in "white" stones. The stones in the top row are Cape Series stones and range from about Crystal to Yellow or Dark Cape (see page 211). There are several grades whiter than the stone on the left. The two stones on the lower row are Brown Series. The stones are shown on a corrugated piece of white paper in a white light at about the angle that they should be graded by eye. The difficulties in reproducing the colours accurately are in the different colour values caused by the camera lighting, the film stock, the ink used in reproduction and finally the paper on which the reproduction is printed, since that also has a tint which is several grades below that of the finest white diamond. Photograph by Peter Parkinson, F.I.I.P., London.

DIAMONDS

by

Eric Bruton, F.G.A.

CHILTON BOOK COMPANY
Radnor, Pennsylvania

Contents

CONTENTS

Acknowledgments for photographs and related information

Grateful thanks are due for pictures to:
De Beers Consolidated Mines – the publicity and photographic staff.
Mr. Frank Beresford and Consolidated Diamond Mines of South-West Africa.
The Anglo-American Corporation.
The Diamond Research Laboratory, Johannesburg.
Mr. R. Webster of the London Gemmological Laboratory.
Dr. E. Gübelin, of Lucerne.
Mr. R. Liddicoat, Director of the G.I.A. Los Angeles Gemological Laboratory.
Mr. R. Crowningshield, Director of the New York Gemological Laboratory.
Mr. H. Tillander, of Helsinki.
Mr. J. T. McNish, of Cape Town.
A. Monnickendam Ltd.
Mr. D. McNeil, Editor of *Jeweler's Circular-Keystone*, U.S.A.
The Editor of *Retail Jeweller*, U.K.
The Editor of *Watchmaker, Jeweller and Silversmith*, U.K.
The Editor of *Industrial Diamond Review*, U.K.
The Secretary of the Gemmological Association of Great Britain.
The Industrial Diamond Information Bureau, London.

My thanks must also be extended to the following for the loan and sight of diamonds, without which this book could not have been written.
De Beers Consolidated Mines.
The Diamond Trading Company.
Diamond Research Laboratory.
Consolidated Diamond Mines of South-West Africa.
Mr. D. Whitehead, of Industrial Diamond Co. (Sales) Ltd.
Mr. Gordon Andrews, of the Gemmological Association of Great Britain.
Mr. Albert Monnickendam, senior, and Mr. Arthur Monnickendam.
Mr. B. W. Anderson, of the London Gemmological Laboratory.
Mr. A. R. Emerson, of Sir John Cass College.
Mr. D. Clark, of D. and P. Clark (Diamonds) Ltd.
Messrs D. Bucks and P. Propper of Polished Diamond Distributors, and many others.

PREFACE

This book is the result of an interest in diamonds that began with a course in gemmology many years ago at the old Chelsea Polytechnic where the first lecturers were Mr. Basil Anderson, director of the London Gemmological Laboratory, and Mr. Robert Webster, long a senior member of the laboratory staff.

It happened that in the 1950s I became Editor of *The Gemmologist*, now alas defunct, and also *Industrial Diamond Review*, which today flourishes under the umbrella of De Beers. Much later, through the urging of Mr. Norman Harper, chairman of the Gemmological Association of Great Britain, who had started in Birmingham the first course in gem diamonds in the world, I found myself running a parallel course at Sir John Cass College in London and in 1970 helped found a similar course at Barcelona University. Examinations for a diploma are held by the Gemmological Association of Great Britain and Professor S. Tolansky is the chief examiner.

Although some excellent books have been written on diamond with approaches ranging from very popular to very technical, there was still no single book that covered all or most of the aspects of gem diamonds, spanning the history of diamond digging and cutting, mining and recovery, cutting methods, grading and valuation, and identification of diamond and its simulants. The object of this book was to amend this omission in a style that could readily be understood by the layman as well as the serious student, as I have found on my 'diamond travels' that the diamond scene tends to be in an organized series of fairly tight compartments, so that, for example, the mining engineer has little information about the precious stones he is responsible for recovering, the geologist is hazy about the market-place, the retailer does not appreciate cutting and grading problems, and most of all, members of the general public do not appreciate that the possession of a diamond today, which is easy, has taken 4,000 years of endeavour – blood, toil, sweat and tears – to produce the modern brilliant-cut gem diamond.

There are very many people in addition to those already named who provided help and information. Of them my greatest thanks are due to Mr. Lionel Burke of De Beers Consolidated Mines in London, who made it possible for me to visit the principle diamond mines in the southern part of Africa to see and to ask my questions, a remarkable experience. Everywhere everyone was uninhibited with information. It is impossible to mention all by name but I must express particular thanks to Mr. Michael Grantham, who represents De Beers in Johannesburg, for his superb organization of visits to mines in four different countries.

In my present capacity of Editor and Publisher of *Retail Jeweller*, I have been fortunate in meeting many other people, too numerous unfortunately to mention by name, who have helped towards the eventual publication of this book.

Finally, my thanks are gratefully given to those who undertook the tiresome task of reading and criticizing the manuscript: Mr. Gordon Andrews, Secretary of the Gemmological Association of Great Britain, and various chapters in galley proof: Mr. Robert Webster, of the London Gemmological Laboratory; Mr. A. Monnickendam, Snr., principal of the cutters and polishers, A. Monnickendam Ltd.; Mr. Alan Jobbins, Chief Geologist, the Geological Museum; Mr. Howard Vaughan, of De Beers; Sir Samuel Fisher, Executive Vice-president of the London Diamond Bourse, Mr. Edmund Goldstein, Chairman of the London Diamond Club; and Mr. Herbert Tillander, Crown Jeweller, Helsinki, Finland, who is also Chairman of the Scandinavian Diamond Nomenclature Committee.

Finally my appreciation is especially due to Professor S. Tolansky for the difficult task he undertook of writing a foreword.

Great Bookham,   ERIC BRUTON
1970

FOREWORD

by Professor S. Tolansky, Department of Physics
Royal Holloway College (University of London)

Diamonds have attracted man's attention for thousands of years. The striking exceptional hardness of the stone called adamas (diamond) was recognized almost in prehistorical times and remarkably enough this unique hardness today plays a formidable part in modern industrial technology.

There has always been an exceptional dichotomy in the evolution of the use and exploitation of diamond. It started off being worn as a talisman, inducing strength and courage by virtue of its hardness, whilst at the same time, even in Biblical times, it was used as a hard tool for engraving and maybe for drilling too. Then as time progressed, by the early Middle Ages it began to be used by the wealthy and the great as a decorative gem, whilst at the same time its uses for glass engraving and glass cutting were developed side by side. By the early nineteenth century the use of diamond as a fiery decorative gem was widespread amongst those who could afford it, yet again its employ as a hard technical material was gathering momentum. Indeed it was certainly being used for rock drilling early in the eighteenth century, if not before this.

The twentieth century saw a great upsurge in this dichotomous use of diamond. Primarily this came about through the discovery of the great new mining sources on the African Continent. To this has been added the invention some fifteen years ago of the manufacture of a true synthetic diamond material suited for grinding wheels.

Now many millions of men and women wear diamonds, mainly, but not exclusively, in rings, brooches and watches and likewise almost the whole of engineering and electrical industries, light and heavy, use considerable numbers of diamond machine tools, somewhere along the production line; from the making of fine lamp bulb filaments, to the smoothing of airplane runways, from manufacture of watches to building of bridges, from making a tiny screw to the building of a mighty oil tanker.

All this fundamental dichotomy is gone into in a most thorough and scholarly manner by Mr. Bruton in this book on diamond which we most heartily welcome. The author is in a rare and strong position for surveying this dual function of diamond in modern society. He has had long experience in the editorial chair, of the production of two journals, the one devoted to diamond as a gem, the other devoted to diamond as an industrial weapon. He has long been familiar with the formidable bibliography in both fields. He has also acquired special knowledge of the extensive diamond mining industry and, to crown it all, he has a most lively interest in the historical evolution and development of the use, the extraction and the exploitation of that king of stones, the diamond. I have enjoyed reading this most attractively written yet very complete general account about diamond and I am convinced that any other reader will equally respond to the infectious enthusiasm of the author.

This book does not set out to deal with the admitted formidable technical complexities of current scientific research on atomic diamond structure, such researches as are concerned, amongst other things with crystal lattices, light absorption and emission, thermal and electrical conductivity, chemical and physical impurities, etching and so on. It will not frighten off the lay reader with any overload of scientific technologies. On the contrary to the student of gemmology and mineralogy, to the practising diamond cutter and polisher, indeed to the non-technically minded diamond merchant, this book should prove to be a boon and something to whet the appetite.

September 1970   S. TOLANSKY

CHAPTER ONE

Diamonds in History

Introduction

As long as about three thousand years ago, man bent down to pick up a glisten-ing pebble and by some chance found it to be different from other stones. From that time, diamond began to acquire magical powers and to be regarded with awe, worship and avarice. More recently it has become an object of extreme scientific curiosity.

Man began to collect diamonds, treasure them, build legends around them, trade in them, use them as tools, treat them as gems, raise loans with them, fight over them, and eventually to give them as symbols of love and trust. His early instinct to treat diamond as unique was true, because today probably more effort goes into discovering the nature of diamond than into research on any other material.

The desire for diamond because of its beauty as a gem, apart from its scientific and industrial uses, has not dimmed over the years but has become much more widespread. A century ago, the possession of a diamond was the prerogative of the rich alone. Since the discovery of huge deposits in Africa, and more recently diamond pipes in Russia, intensive mining and marketing of diamonds has brought them within reach of large sections of the populations of industrial countries, both as gems and in working tools.

Diamond is the hardest substance man has ever discovered and the purest that occurs in Nature. Although very highly prized as a gem, however, it is composed of one of the commonest substances on earth, ordinary carbon. Carbon is found in all living things, plants as well as animals, and in many rocks.

Diamond can be broken with the blow of a hammer, yet will penetrate steel by pressure. It is extremely durable, being able to withstand attack by the strongest acids and alkalis, yet is an unstable form of carbon and will burn or oxidize on the surface if dropped in a fire for a short time. It has a very high melting-point and will cut steel for long periods at near red heat. Yet heated to bright red it will catch fire and convert to carbon dioxide gas.

The Hardness of Diamond

The name 'diamond' is derived from the old French *diamant*, itself derived from the Latin and the Greek adamas, meaning 'unconquerable'. From the eighth century B.C., *adamas* was usually a name for iron or iron alloy, but Ovid may have intended it to mean diamond when he used it in the second half of the first century B.C.

The Roman philosopher, Pliny the Elder, wrote: 'These stones are tested upon the anvil, and will resist the blow to such an extent as to make the iron rebound and the very anvil split asunder.'

I

Fig. 1.1. *Jean Baptiste Tavernier, the French jeweller and traveller who made six trips of several years to the Orient buying and selling. Many famous Indian diamonds passed through his hands. His first trip was made in 1631 in his twenties.*

The belief persisted for centuries. In the year 1476, Swiss mercenaries found diamonds belonging to Charles the Bold, Duke of Burgundy, after the battle of Morat, and struck them with hammers and hatchets to discover whether they were genuine, with the result that they powdered.

Many fine diamond crystals were broken in the same belief by miners of the Indian mines from the fifteenth century to those of the early diamond diggings of South Africa in the last quarter of the nineteenth. It was said by the French jeweller and one of the first 'globe-trotters', Jean Baptiste Tavernier, after he visited the Indian mines in the seventeenth century, that some merchants knew the true facts (Fig. 1.1). They persuaded miners that stones they found were not diamond by breaking them with a hammer, then picked up the pieces after the disappointed miners had left.

'Diamond cut Diamond'

The truth is that, because diamond is the hardest known substance, it has relative brittleness. The two properties are different. Other materials are also brittle because they are hard, such as sewing needles and metal files. The eminent scientist Sir William Crookes used to demonstrate the hardness of diamond by placing a crystal between the jaws of a vice and tightening the vice. Diamond cannot be deformed plastically by normal forces, so the crystal penetrated the hardened steel jaws and did not break – an experiment that had been previously reported by Ibn Mansur in the thirteenth century.

One aspect of the hardness of diamond is, then, its extreme resistance to being deformed. Another is that it cannot be scratched except by other diamonds (and one man-made material called cubic boron azide). But it resists scratching by another diamond in some directions more than in others. A diamond used in one of the harder directions will therefore cut another diamond in one of the 'softer' directions. That, and how to find the hard and 'soft', was a secret kept for centuries by diamond cutters and engravers.

King Charles I of England knew something of this. The night before his execution in 1649, he wrote:

> 'With my own power my majesty they wound
> In the King's name the King's himself uncrowned
> So doth the dust destroy the diamond.'

Diamonds in Social History

The wearing of jewellery is as ancient a custom as any on record and appeared in early societies to be of primary importance after the seeking of food and shelter. It has been conjectured that the wearing of pretty stones was originally motivated by a desire to remember the spring with its promise of food and warmth, and later became the personal adornment a symbol of rank or wealth.

Large diamonds were badges of rank worn by rulers and also convenient portable wealth in the early days of India. Most of the historical diamonds that still exist are Indian, and all have had eventful and sometimes bloody histories. Tavernier brought a number of them to Europe.

The Koh-i-Nûr, or Mountain of Light, has the longest history of all famous diamonds as it was known to be in the possession of the Rajahs of Malwa as long ago as 1304 and was facetted no later than 1530 (Fig. 1.2). It is believed to have been set by the Mogul emperors in the famous Peacock Throne as one of the peacock's eyes. The other eye was the Akbar Shah diamond. The Persian Shah took the diamond when he invaded India and later it came into the hands of the 'Lion of the Punjab' who accepted it in return for military help that he never gave. Eventually it was taken by the East India Company against losses and presented to Queen Victoria.

The 410 carat Regent Diamond (Fig. 1.3) played a part in the French Revolution. It was one of the last big diamonds to be found in India, in 1701. It came to England and was named 'the Pitt', and the major part after recutting was resold to the Regent of France, when it acquired its current name. Later Marie Antoinette wore it and on 17th September, 1792, it was among the French Crown jewels that were stolen during the early stages of the French Revolution. Most of the treasures were quickly recovered but the Regent diamond did not come to light until fifteen months later when it was found in a hole in a beam of a Paris garret.

During the Directoire period, the Regent and other diamonds were pawned

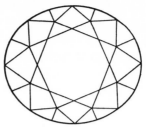

Fig. 1.2. *The Koh-i-Nûr diamond, as it was first cut about 1530, and* (centre) *was recut in 1862 in Amsterdam. The present weight is 108.93 carats, and it is set in the British State Crown.*

Fig. 1.3. *The Regent diamond, from the Indian Partial mine. It was once in England and was known as the Pitt. Now in the Louvre, in Paris, it was one of the last big diamonds to be found in India, in 1701.*

Fig. 1.4. *The Hope diamond, which is thought to be part of the Blue Tavernier from the Kollur mine in India, brought to Europe by Tavernier after he had bought it in 1642. The Hope is now in the Smithsonian Institution Museum in Washington.*

to a Berlin banker for four million francs to keep fourteen French armies in the field. It was redeemed and then used as guarantee for a loan from a Dutchman. After it was again recovered, Napoleon Bonaparte had it set in the hilt of a sword he carried when being proclaimed Emperor of France.

The Hope diamond, to which stories of tragedy have become attached, is supposed to have been part of the famous Blue Tavernier diamond brought to Europe by Tavernier. It was also stolen during the French Revolution, but never recovered. The 44½-carat Hope diamond (Fig. 1.4) is perhaps the largest of three parts into which the Blue Tavernier was cut. Hope's son lost his fortune after inheriting the stone. It was sold and eventually came into the hands of Mrs. Edward B. McLean, who lost her child in an accident, saw her family break up, lost her fortune, then committed suicide.

Diamonds' effect on social history has been mainly because they are possibly the greatest concentrated form of wealth which is negotiable almost anywhere. They have played a part in many upheavals and during recent world wars paid the way for the escape of refugees from totalitarian tyrannies.

From at least the fourth century B.C., India traded in diamonds, taxed them and exported them. There had long been trade between India and Babylon,

Mesopotamia, Syria, Israel, Egypt, Ceylon, and Arabian countries. Diamonds that reached the western part of the Roman Empire were prized for their magical powers, but Rome also re-exported them to China as tool bits set in iron holders for cutting jade and drilling pearls during the first five centuries A.D. There were no superstitions in China to deny this use and, even as tools, they were still regarded as presents fit for kings, according to the Chinese philosopher Lao-tse in the first century A.D.

The Arabs and Persians monopolized trade between the Roman Empire and East Asia and, during the Middle Ages, between Europe and East Asia, until the sea route to India was discovered. It appears that they retained for themselves many of the finest diamonds from India and sold the poorer and smaller ones. The earliest price list of diamonds that has been discovered was issued in the twelfth century by the Arab, Teifaschius.

Fig. 1.5. *An Indian engraved diamond, the Jahangir, which is supposed to have been suspended from the beak of the jewelled peacock of the Mogul Emperor's Peacock Throne.*

Diamond in Literature

It is difficult to isolate references to diamond in early literature because it is not known positively what certain names referred to. The word *jahalom* in the Bible, Exodus, Chap. 28, verse 18, instructing Moses to make a breastplate of judgement set with four rows of stones is translated in the revised edition as diamond, but had it been one it would have been bigger that the Koh-i-Nûr. A reference in Jeremiah, Chap. 17, verse 1, thought to have been written about 600 years later, in 600 B.C., describes an iron pen with a point of a hard mineral. These early materials could have been diamond, but were more likely corundum. By 300 B.C., however, the Indians had certainly learned how to engrave with diamond and perhaps on diamond. An engraved Indian diamond is shown in Fig. 1.5.

The Roman, Pliny the Elder, who was born in A.D. 23 and died investigating the eruption of Vesuvius in A.D. 79, devoted a volume of his *Natural History* to precious stones, in which many rational statements are tangled with legend and myth. He wrote of diamonds: '. . . they resist blows to such an extent that an iron hammer may be split in two and even the anvil itself may be displaced . . . this invincible force, which defies Nature's two most violent forces, iron and fire,

5

can be broken by ram's blood. But it must be steeped in blood that is fresh and warm and, even so, many blows are needed . . .'

'Valley of Diamonds'

Pliny also recorded that diamonds were found in a Valley of Diamonds, a belief that was based on an earlier legend of how Alexander the Great, during his campaign through India about 350 B.C., retrieved diamonds from a pit guarded by snakes whose gaze would kill a man. The snakes were killed by Alexander's soldiers using mirrors so that the snakes' gaze fell on themselves.

Sheeps' carcasses were then thrown into the pit. The diamonds adhered to the fat and vultures lured by the meat picked it up with the diamonds attached. The soldiers followed the vultures to their roosts and recovered the diamonds from nests and droppings. The Valley of Diamonds legend seems to have originated in writings of the Bishop of Constantia, Cyprus (c. 315–403) and was later repeated by Marco Polo.

The story has survived until today in the fable of Sinbad the Sailor, who was thrown into a diamond valley to die. He saved himself when he saw merchants throwing flesh into the valley. Wrapping some diamond-studded flesh round his body, he allowed a vulture to carry him to safety.

Professor Samuel Tolansky, an authority on diamond, has suggested that the Valley of Diamonds legend was deliberately encouraged by Indian diamond merchants in Golconda, the trading centre, to disguise the true sources in river-beds of the surrounding country. He also suggests that the ram's or goat's blood legend may have had a similar purpose, to camouflage the art of cleaving, by which a diamond may be split to divide it by a single blow on certain places on the crystal.

Diamond Cutting

Early descriptions of facetting diamonds refer to polishing and it is presumed that octahedral crystals were left in their natural shape or the angles of the faces were altered by cutting, since they were called point-cut stones (Figs. 1.6 and 1.7). An octahedral face is in fact impossible to polish. Moreover, the process of cleaving produces pointed stones without the necessity for polishing. Grinding to remove the top point of the octahedral crystal to produce what was called the table stone (Fig. 1.8) presumably came later.

The history of cutting and polishing is poorly documented and the art remained a trade secret for many centuries. It is uncertain where cutting originated, whether in Europe or India, as well as which process came first. The origin in Europe was probably in the fourteenth century and in India possibly about the same time because there was an earlier ban for superstitious reasons on shaping diamonds. Superstition probably delayed the development in Europe, too, because the alteration of a diamond was supposed to destroy its magical properties.

Tavernier noted in the seventeenth century that there were considerable differences in the techniques of European and Indian cutters. He also surmised that the Indians used facets to hide flaws.

6

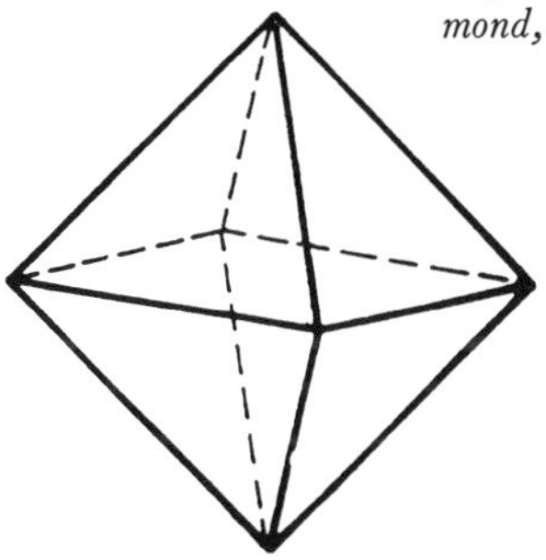

Fig. 1.7. *The point-cut dia-mond, shaped from an octahedral diamond.*

Fig. 1.6. *A natural octahedral diamond crystal of the type called a glassie which was sometimes set in jewellery.*

Fig. 1.8. *A second early form of 'manufactured' cut of gem diamond, the table-cut or table stone, made from a natural octahedron.*

Mysticism and Diamond

Powerful material and spiritual powers have been attributed to gemstones from the earliest days until comparatively recent times. They were believed able to cure diseases, avert calamity, and to be able to ward off evil spirits. It was thought that the arbiter of a man's fate could be carried by him in his purse in the shape of a precious stone.

For many centuries before the spread of monotheism, man was believed to be a microcosm of the universe. He was its counterpart and for every part of his body there was a corresponding part of the universe. At the moment of dissolution of his body in death, his soul if pure, united with the great universal soul — the Buddhist's *karma*. If his soul were impure, it passed through a number of transmigrations during which it animated animals, plants, and even some minerals, until it was purified and was absorbed into the universal soul. That is why gemstones were thought to have life.

These beliefs from ancient India spread through the East, then came to Egypt and to Greece and were influential in Europe in the Middle Ages, particularly through the activities of the alchemists.

Plato, the Greek philosopher, believed that precious stones were truly living beings and were produced by a sort of fermentation as the result of vivifying spirits descending from the stars. Distinguishing diamond from other stones as a kind of kernel formed in gold, he supposed it to be the purest and noblest part of the metal that had condensed into a transparent mass.

Later, Theophrastus, a pupil of Aristotle, divided precious stones into male and female specimens. It was a logical development of the belief in them as living beings.

Precious Stones

In 1501, on the threshold of the Renaissance, Jerome Cardan was born. He deserves a special place in gemmology, for he first defined a precious stone, and as a result, centuries later, led us to the absurdity of the semi-precious stone. Cardan classified all brilliant-appearing stones as gems. He reserved the expression precious stones for those that were not only brilliant but rare and of small dimensions. Precious stones were still further divided into firstly, being brilliant and transparent like the diamond; secondly, those that were opaque like onyx; and thirdly, those 'formed by the conjunction of the two other kinds', an example being jasper. Onyx and jasper are actually similar material.

Cardan's beliefs were influenced by the animism of the previous centuries. He assumed precious stones to be living beings, that were 'engendered', in the same manner as the infant from the 'maternal blood', by juices distilled from precious minerals in the cavities of rocks. The diamond, emerald, and opal, he wrote, were distilled from gold. He added, 'And not only do precious stones live, but they suffer illness, old age, and death.' Even as late as 1876, Indians were told: 'Like men, diamonds are divided into Brahmins, Kshatryas, Vaisyas and Sudras.' The divisions into caste were made by colour.

As a Medicine

Probably the earliest medicines were herbal and animal, but mineral substances were undoubtedly employed at an early date. Many pharmacopoeias acclaimed precious stones as among the most valuable remedies.

Diamond was not among the 'Five Precious Fragments' – the ruby, topaz, emerald, sapphire, and hyacinth (probably the orange-red zircon or hessonite garnet) – but was reckoned to have the power of resisting all poisons. If taken internally, however, it was supposed to reveal itself as a deadly poison. One belief was that a diamond grew dark in the presence of poison because particles emanating from the poison gathered on the surface of the stone, being unable to penetrate it.

Diamond has held this contradictory position in the view of several ancient authors. St. Hildegard, in the tenth century, maintained that a precious stone would only heal a person if held in his hand while making the sign of the cross. It would also heal if taken to bed and warmed by one's body, or if held in the mouth, especially when fasting, if breathed upon, or if worn next to the skin. He added that a diamond held in the mouth of a liar or scold would cure his spiritual defects.

The Hindus believed that only the powder of a flawed diamond was poisonous, causing various ailments and diseases such as lameness, jaundice, pleurisy and leprosy. Powder from diamonds of different colours, they said, had different flavours, from sweet to sour or salty. (There were also reports of the scent of powdered gems.) The powder of the highest quality diamonds, when swallowed, had the opposite effect to that of flawed ones, for it imparted energy, strength, beauty, happiness, and long life.

8

Alphonse X, in his 'Lapidario', declared that diamond was only to be used for chronic cases of bladder disease.

Diamond as a Poison

Emperor Frederick II (1194–1250) died, according to legend, through a fatal dose of powdered diamond. The Turkish Sultan Bejazet (1447–1512) is said to have been poisoned to death by his son, who mixed a large amount of pulverized diamond in his father's food. In 1532, Pope Clement VII was ailing and was prescribed doses of powdered precious stones, including diamond, by his physicians. Apparently he failed to survive the fourteenth spoonful, by which time the bill was 40,000 ducats.

There are other records of the death of prominent people by diamond poisoning. Catherine de Medici's powder tipped into food or drink – the famous *poudre de succession* – is supposed to have been powdered diamond. If it was, there was probably another secret ingredient, possibly arsenic. Catherine was the dominating wife of Henry II of France in the mid-sixteenth century.

The celebrated Italian seventeenth-century goldsmith, Benvenuto Cellini, wrote at length about an attempt on his life by his enemy, P. L. Farnese, son of Paul III, who attempted to poison him by causing powdered diamond to be mixed with his salad. Cellini attributed his escape to the fact that the lapidary who was employed to pulverize the stone kept it for himself and substituted powdered glass for the diamond powder.

It is possible that the belief that diamonds were poisonous was fostered to reduce the risk of stealing, particularly from the mines, by swallowing the stone and recovering it later.

Magic Powers

There were astrological significations of precious stones. In a table of planets given in the 17th century, diamond is equated with the sun thus: Planet: *Sun*. Metal: *gold*. Precious stones: *diamond, sapphire, jacinth, lodestone*.

A curious belief about the diamond was that, if held in the mouth, it caused the teeth to drop out. Jewellers today often advise the owner of a valuable diamond ring to hold it with her teeth while washing her hands, to eliminate the risk of leaving the ring behind.

Diamond was supposed to be of service to lunatics and those possessed of devils. It also repelled the attacks of phantoms and made the sleep of the wearer free from nightmares. It was worn in battle because it dispelled vain fears and made the wearer courageous as well as magnanimous and virtuous.

Another benefit of diamond was its ability to baffle the magic arts and to cause lawsuits to be settled in favour of the wearer. It was not explained what happened when both parties wore diamonds. If a house, orchard, or vineyard were touched at each corner with a diamond, it was thought to be protected from lightning, storms and blight.

A property of some diamonds known in Roman times, if not earlier, and regarded as proof of diamonds' magic, was their ability to glow in the dark after being subjected to strong sunlight for a time, that is their phosphorescence after exposure to ultra-violet light.

The ancients declared that the magic powers of diamond were so superior that a lodestone would lose its magnetism in the presence of diamond. Diamonds when rubbed, will pick up small pieces of paper and other light objects because of the static electrical charge induced in it, is easily proved. (When rubbed on wool it becomes electrically positive.) Probably it was this fact that lively imaginations developed into superior magnetic powers. No one thought of experimenting to discover whether the fact was true. Intellectual theory was supposedly vastly superior to practical experiment, particularly in Greek times. The value of experiment was not generally appreciated until the eighteenth century.

Diamond as a Gem

Diamonds have not always been regarded as dominant gemstones. In early times the Persians certainly preferred pearls, which could be perfect and very beautiful when taken from the oyster, whereas the diamond crystal was insignificant in appearance, relying on its invincible properties for its value. In the Middle Ages, diamond was rated below ruby and emerald and had slipped to seventeenth place in importance in medieval lapidaries as its powers became less credible. Cutting and polishing, as the techniques improved, restored diamond to a high place in the list of gems, but for different reasons.

Attributes of Gems

All gems have three attributes in common. They are beautiful; they are durable; and they are rare. Beauty in some gems relies on colour alone. In others it comes from a display of light, as in the irridescence of opals and pearls, the schiller of moonstone and bronzite – and the fire of diamond. Beauty is also affected by the lustre of the surface. The lustre of diamond is unique and for that reason has been given its own name – adamantine.

Durability is an obvious necessity for a valuable gem. It does not necessarily mean hardness, for pearls are quite soft, yet endure for thousands of years. Diamond is again unique in durability. Few well-known diamonds have been lost for ever. They usually turn up again, even after centuries.

Diamond is the only colourless and transparent gemstone that has great beauty. Colourless zircon is poor by comparison. Only the man-made strontium titanate, that has been appropriately trade named Fabulite, compares with it in appearance, although it is too 'flashy'. Strontium titanate does not have an adamantine lustre, however, and is not very durable because it is damaged relatively easily.

Rarity is a term that must be qualified in relation to value. Rubasse is a rare rock crystal with red spangles in it, but it is not valuable. About seven tons of diamond are mined every year, yet diamond is valuable. By rarity, is meant how far the supply fulfils the demand. For example, the demand for good coloured emerald outstrips the supply, with the result that emerald prices are always rising. The supply of diamond is related to the demand and average prices keep roughly in step with the cost of living.

Despite new finds of gem diamond sources, ultimately the supply of natural diamonds must fail. Nature does not provide endless reserves, so prices will tend to climb. This has happened already with diamonds over a carat in weight, which are becoming harder to come by. Even if diamonds are discovered on other planets, the cost of recovery will keep prices high.

Synthetic Diamonds

What about synthetic diamond, made in the factory; surely that will reduce the value of natural diamonds? The question is frequently asked. Diamonds have been made synthetically in commercial quantities since 1954 and today many tons are manufactured, although no commercial gem diamonds have appeared yet. Gem diamond was first made in 1970 on a laboratory scale by a long and very costly process, by General Electric of America.

When commercial gem diamonds appear on the market they will be expensive. If the price later falls, will this cause the prices of natural gem diamonds to plummet down? Definitely not. Thousands of tons of synthetic ruby and sapphire are made yearly, mainly for industrial uses, but also as gems. The huge numbers of synthetic rubies and sapphires on the market at a few shillings each have not reduced the high prices of the natural stones. The same is true of synthetic emeralds. In fact, the shortage of fine natural emerald has kept the price of synthetic emeralds much higher than the prices of many other attractive natural stones.

Therefore synthetic gem diamonds are not a threat to natural gem diamonds, but might well expand the market and the demand for natural stones and push up prices.

A synthetic stone is exactly the same material as a natural one. A synthetic diamond is like a natural one, a unique structure of carbon atoms. A synthetic ruby, like a natural one, is a particular structure of aluminium oxide. The differences that exist between the natural and synthetic are often extremely small. Often the synthetic is too perfect for Nature to have made.

While it remains possible to identify a natural from a synthetic stone, a price difference will exist. It is often necessary to call in the services of a specialist laboratory to determine whether a stone is natural or synthetic. This is particularly true of synthetic emerald, and appears to be so of synthetic gem diamond.

Synthetics and Simulants

It should at this point be made clear that in gemmology the expression synthetic applies only to a man-made replica of a natural material, so synthetic diamond is real diamond. A copy, which looks identical or very similar but is not the same material, is called an imitation or a simulant. The high-density glass, known as strass or paste, used to copy diamond, is therefore a diamond simulant, or an imitation diamond. It is *not* a synthetic diamond. Strontium titanate and another material, yttrium aluminium garnet, which has the trade name Diamonair,* are oddities. Having no counterparts in Nature, they are not strictly speaking synthetic stones, although for convenience they are called synthetic. When either is used to imitate a diamond, it is used as a diamond simulant.

* The trade name Diamonair has been condemned by some European gemmologists because of its likeness to diamond.

Diamonds in Jewellery

After diamonds were discovered, they were not worn in jewellery if they were worn at all, as they were regarded as talismans. At some point they acquired value in exchange for other goods or for services and therefore became a means of acquiring wealth in a conveniently portable and durable form. Perhaps the first wearers were the princes of India seeking magical protection and then displaying their power and wealth. The diamond had then become a badge of rank.

In the first and second centuries A.D., Romans wore diamond crystals set in gold rings, but for superstitious reasons of protection rather than as jewellery. The early history of the diamond in jewellery still has many mysteries.

One of the earliest pieces, if not the earliest, set with diamonds (uncut) must been a queen's crown – the Holy Crown of Hungary, or Crown of St. Stephen, shown in Fig. 1.9. It is still in existence. Figures on it of the Emperor of the Romans (Michael Dukas) and the King of Hungary (Geza I) indicate that it was a gift from Byzantine to the Hungarian Royal Court between the year 1074, when Geza became king, and 1078, when Dukas lost his throne.

As it was unusual for a king to have his own picture on a crown and the crown itself has the characteristics of one for a queen, therefore the crown may have been intended for Queen Synadene, who came from a Byzantine noble family and was the wife of King Bela I, Geza's father. The diamonds are set, with pearls, in the arches over the crown.

One of the earliest places where diamonds were worn must have been Paris, because it was a centre of goldsmiths as long ago as the seventh century, when three jewellers, Eloi, Alban de Fleury, and Theau, were canonized. Only the monasteries had workshops and made pieces for the priests for a long period, but by the twelfth and thirteenth centuries, secular jewellers had become well established. The earliest reference to diamonds seems to be in 1319, however, when a diamond necklace was said to have been worn by the French Queen Clemence, Hungarian wife of King Louis the Quarreler.

Edward, Prince of Wales, the elder son of Edward III of England, later known as the Black Prince, was very fond of jewels to judge from records that still exist. In 1355, for instance, among his jewel purchases were twenty-seven rings, some set with rubies, some with diamonds, and some with pearls. A crown of gold set with diamonds, rubies, sapphires 'and other great pearls' fell into his hands when the owner, King John II of France, was taken prisoner at Poitiers in 1356.

The Duke of Burgundy gave his mother a ruby brooch surrounded by diamonds and pearls in 1369. In 1396, when King Richard II of England married his second wife Isabella of France (who was 7 years old at the time), he gave her a number of presents, one being a collar of diamonds, rubies, and large pearls. There are many other records of Royal gifts of diamonds from these early times to the present day, but it is difficult to determine from them whether or not the diamonds were facetted or not, that is, when facetting was invented.

A well-publicized gift of diamond jewellery was that of Jacques Coeur, a French diamond merchant of the mid-fifteenth century, to Agnes Sorel, mistress

Fig. 1.9.   *The Crown of St. Stephen, which is perhaps the earliest jewelled piece in existence set with (uncut) diamonds. It is in the Hungarian Crown jewels and is dated between 1074 and 1078.*

of King Charles VII of France (Fig. 1.10). Jacques Coeur was firstly a coin maker who, when young, was exiled for competing with the Royal Mint. He was reinstated after fighting anti-Popery, and became a powerful trader with the East. Agnes Sorel persuaded Jacques Coeur to finance the king's battle against the English and subsequently arranged for him to become the king's financial adviser and later master of the Royal Mint.

Coeur imported stones from India and diamond cutters from Venice and Constantinople. He made diamond necklaces, brooches, and buckles for Agnes Sorel to wear, and she became famed for her jewels.

In the reign of Queen Elizabeth I of England, from 1558 to 1603, it was for some time fashionable among the wealthier to wear rings set with octahedral crystals of diamond with the point of a four-sided pyramid to the front. At one time they became known as scribbling rings after the craze for using them to scribble love messages on glass window-panes. Even the Virgin Queen herself, it is said, exchanged rhymes with Sir Walter Raleigh on a window-pane.

Over the centuries, diamond jewellery has become more and more widespread until today in Britain, three women in four own diamond rings.

Where Diamonds are Found

Pliny remarked that the diamond accompanied gold. Diamonds *are* found with gold, but we know now that they arrive together through the actions of winds and rain over millions of years gradually shaking and sifting them and other heavy minerals together. Diamond does not occur in its original sources with gold. Pliny referred to six types of diamond, but from his descriptions some types were in fact sapphires, which are very heavy and are also found with gold.

As far as is known, all early sources of diamond were in the beds of active or dried up rivers, despite the legends. India was the only known source for over 2,000 years, except for Borneo where diamonds were probably first mined in the sixteenth century. The Brazilian diamond fields were discovered in the gold-mining area of Minas Gerais in 1725.

New discoveries always seem to have been regarded with scepticism. The genuiness of the Brazilian stones was questioned on the London market and as late as 1740 a jeweller declared in print that it was a 'false idea that the (gold) mines of Brazil furnish diamonds'. Even a century later, Portuguese merchants used to take the Brazilian diamonds to Goa, a Portuguese possession in India, to sell them. Mining was carried out so intensively that main areas were almost exhausted in twenty years.

By an extraordinary coincidence, the South African diamond fields were discovered in 1866, by the time that the Brazilian fields had dried up. When the news arrived in Brazil, history repeated itself. The Brazilian merchants refused to believe the fact, and many were ruined. Professor J. R. Gregory, a London University mineralogist, actually spent three weeks in the South African diamond fields and subsequently wrote an article for the *Geological Magazine* of 1868 declaring the story of South African diamonds was false and 'simply a scheme for trying to promote the employment and expenditure of capital in searching for the precious stone in that country'.

Major diamond deposits were found in the arctic areas of Yakutia in Russia

Fig. 1.10. *Agnes Sorel, who, in mid-fifteenth century, popularized the wearing of diamond jewellery in the French court.*

Fig. 1.11.   *A natural diamond of rounded octahedral shape in blue ground, the rock that brings it to the surface from over 120 miles deep in the Earth where it was formed.*

from 1954. Again there was disbelief in some quarters before the diamonds came on to the market in the West, but now the Russian mines have an output second only to South Africa's.

World Production
It has been estimated that only about 130 tons of diamonds have been mined since they were first discovered thousands of years ago. That may seem to many readers to be a large amount of diamond in relation to a half-carat stone in a ring, which weighs about a two hundred and eightieth part of an ounce. The reward of 130 tons of diamond is very small against the effort of discovering the source and mining it. Finding a needle in a haystack is an easy task by comparison.

The present yearly production of diamond is about seven tons. This amount sells for about £300,000,000 as raw material. About 20 per cent only is useful as gem material, yet accounts for at least £250,000,000 of the value. The remaining 80 per cent, plus much more than that amount of synthetic diamond, is consumed by industry.

Jewellers Subsidize Industry
The value of the gem is thus about three times as much as the very much larger quantity of industrial diamonds. If there were not such a strong demand for gem diamonds, the whole cost of mining would be born by scientific and industrial users. The jeweller and the members of the public who buy diamond jewellery are doing industry and their country a considerable service by subsi-

dizing mining. Modern industry would come to a halt without industrial diamond. Diamond is used for all high-precision machining and for drilling oil wells and has a million other uses. But for the young man who buys a diamond ring for his girl, industry would have to pay very much more for its diamonds.

Nearly all diamond sources are in the more remote places of the world and the crystals are usually extremely difficult to recover from old river-beds or beaches beneath the deep sands of the desert, from thousands of feet down in 'volcanic' pipes, some deep under permanent arctic ice, or from under the treacherous ocean waves off the forbidden coast of South West Africa (Figs. 1.11 and 1.12). The amount of sand, earth, rocks, gravels, and other material that has to be removed to recover a diamond varies in different places, but can be in the order of a hundred million to one. Mining and recovery means finding and sorting of 200,000,000 tons of diamondiferous ore in remote places to discover a year's supply of diamond. A carat is a fifth of a metric gramme. There are about 142 in an ounce avoirdupois.

Unwettable but Grease-attracting

A clean diamond cannot be wetted by water. The water just forms into drops and rolls off. On the other hand, grease very easily sticks to it. The discovery of this fact led to the method of extracting diamonds from the rest of the heavy residue from diamond mines and diggings by passing it over a layer of grease to which the diamonds stuck and the rest was washed over by a stream of water.

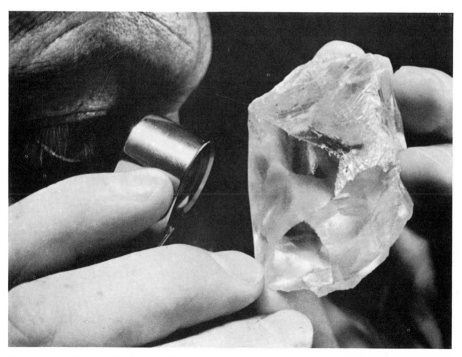

Fig. 1.12. *The Lesotho Brown diamond, a 601.25 carat stone of faint brownish tinge found in 1967 in the Letseng le Draai diggings in Lesotho (formerly Basutoland). It has now been cut into a number of gemstones.*

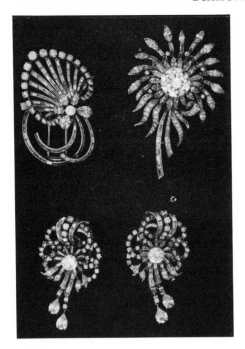

Fig. 1.13. *Diamond brooches in traditional patterns and a diamond ring of Japanese design that won an award in a De Beers design contest. European designers won an exceptional number of awards.*

The affinity of diamond for grease also means that diamond jewellery will pick up grease and oils from the skin of the wearer and should be cleaned regularly in a diamond cleaner or a detergent. It is more important to clean the back than it is the front, not just because that is where the grease is trapped, but because the back facets will not reflect if they are coated with grease.

The Brilliant Cut

The shape of the modern brilliant-cut stone is derived from the shape of the most common form of crystal, the octahedron. For about two centuries, one point was ground or polished off to produce the square table-cut diamond. From around mid-seventeenth century, more facets were added and the shape made rounder. The modern round brilliant-cut gem (Fig. 1.13), with fifty-eight accurately-placed facets, was the result of a book of theory written in 1919. The author worked out the angles that produced the maximum display of light and flashing colour and gave us the modern brilliant-cut stone, which was shallower than the earlier polished diamonds and consequently threw more light back to the person looking at the stone by reducing the leakage of light through the back.

Smaller Diamonds

As a gemstone, diamond is now relatively common. The big South African discoveries, followed by the Russian ones, and the development of modern mining methods are responsible. Diamonds are bound to become more common because the average size of crystals being mined is gradually getting smaller. Most gem diamonds are found along the desert coast of South West Africa, trapped in potholes in the rock under sixty or so feet of sand, parallel to the

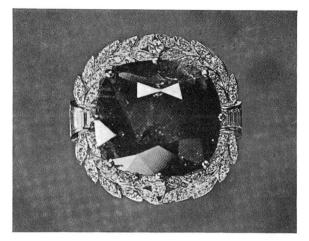

Fig. 1.14. *One of the few famous black diamonds in existence, the Black Orloff, weighing 67.50 carats. It is believed to have come from India and to have been known as the Eye of Brahma.*

long rolling breakers of the sea. Consolidated Diamond Mines of South West Africa find as many as 90 per cent of gems among the crystals they recover. But the average size fell from 0·90 carat in 1967 to 0·84 carat in 1968.

When a full or brilliant-cut diamond is fashioned out of a natural crystal, much weight is lost. Diamonds weighing a carat are often the biggest that can be cut from a crystal weighing two carats. If the crystal is mis-shapen or faulty the recovery will be lower, even as low as a fifth of a carat or less.

Price Stability

It is inevitable therefore that smaller diamonds will be appearing in jewellery and designers will be swinging away from single stone rings and featuring more smaller diamonds. A number of small diamonds is more economical in price for the same area of diamond since diamond prices rise rapidly as weight increases. Very roughly, a diamond twice as heavy and of the same quality as another will cost four times as much, but the area of the top will only increase by about a fifth.

The production of smaller stones from the mines will bring diamond jewellery into reach of many more people.

Trust in Trading

Diamond is the only mineral that still has to be sorted by hand as a last stage in the mining process, however automatic and sophisticated it may be. There is no substitute for the human hand, eye, and brain, in gauging quality and estimating value. There is no other mineral, except perhaps among the very rare earths, that has such a high intrinsic value when mined. Diamond crystals are therefore kept under guard from the moment they are discovered. They remain so through the stages of sorting, cutting, and setting in jewellery, yet they are commonly transmitted from place to place through the ordinary post.

Extreme security precautions have to be taken to protect both crystals and polished stones from crooks. Yet within the trade itself, diamonds of great value pass from hand to hand on a signature and often without even that formality.

Anyone unconnected with the diamond trade is amazed at the extent of the trust placed in each other by buyer and seller. This trust is the keystone that keeps the entire trade in being.

In the rest of the chapters of the book many of the subjects referred to in this preliminary chapter are explored in more detail, but much has to be left unsaid because the subject of this one material is so vast, so much as yet unrelated work has been done on it and so much unrelated history written about it that a lifetime could profitably be spent on the study of diamond alone.

REFERENCES

Natural History, Book 37, by Pliny the Elder (A.D. 77).
Gemmarum et Lapidum Historia, by Anselmus Boetius de Boot. (Lyons, France, 1636).
Antique Gems: their origin, uses and value, by Rev. C. W. King M.A. (London, 1866).
Mani-Mala, or a Treatise on Gems, by Sourindro Mohun Tagore (Bengal, 1876).
Diamond Design, by Marcel Tolkowsky (London, 1919).
A History of the Crown Jewels of Europe, by Lord Twining (London, 1960).
The History and Use of Diamond, by S. Tolansky, F.R.S. (London, 1962).
The History of Diamond Production and the Diamond Trade, by Godehard Lenzen (London, 1970).

CHAPTER TWO

Where Diamonds are Found

All early 'diamond mines' were the alluvial gravels in the banks or beds of active or dried-up rivers in which diamonds and other heavy and hard crystals had been concentrated by the action of flooding water. Alluvial deposits near active rivers were later called river diggings or wet diggings.

Some alluvial gravels containing diamonds were found under the surface in desert regions where rivers had dried up many thousands of years ago. They were called dry diggings. In the second half of the last century, a few dry diggings in Africa were found to be the tops of great columns of a special kind of rock that had diamonds trapped in it, apparently having carried them from their source of origin deep in the earth. These diggings were renamed pipes or pipe mines.

The Indian Mines

Alluvial diamonds were known in India as early as about 800 B.C. The diamonds were found in compact sandstones and conglomerates and in the same materials after they had weathered, as well as in the sands and gravels of river-beds and terraces. Indian diamonds were exported through the port of Alexandria at an early time and there is a reference in the writings of the Alexandrian astronomer Ptolemy (A.D. 90–168) to a diamond river in India.

Tavernier visited a number of mines between 1630 and 1668, and most of our knowledge about them comes from his writings. The most famous workings were at Kollur in the great gorge cut by the river Kristna in the south of the former kingdom of Golconda, now part of the State of Hyderabad. Kollur was where several historical diamonds, including the Koh-i-Nûr, the Regent, and the Tavernier Blue, were found. Tavernier reported that some time before 1650 he found 60,000 men women and children at work there.

The mining area was generally known as Golconda, although Golconda was in fact a fortress and town which was the headquarters of the diamond merchants. Diamonds from the scattered diggings were facetted if necessary at the village of Karwan outside the city walls.

The mines were divided into claims operated by local merchants who paid a levy to the local ruler plus a percentage of the value of stones discovered. The miners worked to a strict religious ritual. Having decided on the place to be worked, they levelled off an area beside it and surrounded this by a two-feet-high wall, with holes or gates in it at intervals around the base. The gates were blocked and earth and gravel from the mining area was dumped in the walled enclosure by women and children. When the mining area had been excavated, usually to a depth of about fourteen feet, water seepage prevented further mining. The water was taken in pitchers and tipped into the walled area to bring the

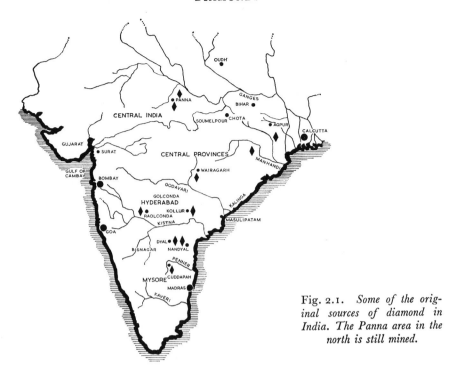

Fig. 2.1. *Some of the original sources of diamond in India. The Panna area in the north is still mined.*

earth and gravel to a consistency of soup, which it reached after one or two days.

The gates were then opened to draw off the water and mud. Sometimes two or three washings were necessary until the hot sun dried off the remaining moisture and left only sand containing diamonds.

The smaller material was winnowed like grain in baskets to allow the lighter elements to be blown away by the wind. The remainder was raked over, which exposed many lumps. The miners broke up the lumps by pounding the whole area with large wooden pestles or rams before winnowing once more. Finally the miners ranged themselves on one side and worked across the sand to pick out any diamonds by hand.

The best stones at Kollur, Tavernier reported, had a green crust on the surface, 'because when cut they proved to be white and of very beautiful water'. Nearly all the world's finest and biggest diamonds came from the Indian mines which were situated in an area of quite different geological formation from those in Africa and Siberia where most diamonds have been found.

It was reported that two new diamond mines were operated in the 1960s, near the original ones in the Golconda area. Sources are shown in Fig. 2.1.

A second early diamond area was in the Karnul district of Madras. The mine was called Ramulkota (Raolconda in Tavernier's record). The miners dug deep pits in the sandstone and used iron rods, crooked at one end, to extract diamond-bearing gravels from veins in the rocks.

A third diamondiferous area was to the north in the small state of Madhya,

Fig. 2.2.   *How some early mines in Panna, India, were worked in pits in the sandstone. Note the armed guards on the right.*

Fig. 2.3. *Some of the earlier mining areas in Brazil, which was the main source of supply in the eighteenth century and first half of the nineteenth century.*

near the town of Panna (Fig. 2.2). More recently, twenty miles south of Panna, at Majgawan, diamond-bearing pipes have been found and the government organizations, the National Mineral Development Corporation, which took control of production in 1960, is developing these resources.

Apparently in early days, the Indians believed that diamonds possessed the magical power of growing like seeds, so old dumps and tailings were worked over many times to see if any new diamonds had been generated in them. In fact, conglomerate and sandstone in which diamonds were trapped broke up after a time on exposure to the weather to release the stones.

Mining in Brazil

Diamonds were first discovered in Brazil at the beginning of the eighteenth century. Crystals had been found by gold miners in gravels of river workings near Tejuco in Minas Gerais, which has since become famous for many other gems too. Gold miners apparently used them as counters while playing cards until an official who had seen diamond crystals in India recognized their nature and sent some to Lisbon. Some of the samples were cut in Amsterdam and found to be as fine diamonds as those found in India.

The official discovery of diamonds in Brazil by the Portuguese, who then occupied the country, is recorded as in 1725. Many other deposits were found and production was increased so much that prices tumbled and the Portuguese Government restricted production almost to a trickle. They made mining a Royal monopoly in 1772. Diamonds in Minas Gerais are found only in rivers that flow through strata composed of itacolumite (flexible sandstone).

Another big discovery occurred in 1844, in Bahia, twenty-two years after Brazil had gained its independence. Unfortunately the deposits were again worked so intensively that they were more or less exhausted in twenty years. Tough, black, impure diamond was found in the Chapida Diamantina area of Bahia. It was often in large lumps of several ounces, was called carbonado, and was of no commercial value at the time but was afterwards discovered to be valuable as an industrial abrasive.

Diamonds usually occur in Brazil in a gravel of rounded quartz pebbles and light coloured sand, known locally as *cascalho*. All the diggings are alluvial, situated in or near river-beds. Sources are shown in Fig. 2.3.

The method of recovery when Brazil was the world's biggest supplier of diamonds, was to dig down to the diamondiferous gravels, which were usually about ten feet deep, and to pile the gravel in heaps near washing huts. The huts were occupied by overseers sitting on high seats. In front were washing troughs, where labourers washed away the finer sands and soil and picked out the diamonds. During the dry season, the waters of rivers were diverted through canals to the troughs, which are shown in Fig. 2.4.

There are still some independent diamond diggers called *garimpeiros* (snipers) in Brazil and in the 1960 the rivers that were still diamondiferous were mined by dredger, using modern placer methods, but Brazil's main contribution to world supply lasted only until three-quarters through the nineteenth century. During 250 years of diamond mining it produced about fifteen million carats, compared with about forty-five million carats *a year* from current world mines.

It seems fortuitous, but probably is a result of economic forces, that as India's

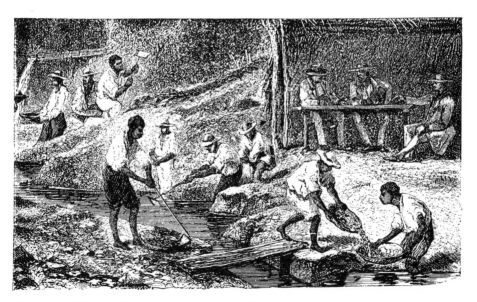

Fig. 2.4. *Diamond diggers in Brazil at work collecting gravel and washing it under the eyes of overseers. The man on the right will swirl his pan in water to cause any diamonds to settle to the centre at the bottom.*

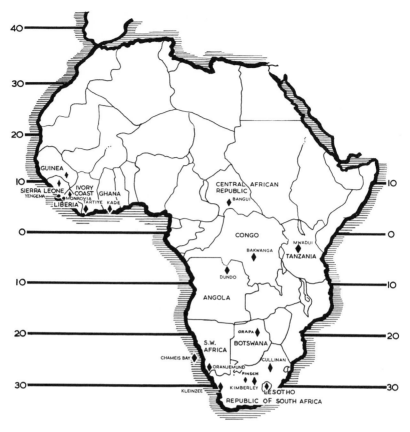

Fig. 2.5. *Main current sources of diamond in Africa. Most gem diamonds come from the coastal deposits in South West Africa. The Congo and Angola fields are largest but almost all the diamonds there are of industrial quality.*

supply of diamonds was running out, deposits were found in Brazil, and just as Brazil's was nearly exhausted, huge supplies were found in Africa.

Diamonds in Africa

Diamonds were first discovered in the interior of South Africa in the land of the Griquas, who were descended from the original Hottentots of Cape Colony. The Griquas had been driven from the Cape by European colonists and had emigrated north, in turn driving away the Bushmen from the area formed by the junction of the Vaal River with the Orange River. See Figs. 2.5 and 2.8.

European hunters gradually found their way northwards and were followed by Dutch farmers, the Boers, trekking with herds of cattle and sheep in search of places suitable to settle. The few who stayed in the lands of the Griquas were followed by hundreds more in the Great Trek from the Cape in 1836, caused by the British decision to free slaves in the middle of a harvest which led to ruination of the crops.

The Voortrekkers appropriated all the territory in the fork of the rivers to found the Orange Free State, and the Griquas, under Adam Kok, were forced across the Vaal River.

The First Diamond

Early pioneers were driven by strong religious convictions and the intention to convert coloured people to their own beliefs. The Berlin Mission Society set up missions on the banks of the River Vaal, one at Pniel and another at Platberg. In the daily diary of the Pniel station is a record of a 5-carat diamond being found in 1859 on the river bank near Platberg by a native and its purchase by a priest for £5. Even today the Berlin Mission sells diamonds found on its concession to licensed buyers in Kimberley.

News of the discovery of the Platberg diamond brought to the area a man named T. B. Kisch, who was an apothecary born in Colesberg and educated in England and whose hobbies were geology and mineralogy. He was perhaps the first European prospector in the area.

The Next Find

The first authenticated find was on the De Kalk farm in the Hope Town district, in Cape Colony just south of the Orange River. Schalk van Niekerk, the step-son of the farmer, had his home on the farm and was a farmer himself, but had to work as a trader as well in order to make a living. Also on the farm was a tiny stone house occupied by a family called Jacobs.

During his trading expeditions, van Niekerk became interested in collecting colourful pebbles from the river and veldt. A land surveyor to whom he showed his collection was intrigued enough to encourage the interest of this unusual farmer by giving him a book on precious stones. Van Niekerk always asked people he met to keep for him any unusual stones they came across and while he was at the Jacobs' house one day, Mrs. Jacobs remembered that her 15-year-old son, Erasmus, had brought home a glittering stone with which the other children had played the game five-stones. Van Niekerk eventually found it lying on the ground outside, below one of the windows.

Turning it in his fingers, he was reminded of the drawing of diamond crystals in the book he had been given. He told Mrs. Jacobs that it might be a diamond and asked if he could buy it, but she said he could keep it. She explained that Erasmus had been sent with Klonkie, a Hottentot shepherd boy, to cut a stick from a tree and while playing afterwards, Klonkie had noticed the stone and had knocked it across to Erasmus, who had brought it home for his sisters.

Remembering that his book said diamonds would scratch glass, van Niekerk tried the stone on one of the panes of glass in the humble Jacobs house and it made a strong mark. The original pane still exists and is now on display in the Colesberg Museum. He took the stone on his next trip to Hope Town and showed it to some friends with an interest in minerals, but none could identify it or even guessed that it might be a diamond. Then he visited two German traders named Gustave and Martin Lilienfeld and while they were looking at the stone, their very junior partner, a young Englishman named James Wykeham, came in. He was shown the stone and after examining it carefully, declared it was probably a diamond.

The stone was taken to the Assistant Commissioner to ask for his advice. He said he knew nothing of precious stones and suggested taking it to Colesberg for identification. Van Niekerk had to return, however, and handed the stone to his wife who put it in her sewing box so that it would not be mislaid.

In March, 1867, a hunter and trader, J. O'Reilly, called at the De Kalk farm on his way to Colesberg with a load of skins, ostrich feathers, and elephant tusks. Van Niekerk met him and showed him the stone, explaining that it belonged to young Erasmus Jacobs and that it had been suggested that it should be shown to the Assistant Commissioner, Lorenzo Boyes, at Colesberg.

O'Reilly has recorded: 'This information gave me an idea. I told van Niekerk I was on my way to Colesberg and if he cared to entrust the stone to me I would take it to Mr. Boyes. He agreed, without making any stipulation concerning the stone should it be of value, and which I at the time never thought of asking about, a lax arrangement which could have got us both into trouble had we not been dealing with honourable men.'

Boyes said he thought the stone was a diamond although James Wykham had only been joking. He sent for T. B. Kisch, the apothecary, and showed it to him. Kisch said he would bet Boyes a new hat that it was a topaz. It was agreed to send the crystal to Dr. Atherstone in Grahamstown, for him to decide, so it was sealed in an envelope and sent by post cart.

The Stone is Tested

Dr. Atherstone was the first to subject the stone to any tests. One was the determination of its specific gravity, which was carried out by a local school-master. It was shown to a priest, who inscribed his initials on a window-pane in the Roman Catholic Presbytery, where they may still be seen, and to a jeweller who said he had no doubt about its being a diamond.

A letter from Dr. Atherstone to Mr. Boyes stated: 'I congratulate you on the stone you sent me. It is a diamond, weight twenty-one and a quarter carats, and is worth £500. It has ruined all the jewellers' files* in Grahamstown. Where this one came from there must be many others. Can I send it to Mr. Southey, the Colonial Secretary?'

The stone was bought for £500 by the Cape Governor, Sir Philip Wodehouse, after M. Heritte, the French Consul in Cape Town, who was regarded as an expert in diamonds, and a visiting Dutch diamond cutter, Louis Hond, had confirmed the identification. It was sent to Messrs. Hunt and Roskell, the Crown Jewellers in London, who also declared it to be a diamond and suggested putting it on show at the Paris Exhibition of 1867.

Schalk van Niekerk was given £350 as his share in the sale and he gave half of this to Mrs. Jacobs. The Governor sold the stone, which became known as the Eureka Diamond (Fig. 2.6).

After losing his bet, Kisch set out again to seek diamonds, near the junction of the Vaal and Orange Rivers, after he had gained a concession from the Griquas north of the Vaal (Fig. 2.7.). Lorenzo Boyes also caught 'diamond fever' and asked for leave of absence to look for them. Both men dug out gravels from the rivers and from their banks, but neither found diamonds.

* A file may be used on a crystal but *never* on a polished diamond.

Fig. 2.7. *The Vaal river in earlier days with Barkly in the distance. The diamond rushes began on the banks of this river.*

Fig. 2.6. *The Eureka diamond, which weighed 10.73 carats after cutting, the first of the authenticated finds in South Africa, which was responsible for making the African diamond deposits known.*

The First Big Find

There are records of two other early finds, but it was an 83½-carat crystal that really started the world-wide rush of fortune seekers to Griqua country. Up to that time, a small population of diggers worked the wet diggings along the Vaal, Orange, and Hartz Rivers, and later the Riet and Modder Rivers. The diggers discovered that many Griquas and some of the Bushmen who were left knew of the stones, but not of course that they were diamonds.

The 83½-carat crystal that eventually became known as the Star of South Africa, was picked up on the Zandfontein Farm in March, 1869, by a Griqua shepherd boy named Booi, while trekking with a few fat-tailed sheep to find work. He asked a farmer named Duvenhage if he might stay the night and offered the stone as payment. The farmer sent him on his way, saying he was no van Niekerk. Booi found a farmer near the Orange River who let him rest there. He offered the stone in payment for some goods to a shop assistant who sent him to talk to van Niekerk.

Van Niekerk must have had a shock when he saw the huge stone, but he thought it was a diamond. He took a chance and gave Booi everything he could lay his hands on in exchange – the horse he was riding, ten oxen and a wagon he had just hauled from Cape Town, even 500 fat-tailed sheep belonging to his father-in-law. These were riches beyond belief to Booi and no doubt made van Niekerk even better known as a fair man to whom one should take stones thought to be diamonds.

Van Niekerk showed this stone also to James Wykham, who said he would risk £5,000 of his own money in buying it. The other two partners of the business, the Lilienfelds, had a look, but were doubtful about it. By an astonishing coincidence, the Dutch diamond cutter, Louis Hond, happened to arrive. He studied the stone and weighed it and then called the traders into a private conference from which van Niekerk was excluded. He returned with an offer from the group of them for £11,300, which van Niekerk accepted on the spot in case they should change their minds.

The traders sold the stone in London for £25,000 in 1870, which was the price forecast by Louis Hond. Before the stone was dispatched, it was placed on the table of Parliament House in Cape Town and the Colonial Secretary pointed to it and made the prophetic announcement, 'This diamond, gentlemen, is the rock upon which the future success of South Africa will be built.'

Move to Dry Diggings

Booi had found the Star of South Africa on a farm far away from the river diggings and as soon as the news spread, diggers began to abandon their river claims, and invade the farms to search for dry diggings. Farmers sold permits and often made more profit than the diggers. Some farmers hated the diggers' intrusions but discovered that it was almost impossible to prevent the rush of humanity. One of the first finds was of an 8-carat stone on the property of the man who would not accept the Star of South Africa in exchange for a night spent on his farmland.

Adventurers of all kinds, gold miners from Canada and Australia, Europeans in every walk of life, deserting seamen, honest men and riff-raff began to pour into South Africa on every ship. Many had then to earn enough money to make the long trek at about ten miles a day over the veld, across the desert of the Karoo, over the mountains, and the scorched, rocky land beyond, to arrive two to four months later on the South banks of the Orange River in the north of Cape Colony. Some went over the Orange into the Orange Free State, and others north to the banks of the Vaal and across it into the land of the Griquas. Fast passenger coaches reduced the time to ten days after 1870 for those with money.

A very small sprinkling of men had some diamond experience in India, Borneo, or Brazil, but most knew nothing of mining. Soon they abandoned their normal clothes and adopted the rough breeches and wide-brimmed hats of the Boers. They even grew whiskers, like the Boers, to protect their faces from the sun and from the biting sand in the wind, and those who could afford it carried revolvers at their waists.

Hope Town

It was usual to make at first for Hope Town, which had become a rough and bustling frontier town where would-be miners could buy picks, buckets, spades, and sieves. From there, not far off the river, they went out into the semi-desert and the farms to prospect. Many thousands of diggers became scattered over a huge territory, working haphazardly and digging holes that were in many cases much too shallow to penetrate to any diamondiferous gravels even if they existed. There was constant trouble with farmers over prospecting rights and because sheep fell into prospect holes and were crippled or died. There were battles, too, over the livestock that disappeared into diggers' cooking-pots and continuous squabbles and fights over the very few sources of water.

The dry diggings were being worked fairly extensively at this time, and the newcomers had little luck owing largely to their inexperience and the size of the territory over which they were spread. This led to a movement back towards the river diggings, which became so jammed that there was utter chaos in the better areas, where there were diggers' camps, and thousands of sheep, oxen, horses, donkeys, cattle, wagons and equipment among the piles of discarded gravels.

Fine diamonds were being found in some areas, but others were barren. The invasion of newcomers brought crooks who paid a few pounds for useless claims, salted them with a few crystals, and resold them at large profits. The lack of

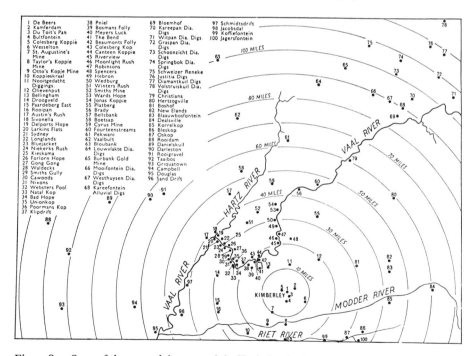

Fig. 2.8.   *Some of the many claims around the Vaal river in the 1870s and 80s. The pipe mine in the Kimberley area, became by far the most productive.*

policing resulted in much thieving of poultry, cattle and other goods. The demand for timber for shacks and fires was so great that trees everywhere were cut down and stolen from the farms until not a tree existed for miles around the rivers.

As many as 10,000 claims were being worked along the Vaal by 1870. The various camps and claims had their own names, sometimes referring to the digger's name or fortune, such as Forlorn Hope, Waldeck's Plant, Poorman's Kopje, Webster's Pool, and the rich Gong Gong, which is still being worked. Many are shown in the plan in Fig. 2.8.

The Standard Bank helped to provide security for diamonds and money when they set up a branch with a safe, at Klipdrift, opposite Pniel, in 1870. In the same year a judge with the forbidding name of Lynch arrived in Pniel Camp.

The Diggers' Republic

Before this time, many Boers had crossed the Vaal River and annexed much of the Griqua lands to found another independent state, the Transvaal. The lands along the river had remained in the hands of Griqua chiefs, however, some of whom had granted concessions to diggers. President Pretorius and the Transvaal Government began to cast envious eyes on the riches in the earth and in 1870 claimed all the diamondiferous areas along the northern bank of the Vaal down to the junction with the Hartz River. The Orange Free State also laid claim to lands along the rivers. The diggers cared little who were the owners provided that they could buy stakes and work the ground.

The Transvaal Government made the incredibly naïve move of not only claiming the area but of giving the concession for mining it to a group of local men. The diggers' reaction was to refer the Transvaal Government to an agreement made between one of their original number, Stafford Parker, and the Griqua chief, Jan Bloem, at Nooitgedacht. A Mutual Protection Committee was formed at a big meeting of river diggers and at a subsequent meeting at Klipdrift, it was decided to found a Diggers' Republic in the same way as the Boers had formed their two independent farmers' republics. Stafford Parker, who was a claim owner, ex-policeman, ex-seaman, one-time gold-miner, father of eighteen children, and owner of the local dance-hall, was elected first President (Fig. 2.9).

Stafford Parker took his duties seriously. He wore a top-hat and frock-coat he had purchased on impulse while in London. He appointed an ex-butcher as State Punisher and introduced flogging for theft of stock and diamonds. Card cheats were ducked in the river and petty thieves had to parade through the camps ringing bells and carrying cards labelled 'thief'. Another punishment was to be hauled across the river by a rope tied round the wrists and attached to the stern of a boat, similarly to keel-hauling. Parker also made it compulsory for diggers to train for military service. The flag of the Diggers' Republic showed a horse, with a Union Jack in one corner.

President Pretorius of the Transvaal, with a small armed force and the three concessionaries, travelled to the diggings to claim the land, but had to turn tail when Parker's 'army' advanced on them. Pretorius then tried to make a deal with Parker but was unsuccessful. In the meantime, the British Government in

Fig. 2.9. *Stafford Parker, first President of the short-lived Diggers' Republic.*

Cape Province ordered its agent on the spot to disarm the diggers, which was another ingenuous directive. The British had earlier annexed the territories taken by the Boers – the Orange Free State and the Transvaal – but had abandoned them because of the expense involved. They, too, had become interested again when diamonds were found in quantity.

President Brand of the Orange Free State claimed the Vaal River diggings from the Griqua chief, Nicholas Waterboer, including the land of the Berlin Mission Society on the southern bank. Diggers refused his demands too, so he sent a unit of commando to Waldeck's Plant, downstream of Pniel. Within a short time the commandos were confronted by thousands of armed diggers. Stafford Parker arrived to consult the commando leaders. In the meantime the men of the commando unit began talking to the diggers and finished the Free State's attempt at annexation in a drinking spree that lasted several days.

Waterboer had lawful claims to the territory and had granted concessions to the diggers. There were many confusing manœuvres and eventually legal action. A Court of Arbitration was set up which included a referee, a representative of the British Government and one of the Transvaal.

The decision was in favour of the Griqua chief, which angered not only President Brand, but President Pretorius in the Transvaal, who tried again to make an agreement with the diggers. His failure cost him the presidency, as he was forced on this issue to resign. Waterboer asked the British to take over his country, a manœuvre it now became obvious was planned, for the Griqua chief received a large pension and his territory became a Crown Colony in October, 1871, being renamed Griqualand West.

Many diggers wanted to fight even the British Government to retain their republic, but Stafford Parker declared, 'You cannot fight your own Queen', and the Diggers' Republic ended.

The First Pipe Mines

The first source of diamonds in the Orange Free State was discovered in July, 1870, on the farm Koffiefontein, on a bank of the Riet River, north-west of Fauresmith (Fig. 2.10). On that day, a transport driver named Bam, while camped close to the river, picked up a stone which he thought might be a diamond. Bam continued on his journey to the Vaal, where the stone was positively identified, but the river diggers were sceptical about his having found it so far away. Bam gathered together some friends and they returned to Koffiefontein and dug successfully for a number of years almost undisturbed. The workings of one of the party was so deep by 1874 that he had installed a horse-driven whim to raise buckets of ground. Up to this time only relatively shallow sources had been found.

Fig. 2.10. *Koffiefontein, the first pipe found, as it was when abandoned after earlier working was finished. It was reopened in 1971.*

The diggings turned out to be an original source of diamonds, the first known pipe of blue ground from deep in the earth, which was weathered to yellow ground at the top, and was covered with overburden to the surface. The diggers at this time knew little or nothing about the origin of diamonds, but the finding later of other deep mines brought in the financiers, who realized that to exploit such rich sources of diamond, money and organization were essential. When the Koffiefontein pipe became too deep for individual diggers to mine successfully, they sold the rights to Alfred Mosely, who formed a company to exploit it in 1891. In the same year, a 136-carat stone was found there, which made many more people aware of its existence. Eventually it was purchased by the De Beers Mining Company and worked until 1931. It was reopened in 1971.

One man who heard about the Koffiefontein finds was de Kerk, foreman of the farm Jagersfontein about six miles from Fauresmith. The farm was in a valley through which ran a stream, which was dried out for most of the year. Having learned the rudiments of diamond recovery from Vaal river men passing through, de Kerk decided to try his luck in the river bed. He dug down several feet to the river bedrock and concentrated the gravels he found there with an ordinary garden seive and a tank of water. In August, 1870, he found a 50-carat diamond.

A few Vaal river diggers heard about the find and tried the area, but the occurrence was patchy. The owner of the farm, Miss Visser, charged what was at the time the high fee of £2 a month for a claim, which discouraged more extensive searching. Some diggers remained, however, and found themselves being drawn towards one area. Around 1878, it became evident that the diggings were not alluvial, as was naturally assumed, but the relatively small area with higher yields of good-quality stones was the mouth of a pipe.

The open cast working of the Jagersfontein pipe was easier than others at first because the hard basalt rock around it eliminated most of the problem of surrounding reef falling into the hole as it was worked deeper.

The Excelsior Diamond

J. T. McNish tells the story of an agreement for the owners of the Jagersfontein mine to sell to Wernher, Beit and Co., all diamonds found between July 1892, and midnight 30th June, 1893. Before the time ran out, an overseer had become suspicious of one of the coloured labourers, but had been unable to find anything positively wrong. Half an hour before midnight, the labourer took fright and gave himself up to the mine overseer. He produced a top quality carat diamond that measured $2\frac{1}{2}$ inches by 2 inches and was 1 inch thick! It was at that time the largest ever found. It weighed 972 carats and was subsequently named the Excelsior (Fig. 2.11).

Despite the earlier suspicions of him, the labourer was rewarded with £500, a horse and equipment, and released from his contract. Wernher, Beit and Co., gained the crystal for a fraction of its worth because the contract specified a relatively low price per carat for all stones found. The Excelsior lay in their safe for thirty-three years awaiting a buyer.

In 1910, a 1020-ft. shaft was sunk beside the pipe and another added later, for

Fig. 2.11.   *The Excelsior diamond, that weighed 972 carats in the rough, when found in the Jagersfontein mine. For a time it was the largest known.*

underground working. The pipe was closed for a time during the world depression of 1930 and was not worked during the Second World War when the buildings were used as an internment camp. It has been worked for a number of years, however, but was closed again in 1971.

More Pipe Mines Discovered

In 1867, a Yorkshireman named William Anderson went to Durban to prospect in Africa for gold as an employee of the London and Limpopo Gold Mining Co. Although he found traces of gold, his interest turned to diamonds and he went to the Vaal diggings. A short time there, however, persuaded him that their future was limited, so, having heard of the stones bought by Van Niekerk which had been found on the open veld, he decided to leave the river diggings and try his luck elsewhere. He began by examining the prospecting pits of other diggers and eventually came to the farm, Dorstfontein, owned by Adrian J. van Wyk. It had been bought by van Wyk from another farmer, Abraham du Toit, who himself had purchased it from the Free State Government in 1860.

Van Wyk had built himself a mud-walled hut on the edge of a pan (pond) which was filled with brackish water in the wet season and was an area of cracked mud in the dry season. Anderson asked for permission to dig, but was refused, as van Wyk had no wish to see the place overrun by diggers. Nevertheless, Anderson became friendly with the Boer farmer, whose children one day showed him some stones in the mud walls of the hut. He recognized with excitement that they were diamonds and asked the children to point out the place from which the mud had been dug.

This convinced him that there was an important source of diamonds on the farm, but he kept the knowledge to himself and made a visit to a neighbouring farm, Bultfontein, where he persuaded the owner, Cornelius du Plooy, with whom he had become acquainted, to let him dig. There, too, he found diamonds in the mud of the farm's pan.

Anderson's next move was to find friends who would back him in a venture to exploit both Bultfontein and the pan on the Dorstfontein farm, which eventually became known as Du Toit's Pan (Fig. 2.12). If Anderson had been successful in his plans, he would have owned two of the richest diamond pipes in what was later named Kimberley. They are still being mined intensively today. He would have become a millionaire many times over. Unfortunately, as so often happens, one of his friends was unable to keep the secret and the news spread throughout the Vaal diggings, causing a rush of diggers to Du Toit's Pan in 1870. Anderson was able to make a stake, but as far as is known, his ground was not particularly profitable.

Biggest Rush to the Dry Diggings

News of the dry diggings spread not only through the diggers' communities but throughout the world and very soon there were thousands more adventurers from most of the European countries and from Australia, America, Canada, and New Zealand on the way to the new dry diggings in South Africa. Soon after the end of 1870, the river camps, including Pniel and Klipdrift, were practically deserted.

Chaos reigned wherever there were diamonds in the veld. Farming became impossible. Trees, livestock, vegetation all disappeared. Van Wyk was so distressed that he sold his land for £2,000 to the London and South African Exploration Co., which was represented locally by Henry Webb and Martin Lilienfeld, one of the people who had bought the Star of South Africa from van Niekerk in 1869.

At this time, the farm was seething with diggers and would-be diggers pegging claims, fighting over them and working them. When Webb told diggers to leave because the company he represented had bought the land, he found a revolt on his hands despite his threats to call in the police. He soon realized the situation was uncontrollable. The diggers wanted the area to be declared a public diggings. Webb was asked to attend a meeting of the Diggers' Mutual Protection Association Committee, which he managed to delay until the directors of his company arrived. The result was an agreement that diggers could stake claims anywhere except in the immediate area of Webb's house. Webb declared later that he only signed because he was threatened. It was at this meeting that the mine was named Du Toit's Pan.

Meanwhile, on the neighbouring farm of Bultfontein, the owner du Plooy had been to the Vaal River to see the diggings for himself and had tried searching for diamonds on his own land, but without much success. Very soon after Du Toit's Pan was overrun, there were approaches to du Plooy to allow claims on his land and late in 1870 diggers began prospecting without permission. Du Plooy knew that he would soon be faced with the same problem as his neighbour, unable to farm the land, and he began to look for a buyer.

He was offered £2,000 by a land speculator and when Martin Lilienfeld, now representing the Hope Town Diamond Mining Co., heard about the offer he

Dutoitspan Mine. H.B. Webbs Claim. 1880.

Fig. 2.12.　*The Dutoitspan mine in 1880, showing the claims worked to different levels.*

Bulfontein Mine. Hope & Hadden 1879.

Fig. 2.13.　*Claims in the Bultfontein pipe mine, on the next farm to Dutoitspan, in 1879.*

went to du Plooy and persuaded the religious farmer that as the offer had been made on a Sunday, it was illegal. He offered £2,600 for the land, with an indemnity against court action. Legal action was in fact taken by the first buyer, who won £500 and costs but lost one of the world's biggest diamond pipes.

The Hope Town Diamond Co. began mining Bultfontein themselves, employing a large number of native Africans. When the Du Toit's Pan Diggers Committee heard about this, they decided it was unfair because it eliminated claim pegging. The two companies approached each other for self-protection and amalgamated under the London and South African Exploration Co., with Henry Webb in charge to work both mines. Unable to clear the diggers from Du Toit's Pan, they concentrated on Bultfontein (Fig. 2.13).

The Government steps in

In the meantime, unsuspected by the company, the government in Bloemfontein was putting the finishing touches to a law that was to explode like a land mine among owners of diamondiferous land. In 1871, the government decreed that owners of property where diamonds were found had to declare the areas as public diggings. If they did not, the ground would be confiscated at the compensation of £1 per morgen.* All finds of diamonds had to be reported to government inspectors who would be appointed to control both diggings and diggers. The government would then take half of what owners of land earned in issuing claim licences. Certain conditions were imposed on, and protection granted to diggers.

One result was that the Exploration Co., lost all their digging rights, half of what revenue they could get from allowing claims, and in addition had to pay 10 per cent of what was left to the Diggers' Committee. Another result was that as soon as the news was known, there was a mad rush to Bultfontein.

In effect, the British annexed the diamondiferous farms Vooruitzicht, Bultfontein, Du Toit's Pan (Dorstfontein), Kenilworth, and Wesselton (Benaaudheidsfontein), but not Koffiefontein and Jagersfontein which lay outside the limits of the government's land survey.

Into Yellow Ground

At this time, only the surfaces of the dry diggings which were on pipes were being scratched. It was not until the end of 1871 that a digger went through the overburden of limestone to the decomposed yellow ground where the diamond concentration was much higher. About 6,000 diggers were active on the two farms at this time. Diamonds of over 100 carats were frequently found in 'The Pan'. Claims changed hands for high prices but not all were rich or even payable. Some were given away when they turned out apparently to be barren, and the following day the new owner would find a fortune.

Rough hotels, canteens, shops, and bars were set up for the multitude of diggers who lived in tents and shacks. Prices of goods were high and sometimes outrageous when transport was difficult and supplies short. Most of the time a haze of dust hung over the diggings but when the rains came the diggings became flooded and all work had to stop. When people died they were buried in a

* A morgen is 2·1165 acres.

cemetery near the Bultfontein diggings. Some strange customs originated in communities of diggers. J. T. McNish records that it was the practice of Vaal river diggers to build cairns of stones surmounted by a black flag on a stick along the river banks for their dead.

The de Beers' Farm

On a neighbouring farm to Bultfontein, known as Vooruitzicht, a lone Dutch digger called Corneilsa had been allowed to work a claim on condition that he paid 25 per cent of all he received to the owners of the farm, the de Beers brothers (Fig. 2.14). News of this seeped to a Vaal river digger, Richard Jackson, who eventually decided to form a party of four to investigate. The

Fig. 2.14.   *Johannes Nicholas, as one of the de Beers brothers who bought the Vooruitzicht farm for £50 and sold it for £6,300. About £590 million worth of diamonds have been found there.*

party found Corneilsa, who innocently welcomed them and introduced them to the farmers.

Jackson's party returned to the Vaal and suggested to several friends that they form a larger party, but the news got out and the biggest rush to date started to the de Beers' farm. Horses and wagons and mules were literally raced neck and neck across the veld and apparently Jackson and his friends only beat the main body of the rush by a hundred yards or so to hammer in their pegs. Within hours, the whole area was pegged out beyond the Vooruitzicht farm border, regardless of what might have been the owners' wishes, and into parts of the neighbouring Kaufersdam and Dorstfontein farms.

Jackson found his own six claims worthless as they were just outside the circle of what was a new pipe mine, and he abandoned them with nothing left but his pick and shovel.

Corneilsa took fright at the ruthless rush for land and sold his claim for £110. The de Beers brothers, bewildered by the madness around them, on 19th October, 1871, sold the farm to a syndicate for £6,300, which was a large sum compared with the £50 they had paid for the farm eleven years earlier. Afterwards they complained that they had been tricked and should have received a new wagon and equipment as well! Later, the syndicate sold the farm to the Cape Government for £100,000. To date, about £590 million worth of diamonds have been recovered from the farm, which later came into the ownership of De Beers Consolidated Mines.

The 'Big Hole' of Kimberley

Among the men who arrived at the de Beers farm was a man named Fleetwood Rawstone, who led a group known as the Colesberg Party after the place from which they had originally come. The party had been late arrivals, but Rawstone had bought a claim that they had worked with success, until Rawstone lost it gambling (Fig. 2.15).

Dispirited, the party set off again and camped on the edge of a depression not very far from the de Beers diggings to the west. They were so unlucky there, that some members returned to find employment on other diggings. Rawstone had a cook-boy called Damon who had grown up with his family. Damon was reliable, even in bad times, except when he managed to get hold of alcohol.

At the time that the party, who had begun to call themselves the 'Red Cap Company' because they wore red bags on their heads, were testing this ground and finding nothing, Damon came across a friend with whom he got drunk and became more obstreperous than usual. Rawstone dismissed him, but relented when Damon pleaded for his job and sent him to start a prospect pit in a previously abandoned area.

A few days later, on the Saturday evening of 15th July, 1871, according to the story recorded by one of the Red Cap survivors years later, Damon came to the tent where Fleetwood Rawstone and some of the others were playing bridge and said quietly, 'Fleet, I want to see you.' Irritably, Rawstone told him to come in and Damon opened his hand to disclose three diamonds.

The effect was electric. The card table was overthrown and the players rushed for their pegs and hammers. Claims were marked out for all members of the party, including those who had left, around Damon's pit, which was under a camelthorn tree in the knee-high grass. The next day, Sunday, Rawstone reported the discovery officially to the government surveyor, but already the news had spread and a big new rush was on. On the Monday the government surveyor was already recording and checking claims.

The mine was first called the 'New Rush' and afterwards became known as the Kimberley Mine, and finally the 'Big Hole' of Kimberley. It was worked until 1914. Before then, the thirty-eight-acre hole had become about a mile round the edge and about a quarter of a mile deep. Shafts were sunk to mine it from underground to a depth of 3,601 feet. The story of its mining is told in Chapter Four. About twenty-five million tons of ground were dug out to recover about three tons of diamond (14·5 million carats) worth about £50 million (Fig. 3.6).

Rawstone was unlucky to the last. Of his four claims, two were inside the area of the pipe and two outside, but even the diamondiferous ones were very poor and he hardly paid his way from them. Others in the party were more fortunate. All members of the Red Cap Party were awarded claims although some had not been present when the find was made. One, T. B. Kisch, was mentioned earlier as the first known European to prospect for diamonds in Africa.

Fig. 2.15. *The Red Cap Company, under Fleetwood Rawstone, who found what became the Kimberley mine – now called the Big Hole. Rawstone made a bad claim and gained nothing from the £50 millions' worth of diamonds found there. Damon is on the left.*

Fig. 2.16. *At Nooitgedacht, on the banks of the Vaal river, independent licensed diggers still work by the traditional methods, except for using trucks. Pegs in the foreground show staked claims.*

Present Small Diggings

Most of the inland alluvial diggings, dry diggings in dried-out river beds and banks in South Africa, which were the most numerous of all, are today exhausted, but some diamonds are still found in the most productive of them at Barkly West, Bloemhof, and Lichtenburg. A handful of individual diggers also still works about six square miles of bushland called Nooitgedacht on the Vaal River near Kimberley which is owned by De Beers Consolidated Mines. No new diggers' licences have been issued since 1945 and the prospectors and their labourers still live and work in the conditions of the early frontier (Fig. 2.16).

River claims were first 20 feet square. Later they were made 30 Cape feet square, and eventually 30 by 60 feet. Claims at the dry diggings, i.e. the pipe mines, were always 30 feet square, but the English foot was used at Dutoitspan and Bultfontein, and the Cape foot at the De Beers, Kimberley, and Jagerfontein mines, which made the claims there 31 English feet square.

The Diggers' Press

One of the earliest arrivals on the original Vaal fields was R. W. Murray, co-founder of the *Cape Argus* newspaper in 1857. In August, 1870, he produced the first diggers' publication, *The Diamond Field*, at Pniel. On the following day, a rival appeared, *The Diamond News*, published by Richards, Glanville and Co., who were publishers of the old *Grahamstown Journal*. The company's printing press was carted after the diggers to Du Toits Pan, and then to the New Rush. The name was changed to *The Diamond and Vaal Advertiser*, and again on a change of ownership in the 1870s to *The Diamond Fields Advertiser*. It is still published under the last name as a daily newspaper from Kimberley. *The Diamond News* is now a trade paper, also published from Kimberley.

REFERENCES

Diamonds and Precious Stones, by Louis Dieulafait (London, 1874).
The Diamond Fields Advertiser, Kimberley. Various issues.
The Diamond News, Kimberley. Various issues.
Early Diamond Days, by Oswald Doughty (London, 1963).
The Road to El Dorado, by J. T. McNish (Cape Town, 1968).

CHAPTER THREE

The Big Mining Companies

Cecil Rhodes at Kimberley

The last twenty years of the nineteenth century saw the rise of the big mining companies and gradual elimination of individual diggers in South Africa. The man who had most influence on the course of African history and on the diamond industry in particular, and gave his name to Rhodesia, sailed into Durban in a small barque after a seventy days' journey from England. The date was 1st September, 1870, two and a half months after the New Rush. Cecil Rhodes (Fig. 3.1) had been sent to a better climate at the age of 17 because of his poor health and intended to join his elder brother Herbert, who was farming in Natal, but arrived to find that Herbert had caught 'diamond fever' and had left for the river diggings, where he had made a rich strike.

Cecil stayed on the farm, got to know a number of important people, and lived off an income he made by selling gold shares on commission. In 1871, Herbert returned to find that his younger brother had leased a farm called Lion's Kloof. The two brothers cleared the area for cotton growing, but Herbert was drawn again to the diamond fields as more news came through of big fortunes being made. He departed at short notice leaving behind the advice to wind up the farm and follow him. This Cecil Rhodes did, and arrived on the fields himself in May, 1871. He tried unsuccessfully to buy a claim at the de Beers' diggings and then moved to an area near Fleetwood Rawstone's camp, where he employed some Zulus to dig for him. He was unlucky, however, and had to resort to selling ice-cream, and then water, in order to survive.

As the 1870s continued, the difficulties for individual diggers in the pipe mines became enormous. At first one person was allowed officially to work two claims of 30 feet (or 31 feet) square. Then, in 1874 the number of claims permitted was increased to ten. In 1876, the restriction was removed altogether, mainly because of the difficulties of working separate claims in a concentrated area of yellow ground which reduced in diameter as the diggings became deeper. Removal of the restriction made amalgamations possible.

Cecil Rhodes went into partnership with two Englishmen, Charles D. Rudd and Wallace Anderson, and raised £900 to buy a pump in Port Elizabeth which they hired to diggers whose claims were flooded, earning a considerable sum of money. Rhodes again had serious health problems and this time he returned to England to recover. He was 21 years old. While in England, he borrowed money from his aunt to take a degree in law at Oxford University.

He returned to South Africa in 1873 and managed to buy one claim in the de Beers mine. His profits from the pump venture went to further claims and to enter into partnership with owners who did not want to sell out entirely, until by 1880, he was one of the largest owners.

Fig. 3.1.   *Cecil J. Rhodes, visionary, pioneer, and financier, who formulated diamond marketing policy.*

In 1880 and 1881 there was a period of reckless company promotion and share rigging, combined with great difficulties in working claims, that led to more amalgamations. Most active still in buying claims was Rhodes, who in 1880 had formed the De Beers Mining Co. Ltd., working with two other groups. It took him until 1887 to gain complete control, as some small companies held on to their shares to the end.

Barney Barnato
The same year that Rhodes returned to South Africa, 1873, another man who was to have a considerable influence on the course of events also arrived at the diamond fields. His name was Barney Barnato (Fig. 3.2) and he was the opposite of Rhodes in almost every respect. Rhodes was delicate in health, tall and fair in appearance, and cold and scholarly in manner. Barnato was almost the same

age, but robust in health, short and dark, uneducated, and rumbustious in manner.

Barnato also came out to join his elder brother, Harry. Their real surname was Isaacs, but they had changed it when Barney, at the age of 14, had partnered his brother in a variety act. His prompt to come on stage were the words 'And Barney, too'. This became a nickname Barnato, which both brothers adopted as their surname.

Fig. 3.2.   *Barney Barnato, photographed after he had formed Barnato Diamond Mining, his first company, with a capital of £300,000.*

Barney arrived on the fields at the age of 18, with sixty boxes of doubtful cigars as capital, in the middle of a slump in prices to find his brother almost destitute. He had to turn his hand to selling anything he could get hold of. He also set up a boxing ring to make a little money taking on all-comers for bets. The original booth is now set up in the extensive museum maintained by De Beers on the edge of the Big Hole in Kimberley. He managed to save £30 and with this amount of capital he set up in business as a kopje walloper, as diamond dealers were called, in partnership with a man named Louis Cohen.

When the diggers were abandoning their claims in the Kimberley Mine because they thought that the diamonds were running out at the end of the yellow ground, Barney gave up buying stones and rejoined his brother as Barnato Brothers. Having heard the arguments of the geologists who thought the hard blue ground under the yellow ground should also contain diamonds, and the opposing views of many diggers who said it was hard bedrock like they had found under gravel and sand in alluvial diggings and was barren, Barnato Brothers decided to take a chance and buy up claims as near as possible to the centre of the diggings. In 1880, they formed the Barnato Mining Co., which later merged with the Kimberley Central Mining Co., and bought out the remaining six claims in the centre of the mine from a man named Stewart. In

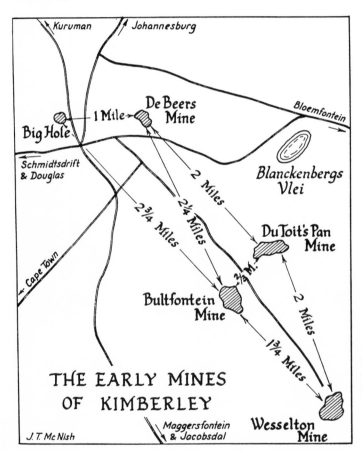

Fig. 3.3. *The pipe mines that became the town of Kimberley.*

Fig. 3.4. *Claims in the Kimberley mine in 1883, showing the French company's key position next to Barnato's Kimberley Central.*

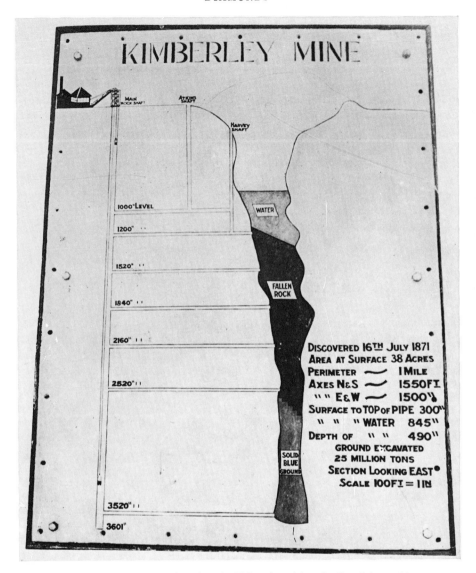

Fig. 3.5. *A notice board at the Big Hole today giving details of the workings.*

1883–4, Kimberley Central, under Barney Barnato's control, was the first to sink shafts into the centre of the mine.

By 1887 the mining operations in Kimberley – the town that had grown from the original mining camps around the group of four pipe mines, Kimberley, De Beers, Dutoitspan, and Bultfontein – were concentrated in the hands of three main groups (Fig. 3.3.). Rhodes was the chairman of De Beers Mines and Barnato was the most influential figure in the Kimberley Mine. The third group, the Compagnie Française des Mines de Diamant du Cap de Bon Espèrance, had the next most important holding in the Kimberley Mine (Fig. 3.4 to 6).

Rhodes with financial backing from his friend Alfred Beit and from Roths-
childs in London, made an offer of £1,400,000 for the French company. When
Barnato heard of this, he immediately thought Rhodes was poaching on this
territory and made a counter offer of £1,750,000.

Rhodes, typically, did not compete, but went to Barnato with the suggestion
that they co-operate. If he were allowed to buy at the lower price, he said, he
would sell the French company to Barnato for a fifth interest in Kimberley
Central and £300,000 in cash. Barnato agreed, sure that the minority holding
Rhodes would gain could easily be contained.

Barnato grossly underrated Rhodes. A financial battle for control of Kimberley Central developed between them with rival bids being made for the
remaining holdings. As the prices of shares in the mining companies shot up, the
prices of diamonds were dropping owing to a slump in sales at the same time as
high production from Africa. At one time top grade stones were as low as 10s. a
carat.

De Beers Consolidated Mines

Barnato was the first to break and agreed to give his shares in Kimberley Central
to Rhodes in exchange for a block of shares with less influence in a new company
called De Beers Consolidated Mines, Ltd., formed by Rhodes in 1888 to control
both pipes and to consolidate all the diamond mining interests and control the
output. The De Beers Mine is shown in Fig. 3.7.

Some shareholders in Kimberley Central were so dissatisfied with the agreement that they took the matter to court on the grounds that the Kimberley
Central charter provided that it should merge only with a similar mining
company and that De Beers Consolidated was not similar as its charter was to
build an empire and even permitted it to 'take steps for good government of any
territory, raise and maintain a standing army, and undertake warlike operations'.

The court decided in favour of the dissident shareholders, but without altering
the outcome, because Rhodes and Barnato liquidated Kimberley Central and
sold the assets to De Beers. Then they handed to the liquidators for distribution
to the shareholders in Kimberley Central a cheque for £5,338,650. The
cancelled cheque was framed and still hangs in the De Beers boardroom at
Kimberley.

Two years before the formation of De Beers Consolidated Mines, Rhodes had
visited the Rand by ox wagon to investigate the goldfields, but had returned to
Kimberley on hearing of a friend who was dying. He considered and turned
down the chance of buying a farm for £250 that was worth £2 million only two
years later. He became Prime Minister of South Africa at the age of 37. Barnato,
who was a year older, took a big part in developing the Rand gold fields, but
gradually broke down in mental health under the strain of running his huge
financial empire and at the age of 44 jumped overboard from the ship on which
he was travelling to England.

Rhodes was Premier again in 1896. The Jameson Raid followed and his
retirement from politics. In 1899, the Boer War broke out when the independent
Boer States invaded the Cape. Rhodes was detained in a cottage in Muizenberg,
near Cape Town, where he died before the war had ended.

51

Fig. 3.6.   *The Big Hole, or Kimberley Mine, today. The town of Kimberley reaches almost to its edge. It is probably the biggest man-made hole.*

The Town of Kimberley

The Boer and diggers' names for the Colesberg party's find did not survive long under England's dignified Victorian administration and on 5th June, 1873, a proclamation announced: The encampment and town heretofore known as De Beers New Rush the Colesberg Kopje No. 2, or Vooruitzigt, shall henceforth be and be described as the town of Kimberley (Fig. 3.8). The Earl of Kimberley was at the time the British Secretary for the Colonies.

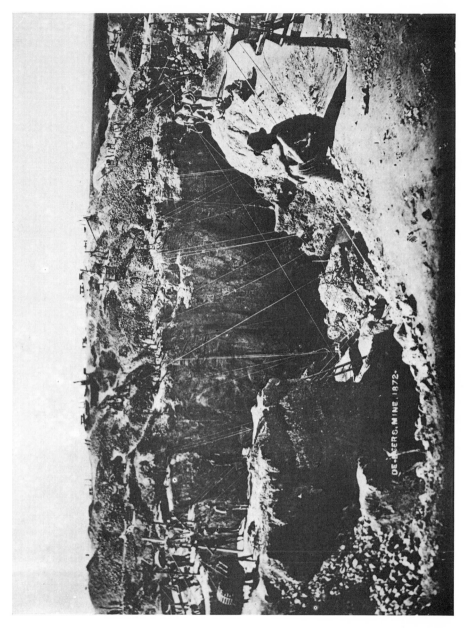

Fig. 3.7.   *De Beers mine in 1872, after it had become so deep that cables and buckets had to be used to bring up the ground. A man winding up a bucket can be seen on the left.*

Four years later, the novelist Anthony Trollope visited the diggings and wrote of Kimberley: I cannot say that Kimberley is an alluring town – perhaps as little so as any town that I have ever visited. . . . The town is built of corrugated iron. It is probably the most hideous that has yet come to man's hands. . . . It is difficult to conceive the existence of a town in which every plank used has to be dragged 500 miles by oxen; but such has been the case at Kimberley.

Another visitor said that the first view was of a white sheen of tents along the ridge. The only regular road was the main street. The rest were paths between the tents and tin houses that diggers moved wherever they wished. In 1968, a huge rubbish dump was examined in Kimberley and found to contain early beer bottles from six different bottling factories and also large numbers of caviar jars. The owner of the dump was selling 'claims' to those interested in looking for relics of old Kimberley.

The camp around the old De Beers mine near by soon fused into Kimberley, and later houses first straggled along and then extended along the track to Dutoitspan, about two miles away, until the two settlements became one (Fig. 3.3).

Kimberley is high, being on the plateau of South Africa, about 4,000 feet above sea-level, and is today a flourishing town in a semi-desert area, but still retains much of its old mining atmosphere. Town buildings extend almost to the

Fig. 3.8.   *Jam of ox wagons at Kimberley in 1880–85, after bringing supplies across the desert.*

edge of the exhausted Big Hole. The big holes of the other mines are security areas because the mines are still in production.

Some of the old timber and corrugated iron buildings still exist. If an old building is demolished, one of the few remaining licenced diggers will usually obtain the right to work the site which he will proceed to do in the traditional manner of the pioneers, even in the middle of the bustling traffic, often making rewarding finds.

One of the finest of the old buildings being preserved is the headquarters of De Beers Consolidated Mines, who have resisted the temptation to have a modern steel and concrete block in its place (Fig. 3.9). Kimberley always remained a very English town until recent times when a big railway depot was set up and the Afrikaans population rapidly increased.

The Wesselton and Premier Mines
On the edge of Kimberley is another pipe mine about two miles east of Dutoit-span. It was discovered in December, 1891, on the farm Benaaudheidsfontein, and was named the Wesselton. It is still very actively mined.

Finding of the Wesselton pipe sparked off another search for kimberlite, as blue and yellow ground were named, but by 1898, after many unpayable

Fig. 3.9.   *De Beers Consolidated Mines still occupy, in Stockdale Street, one of Kimberley's oldest buildings. Even the early atmosphere is still preserved.*

kimberlite areas had been located, most prospectors decided that no more big finds were likely. That was the year, however, that an ex-bricklayer named Thomas Cullinan, who had made a small fortune building, decided to go prospecting in the Pretoria area a long way from Kimberley. He met a man who had picked up a 3-carat diamond on a farm, and on looking around, he noticed a kopje (hill) like those he had seen in the Kimberley area. The farm, Elands-fontein, was about twenty miles north-east of Pretoria.

Cullinan tried to buy the farm, but the farmer, an old Boer named Joachim Prinsloo, refused to sell because he had already been driven out of two farms, Madderfontein where gold had been struck, and another where diamonds had been found. This time Prinsloo was determined not to move as he was completely uninterested in money. Cullinan had to wait until Prinsloo died, which was not long afterwards, until he was able to buy the farm for £52,000 from the old man's daughter.

In 1903, the kopje was identified as the mouth of a pipe that was the biggest known up to that time, the giant Premier mine. It was 2,900 feet long by 1,400 wide and there were 3,570 claims on it, each 31 feet by 31 feet. The size of it gave Rhodes' partner, Alfred Beit, a severe shock, as he believed it could undermine the Rhodes empire. Eventually, however, it came under the control of De Beers Consolidated Mines.

It was here that the biggest diamond of all time was found on 25th January 1905, by the surface manager, F. G. S. Wells, projecting from a mine wall. It was named the Cullinan, after the owner of the mine, and weighed 3,106 metric

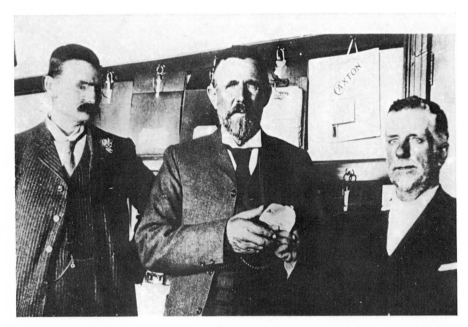

Fig. 3.10. *William McHardy, general manager of the Premier Mine in 1905, holding the Cullinan diamond, the largest ever found. On the left of the picture is Sir Thomas Cullinan and on the right 'Daddy' Wells, surface manager, who found the stone.*

carats, being about a pound and a half in weight. It was cut into 105 stones, the biggest of which are still the two biggest polished diamonds in the world (Figs. 3.10 and 17.10 and Appendix 3). Three very large pipe mines were subsequently found in Africa, the Williamson in Tanzania, the Finsch in the Republic of South Africa, and A.K.1 in Botswana, and are referred to elsewhere in this book.

Diamonds on the Beaches

The country where most of the world's gem diamonds are discovered today is a strip of wild, bare sandy coast running northwards from the mouth of the Orange River in the former German territory of South West Africa, now a protectorate of South Africa (Fig. 3.11). The river is the boundary between the two countries. The strip of land lies within the Namib Desert area, which has scrubby vegetation at times of the year but no surface water. In the summer, herds of gemsbok and springbok come into the desert, and many Bushmen still manage to exist in the interior.

In 1863 or 1864, a Hottentot chief, David Christiaan, gave a mineral concession to De Pass, Spence and Company of Cape Town, covering a strip of coast twenty miles wide extending from Angra Pequene (which became the town of Luderitz) south to the Orange River. Working through the Pomona Syndicate, the company mined lead for a time, but found it unprofitable.* In 1884, South West Africa was annexed by Bismark and declared a German protectorate. Kimberlite pipes were found in the Gibeon district, but were not diamondiferous.

The Germans built a railway from Luderitz which was at times blocked by 'walking sands' – drifts built up by the wind. One day in 1908, a coloured man, Zacharias Lewala, who had worked previously for De Beers in Kimberley, was shovelling sand near Kolmanskop, when he saw some crystals that he recognized as diamonds. They were shown to a railway official, August Stauch, who persuaded the German Colonial Company to grant him claims in the area. This started such a rush that within four months of the first find, the whole area north of Pomona had been pegged.

Soon it was discovered that diamonds occurred in a strip of coast from Marmosa to Conception nearly 300 miles long and from two to twelve miles wide. So rich was the ground in some parts that diamonds lay on the surface, where winds had blown the sands away. In the Idatal Valley bottom, the Germans employed African labourers to crawl on their hands and knees in a line to pick up the crystals, as shown in Fig. 3.12. In six years, the area yielded about £9 millions worth of diamonds (Fig. 3.13 and 3.14).

In September 1908, soon after the rush, the German Government decreed the area *Sperrgebeit* – forbidden territory – which meant that from the north of the Orange River to latitude 26° north, and inland for 100 kilometers from the Atlantic Ocean, no general prospecting was allowed by anyone except the Deutsche Diamanten Gesellschaft. In 1909, a marketing company, Diamond Regie, was formed, based in Berlin. (In fact, coastal diamonds occur from about five miles north of the river mouth.)

Mining all but stopped when war was declared in 1914. A year later the

* The facts of this historical background are based on research by Frank Beresford, of Consolidated Diamond Mines of South West Africa.

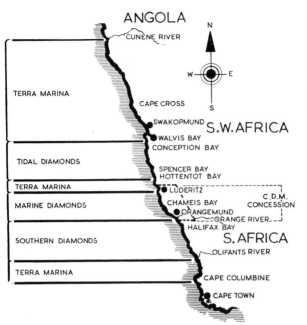

ANGOLA

CUNENE RIVER

N
W   E
S

TERRA MARINA

CAPE CROSS

SWAKOPMUND

S.W.AFRICA

WALVIS BAY
CONCEPTION BAY

TIDAL DIAMONDS

SPENCER BAY
HOTTENTOT BAY

TERRA MARINA

LUDERITZ

MARINE DIAMONDS

CHAMEIS BAY

C.D.M.
CONCESSION

ORANGEMUND
ORANGE RIVER

HALIFAX BAY

SOUTHERN DIAMONDS

S. AFRICA

OLIFANTS RIVER

TERRA MARINA

CAPE COLUMBINE

CAPE TOWN

Fig. 3.11. *The coast of South West Africa, where over 80 per cent of the diamonds found are of gem quality. There are deposits under the sands on the beaches and also in the sea, where the concessions are shown on the map.*

Fig. 3.12. *During the early days of the century, the German mining companies employed labourers to crawl along the coastal sands to look for diamonds near Luderitz.*

Fig. 3.13. *Camel transport at the police post and water hole at Bogenvels in 1912 after the area had been declared Sperrgebeit – forbidden territory.*

German administration was overthrown and the South African Government took control, allowing restricted mining by nine German companies, who did well until 1920, when a slump in demand began to affect production. At this point, Ernest Oppenheimer, who was later to become the chairman of De Beers, negotiated with the companies, which resulted in the formation of Consolidated Diamond Mines of South West Africa Ltd., in the same year.

Some time earlier, in 1909, a German prospector, F. W. Martens, had found a few diamonds in the extreme south of the Sperrgebiet, near Alexander Bay. During the following year, two other prospectors dug inspection pits on the farm Sandkrall on the north bank of the river. Unfortunately for them, they missed immensely rich deposits by about seventy yards. The gravels were discovered in 1927, after a find near Port Nolloth in 1925 by J. E. Carstens reawakened interest in the area.

The man most responsible for working the deposits and discovering something of their nature was a brilliant geologist named Dr. Hans Merensky, who formed the H.M. Association in January, 1927, to buy from two solicitors' claims at Alexander Bay a few miles south of the Orange River in north-west Naquamaland.

The three partners in the Association put up £30,000 to buy the claims and it seems that there was no written contract, only a record in the minute book.* As soon as it became clear that the syndicate had control of rich deposits, Ernest Oppenheimer, who was a friend of Merensky and who was steadily acquiring

* Communication from the Anglo-American Corporation of Johannesburg.

Fig. 3.14. *The first train to run between Elizabeth Bay and Bogenvels in about 1912.*

diamond interests, bought the holding of one of the partners in June the same year for £500,000 on behalf of the Anglo-American Corporation.

In November, 1928, Merensky sold his entire holding to Anglo-American for £1,006,000, which gave them a 74 per cent holding. Ernest Oppenheimer remarked afterwards, 'It isn't often a man comes to a meeting without sixpence in his pocket and leaves it owning a million.'

As soon as Merensky had discovered the richness of the claims, he had instructed all his employees to obtain prospector's licences and to peg claims, but the local magistrate had refused to issue the necessary certificates, which led to a long dispute, partly resolved by the passing of the Precious Stones Act in November 1927, after which the H.M. Association appointed Consolidated Diamond Mines of South West Africa as technical advisors.

The Oyster Line

Merensky's name is associated with his discovery of the connection between diamonds and oyster fossils. After one of his prospectors had reported finding some diamonds among fossilized oyster shells, Merensky told the diggers to follow the trail of oyster shells and they turned up some superb stones. The diggings became known as 'the oyster line', a line parallel to the sea below which oysters used to breed.

The line was in fact associated with a ledge or terrace where diamonds were trapped. News of the discovery led to wild rumours that diamonds had been found in oysters, like pearls!

Continuing disputes over rights led to a government survey which distinguished six formations towards the sea:

1. The oyster line.
2. The extension of the oyster line.
3. The operculum (another shell fish) bed line.
4. The pebbly limestone line.
5. An area near the Orange River consisting of river gravel instead of shingle like the others.
6. The Buchenberg area.

Soon after news of the Alexander Bay discoveries reached them, Consolidated Diamond Mines began to prospect for similar lines north of the Orange River in their own territory. There were greater difficulties owing to the much thicker overburden of sand, but by mid-1928, they had traced the main terraces for a considerable distance up the coast. Today these diggings are still the richest of all for gem diamonds (Fig. 3.15).

It was discovered later that there were double deposits at the mouth of the Orange River where sea and river deposits overlaid each other.

Further prospecting provided an estimate in 1930 that there were more than two and a half million carats of diamonds in the strip of land from the Orange mouth twenty-five miles northwards, but the excitement was short-lived because production had to be suspended between 1931 and 1935 during the world trade depression.

Fig. 3.15.   *After Consolidated Diamond Mines took over they introduced more mechanical means of stripping the sand from beaches. This was at Elizabeth Bay.*

Oranjemund Founded

Mining was restarted in 1935 and C.D.M., by then mining the whole coast from their headquarters in Luderitz, gradually moved their main operations to the south. It was decided to build a town in the desert at the southern end of the concession, just by the mouth of the river, which gave the town its name, Oranjemund. In 1943, C.D.M. moved and now the town, shown in Fig. 3.16, has grown so much that it houses about 2,500 Europeans and about 3,500 Africans, mostly from Ovamboland. It is completely isolated from the outside world, not only by its remote position surrounded by sand, but by the all-enveloping security precautions, yet many people like the isolation and insularity so much that they have spent decades of their lives happily in the town.

There is a town centre with shops and a power station that is the largest diesel plant in southern Africa, fed by fuel oil delivered twice yearly by oil tankers and pumped through a two miles long undersea pipeline. There is a hospital, infant schools, a golf course and a sailing lake in some old diamond diggings. In 1951, the building of the Ernest Oppenheimer bridge over the river brought Oranjemund a little more into touch with the outside world.

Diamonds in Namaqualand

The finds along the coast north of the river started prospecting to the south of the Merensky claims farther into South African territory. Farms along the coast for about 100 miles south of Alexander Bay were found to be diamondiferous by the H.M. Association, Anglo-American, Barnato Brothers, and the Consolidated Union Selection Trust.

In 1928, they formed their interests into the Cape Coast Exploration Company, controlling the coast from Alexander Bay to the Great Brak River, about 120 miles. Prospecting was at first prohibited under the Precious Stones Act, to prevent over-production of diamonds, but later some deposits were worked and the area became the State Alluvial Diggings under the Act.

About the same time, more alluvial deposits were found in the western Transvaal, and despite the agreements made to control the market by members of the Diamond Syndicate, too many diamonds were reaching the market at the same time. How the market was gradually brought under control is described in Chapter Fourteen.

Other Discoveries in Africa

When diamonds were picked out of the gravels of the Kiminina River near the Mai Munene waterfall in 1910, it was little suspected that they would lead to the discovery of the world's biggest source of diamonds. The diamond field was in the Belgian Congo and was so large that it extended into the neighbouring country of Angola, which is held by the Portuguese. The estimated size of the fields, which comprise many ancient river beds, is 150,000 square miles (approx. 390,000 sq. km.)

The concession for mining in the Belgian Congo was awarded to the Société Internationale Forestière et Minière du Congo, or Forminière for short, but since the Congo became a republic has been worked by the government with the

Fig. 3.16. *Oranjemund, the town in the coastal desert, built by Consolidated Diamond Mines of South West Africa as it is today.*

Fig. 3.17. *Gravels being panned on the banks of the river Sewa in Sierra Leone to recover alluvial diamonds, which are in gravels only four or five feet below the surface.*

help of technical advisors from the diamond mining industry. The Angola part of the fields were worked by a subsidiary of Forminière known as Diamag, the Companhia de Diamantes de Angola.

Most of the output is of industrial diamonds and although these are usually small in size, large stones of up to about 40 carats do occur. The centre of the

Congo workings is the town of Tshikapa, in the Kasai region of the country, and the gravels are excavated from about fifty large pits. Extraction of diamonds was carried out under the Forminière rule by tromelling to remove the large pebbles and the sand, and passing the concentrate through an electro-magnetic extractor, over grease tables and finally hand sorting. Diamonds were picked off the grease tables by Congolese, using tweezers.

A curious mining official washed some of the gravel from the trommels used to cover paths in the city. He found that they had a content of 20 to 25 carats of large diamonds per cubic metre! Because of the number of large diamonds rejected, it was decided to instal a crusher to reduce all the large rejected material and to repass it through the recovery plant. Any large diamonds are therefore crushed.

The diamond fields of the Gold Coast, now Ghana, were discovered in 1919, when Sir Albert Kitson picked up a crystal at Abomoso near the Birim River. An important source of better quality in Sierra Leone gravels was found after a geological survey had located two diamonds in quartz gravels on the bank of the Gbobora River. Consolidated African Selection Trust were granted prospecting rights and found further rich fields. (Fig. 3.17.)

The alluvial diamond areas of Guinea, formerly French Guinea, are an extension of the same fields.

A bigger pipe mine than the Premier was found in Tanganyika (now Tanzania) and named the Williamson after its discoverer and owner (Fig. 6.2). It now produces about half a million carats a year, about half being of gem quality. Some of the stones are pinkish or pink in colour and one of these, of 54 carats in the rough, was cut to 26·60 carat and presented in a brooch to Princess Elizabeth when she was married.

There are also alluvial deposits in Tanzania, found originally in 1910 south of Lake Victoria, but not worked until 1925.

In the 1950s an even larger pipe was found about 100 miles west of Kimberley by A. T. Fincham. Further pipe finds were made in Botswana, formerly Bechuanaland, in 1968. More details of these later pipes are given in Chapters Four and Six.

Deposits in Other Countries

These are diamonds of good quality in some rivers of Guyana, formerly British Guiana, in difficult and remote terrain, which are recovered by 'pork-knockers' using relatively primitive methods. Venezuela, also in South America, produces diamonds which often have a greenish coating although the colour inside may be fine.

Borneo, a very old source, and Indonesia, still mine some stones. There is a little production in Australia, from which come particularly hard stones owing to twinning or 'knots' in the crystals, and isolated small occurrences in the U.S.A.

Deposits in Russia

Diamonds were occasionally found in placer deposits in the Ural Mountains of Russia by gold miners, but when prospectors explored the region it became evident that there were no pipes. From 1938, systematic prospecting was carried

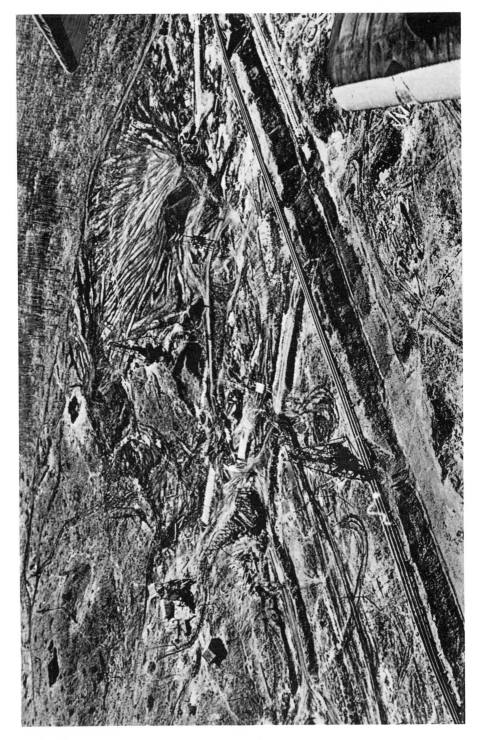

Fig 3.18. *The Mir pipe in the arctic regions of Russia after work had begun stripping off the overburden.*

out in the vast territory between the Yenisei and Lena Rivers in Siberia, because geologists had declared it to be a similar platform zone to the diamondiferous regions of Africa and India.

In 1947, a big expedition was set up to explore central and eastern Siberia and a year later the first diamonds were found in the upper reaches of the Nizhnaya Tunguska River. Many geological parties were sent into the basins of the rivers, into the Siberian forests, and through the mountain ranges, where the summers are hot and wet and the winter temperatures are rarely above $-40°$ C. Alluvial deposits were found in several areas including the bed of the Vilyui River, but no pipes.

After the discovery of pyrope garnets in 1953 indicating the presence of diamonds, prospecting was concentrated in the same neighbourhood, which led to the finding of the first kimberlite pipe in the upper Markha River during the following year by a woman mineralogist from Leningrad, L. A. Popugayeva. The pipe was named Zarnitza (Dawn).

In the years from 1954, about 400 pipes and seams were located, but only about one in forty or so was diamondiferous. The richest pipe is the Mir (Peace) in the basin of the Lesser Batuobiya tributary to the Vilyui. The Mir pipe is oval in section, about 400 metres by 600 metres in size at the top and over 1,000 metres deep with sides that slope at between 60 and $75°$ (Fig. 3.18).

Enormous mining problems have been overcome because the soil is permanently frozen to as deep as 350 metres and only the top one or two metres thaw in the summer. The permafrost affects alluvial as well as pipe deposits because the gravels are cemented with ice even in summer.

A big self-contained mining town has been built around what was an original tented community of miners and construction workers around the Mir pipe. The

Fig. 3.19. *The town of Mirny in Yakutia, USSR, that has been built for workers at the diamond mine.*

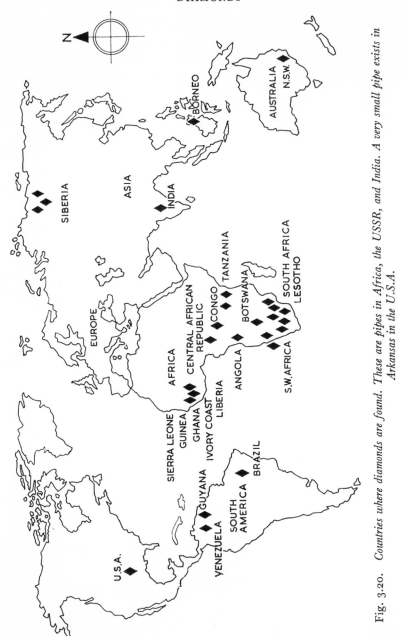

Fig. 3.20. Countries where diamonds are found. These are pipes in Africa, the USSR, and India. A very small pipe exists in Arkansas in the U.S.A.

town is known as Mirny and is said to depend for all its power needs on an arctic atomic power station (Fig. 3.19).

As soon as production at the mines became significant, a diamond laboratory was set up and also the first of several large diamond-cutting works was built at Svedtlovsk.

Second to the Mir in size is the Udachnaya (Success) pipe, discovered also in

1954, but on the Arctic Circle, about 300 miles to the north of the Mir, in the basin of the Daaldyn tributary of the Markha River. Mining began in 1969, following plans by the Yukatulmaz, the diamond trust set up in 1957 to plan the industry.

In 1959, another diamond pipe was located near the Mir and named the Sputnik. Two years after that there was another pipe find about 300 miles north of Mirny on the Arctic Circle, which was named Aikhal (Glory). Rich deposits have been located even further into the Arctic Circle at Anabar Tundra.

There are six central treatment plants in operation and from 30 to 35 per cent of production is said to be of gem quality, nearly all exported to the West. The largest diamond reported weighed 166 carats and was unearthed by a prospector near Mirny in 1968. U.S.S.R. diamond production is not disclosed, following the usual communist practice of controlling all information, but was believed to be in the neighbourhood of 1·6 million carats of gem diamonds and 6·4 million carats of industrials in 1968.

REFERENCES

The Diamond News and S. A. Jeweller, Kimberley. Various issues.
The Gemmologist, London. Various issues.
Optima, Johannesburg. Various issues.
Graves and Guineas, by J. T. McNish (Cape Town, 1969).
Cecil Rhodes, by Sir T. E. Fuller (London, 1910).
Ace of Diamonds – The Story of Solomon Barnato Joel, by Stanhope Joel (London, 1958).
The Great Barnato, by Stanley Jackson (London, 1970).

CHAPTER FOUR

Mining and Recovery Methods

Early diamond diggers in South Africa introduced some basic methods of recovery that have changed only in scale and sophistication in modern days.

At the river diggings, pits were dug down to the gravels which were extracted by pick and shovel (Fig. 4.1). On dry days, gravel was sifted immediately by a man with a round sieve, like an ordinary garden sieve. The sieve had a large mesh so that it retained only pebbles over about an inch across, which after inspection were thrown away. Diamonds were unlikely to be of this size, but any that were could easily be seen and recovered.

What passed through the sieve was sifted through a finer sieve to get rid of the sand. Any diamonds the size of sand were not worth recovering. The fraction left – the 'middlings' – was taken to the river to be washed in a fine sieve to remove any remaining fine silt and dirt, and the remainder was searched for diamonds. The procedure was not possible on wet days, so the whole of the material dug up was washed while being sieved.

Recovery soon became divided into three main operations; screening (sieving), washing, and hand-sorting. Screening remained crude, although some miners arranged sieves of different mesh in tiers of three until a Californian gold digger working in the diamond fields invented a simple sifting machine. His name was J. L. Babe, and he went to South Africa in 1865, before Vaal River diamonds were found, as a representative of the Winchester Repeating Rifle Co.

The 'Baby'

Babe invented a rocking sieve around 1870 which became known after him as the Baby or Yankee baby. By selling it and using it himself on the diggings, he was so successful that he was able to retire to America in 1873. The baby comprised two sieves, one above the other. The main one was in a large rectangular frame hung from four rawhide thongs or light chains from four posts planted in the ground. It was fed through a smaller sieve about two feet square with a mesh that allowed through it stones up to about half an inch across. The total effect was that the larger material was discarded at one end of the baby and the fine tailings underneath. Off the other end came the middlings, which were then washed and sorted. Babe had his machine made in Colesberg. Fig. 4.2. shows a rocking screen made at some later date.

Washing could be carried out before or after screening, depending upon the deposit – how much fine material or earth was in it – and upon the availability and cost of water.

A form of cradle was also used for washing. There were many types, the construction of which depended on the material that was available. The simplest

Fig. 4.1. *Digging a prospecting pit at the corner of a claim to determine the depth of the layer of diamondiferous gravel.*

was a discarded box, in which gin bottles had been sent from England, mounted on top of another gin box so that it could be rocked from side to side by levers, as shown in Fig. 4.3 It was used for dry sieving, but for washing as well, when water was poured on the top from a bucket. More elaborate cradles were devised which did the job of sieving as well as washing.

71

Fig. 4.2.   *A form of rocking cradle to separate smaller pebbles including diamonds from larger ones.*

Fig. 4.3.   *Diggers on the banks of the Vaal river in the early days. On the left two boxes are being used as a rocking sieve where gravel is also washed. In the centre and on the right are picking tables.*

The Long Tom

Australian diggers introduced a form of washer used for alluvial gold which also did some sorting and was known as the long tom. It was a long sloping trough with riffles (small pieces of wood) nailed transversely across it from one end to the other. The gravel was dumped on the higher end and washed down by a stream of water from buckets or a pump. Small and light material including sand was washed down over the riffles, and so were some of the larger but lightweight elements, but diamonds were trapped.

Concentrating in Water

Water was used as a means of concentrating the heavier fraction of the gravels. The term concentrating means separating the material of higher relative density. This heavier fraction of gravel is called the concentrate, and obviously most concentrates can be further concentrated.

The sieving method introduced into the diamond fields was already known to gold miners and is still in use in various parts of the world by both gold and diamond miners.

Deposit that has been screened and washed is emptied in a convenient quantity into a sieve, which is about two feet six inches across and has a bottom of fine mesh. The sieve is held in a tub of water or in the river, where it is sharply twisted one way then the other a few times and then moved more gently up and down in a jigging motion. The actions are repeated until the lighter gravels come to the top of the sieve and the heavier ones are concentrated in the middle at the bottom. A sieve is shown in Fig. 4.4.

The sieve is lifted out of the water and taken to the picking table where it is deftly turned over and the contents dumped on the table like a child making a mud pie. When the sieve is lifted off, the gravel is left, shining wet, in the shape of a large flat cake. The picker examines the stones on the top in the middle of the pile, and picks out any diamond crystals. Then, to make sure that no diamonds

Fig. 4.4. *A sieve, twisted in water to bring diamonds to the centre of a pile of concentrate, has here been upturned to empty its contents on the picking table, with heaviest material at the top in the centre.*

have remained in the rest of the gravel, he goes through the 'cake' of gravel, slice at a time (Fig. 4.4).

To do this, he uses a home-made tool, usually a triangular piece of iron or aluminium about six inches long by three inches or less wide. With the tool, he cuts off a section of the gravel and spreads it across the sorting table, examining the multicoloured concentrate for diamonds. Then he sweeps this layer on to the ground and takes another section of the heap until it has gone.

The Picking Table

The picking table was at first nothing more than an inverted packing-case. It was soon displaced by a rough table or trestle table covered with a sheet of iron, usually an old enamelled advertisement or a flattened tin container, nailed on. Some diggers used sacking as a top cover. Usually there were strips nailed along three sides to prevent gravel from rolling off. Others made a booth with a back, sides and a top to reduce the sun's brightness.

Exactly the same methods are used by individual diggers today, although the sieve may be a little different. In Guyana, for example, a cone-shaped pan, like a metal dustbin top, is used instead of a sieve. At Nooitgedacht, on the Vaal River banks, the method has not changed at all.

In the later days of the river diggings, rotary washing pans were introduced. They had been developed at the dry diggings as described on the following pages. Hand-operated rotary washing pans are also still in use today on individual claims.

Mining at the Dry Diggings

When the dry diggings were first discovered, they were thought to be the same kind of deposits as the river ones and the same methods of recovery were employed. It was naturally supposed that the deposits were of only limited depth, and claims were allowed next to each other, just like those by the rivers.

By the time that the 'New Rush' (now the Kimberley Big Hole) was found in 1871, it was known that deposits went down to a considerable depth, so it was decided that each claim would contribute a strip of $7\frac{1}{2}$ feet which would not be worked for the general benefit. This resulted in a series of roadways 15 feet wide and 45 feet apart. The idea was practicable at first, but as soon as the claims were dug deeply with almost vertical sides, the roads began to fall in. The whole area was weathered yellow ground, which became very friable as it weathered even further after exposure to the air. A view of the mine in 1872 is seen in Fig. 4.5.

The ground being mined was dug with picks and shovels and loaded into sacks, which were carried by labourers up steps cut in the side of the claim and emptied by the side of the road (Fig. 4.6). The sacks were taken to the edge of the mine and the ground broken up, screened and sorted there. Some claims had sloping ramps up which hand trucks of ground were pushed. Others used a pulley and block for hauling up the ground in buckets.

Haulage Systems at Kimberley

By 1872, the roads had become unsafe for use and after two years they had

Fig. 4.5. *The Kimberley mine in 1872 when roads left between claims were beginning to crumble at the edges.*

Fig. 4.6. *Chains of labourers working in the west side of the Kimberley mine when it was still worked by open cast methods.*

disappeared altogether. Aerial gear was then devised for bringing yellow ground from each separate claim to the surface at the edge of the mine.

The first arrangement was a pulley fixed above, at the edge of the hole, and a second one on the claim below. An endless rope ran round the pair of pulleys and to this the bucket, made of hide, was attached. A digger at the top wound his pulley to bring up the loaded bucket. There were at one time thousands of these lines from the claim, as shown in Fig. 4.7, taken in 1876.

The ropes and buckets were replaced by iron or steel cables and large steel bucket-shaped bins. A still later arrangement was a trolley which ran on the cables. The trolley was a frame with four wheels carrying a container. The wheels ran on two parallel cables the appropriate distance apart (Fig. 4.8). A separate rope attached to the wheeled frame pulled it up the sloping cables. This rope was wound round a whim (large horizontal drum) at the edge of the hole. The many whims around the edge were turned by gangs of labourers or by horses. Later steam engines were introduced (Fig. 4.9).

At the claim, now hundreds of feet below ground level, the container was filled from a platform. At the top, it was automatically discharged into a bin. Aerial gear for extracting blue ground was in use at the Jagersfontein mine as late as the turn of the twentieth century.

With some open-cast mines, flooding was a serious problem, owing to the crude and insufficient methods of pumping out water. The Wesselton Mine suffered particularly.

Fig. 4.7. *Staging in several tiers round the edge of the Kimberley mine in 1876 to hold cables up which hide and metal buckets of ore were drawn.*

Fig. 4.8. *More elaborate cable systems with trolleys running on wires replaced some of the earlier buckets.*

Methods of Washing

There was no washing at first at the dry diggings, as the areas were in semi-desert. The yellow ground was pulverised by sledge-hammers and shovelled into rectangular hand sieves with $\frac{1}{8}$ inch holes in them. What passed through the holes was thrown away and what remained went to the picking tables.

The method was so inefficient that in recent times the piles of tailings left by

77

Fig. 4.9. *The top edge of the Kimberley mine in 1875 showing whims turned by horses to draw up the buckets of ore.*

early diggers have been found quite rich when reworked. In some areas, old tailings have been worked over three times as extraction methods improved.

Soon various types of washing were introduced based on those in use at the wet diggings, although provision of water for them was usually a problem. Before washing, yellow ground was passed through a revolving sieve known as a cylinder or a trommel. It was a sloping tube of steel with 1-inch to $1\frac{1}{4}$-inch holes in it, which was rotated by a handle. The ground to be washed passed through the holes and the larger lumps that went straight through the trommel were discarded. The trommel is still in use today for prospecting in South West Africa and elsewhere (Fig. 4.10).

The Rotary Pan

By about 1875, hand-driven rotary washing pans had come into use. The inventor may have been a J. Mackay. The rotary washing pan was simple in concept, but its exact operating principles even today are not fully understood and are being studied by the Diamond Research Laboratory in Johannesburg.

In its more developed form, the washing pan was an annular container, four feet across and about nine inches deep. In the central hole was a vertical axle on which four arms in the form of a cross were pivoted. From the arms rows of knives extended downwards into the pan, like rakes, as shown in Fig. 5.5.

The ground was shovelled into the annular pan, which was filled with water. The rakes were turned by winding a handle, with the result that the water and gravels were swilled round (Fig. 4.11). Water flowed over the edge, taking with

Fig. 4.10. *A trommel used at the turn of the century for sifting gravel. It was rotated by a handle.*

it the lighter materials held in suspension in the muddy water, or puddle as it was called. Diamonds and other heavy minerals settled to the bottom. After each load, the pan was emptied for picking over. (Fig. 4.12.)

Rotary washing pans are still used in Kimberley and elsewhere. The modern version is power-driven and much larger. The puddle is a thick muddy liquid of decomposed kimberlite and water with a specific gravity kept at about 1·15 to 1·25. The strange fact is that lumps of kimberlite with a specific gravity of 2·7

Fig. 4.11. *The original form of washing pan, which floated off most of the lighter material and caused diamonds and other heavy material to settle in the bottom.*

79

Fig. 4.12.   *Washing pans at the pipe mines in the early days operated by horse whims and later by steam.*

float *upwards* and over the central weir. In some parts of Africa, rotary pans containing only clear water are used to float fractions which would sink in still water.

Mining Blue Ground

Ground from the tops of pipe mines was kimberlite converted to yellow ground by the weathering agencies of air and percolating water, which was therefore easily broken up for sieving and washing. After diggers had reached a certain depth, they met the much harder unaltered kimberlite known as blue ground. At the Kimberley Mine this occurred at about eighty feet down.

Thinking they had come to the end of the diamondiferous area, a number of diggers sold their claims. Those who remained found the broken blue ground could not easily be pulverized to release the diamonds. It was noticed, however that lumps of blue ground thrown aside from the trommels began to break up after a time.

The blue ground from the upper workings was therefore spread out over large areas around the mine and took about three months to disintegrate (Fig. 4.13). The most favourable conditions for weathering were alternate very dry and heavy rain periods. When the weather did not help, the blue ground was broken into smaller lumps by gangs of labourers using the backs of shovels or mallets. At times it was artificially watered.

The surrounding country rock near the surface of pipes was so soft that the

Fig. 4.13.   *The French Company's washing plant at Kimberley before the turn of the century. In the background are the 'floors' where blue ground was spread out to be broken down by the weather.*

Fig. 4.14.   *The Kimberley Central Company sunk a mine shaft in the interior of the Kimberley pipe, which was the first attempt to mine diamonds from underground.*

sides of all the pipes in Kimberley were continuously crumbling. The reef fell into the holes more rapidly than it could be cleared away. By 1882, three tons of debris had to be removed to extract one ton of blue ground from the Kimberley Mine. At the De Beers Mine, after miners had seen what had happened at the Kimberley Mine, an attempt was made to cut back the sides, but this proved almost impossible by the methods then available. At Dutoitspan, a rim of blue ground was left as a kind of protecting wall, but one day all the walls collapsed, luckily when the mine was almost empty of workers.

Underground Mining

On the suggestion of a contractor, Edward Jones, about 1883, it was decided to attempt to mine the Kimberley hole by sinking a shaft. There was insufficient money to sink a shaft from outside, so Mr. Jones developed one from inside, through the rubble on the top of the blue ground. It proved practicable, and several other shafts were sunk in other parts of the mine (Fig. 4.14).

After the Kimberley Mine came under control of Cecil Rhodes, sufficient capital was provided to sink a shaft from outside the pipe and underground workings had reached a depth of 3,601 feet when operations finished in 1914.

The first system of underground working was a form of pillar-and-stall mining. Eventually, the blue ground became honeycombed with chambers and the pillars began to collapse under the pressure of rubble above. The mine was evacuated and a fresh start had to be made.

The next method, known as the Gouldie system, involved cutting chambers in a staggered plan so that the top of the blue ground formed a kind of hump

Fig. 4.15. *De Beers directors photographed in September 1891. At the back are William H. Craven, Gardner F. Williams, and Ludwig Breitmeyer and in the front, John Morrogh, Francis Oats, B. I. Barnato, Charles E. Nind, and Woolf Joel.*

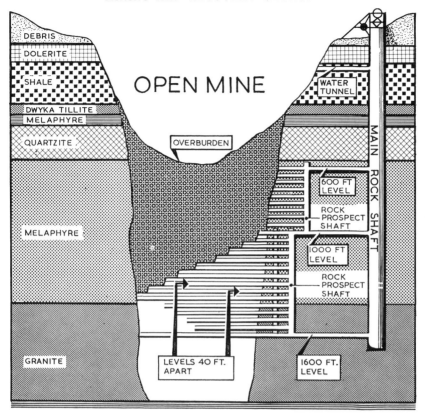

Fig. 4.16. *Principle of chambering in a pipe mine. The blue ground is the white area.*

underneath the overburden, which was supported at the sides like an arch, thus relieving the pressure.

As any pipe is mined from underground, the overburden of shale and rubble mixed with blue ground, gradually descends in the pipe as seen from the surface. The overburden causes pressure on the underground workings, of course, and it is important to prevent any more reef falling into the ever-deepening hole.

The Gouldie system became impractical in the Big Hole of Kimberley at greater depths owing to the various other systems being worked on adjacent claims regardless of safety.

Chambering

After 1887, when the De Beers Mining Company was formed, the General Manager, Gardner Williams (Fig. 4.15), developed about 1890 a uniform mining system for the whole mine known as chambering. Haulage levels were established at 600, 1,000, and 1,600 feet down from the main rock shaft which was itself sunk through the country rock by the side of the diamond pipe (Fig. 4.16).

The main shaft is normally one of two shafts which are sunk about 1,000 feet from the edge of a pipe. It is mainly for haulage and the other is for ventilation also. Main shafts of mines are rectangular in section and today have five compartments, with cages for taking miners up and down and skips for bringing ore to the surface.

Every 40 feet down, chambering levels were established, and at each chambering level a series of parallel tunnels were driven across the pipe to the other side. These tunnels are the 'chambers'. They are 40 feet high and 12 feet wide with 10-feet wide 'pillars' between them. The chambers on the level below are staggered, so that they are beneath the chambers on the level above. The corners of a chamber roof are blasted over a certain length so that the pillar above breaks up and collapses into the chamber, from where it is loaded into cars and taken away for haulage to the surface.

Mining is carried out first from the ends of the top series of tunnels, working from the centre outwards and gradually working backwards as the tunnels fill with rubble from above. As the tunnels fill on one level, mining begins on the next level below, and so on until mining is going on at several different levels, each being in advance of the one below.

Eight tons per shift can be removed by chambering, but it requires a large labour force and by 1970 only the Wesselton mine still employed it (Fig. 4.17).

Block Caving
After a De Beers official had seen a method known as block caving in use in

Fig. 4.17.   *Loading blue ground into a hand truck after chambering.*

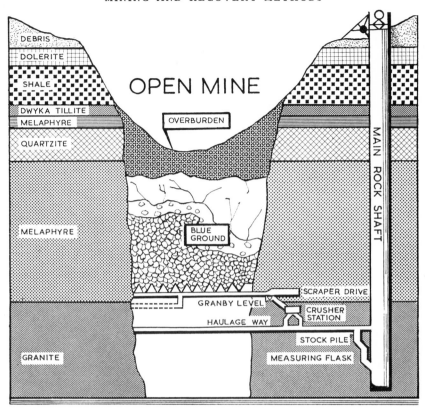

Fig. 4.18. *Principle of block caving where the blue ground (shown white) is undermined and breaks up to fall into draw points.*

other mining operations in Canada and the U.S.A., it was decided to try it on an easily accessible block of unmined blue ground in the Bultfontein Mine. It was so successful that in 1955 a decision was made to change over generally to block caving. Jagersfontein was the first mine to be completely converted, in 1958, and now all the Kimberley pipes, too, except Wesselton, are worked in this way.

Block caving reduced considerably the number of levels and shafts and the labour needs, and lends itself to continuous working and mechanization. It is also much safer for the miners and greatly reduces the pilfering of diamonds. It has been found that blue ground fractures more easily as depth increases, which favours block caving and makes chambering less practical.

In block caving, a mine level is established at a depth which may be 400 to 600 feet below the top of the blue ground in the pipe, according to local conditions. A haulage tunnel for electric locos is driven right round the pipe and about thirty feet away from it in the country rock surrounding the pipe. At intervals around the haulage level, short shafts – called raises – are driven upwards. From these, a series of parallel tunnels – scraper drifts – are driven across the pipe at 45-feet intervals. At the ends of each scraper drift a chamber is cut to house a winch and tackle. Finally another tunnel is cut round the pipe again, connecting each winch chamber to the next (Fig. 4.18).

85

Fig. 4.19.   *The actual stirrup that draws the blue ground through the scraper drift. On the right and left can be seen a draw points through which broken blue ground has come from the pipe.*

Fig. 4.20. (below)   *Winch drawing blue ground through a scraper drift in the Bultfontein pipe.*

The scraper drifts are lined with concrete, leaving square openings – draw points – alternatively on each side of a tunnel at intervals of about eleven feet (Fig. 4.19). Through these openings, blue ground is removed to form funnels in the blue ground of the pipe above. The entire area of blue ground above the funnels is then mined out to a height of about seven feet to form a huge cave.

The roof of the cave begins to break up under the pressure of the blue ground and overburden gradually being squeezed down the pipe by its own weight. Blue ground flakes off the roof of the cave and fills the funnels and draw points to the scraper drifts, until the entire cave is filled with broken ground, which helps to support the roof. The ground that comes through the draw points into the scraper drifts is extracted by large stirrup-shaped scrapers that are hauled by chains back and forth through each drift by electric-powered winches (Fig. 4.20). The blue ground scraped through each drift drops directly through a hopper into trucks, which take it to an underground crushing plant. From there it is hauled by electric locomotive to skips, which take it to the surface.

Caving and drawing off continue at a calculated rate and eventually the roof of the cave breaks through to the overburden on top of the pipe. This occurs when about 60 to 70 per cent of the blue ground has been drawn off. The drawing off continues until the waste overburden has descended the 400 to 600 feet down the pipe and begins to appear at the draw points. Before then, however, a new level has been established 400 to 600 feet below for the next block caving operation.

Fig. 4.21. *Granby trucks used for taking blue ground from the scraper drifts to the underground crushing plant for the two pipes Bultfontein and Dutoitspan in Kimberley that are linked underground.*

87

Fig. 4.22.   *The Finsch pipe from the air. It is being worked by open cast methods. The treatment plant is in the foreground. The pipe is at Lime Acres.*

Block Caving in Use

The first scraper drift level at Jagersfontein was at 1,870 feet, 400 feet below the top of the blue ground in the pipe.

When Bultfontein was converted, it was connected to Dutoitspan underground, since the pipes are adjacent. The same haulage system is employed for both mines and the production is delivered to the same hoisting shaft at Bultfontein. This underground tramming system (Fig. 4.21) is 1,900 feet below ground and 2,220 feet long. Dutoitspan is mined in two sections owing to an unpayable volume of blue ground between them.

The main hoisting shaft at Bultfontein was renovated when the two mines were connected underground and was fitted with 13-ton automatic express skips which deliver blue ground to the surface, after which it is taken by conveyor-belt to the central treatment plant.

Currently all the Kimberley mines except the Big Hole, which is exhausted, have underground workings. They number four – Bultfontein, Dutoitspan, Wesselton, and De Beers. The Premier near Pretoria, is mined by a combination method. Jagersfontein is also mined from underground, but is to be closed, and the nearby Koffiefontein Mine, also in the Orange Free State, will be underground mined from 1971.

All other known pipes are open-cast mined at present.

Modern Open-cast Mining

All pipe mines are first worked from the top by what is known as the open-cast method. Once it was haphazard; now it is systematic. Before mining proper is begun, the pipe is very thoroughly sampled by geologists, to plot its payability, using a sampling recovery plant on the spot.

The Finsch pipe is a good example of the present open-cast method of mining All excavation is mechanized. Because it is easier to excavate in straight lines, the worked shape is a polygon, as may be seen in Fig. 4.22. Excavation of yellow ground is deepest in the middle and proceeds in a way to produce a spiral road out of the mine, up and down which trucks are driven to remove the deposit.

The pipe itself is about forty-five acres in extent and will be open-cast mined for several years, although the removal rate of ground at the end of 1968 was 27,000 loads of rock and 18,000 loads of yellow ground (a load is 10 cubic feet *in situ*) by electric shovels and 35-ton dumper trucks working twenty-four hours a day.

The top of the pipe lay under about sixteen feet of ironstone rubbish and a further 13 feet of mixed kimberlite and ironstone known locally as the 'contact zone'. Sampling has shown that the yellow ground becomes less weathered with depth until at about 300 feet it is unaltered blue ground. It is fairly uniform in appearance and carries inclusions of amygdaloidal lava, diabase, shale, and mudstone, as well as the usual accessory minerals. The sides of the pipe are roughly vertical for about 1,000 feet down.

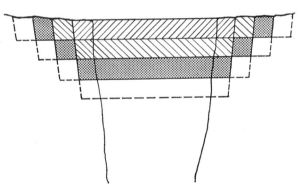

Fig. 4.23. *Economics of open cast mining. As further material from the surrounding country rock has to be removed to prevent its falling in, there comes a point when it is more economical to mine underground. An exploratory shaft was sunk by the Finsch in 1970.*

While removing yellow ground, the sides of country rock are cut back in steps to remove the risk of rubbish falling in, as happened during all the early open-cast workings. This also improves conditions for the time when underground working is resorted to. All the earlier pipes now being worked from underground have, on top of the blue ground a heavy layer of reef which increases the pressure on the workings below. The sides of the De Beers Mine in Kimberley, which had been cut back ineffectively in the early days, were cut back in terraces again in 1968–9 to prevent more falls of reef down the hole which is worked from underground.

The economics of open-cast mining depend on the ratio of country rock to kimberlite being removed. The deeper the hole, the higher the ratio of country rock to kimberlite, as shown in Fig. 4.23, and the lower the diamond load ratio. The steeper the repose angle of the walls can be made, the more economic the mine from this point of view.

The Finsch mine will be lowered to a depth of about 900 feet before working starts from underground.

Benching

A method of mining which is partly open-cast and partly underground is carried out at the Premier Mine in the Transvaal, where it was introduced in 1945 when the mine was reopened after it had been shut at the end of open-cast working to a depth of 610 feet.

The Premier pipe is elliptical at the mouth, about 2,800 feet by 1,400 feet and in the centre of the upper regions is a huge block of quartzite which divides it into two down to over 1,000 feet. The block is believed to have fallen into kimberlite when it was plastic.

The blue ground is blasted in a series of benches in each half of the pipe and falls into cones made in the blue ground below to a grizzly level and ore passes to haulage ways on the 1,060 feet level. The kimberlite is crushed to under six-inch pieces below ground before being hauled to the surface. Benching is also known as slot mining (Fig. 4.24).

Modern Alluvial Mining

The most efficient methods of alluvial mining are those of Consolidated Diamond Mines of South West Africa Limited, along the coast of South West Africa

Fig. 4.24. *The Premier mine where a combination of surface and underground methods called benching is used.*

Fig. 4.25. *Removing sand by scrapers and bull-dozers on the beaches of South West Africa on the Consolidated Diamond Mines concession.*

northwards for about fifty miles from the mouth of the Orange River to Affen-ruchen (Fig. 3.11). The diamonds are about 90 per cent gem quality and re-covery is said to be almost 100 per cent efficient. The diamond deposits lie on a narrow bedrock parallel to the coast. The most fully developed strips have four wave-cut shelves – called terraces – where diamondiferous gravels are trapped. The shelves were caused by wave action and left when the sea advanced or retreated over long periods of time.

It is assumed that the diamonds came down the Orange River because the distribution along the coast drops in a typical curve from the river mouth northwards up the coast. The diamonds were carried in the sea by wind-driven currents and thrown up on the beaches by wave action.

Gravel and conglomerate containing diamonds is covered with marine sand and sandstone, and in some places by compacted red sand and calcrete, which is rather like a soft natural limestone concrete. Over this is a layer of sand that may be as deep as 30 feet.

The major part of mining is in fact a gigantic earth-moving operation. The sand has to be stripped off before the gravels are reached. Mining is carried out by opening the sides of prospection trenches (see page 121), where the over-burden is thinnest, driven at right angles to the coast.

The first mechanization of overburden removal was to use bucket excavators, which could move 80 to 100 tons of sand an hour. The sand was discharged into mule-drawn trucks to be taken away. After the Second World War, Sherman tanks, with their gun turrets removed, were employed as tractors, and after 1954, diesel-driven scrapers with huge pneumatic tyres were introduced. The smaller scrapers work in pairs with a pusher crawler tractor. The biggest scrapers, which can remove sand at the rate of 450 cubic metres an hour, need two bulldozers in tandem to push them while scraping up the sand (Fig. 4.25).

After the primary and secondary sand and soil overburden have been removed, the exposed terraces of gravel are loaded, by means of excavators or front end loaders, into rear dump trucks, which will carry twenty-five tons each.

The gravels were transported to one of the eighteen permanent field screening plants sited along the coast where oversize and undersize material was rejected by vibrating grizzlies and screens and the remainder, amounting to about 20 per cent of the gravels, taken by diesel loco-drawn trucks along a coastal railway, or by road transport, to a central treatment plant.

In some areas, the diamonds are found in a hard, compacted conglomerate, which has to be drilled and blasted. It is stockpiled, and when convenient, crushed to release the diamonds, after which it is treated in the normal way.

From 1970, the field screening plants were replaced by four recovery plants,

Fig. 4.26. *The sand has been removed in the middle distance and piled in the far distance. The scraper has piled up diamond-bearing gravels on the left* (upper left to centre of picture). *In the foreground, the bedrock is being cleaned to remove any remaining gravel.*

each with a heavy media separator, to which gravels are taken by dumper trucks. Concentrate, amounting to about 1 per cent of the gravels treated, is taken from these recovery plants by locked trucks to the central treatment plant. The field screening plants used to send on about 10 per cent as concentrate.

The sizes of the small and large material discarded depend on the locality of the working and the size of the diamonds likely to be recovered.

The terrace depths vary from about twelve inches to twelve feet. When the depth is less than three feet, the gravels are bulldozed into piles. When deeper, the gravels are removed by excavators into dumpers.

As the bedrock is so uneven, as may be seen in Fig. 4.26, the potholes and gullies have to be emptied by hand and most of the African labour force is engaged on this job. The usual method is to break up any hard material by compressed-air drills and to use shovels to throw the gravel on to a conveyor belt set up on the spot.

Final cleaning of the bedrock is by using small bristle brushes (one may be seen in Fig. 4.27) to sweep out gravel. Vacuum extractors called Vacuveyors (Fig. 4.28) have been developed to reduce the labour of sweeping, but they are not adaptable to all areas. The potholes and gullies worn by the sea in the fairly soft schist bedrock are in some places ten feet or more deep. Diamonds tend to

Fig. 4.27. *Potholes in the bedrock trap heavy materials, including diamond, and have to be cleared by hand. Final clearing is done by a small brush, being used on the right.*

Fig. 4.28. *A suction hose called the Vacuveyor is used in some circumstances to empty potholes of sand and gravel.*

concentrate in these or on or near a footwall, i.e. the foot of one of the wave-cut shelves in the bedrock.

Marine Diamond Mining

It had been known from near the beginning of the century that diamonds were to be found on the coastal desert strip, the C.D.M. concession just referred to. Prospectors discovered diamond-bearing gravels extending under beaches between present high and low tide marks. It was, however, very difficult to mine these areas because of flooding, so they were left.

There was much speculation on whether diamonds would be found under the sea. It was argued that the diamonds in the beaches came down the Orange River and were taken up the coast by the sea, and therefore some diamonds must have been trapped in potholes *en route*.

The interest in undersea diamonds of an American oil man, S. V. Collins, was aroused after he had bid (unsuccessfully) for laying an underwater pipeline for delivering oil from tankers to the C.D.M. town in the desert, Oranjemund.

In 1962, he obtained a mining concession for a 170 mile strip off the coast from the Orange River to Luderitz, and formed the Marine Diamond Corporation to mine it. An expensive operation was launched to prospect the sea-bed and several special vessels built to bring up diamonds by a vacuum sweeping technique that was developed.

Fig. 4.29. *Pomona, the recovery barge for undersea diamonds, at work off the coast of South West Africa. The suction dredges are over the front of the barge on the left. The structure at the back contains the living quarters and on top is a helicopter landing platform.*

Diamonds were recovered but were costing more to recover than they were worth. In 1963 and 1965 De Beers concluded agreements with the Marine Diamond Corporation for C.D.M. to take part in the sea-mining operation and to transfer C.D.M.'s tidal strip concession to the Marine Diamond Corporation.

The prospecting vessel *Rockeater*, fitted out with undersea drills was used to plot the payable areas of sea-bed. Contour maps were prepared showing the average diamond content. After Sammy Collins's experience with several barges, one of which was wrecked and another beached, the 300-feet long *Pomona*, shown in Fig. 4.29, was built and commissioned. *Pomona* works continuously night and day with two shifts of workers living on board while a third shift is on leave. It is serviced by a number of other vessels, several aircraft and two helicopters.

Pomona is towed to areas where *Rockeater* has found the gravels under the sea to be payable. It is exactly located by radar beamed on fixed reflectors along the shore. It is then anchored by long lines from the rear and by long lines to anchors on each side to the front in Y-formation. The rear anchor lines are kept taut by the barge's propellors and the lines are gradually let out so that the barge moves forwards.

At the same time, the forward anchor lines are shortened on the port and then on the starboard side alternately, so that as the barge moves forward it also sweeps slowly across the area.

Over the front are four vacuum tubes (Fig. 4.30), two large ones ahead, followed by two smaller ones to pick up anything left by the main tubes. The vacuum tubes now have large flared-out steel heads, in each of which are water nozzles and a suction head. The action is to employ water jets to blow away the overburden of sand and silt and then, when the head has settled through it to the gravel or bedrock, to suck up the gravel into the barge.

An added complication is the frequent heavy swell along the coast which may cause the barge to move up and down as much as 30 feet. The suction dredges still have to be kept stationary in the sea-bed, and this is achieved by a system of cables holding the tubes at one end and counterweights at the other.

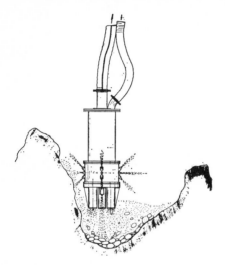

Fig. 4.30. *The head of a suction dredge used from Po-mona. Water jets remove sand and silt and suction draws up gravel including any diamonds.*

The gravel is drawn into the barge with a considerable amount of sea-water which is largely removed by dewatering cyclones and delivered back into the sea. Normal methods of concentration of gravels are used until the last stage, when an adaption of the old-timer's jig concentrates diamonds on the top of a pile of wet gravel on a picking table below decks. Other methods are unsuitable because of the movement of the barge.

Tidal Mining

The problem of mining in the tidal area was that of building dams that would withstand the sea long enough for the area to be mined. Coffer dams, or pad-docks, as shown in Fig. 4.31, were bulldozed from the sand, in various shapes, some reinforced with tarpaulins and sheets of vinyl.

Some lasted a few days, others only a few hours. The secret of making them endure longer was discovered almost by accident. It was a question of extending the front wall in a certain way. At the present time, the front wall of a series of paddocks is made continuous, about half-way between high and low tides. It is about 40 feet thick and high enough to cope with swells of 30 feet. Walls in some places have to be made up to 100 feet thick. Special concrete blocks have been found effective for constructing coffer dams.

Water is pumped out if necessary and the area is mined in the same way as the

Fig. 4.31.   *Mining in the tidal strip by building dams before removing overburden. More of the series of dams can be seen on the left.*

beaches above the high water mark. As each dam is mined out, work is started on the next, while another adjacent is being prepared. Behind the line of working the sea gradually reclaims the dams as can be seen in Fig. 4.31.

The lower half of the beach will eventually be mined separately and presents a much more formidable task in holding back the sea.

REFERENCES

Early Diamond Days, by Oswald Doughty (London, 1963).
De Beers Consolidated Mines Limited Annual Reports.
Publications of the mining companies.
'Some Account of Diamond Winning Practices in Southern Africa', by R. J. Adamson (*Industrial Diamond Review*).
Symposium: Modern Practices in Diamond Mining in Southern Africa. The South African Institute of Mining and Metallurgy, Johannesburg, 1961.
Science and Technology of Industrial Diamonds Vol. 2. Edited by John Burls (London, 1967).

CHAPTER FIVE

Extracting Diamonds

The discovery of pipes and amalgamation of mining interests meant bigger scale operations and eventual separation of the operations into two sections, (1) mining kimberlite, and (2) treating it to recover diamonds from it.

Until efficient mechanical crushers were generally introduced in this century, blue ground was still spread out on the surface to weather (Fig. 4.13). In the 1890s De Beers hired from the government 1,000 convicts to break it up with picks and hammers. Later, steam harrows were introduced to plough over the floors. It was found that the deeper the level from which the blue ground came, the longer it took to disintegrate, at this time from nine to twelve months. Some blue kimberlite, called hard blue or hardbank, did not weather and was picked off the floors and crushed by a mechanical crusher. After the blue ground had disintegrated, it was thoroughly wetted and taken away to be washed and seived. Today, primary crushing is normally carried out underground as a final stage of mining before delivery of the ore to the treatment plant.

Just before the end of the nineteenth century, concentration of the heavy minerals including diamond was carried out by a machine that had replaced hand-jigging and was known locally as a pulsator.

The disintegrated blue ground was delivered on top of a bed of 'bullets' on a sieve in water which was given a rapid pulsating movement. The heavier elements of the deposit gradually descended between the bullets to the bottom and the lighter ones were floated to the top, where they were carried by the water over the edge of the sieve to waste. The heavier fraction containing diamonds fell through the bottom of the sieve. (The pulsator method is still in use today in an improved form for concentrating sand containing tiny diamonds, which is released when kimberlite is crushed).

Diamonds were picked by hand from the resulting concentrate by teams of trained workers.

Grease Table Invented

About 1896, F. B. Kirsten, an employee of De Beers, discovered that diamonds in the concentrate were non-wettable and stuck to grease, while all the other minerals were washed over it. G. F. Labram, chief engineer of the company, devised a sloping table with five steps to take advantage of this fact. The top was covered with a layer of about a quarter of an inch of axle grease. A stream of water carrying the concentrate passed down the table and the grease trapped any diamonds in it (Fig. 5.1).

The grease table was introduced as the last stage of processing before hand sorting and reduced considerably the labour of sorting and the risk of stones being stolen.

Treatment Plants

Today large mining concerns set up treatment plants to deal with kimberlite or gravels from one or more sources. A treatment plant subjects material fed into it to a series of concentrating processes until everything but diamonds has been rejected. The main principles employed are washing, sorting gravels by size, and sorting gravels by gravity, after which the diamonds are extracted by a technical process. Finally, there is a hand-sorting.

Fig. 5.1. *Most diamonds cannot be wetted, neither can grease. If diamond-bearing concentrate is sluiced over a sloping and vibrating table covered with grease, diamonds stick to the grease and the rest of the material is carried off the bottom of the table as waste. Some concentrate has to be given a previous treatment to make the diamonds non-wettable.*

In South West Africa for the marine deposits, and in Kimberley for the deep mines, large central treatment plants have been established. They differ from each other in certain ways because alluvial diamonds are being recovered from loose gravels in which Nature has already partly concentrated them, and pipe diamonds from solid kimberlite in which they are dispersed. Also, treatment plants at different mines and diggings have to be adapted to local conditions.

Here, therefore, the principle machines employed will be described. How they may be linked to form plants may be seen in Fig. 5.2 and Fig. 5.3, which

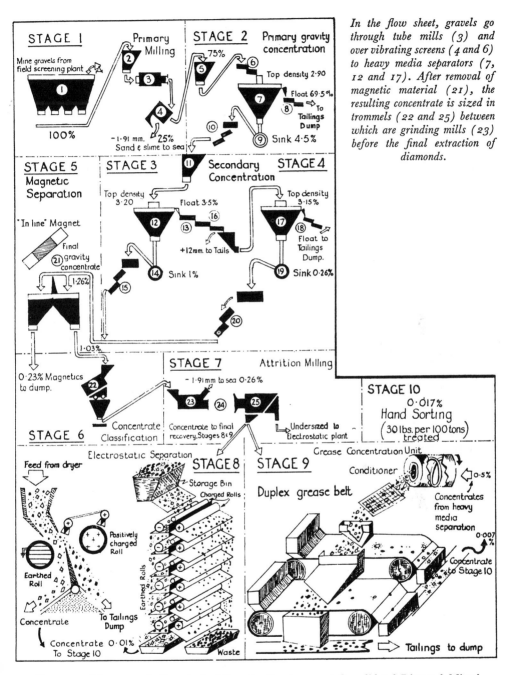

In the flow sheet, gravels go through tube mills (3) and over vibrating screens (4 and 6) to heavy media separators (7, 12 and 17). After removal of magnetic material (21), the resulting concentrate is sized in trommels (22 and 25) between which are grinding mills (23) before the final extraction of diamonds.

Fig. 5.2. *Diagrammatic flow sheet of the extraction process at Consolidated Diamond Mines' central treatment plant.*

show the C.D.M., diagramatically, and the Kimberley, Central Treatment Plants respectively.

Crushing and Milling

The first stage is often to crush the rock or conglomerate in which the diamonds are held. This has to be done with care to avoid crushing the diamonds themselves as they are released. Crushing is, of course, omitted when the diamonds are in loose shingle.

For some deposits, milling is more effective than crushing. Milling comprises putting the diamondiferous material in large rotating drums with water and rocks so that the material is gradually broken down to release the crystals.

Fig. 5.3.   *The central treatment plant at Kimberley which extracts diamonds from the pipe mines. The waste material – the tailings – is dumped near the plant as seen in the foreground.*

Scrubbing is a similar but less violent process employed when an alluvial deposit is bound by hard clay. The deposit is tumbled over with water in large drums. This also has a washing action, of course.

Washing and Screening

Washing is an important process to remove fine material. It is usually combined with another process, such as screening. Screening is simply passing the gravels or crushed rock through a screen of known size. The material that passes through or does not pass through may be the rejected tailings, according to the size of the mesh chosen (Fig. 5.4).

Fig. 5.4. *Part of the screening and washing section of a treatment plant. From some screens the concentrate that passes over is waste and from others the concentrate that passes through is waste.*

Fig. 5.5. *A modern washing pan whose paddles rotate broken blue ground. The blue ground floats over the central weir and the concentrate containing diamonds is extracted from the bottom.*

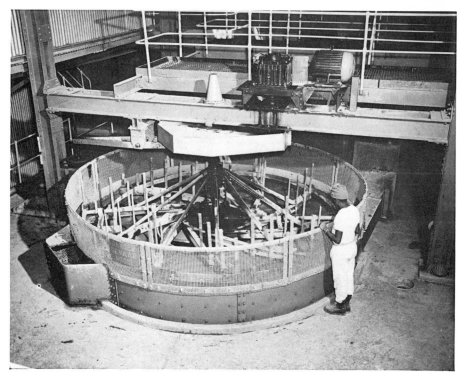

The coarsest screen is merely a row of widely spaced, strong steel bars, known as a grizzly, to separate large lumps of rock that need to be crushed before entering a plant. The finest screen is employed to let through only water and the finest sand.

Sometimes the gravels being concentrated contain a high proportion of a material that can be extracted by a process specially introduced for the purpose. For example, in mines where there is a high proportion of ironstone, the gravel is fed to a moving belt which passes under a powerful electro-magnet. The gravels, including ironstone, affected by magnetism, can be made to fall off the end of the belt in a different trajectory to a waste chute.

Sometimes the gravels contain a high proportion of shells and other soft limestone. This is often best removed by ball-milling, the material being passed through rotating drums containing water and pebbles, to break up the shells into fine material and reject them as slime. Ball-milling is used to clean diamond surfaces as well as to break up friable material.

The most important process of concentration is by gravity. The principle machine is the rotary washing pan, in the form described on page 78, but still in use in larger, power-driven versions today. The general mode of operation has not changed (Fig. 5.5).

The rotary washing pans at Kimberley extract one ton of concentrate for every twenty-three tons of tailings swept over the weir. The concentrate is extracted continuously from the bottom of each pan by an Achimedes screw extractor, which avoids having to stop and empty the pan.

Heavy Media Separator

In 1950, heavy media separation cones were installed at several plants. This kind of separator uses a slurry – a heavy liquid. The slurry is fine ferro-silicon powder suspended in water to give it a density of 2·7 to 3·1. The density can be accurately controlled to the figure required by automatic means.

At C.D.M., in South West Africa, the separators are cone-shaped tanks 12 feet across at the top containing slurry with an S.G. controlled to 2·9. About 95 per cent of the ore fed into the top of the cone has a density less than this and floats over the rim of the tank as tailings. The material with a density over 3·2 which includes diamonds, sinks to the bottom of the cone and is removed up a pipe by an air lift (Fig. 5.6).

The concentrate from the heavy media separator is taken to a smaller secondary heavy media separator containing slurry with a density of 3·25 which provides an even smaller concentrate before final extraction of diamonds.

Another form of heavy media separator employs a kind of paddle wheel to raise the concentrate that has settled to the bottom of the slurry inside it.

The Hydro-cyclone

The hydro-cyclone is the latest means of concentrating gravels. It employs the same principle as the heavy media separator, but is more efficient. The principle is shown in Fig. 5.7. The ferro-silicon slurry is continuously circulated and closely controlled to an exact specific gravity. A centrifuge effect is employed by

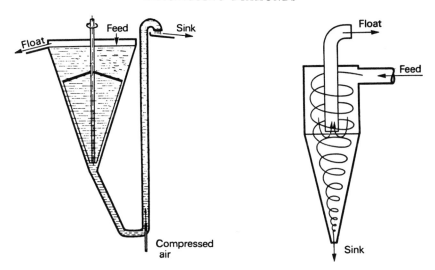

Fig. 5.6. *Principle of the heavy media separator. Gravels or broken blue ground is fed into the top. Light materials float off the top of the heavy liquid in the separator and heavier ones including diamonds sink to the bottom and are extracted.* Fig. 5.7. *(right) Principle of the hydro-cyclone. Gravel and broken blue ground fed in from the side are centrifuged, when the heavy faction sinks and the lighter one is extracted from the top.*

feeding in the concentrate and ore so that the heavier fraction moves to the outside and down the conical tank, and the light fraction comes to the middle and is forced upwards where it is floated off.

Greased Surface Concentrators

The grease table separator mentioned on page 99, was developed and became the principal method of final recovery at the diamond pipes. The early sloping grease table was developed into a heavy aluminium plate with several steps across it, vibrated rapidly from side to side by an electro-magnetic motor. Concentrate is passed rapidly down the grease tables with plenty of water.

Most of the diamonds are trapped in a band very near the top of the grease-covered table. The stream of gangue (the rest of the concentrate) tumbling over them tends to push them firmly into the grease. At intervals, the process is stopped and the grease scraped off with a knife. It is put into wire baskets which are placed in a boiler to melt away the grease (Fig. 5.8).

The diamonds are finally hand sorted to remove the small amount of salse (other materials including apatite, garnet, calcite, quartz, etc.) that gets through even the grease process, and are finally boiled in hydrochloric and sulphuric acid (or hydrofluoric acid) to clean them before they go to the Diamond Producers' Association for sorting and valuation.

The Grease Belt

The Diamond Research Laboratory designed an improved form of grease

Fig. 5.8.   *After the grease on a grease table has trapped diamonds it is scraped off and put into drums. The grease is boiled off to leave the diamonds and other material that might have been trapped.*

surface concentrator which has replaced the table at the Central Treatment Plants at C.D.M., and in Kimberley. It employs a grease belt about a yard wide running over two rollers as shown in Fig. 5.9. The advantage is that the belts do not have to be stopped at short intervals like the grease table, to remove grease and diamonds and to resurface it with grease. The grease is applied automatically and also scraped off automatically, with any adhering diamonds.

The concentrate, with a strong flow of water, is fed across the belt, which is mounted so that it tilts sideways. Diamonds trapped by the grease are taken across the flow of concentrate by the movement of the belt and scraped off by a heated scraper blade as the belt goes round the end roller, as shown in Fig. 5.2 and 5.9.

Earlier grease belts were mounted in pairs, one below the other, so that any diamonds washed over the first were trapped by the second. It was found that the system was so efficient that the second belt was unnecessary. A further development was a very much larger single belt, the middle section of which was vibrated to encourage the diamonds to stick to the grease. One of these is installed at the Finsch treatment plant.

Conditioning Treatment

Not all diamonds are unwettable and stick to grease. Those from the marine terraces of South West Africa behaved in the same way as the gangue, and were washed over grease. The reason was found to be due to a molecular thick salt coating on the crystals. It was found that a pre-treatment of the concentrate by fish acid oil and caustic soda made the diamond non-wettable and therefore able to stick to grease, but left the gangue unaffected.

Coatings of other kinds on diamonds from pipe mines sometimes have the same effect and make conditioning of the concentrate necessary before grease tables or belts can be used for final recovery. Diamonds from the Finsch and from the Williamson pipe mines need conditioning. The Tusilo plant in Angola is another with a conditioning plant.

The chemical reagent now most used is maize acid oil with caustic soda to saponify it, but there are other soap solutions that will cause the chemical action desired.

Fig. 5.9. *The grease belt has largely superseded grease tables. The diamond-bearing concentrate is sluiced across the moving grease belt, which traps diamonds and carries them to the end (foreground) where a knife scrapes them off. At the other end of the endless belt, fresh grease is applied automatically. Originally two belts were used to make sure all diamonds were trapped, as shown in stage nine, Fig. 5.2, but one belt only has been found highly effective.*

Recovery of Small Diamonds

As diamond prices rise, so the recovery of smaller and smaller diamonds becomes economical. The small ones which are economically not worth recovering are sieved out and end as tailings. After certain periods of time, therefore, tailing dumps become worth re-treating to recover diamonds thrown away at earlier times.

It was known that recovery of small crystals was not economically possible by grease belt, even after treating the concentrate with a reagent, because so much of the small gangue was made non-wettable too and stuck to the belt. The solution found was to put the small concentrate through an attrition mill, which gradually ground down all the minerals except diamond into a slime. This method is applied to concentrates that have passed over the grease table or belt and are known to contain untrapped small diamonds.

Electrostatic Separation

Before the grease belt and preconditioning of concentrate was introduced at the alluvial mines in South West Africa, the principle method of final recovery was electrostatic sorting. It was developed from 1947 by the Diamond Research Laboratory, and became the basic system at most alluvial mines in Africa, but it was also used at certain pipe mines for the recovery of small diamonds below 10 mesh (about 1·65 mm.).

The concentrate was divided into four sizes and then passed through pebble mills to make sure that the surface of gravels and diamonds were well polished. The fine fraction (under $\frac{1}{4}$ inch) went through a drying kiln and on to a high voltage electrostatic separation plant. This plant comprises a series of horizontal rollers in vertical columns. The rollers on one side are earthed and those on the other are positively charged. On each side is a series of chutes, leaving a clear passage between the vertical banks of rollers, as shown in Fig. 5.2.

Diamonds are electrical insulators, so when a stream of hot, dry, diamondiferous gravel is allowed to fall between the rollers, the diamonds fall straight down, while the gravels become charged and attracted towards the positively-charged rollers, which deflect them down tailing chutes.

Skin Flotation Recovery

Very small stones, micro-diamonds, are separated from the equally fine concentrate by placing the concentrate in the bottom of a Pyrex beaker and boiling it in concentrated hydrochloric acid, diluted with about three times the volume of water. Careful decanting and stirring causes the tiny diamonds to rise to the top and form a 'raft' on the top of the liquid held by surface tension, from which they may be skimmed off.

X-ray Separation

In 1958, the Russians stated that they had developed a separation technique for their new mines in Yakutia. It was based on the fact that most diamonds – perhaps all from certain sources – fluoresce when irradiated by X-rays, whereas nearly all accompanying minerals in a concentrate do not. The concentrate is

Fig. 5.10. *Optical separation units, which are similar in principle to X-ray units.*

fed into the recovery machine and passes in a stream in the dark under an X-ray beam. Any diamond lights up, which triggers a photo-electric cell causing a gate to open and deflect the diamond into a separate chute.

An X-ray sorting machine has been developed by Gunsons Sortex Limited of London, based on machines they have developed for sorting agricultural seeds. These have been installed to date with success at the Finsch, C.D.M., and Kimberley Central treatment plants.

A V-belt feeds the concentrate under an X-ray beam. When any diamond fluoresces, a photomultiplier tube causes an air jet to deflect the stone into a separate chute, as shown diagramatically in Fig. 5.11.

The X-ray recovery system has proved so effective that it will probably become the principal method, as soon as a way is invented of treating the concentrate in a broad band instead of a narrow stream. In some mines, calcite can get through to the final concentrate. Calcite fluoresces, too, but with different colours from diamond, so a colour filter is used to prevent any pieces of calcite from triggering the air jet. When there is much calcite, it can be eliminated at an earlier stage by milling.

Testing Recovery Efficiency

When the proportion of diamond to ore is in the neighbourhood of 20,000,000 to one, as is quite common, the loss of very few diamonds by the recovery process makes all the difference between profit and loss. In 1954, the Metallurgical Department of the Anglo-American Corporation of South Africa, devised a relatively simple system of testing a whole plant during one cycle of its operation.

They took some test diamonds and drilled small blind holes in them. The holes were loaded with radio-active cobalt-60 and sealed with Canadian balsam. The

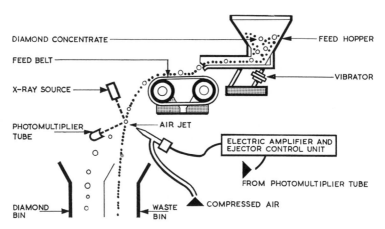

Fig. 5.11. *Principle of the X-ray separation units used by De Beers Consolidated Mines. Any diamond will fluoresce under X-rays and this light triggers an air jet that blows the diamond into a collection chute.*

heavier cobalt and lighter basalt kept the specific gravity of the diamond at 3·5. The diamonds were introduced into the ore and tracked through the plant with scintillometers.

As well as prepared diamonds, octahedra made of a zinc-aluminium alloy to an S.G. of 3·5 are also used after being irradiated in a nuclear pile to make them radioactive. Most mines employ this technique for measuring the efficiency of their recovery process.

Optical Separation

The Diamond Research Laboratory's X-ray separator has features in common with the optical separator the Laboratory developed from 1957. The object of the optical separator is, however, to provide a check on the tailings from the grease and electrostatic machines, to see how many diamonds, if any, have got through. The optical separator, besides indicating the general efficiency of a process, also quickly identifies a faulty separating machine.

The machine carries tailings from a plant by belt under a beam of light in the dark. A diamond reflects some light and operates a photomultiplier which causes a gate to deflect the stone to a separate outlet. The rest of the gravel, being dark, does not operate the photocell.

Fig. 5.12.   *One day's output of diamonds from Consolidated Diamond Mines of South West Africa. About ninety per cent are of gem quality and the total is about 4,000 carats.*

The optical separator is also employed in the industrial diamond sorting rooms in Kimberley. By using light filters, industrial diamonds may be rapidly sorted into groups of different colour. (Fig. 5.10.)

Fig. 5.12 shows a day's recovery from the C.D.M. plant. Over 80 per cent of the rough is gem quality.

REFERENCE

Occurrence, Mining, and Recovery of Diamonds (De Beers Consolidated Mines, London 1969).

CHAPTER SIX

Prospecting Methods

The old-time prospector's favourite expression was, 'Gold is where you find it.' It was originally true, perhaps, of every mineral. Certainly the first diamonds in any country were found by chance. Any discovery drew other seekers to the area. From this, a sound prospecting philosophy arose: work outwards from known mineral deposits.

In India, Brazil, Russia, Africa, South America, Borneo, Australia, and other places where diamonds occur, someone originally picked up an unusual pebble that was subsequently identified as diamond – sometime later a rush began. Early finds were near the gravels of river beds, so prospectors naturally followed river banks and beds as they explored outwards from the original discovery.

Some of the earliest mining areas were probably wet diggings in the beds and banks of active rivers. Dry diggings were inland and often in semi-desert areas. It became apparent that these were the beds of rivers that had dried up thoussands, or even millions of years ago. Although the gravel of the original find was probably exposed, prospectors naturally tried to discover the original course of the river, if it had become covered with rocks and soil, by sinking inspection pits.

It became evident during digging and recovery that diamonds were almost invariably accompanied by other heavy minerals, including garnets, ilmenites, zircons, and chrome diopsides. As the accompanying minerals were much more plentiful than diamonds, it was easier to search first for them. These red, green, and yellowish minerals are generally known as diamond indicators or indicator minerals. The Russians in recent times have named them *sputniki*, as they are little 'artificial satellites' to diamond deposits.

A mine is, of course, a wasting asset. Any miner or mining company is anxious to stay in business. Prospecting therefore becomes inseparable from mining.

Traditional Prospecting
In the old days, the prospector was usually an independent adventurer who was looking for any kind of mineral that would be rewarding. With his pick and shovel strapped to a mule's pack, he could cover all kinds of terrain, but he depended upon diamonds and other minerals being on the surface or not very deep below it. After finding a deposit, he would work it out to raise money to set off on the next trip – if he did not make the fortune that was always waiting around the corner.

In the early diamond digging days of South Africa, it was common for several diggers to form themselves into a party with a single prospector to guide them. Very few indeed of these prospectors knew much about systematic prospecting however, as even the source of diamonds was unknown. The discovery of kimberlite pipes bringing them from deep in the earth provided the prospector

Fig. 6.1.   *A. T. Fincham, the prospector who found the diamond pipe afterwards called the Finsch in South Africa. In 1963 he sold his rights in it to De Beers for two and a quarter million pounds.*

with a new objective, to find areas of kimberlite, which in its decomposed form on or near the surface, he could recognize.

Yellow ground usually held more moisture than the surrounding sandy ground. Also it covered a roughly circular area which might be slightly above or below the level of the surrounding country. When a little lower, it sometimes became a *pan* – to use the Boer name for a pond on a farm. Areas of yellow ground that were small flat hills, perhaps only a few feet high, were known as *kopjes*, also in the Afrikaaner's tongue. Because of the higher moisture content of the yellow ground, there was sometimes more vegetation on a kopje of yellow ground than there was surrounding it, or on other kopjes.

There is an artificial obstacle today to prospecting in most countries where diamonds have been found. Either to do so is illegal and a right only of the state, or the prospector has to obtain a licence, which is not always readily granted.

Freelance prospectors have some spectacular successes, nevertheless. One was A. T. Fincham, who discovered a huge forty-five-acre pipe in the semi-desert Postmasburg area about 100 miles north-east of Kimberley. He sold his rights in 1963 to De Beers for £2¼ million and the diggings became the Finsch Mine, named after Fincham and his partner, E. Schwabel. See Figs. 6.1. and 4.22.

Scientific Prospecting

Earlier in the century, especially where industrially significant minerals were being sought, geologists had taken a hand in prospecting decisions. They studied the nature of deposits, the geology of the area, and the mechanics of transportation. They tried to deduce the locations of original sources, or to discover other areas where similar deposits might be found. This is a long way from the 'gold is where you find it' approach.

One of the geologists to apply such methods to diamond prospecting was Dr. John T. Williamson, a Canadian who had worked on the Rand in South Africa for a time and became interested in diamonds. (Fig. 6.2.) He theorized the location of the pipe from which alluvial diamonds in Tanganyika (now Tanzania) originated. After nine years of prospecting, he discovered it in 1942–3 at Mwadui, about ninety miles from Lake Victoria. The pipe was about eight times bigger than the Premier Mine, near Pretoria, the biggest then known in Africa.

Modern Prospecting

Pack-saddle mules and donkeys are still used for prospecting by individuals and even larger concerns when they are the best way of covering the terrain. Since geologists have controlled the bigger prospecting operations, however, the pack-animal has been superseded by the internal combustion engine and the lone prospector by teams of university-trained geologists as in the massive search mounted by the Russians to find pipes in Yakutia.

De Beers have their own prospecting company for diamonds that operates in a number of countries where prospecting rights have been obtained and are

Fig. 6.2 *Dr. John Thorburn Williamson who found the big Williamson pipe in Tanganyika in 1942–3 after prospecting for many years. He set up his own company to mine it. After his death it was acquired by De Beers and the Tanzanian government.*

considered worth exploiting. One country where the search is becoming more intense is Canada. Kimberlite has been found in a number of areas including Kirkland Lake in western Ontario, which seems most promising. Systematic prospecting is also being carried out in Australia.

In 1968 De Beers Prospecting Unit was exceptionally successful when it located a number of new kimberlite pipes, some diamondiferous, in Botswana (formerly Bechuanaland) by scientific methods.

An operation like this starts at headquarters in Johannesburg, where a geological study is made of the country. The places where diamonds have already been found are plotted on a map. Attempts are made to correlate the finds in order to make an informed guess about the situation of major diamond deposits. It is decided for one reason or another to concentrate on certain areas and the logistics of the operation are planned.

Although there is an apparent whimsicality in the distribution of all minerals, and of diamonds in particular, major diamond deposits of which seem to occur in areas remote from civilization. For desert areas, aircraft and desert vehicles are employed by the prospecting unit, using aerial photographs and geophysical detection devices.

Prospecting in the Kalahari

In Botswana, De Beers Prospecting Unit is operating in the Kalahari Desert, the great infertile tract covering about 20,000 square miles between the Orange River and the Zambesi and inhabited mainly by a thin sprinkling of Bushmen. The first problem was knowing where to start, because seeking a pipe under a great overburden of sand without a very strong indication of its presence, would be a highly uneconomic proposition.

The discovery of the first major diamondiferous pipe, known as AK1, is an excellent example of the combinations of geological knowledge, and deduction, hunch, hard work, and luck. The first pipe in Botswana had been found by the unit in 1965, in Bakgatla tribal territory beyond Mochudi in the bush, only a few hours' travel from the capital, Gaborone. It was about 400 feet in diameter, but unfortunately contained no diamonds. There was no surface indication – no depression or hump – and the top of the kimberlite was twenty to twenty-five feet below an overburden of ferruginous gravel and sand.

To find the pipe, Dr. Gavin Lamont, the geologist in charge of the field operation, employed a blanket sampling method which was made possible by some acute observation. It was noted that ant colonies had inhabited the desert for thousands of years. They bored many feet down into the ground for material that they brought up to make their ant-hills. As colonies of billions and billions of ants over the centuries grew and died, the huge ant-hills were destroyed by the elements to help form the top surface of the desert. This surface contained samples of material brought up by the ants from various depths.

If kimberlite were below the surface there should be indicators including pyropes (garnets) and ilmenites, on top. The indicators are found as small broken and worn crystals within a quarter of an inch of or on the surface, where they have been exposed by wind.

Sampling consists of taking surface samples and counting the number of indicator minerals in the sample. The number rises very significantly over a pipe, from say, less than a dozen to thousands. Fig. 6.3 shows a new ant hole from which ants are still bringing up indicator minerals and, on extremely rare occasions, small diamonds. Fig. 6·5 illustrates the size of the pyropes and ilmenites.

Reconnaisance sampling is carried out systematically by setting up a camp in the bush in the area to be tested. A base line is established by cutting down any vegetation in the way, mostly thorn bushes, and driving trucks through to form a wide path. The trucks also take samples as they go. From this, a grid is set out by pacing out the area using a measuring wheel and marker posts. Base lines are about 10·5 metres apart and are pegged at one metre intervals.

At every ten to fifteen paces on the grid a sample of the top layer of sand – the deflation layer – is taken with a small scoop and transferred to a container known as a soil splitter, which retains only half of the sample to reduce the amount to be treated. When 10 to 15 lb. has been collected, the sample is sealed and marked with an identification number and returned to camp, where the heavy minerals are separated by sieving in water in the traditional way and by obtaining a concentrate using bromoform as a heavy liquid. The sieving is to eliminate the sand and very small heavy minerals that may have been transported by wind and would confuse the sampling. The concentrate is examined under a microscope and the brownish-black, manganese-rich ilmenites and pale orange to red pyropes are extracted and counted.

Reconnaissance teams comprise a number of trained workers (one is seen with his scoop and soil splitter in Fig. 6.6) under a geologist. A team can cover ten square miles a day, and since teams usually work in threes, as a field unit, they

Fig. 6.3. (below) *Ant hole in the Kalahari desert. Billions of billions of ants bring to the surface material including garnets, ilmenites, and even very rarely small diamonds.* Fig. 6.4. (right) *The top of a large ant hill: the prospecting truck behind is standing on part that has broken down. Material in the ant-hill from underground becomes the surface as the anthill breaks up.*

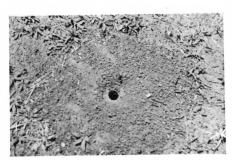

can sample thirty square miles a day. A reconnaissance field unit can cover the astonishingly large area of 450 square miles a month, which includes about three moves. The unit is supplied from a base, but field units in the Kalahari desert have small bonuses in the occasional finds of ostrich eggs, which being the size of about two dozen hens' eggs, make enormous omelets, and even the discovery occasionally of truffles!

The diamond company CAST had found diamonds in the north-east of Botswana, in river terraces that were only about six inches of gravel. The deposits were not workable. This was another traditional starting point in Botswana for Dr. Lamont – diamonds are where you find them. He carried out sampling operations upstream to the end of the valley where the river had its source, and found a few diamonds, including a 2½-carat white crystal, but no indication of the origin of the deposit.

The diamonds in a river-bed must have come from a pipe, yet there was no pipe anywhere near the source of the river. The only conclusion he could come to was that the present river source was not the original one. At this point, geological knowledge and inspiration led him to the theory that the ridge where the present river had its source was relatively recent in geological terms; it was a warp in the Earth that at some time in the past had risen across the old river, cutting it in two and sending the original head flowing in the opposite direction.

He tried to determine the area where the decapitated position of the river lay, by the sampling methods described. Within a year he had found several pipes including the major AK1, which is about five times the size of the Finsch Mine in area (Fig. 6.7).

The full code name for the pipe is 2125AK1. For sampling purposes the areas between lines of latitude and longitude are divided into four, called A, B, C and D. The first kimberlite pipe (K1) found in area A between latitude 21–22° and longitude 25–26° was therefore coded 2125AK1, or AK1 for short. It is in the area of Orapa near Letlhkane about 210 miles from Gaborone, in country

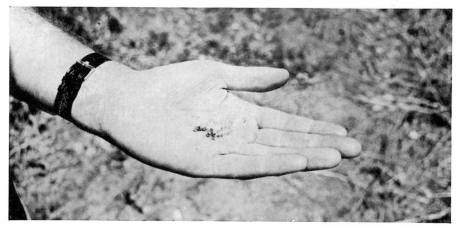

Fig. 6.5.   *Garnets and ilmenites found on the surface of the desert sand.*

explored by David Livingstone. The nearest railhead is 176 miles away (Fig. 6.8).

By great good fortune the full depth of Kalahari Desert sand ends in an escarpment about thirty to fifty feet high only a mile or so from the pipe. If the 5,000-feet pipe had been covered by this thickness of sand, it would probably not have been found. After Dr. Lamont received an excited message about the garnets and ilmenites from the field geologist, Manfred Marx – 'We're up to 1,200 and still counting' – a more concentrated survey operation was set up to determine the limits of the pipe.

The next stage was to determine payability. A sampling plant larger than the whole recovery plant at most mines was set up on the spot to sample the ground taken from inspecting pits sunk in different parts of the pipe. When this work is completed under the supervision of geologists from the Diamond Research Laboratory, Johannesburg, the mine will be handed over to the miners for open-cast working.

From the air, the area of the pipe can be recognized by a difference in colour of the vegetation which springs up after the rains. The country rock in the area

Fig. 6.6. *One of a team of men who takes samples from the surface with spade and soil-splitter so that the number of indicator minerals – garnets and ilmenites – can be counted.*

Fig. 6.7. *Dr. Gavin Lamont and Mr. Manfred Marx at the site where they discovered the big diamond pipe in Orapa, on the edge of the Kalahari desert, after covering hundreds of square miles of country.*

is basalt and there is a capping of calcrete (a limestone conglomerate) to a depth of about fifteen feet over the top of the pipe. The calcrete removed has been laid near by as an airstrip.

The Russians have not published details of their prospecting methods, but they undoubtedly rest on the same basic principles.

Sampling

Prospecting is sampling on a very broad basis. As deposits are found, sampling

119

becomes more precise to determine the limits of the deposits. Then it is even more exactly controlled, to plot the average densities of diamond to discover the richest area to exploit first.

The traditional method of sampling, by sinking a square-shaped inspection pit until the diamondiferous gravel is reached, is still employed. The gravel is extracted and washed and the diamond recovered related to the volume of overburden and gravel, or just the gravel, to give a concentration figure.

One method for sampling beaches is to use Benoto drills (Fig. 6.9). One of these will drill down to about 100 feet by means of a steel caisson about thirty-four inches in diameter. The sample is pulled up through the middle of the caisson by a grab.

In suitable terrain, sampling has been speeded up by the use of the sampling auger, which screws its way into the ground and lifts out a sample. It is mounted on an auger wagon that can be quickly moved to an area and will surface samples from depths of 10, 15, 20 and 25 feet within a few minutes. It will produce more samples in a day than a party of twenty diggers in a month.

At the marine terraces above the high-tide mark along the coast of South West Africa mined by Consolidated Diamond Mines, initial prospecting is carried out by sinking a series of boreholes to find the depth of overburden, the depth of the gravel, and the contours of the bedrock. A conventional jumper

Fig. 6.8.   *The pilot treatment plant set up at the Orapa diamond pipe in central Botswana to treat about 275 tons a day. The pipe, being developed by De Beers, was scheduled to come into production in mid 1971.*

Fig. 6.9. *Foreshore prospecting by Consolidated Diamond Mines of South West Africa. A Benoto drill is in action accompanied by a front-end loader on the right.*

type well drill is used. The holes are drilled in rows at right angles to the coast line.

When a deposit is found to be workable, a trench a metre wide at the top of the gravel is dug, also at right angles to the coast. It may be any distance from a few hundred to over 3,000 metres in length. The trench is divided into lengths which contain 2½ cubic metres of gravel. The contents of each such zone are separately trommeled and jigged and the concentration sorted by hand. From the figures, the diamond deposit concentration can be plotted. Inspection trenches are sunk 500 metres apart and mining comprises opening out the trenches from each side.

Sampling deposits under the sea of the South West African coast is carried out by basically the same method of drilling, except that it is very much more difficult. A special prospecting ship *Rockeater* is equipped for drilling under water and bringing up samples showing the depth of overburden and gravel and whether there are diamonds (Fig. 6.10).

Yellow ground and blue ground are sampled in the same way as gravels. When a new pipe is discovered, the method of sinking a pit through the overburden to the yellow ground is identical to sinking one through overburden to a gravel deposit. Within a pipe, a load of blue ground is removed and sampled.

The problem in diamond sampling is that assaying in the way that most mineral deposits are estimated is impossible, because of the way in which alluvial diamonds become concentrated. Bulk sampling has to be resorted to. The same

Fig. 6.10. *Rockeater, the diamond prospecting vessel under contract to De Beers which is equipped to search for diamond deposits on the sea bed off the South West African coast.*

is true of underground sampling in pipe deposits. There are frequently parts of a diamondiferous pipe where there are few or no diamonds. Another difficulty is that the weight of diamonds recovered is insufficient information to estimate the value of a deposit. So much depends on the size and quality of individual stones that they have to be individually examined to make an estimate of real value.

A further problem is that the treatment plant on larger operations, where twenty-five to thirty tons of blue ground are being sampled at a time, has to be thoroughly cleaned through after every sampling, an operation that may take many hours.

CHAPTER SEVEN

How the Market Operates

It has been found that control of the diamond market to keep prices as stable as possible suits all concerned, the primary producers, the governments of the mining countries, the diamond market, the jewellery trade, and the consumers. The policy appears to be as much benefit to the communist government of the U.S.S.R., as to the various shades of capitalist and socialist governments in Europe and Africa. In the U.S.A., where there is a strong antipathy to monopolies, control existing in the diamond market has been under attack from time to time, but no better method has been suggested.

When Cecil Rhodes gained control of the diamond fields in Kimberley, he directed some energy towards stabilizing the prices paid for stones, being keenly aware that overproduction in a market that was slow to expand and was sensitive to any recession or depression of trade in general would have a severe effect on the mines and miners. It was he who laid down the dictum of equating the supply to the demand.

It was immediately successful because De Beers Consolidated Mines received an average of 18s. 8¾d. a carat in 1889, while in 1890 when consolidation of the four mines of De Beers, Kimberley, Dutoitspan and Bultfontein, was practically complete, they received 32s. 6¾d. a carat.

Barney Barnato's Bucket

As well as wanting to prevent price-cutting of rough diamonds, Rhodes needed capital to buy more Kimberley Central shares. He invited Barnato among other prominent merchants to his board room to inspect about 220,000 carats of rough laid out in 160 piles sorted into different qualities. No-one had seen before such a sight. Rhodes said the value was in the neighbourhood of £500,000, but he would not sell under £700,000. An argument developed and Rhodes withdrew.

At last the merchants agreed amongst themselves to pay the price and split the collection with the largest part going to Barnato Brothers. Rhodes was called and the merchants told him that they had agreed with reluctance to his price. He urged them not to resell quickly, which would upset the market, and then, to their astonishment, lifted one end of the table so that all the stones cascaded into a concealed bucket the other end.

'I've always wanted to see a bucketful of diamonds', Rhodes said to Barney, and suggested they walk to Barnato Brothers' office carrying it between them. Barnato instantly guessed the reason for the dramatic gesture, as it would take at least six weeks to resort the stones which would keep them off the market, but could not resist the theatrical walk suggested by Rhodes. When the stones were eventually sold by the merchants, the market prices had risen and Rhodes was proved right, but Barnato was still blind to the dangers of large quantities of stones being dumped on the market. The time was just before the battle began between Rhodes and Barnato for control of Kimberley Central.

Rhodes dominated the African industry for about thirty years until he died in 1902. By coincidence this was the year in which a young man named Ernest Oppenheimer, later Sir Ernest, arrived in Kimberley as a diamond buyer for A. Dunkelsbuhler and Co., of Hatton Garden, and began an extraordinary career that led to his domination of the world's diamond industry.

After Rhodes had managed to consolidate various diamond interests into De Beers Consolidated Mines in 1888, a serious attempt was made by a syndicate of diamond merchants in Kimberley and London to establish a sound marketing policy. It was largely successful until it was disturbed by finds and rapidly increasing production from the Belgian Congo, Angola, and German South West Africa and elsewhere. Problems of financing the new producers also arose.

Sir Ernest Oppenheimer had, in 1917, set up the Anglo-American Corporation to exploit the gold fields in the far east Rand. In 1921, he gained control of the South West African deposits and formed Consolidated Diamond Mines of South West Africa, through Anglo-American.

By means of C.D.M. he became a director of De Beers and was appointed chairman in 1929, ironically just as the world had moved into the most serious

Fig. 7.1. *The late Sir Ernest Oppenheimer, who, with others, created Consolidated Diamond Mines. He became Chairman of De Beers Consolidated Mines in 1929.*

Fig. 7.2. *Mr. Harry Oppen-heimer, who became chairman of De Beers Consolidated Mines after his father's death. With Sir Philip Oppen-heimer, head of the Central Selling Organization in Lon-don, he continues the policy of international cooperation.*

depression it had known, when the diamond syndicate had big financial prob-lems and the total collapse of the diamond market seemed inevitable.

For a long time, he had favoured a single sales channel for diamonds. To this end, he formed the Diamond Corporation, which with other producers became responsible for a stability that has persisted to the present time.

Cycle of Slumps

The diamond trade was subject to slumps on average once every eight years and the situation was aggravated in the middle 1920s by the discovery of deposits of high quality diamonds at the Lichtenburg alluvial fields, the Namaqualand coastal deposits, and in the German South West African coastal strip. Kimber-ley, because of the cost of the deep workings, could not compete with the new sources and prices were falling.

During the world depression in the early 1930s, the demand for diamonds almost came to a halt. Conditions were so bad that, in the first half of 1933, De Beers could not even sell diamonds worth £600,000 to cover their bare running expenses. They were forced to close down all the mines, and in 1934 Kimberley was described by a visitor as 'almost a ghost city and a most depressing place with numerous empty villas, houses and shops'.

As a result of these ruinous conditions, Oppenheimer was able to persuade other producers in all countries that the only way to cushion the trade against the cycle of boom and slump was to control production and to regulate sales through one channel. He was able to bring producers together to form, with the co-operation of the government, the Diamond Producers' Association.

After the death of Sir Ernest, in 1957, his son Harry Oppenheimer (Fig. 7.2) continued the same policy with as much success as his father and Cecil Rhodes before him, despite the complications of political change and new deposits that have been found in the U.S.S.R.

Diamond Producers' Association

The Diamond Producers' Association formulates policy and sets quotas. It comprises the principle producers in the De Beers group in South and South West Africa; the Diamond Corporation, which is a De Beers subsidiary; and the South African Government, which is a producer because it owns the State Diggings in Namaqualand. The Association makes marketing agreements with outside producers through the Diamond Corporation.

Central Selling Organization

In 1934, the Diamond Trading Company was formed to carry out the actual selling of diamonds. This and the D.P.A. became the nucleus of what is called The Central Selling Organization, a group of marketing companies through which all the principal diamond producers sell diamonds on a co-operative basis.

All diamonds that the C.S.O. handles are first sent by the mines to the D.P.A. offices in Johannesburg or to the Diamond Corporation offices in London. They are divided into two groups – gem and industrial – each of which is sold through different organizations.

The Sights

The gem diamonds are sold, via the Diamond Purchasing and Trading Company, to the Diamond Trading Company, which sorts them into individual parcels to be offered to invited buyers ten times a year at sales known as sights. About 80 per cent of the world's gem diamonds pass through this system. Nearly all the rough stones pass through London, but some allocated to the South African cutting industry are sold through sights in Johannesburg.

The parcels of rough are made up as near as possible to the requirements of each individual buyer. The buyer states the quantities, shapes, and sizes he requires. He is given the full range of goods but cannot make his own selections. Each diamond is examined at least twice before arriving at its final valuation, and, while prices are fixed and there is no element of bargaining, should a mistake occur in valuation, it will be rectified.

The dealers allowed to buy direct number about 220 and are cutters and a few merchants from a number of countries (Fig. 7.3). If a buyer does not want the full range of goods, he still has to buy the whole parcel. He will then have to sell subsequently, if he can, the stones he does not want.

Parcels from the Sights

Buyers attending sights sort their parcels into rough stones they want to keep and those they want to sell, if they are cutters. If they are rough dealers, they break down their parcels into different categories for their own customers.

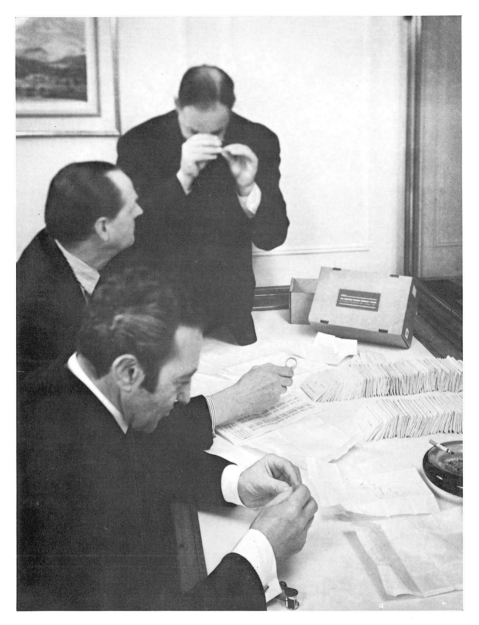

Fig. 7.3. *Buyers at the sights in London examine the contents of a parcel of diamonds. The only question is that of correct valuation.*

Some idea of the value of original parcels offered at sights may be gained by the fact that the annual value of all sales of rough by the C.S.O. was over £300,000,000 in 1969, of which, say, £250,000,000 was for gem diamonds (the actual figure is no longer disclosed). This is sold to 220 customers at ten sights a year, which gives an average of over £100,000 a parcel per customer. Not all buyers have ten sights, however.

All rough gem diamonds eventually find their way through various channels, if not direct, to the cutting trade. Some difficult stones such as coated crystals and those with signs of strain in the crystal (seen by examining it between crossed polaroids as described on page 308), may 'stick' for a long time before a purchaser willing to take a chance is found.

How Prices are Controlled

The Central Selling Organization's policy is not to force unwanted parcels of stones on buyers, but, when demand is good, parcels are always accepted, although the contents may not be just what the buyers prefer. If buyers in general become reluctant to take goods they cannot sell, the C.S.O. will stockpile stones to defend its prices.

During the 1960s, demand expanded so that the opposite situation existed and buyers at the sights were able to resell at increasing prices. The C.S.O. makes occasional overall increases in the price of rough, usually by small amounts averaging up to 5 per cent. Different qualities and sizes are altered differently in price according to supply and demand. In 1970, world demand fell and the C.S.O. had to stockpile.

If demand falls badly, the Diamond Producers' Association can allocate sales quotas to each of its producing members and also instruct the Diamond Corporation to limit its purchases from producers who have agreements with the D.P.A. There have been two occasions since the discoveries of diamonds in South African when a trade depression has closed mines. The recession of 1958, was dealt with by temporary stockpiling by the C.S.O., while the producers continued on the same scales of mining.

Because the system of control is broad, temporary market fluctuations are ignored and there are occasions when the Diamond Trading Company is selling above open market prices and sometimes below. When diamonds are sold, a percentage of the price is retained by the Central Selling Organization to cover handling and marketing, and the rest goes back to the mines. As the C.S.O.'s expenses vary according to the stocks they have to hold, there are times when their funds build up and they make extra payments to the producers.

The C.S.O. has built up a financial reserve fund from about 1950. Later De Beers Investment Trust acted as an additional reserve fund and at present there is a series of four that can back the C.S.O. with funds amounting to hundreds of millions of pounds sterling.

Reorganization of the C.S.O.

Many newly independent African states objected to trading with companies operating from South Africa and much reorganization of the Central Selling Organization was necessary in 1963. Buying operations in certain countries were transferred to the Diamond Corporation. In Sierra Leone, the Diamond Corporation of West Africa Limited buys all the production of individual diggers and a large proportion of the Sierra Leone Selection Trust's production. There are special arrangements for buying in the Congo and in Angola.

Fig. 7.4.   *A licensed buyer, Mr. Jack Young, shown some stones found by diggers in Lesotho. He will weigh and study them if he decides to make an offer.*

The Russians made an agreement in 1959 with De Beers to market Russian diamonds through the C.S.O., but because of the Soviet trade boycott of South Africa, the contract was not renewed, and alternative arrangements for marketing were made in 1963.

The C.S.O. buys diamonds on the open market in various towns in West Africa, among which Monrovia in Liberia is usually the biggest free market. It also buys from Venezuela.

Sales outside the C.S.O.

Of the 20 per cent of the world's diamonds the C.S.O. does not handle, the most important supply is from Ghana, where a government Diamond Marketing Board grades, values, and prices (mostly industrial) rough and sells to licensed buyers.

Part of the Sierra Leone Selection Trust supply also goes to specified buyers direct. Individual diggers and small mines in South Africa, South West Africa, and Lesotho, sell to licensed buyers. The Central African Republic, the Ivory Coast, Guinea, and the South American states of Guyana, Venezuela, and Brazil sell outside the C.S.O. The small Indian production is also outside.

Also outside control are unrecorded but probably large numbers of diamonds found and sold illegally in many producing countries to end up in cutting centres.

129

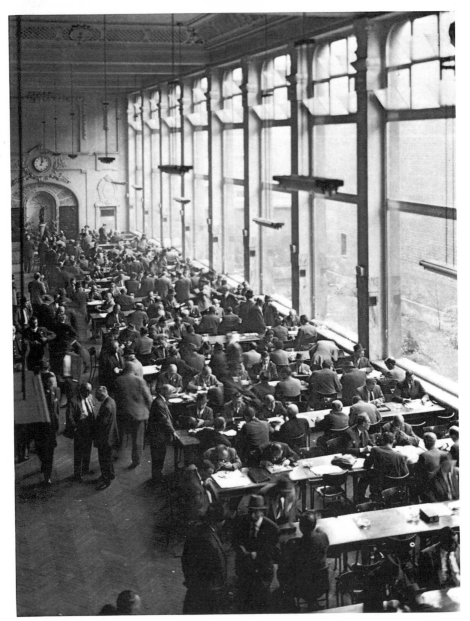

Fig. 7.5. *The bustling Diamond Bourse in Antwerp, where buyers, sellers, and brokers study stones in natural daylight from long windows. This Bourse, which has been renovated since the picture was taken, is one of four diamond exchanges in Antwerp, the busiest diamond trading centre for polished stones.*

The licensed buyer has an exciting life. He has to be born with a gamblers' streak as well as to acquire a deep knowledge of diamonds. He must create a private information network among diggers and their friends to relay swiftly to him news of important finds. He will make personal judgements of the value of

Fig. 7.6.   *Polished stones being checked for weight at the new Diamond Bourse at Tel Aviv in Israel.*

rough diamonds that can run into tens of thousands of pounds and will pay cash on such hunches, without knowing what other buyers have bid. Licensed buyers are shown in Figs. 7.4 and 14.12.

Industrial Diamonds

Industrial diamonds are bought by the Diamond Corporation from South Africa and elsewhere and marketed via Industrial Distributors (1964) Limited, through Industrial Distributors (Sales) Limited. There are no quota arrangements for industrials, but prices are fixed with the buyers. The marketing companies do hold stocks when the market falls, however, to keep prices steady.

Synthetic diamonds from the manufacturing plants in the Irish Republic and South Africa are marketed through a subsidiary of the industrial companies, Industrial Grit Distributors Limited.

The Clubs and Bourses

The diamond wholesale trade, which distributes both rough and polished stones to buyers all over the world, is a very ancient market organized in the form of Clubs and Bourses in the main diamond cities including Antwerp, New York, Tel Aviv, London, Amsterdam, and elsewhere. The Diamond Club is mainly for dealing in crystals and the Diamond Bourse for dealing in polished stones. Each has a huge room with tall windows facing away from the sun with rectangular tables and benches under them. Small groups of dealers at the tables mull over and examine stones. Others stand or wander in groups talking about diamonds and the trade (Figs 7.5 and 7.6).

A Diamond Club or a Diamond Bourse – there is one of each in Hatton Garden – will be a member of the World Federation of Diamond Bourses, which sees that its rules are consistent and strictly applied. For example, a member who is made bankrupt automatically loses his membership and is only allowed back if it is considered that he has made reasonable arrangements to pay his debts. If a member is disbarred, his name is circulated (on green slips) to affiliated Clubs and Bourses all over the world and posted on their notice-boards.

The strict exclusion of possible defaulters is essential because the trade depends upon credit and mutual trust.

Buyers and sellers sit opposite each other like chess players and, after the stones have been studied, cautious bargaining is begun and a price is reached. If the seller is a broker, the stones are sealed by the man who has made the offer.

The diamond paper holding the actual stones is an 'envelope' folded in a particular way (See Appendix 1), often with a translucent pale-blue lining paper for brilliant-cut diamonds and an opaque black one for rose-cut diamonds. The broker transmits the offer to the original seller and, whether it is accepted or not, only the potential buyer may break his own seal. Payment is made on a fixed day, also verbally agreed. After the deal is made, the sealed package is taken to the Diamond Club or Bourse office where it is officially weighed and placed inside a sealed envelope with a note of the weight inside and the date and the weight written on the outside.

Any disputes are brought before a Board of Arbitrators, when a small fee is deposited by the claimant. Any member who fails to abide by a final decision is disbarred, but there is usually a right of appeal.

Of course, not all diamonds are sold in this way. Some are sold direct much like other commodities, singly and in larger quantities. Many larger diamond dealers have offices in which they transact business, but parcels and particularly single stones are always being passed through different hands by the traditional channel and a dealer looking for, say, a stone to match another, or one of particular size and shape, will probably go to a Diamond Club or Diamond Bourse to locate it.

The Jewellery Trade

Most diamonds pass to jewellery manufacturers or designers and through the retail trade to the public. Unfortunately, very few members of the public and even some jewellers do not appreciate the fact that every diamond differs in quality and that there is a wide range in price for stones of the same size but different whiteness, clarity, and quality of cutting. As with other commodities, unless fraud is intended, one generally gets the value one pays for, although a salesman's 'puffs' may appear to upgrade the quality.

Expressing Quality

The basic elements of quality have been cleverly publicised by De Beers under the name 'the Four Cs'. Three of them refer to quality. They are *Clarity, Colour* and *Cut*. Of these, the first two have most affect on price, except when the cut is very bad.

The word clarity was chosen not just because it began with C but because it is a much better word than purity for the jeweller to use. By saying a diamond is pure or perfect implies that others are impure or imperfect, whereas a stone of different clarity or colour is really one created in a slightly different way by Nature. The inclusions that lower the clarity of a diamond are commonly called carbon spots. They are actually nothing of the kind. Most are small fissures caused during the natural growth of the stone, or small pieces of the original minerals with which the diamond grew – Nature's fingerprints and 'hallmarks' of its genuineness.

Colour is the most difficult of the three quality factors to judge, since it requires entirely subjective decisions. In this sense, colour means the exact tint of what would normally be called white. Even white is not right, because the finest colour is transparent and colourless. The finest colour used to be described as 'of first water', which means as pure as clear, limpid stream water. (Stones tinged with yellow were called by-water or bye.)

The accuracy of cutting affects quality because a brilliant-cut stone must be correctly proportioned and finely polished to provide maximum brilliance. A stone of poorer colour or clarity is often cut to less perfect proportion, however, to retain maximum weight, and therefore more value, than it would otherwise have.

Price of Diamonds

The fourth of the four Cs is *Carat Weight*. This obviously affects price. Most people know that the price of diamonds goes up as the weight goes up and also as the quality goes up. What is not usually realized is that the *price per carat* increases.

In practice this favours those who want a large show of diamonds rather than a single stone in a ring or other jewellery. For example, four diamonds each weighing a quarter of a carat each have a larger superficial area than one diamond weighing 1 carat. If they were of exactly the same quality as the 1-carat stone, they would still be much lower priced because the price per carat of quarter-carat stones is much lower than the price per carat of 1-carat stones.

It also explains why diamonds are good supporting stones for rings with coloured main stones. The price of the coloured stone will probably be much the same per carat within fairly wide limits of weight, so a large one will not be too expensive. A number of small diamonds around it will give a good show of diamonds at a relatively low price.

Large diamonds have great intrinsic beauty if effectively cut, but they are being found much less frequently. There is no doubt that smaller gem diamonds are coming from most of the world's diamond sources and that designers and manufacturers of jewellery will have to use smaller stones increasingly in their jewellery as the years go by.

The Myth of the 'Concrete Coast'

From time to time the myth of great hoards of diamonds being held back to keep up prices is recirculated. The implication is that the price is artificially inflated and liable to sudden drop. Like most myths, it has an element of truth. It appears in many forms, one of the most delightful being the belief that many square miles of desert along the Skeleton Coast of South West Africa are concreted over and guarded by the forces of Nature as well as security men to stop anyone from picking up the billions of pounds worth of diamonds that lie there on the sand. Tales are told of bleached bones in the desert and shipwrecks of those who tried to reach the treasure.

The truth is that early in the century, diamonds did lie on the sand of the desert, as described in Chapter Three, and many fortunes were made by Germans who at that time occupied the area. The area is still a restricted diamond concession. It is also true that during the great depression of the 1930s, De Beers Consolidated Mines had to hoard about ten million carats of diamonds in milk cans because they could not sell them. In the 1960s, however, world demand began to outstrip supply. Old mines were being reopened and new ones worked twenty-four hours a day to keep pace with demand and keep the price of diamond from rising too high. Old ones, Koffiefontein for example, were still being opened in 1970.

Display

It is not the purpose of this book to refer to windows and shop display directly, but there are some fundamentals of lighting that must be considered for the most effective display of diamonds. The diamond is at its best when it is lit by one point-source of white artificial light in not too bright general surroundings and it is moved. The brilliance and flashes of fire are then most evident.

It has been truly said in the past that diamonds were designed for candle light. Candle light is unfortunately yellowish in colour but the flicker makes diamonds flash.

Diamonds usually look worse in fluorescent lighting (although rubies can look better). The colour balance of the fluorescent tube may be reasonably accurate in relation to daylight, but the length of the tube and the low intensity of the light reduce the brilliance and fire of the stone.

White tungsten lights of high intensity are much better for window and shop display. Low voltage spot lights run off a transformer system are as effective and generate less heat. Halogen bulbs are very good because the light is white and of very high intensity.

Movement makes the diamond flash with the colours of the rainbow. Some window displays are kept vibrating by passing traffic, and this effect should not be eliminated as far as diamonds are concerned. It is sometimes impractical or tasteless to have a moving display in a jeweller's shop, although there are satisfactory ways of tackling the problem. Jewellery has occasionally been made over very many years with the diamonds mounted on fine springs so that they vibrate and flash in wear.

The Diamond Room

A special diamond room for selling diamonds in a retail shop should be darkened and lit artifically in the way just described. The table or counter may have a low power magnifier mounted on it for the customer's use. Diagrams to explain the four Cs are useful and, of course, pictures of mining and other aids which give customers confidence in diamonds.

The jeweller himself may use the same room for grading and pricing his stock and also for buying from brokers and dealers. In that case, it should have a window facing away from the sun and a table under it with white blotting paper on it for judging colour. The window may be kept curtained when the room is used for selling.

There is no anomaly in using daylight to grade a stone to discover which stones are best in artificial light, where they are principally worn.

Some jewellers possess special diamond microscopes for grading and light boxes for evaluating colour when daylight is not available. The diamond room is where such instruments may be displayed as well as used by the jeweller for grading his stock.

In the U.S.A., and in West Germany, instruments are sometimes used to show customers features of diamonds, that is, as a selling aid. In Germany, particularly, diamond grading equipment plus a certificate showing successful completion of a course in grading are publicized by certain retailers to establish themselves quickly as 'diamond experts' and to gain public confidence.

Principles of Selling

There are two schools of thought about the principles of selling diamonds, either loose or in jewellery, when the diamond is important. One says that it is wrong to go into detail about the diamond, as it will only confuse the customer, who is buying jewellery for a purely emotional reason. The other is that it is important to give the customer the basic facts because he or she will then be more likely to buy diamonds of higher quality, which is better for the customer as well as for the jeweller.

The truth probably lies in another direction, that there are two broad groups of customer, those who buy mainly for emotional reasons and those who buy mainly for practical ones. The more first group buy because the diamond or jewellery is a symbol of what they want for themselves or for the person to whom it is being given. It may represent an emotional occasion such as an engagement, anniversary, birth of a child, and so on, or success in business or some other enterprise. The more practical people buy as an 'investment', a hedge against misfortune, a gift to ensure certain favours or services, or because a certain social occasion needs important jewellery to create an impression.

Often there is an element of both the emotional and the practical in purchase. A man may be buying diamond jewellery for his wife. She is concerned mainly with the emotional possession of a lovely piece of jewellery, but there is the practical element of whether it is suitable for wearing on all or just some occasions. Her husband is concerned in a practical way about whether or not he is spending his money wisely and also with the emotional need for his own success to be displayed to others through the richness or good taste of the jewellery his wife wears.

The salesman's problem is to isolate the person who is most likely to make the final decision and to adjust his attitudes to whether the emotional or the practical attitudes are uppermost during the sale.

What is normally common to both extremes of customer, and to all the shades in between, is a need for reassurance about the knowledge and competence of the salesman and the reputation of the shop. These are matters of training and experience in the case of the salesman, and of fair trading, courteous efficient service, reassurance through window display, and above all, recommendation by other customers, in the case of the shop.

CHAPTER EIGHT

Sorting Crystals

Before diamonds are sold by the mines they have to be given prices. The first step in valuation is to sort them into different grades of usefulness or desirability. A gem diamond is subject to sorting or grading many times during its existence. It is sorted by the miners, by the Diamond Trading Company, by the cutter, by the jewellery manufacturer, and by the retailer. An industrial stone is sorted only in its early life.

Generally the word sorting is applied to crystals, which are divided into groups with similar commercial characteristics. The word grading is usually applied to polished stones, which are separated into much finer degrees of quality. An early sorting office in Kimberley is shown in Fig. 8.1.

It is important to remember that sorting and grading are carried out for commercial reasons. If the market changes, a stone that previously fitted one category might be transferred to another.

Another basic fact is that different categories of sorting and grading are

Fig. 8.1. *Two diamond sorters in Kimberley's earlier days working on piles of rough with the aid of sieves to grade crystals into size groups.*

man-made. Nature provides a continuous band of (1) sizes, (2) shapes, (3) colours, and (4) varieties of inclusion. Any group of any of these four characteristics will merge into an adjoining group. Consequently, there will always be disputed borderline cases.

Sorting Crystals at the Mines

Gem mining, and particularly diamond mining, is different from almost all other forms of mining for minerals because the end product is, and always has been, sorted by hand into a very large number of categories. In other mining activities, such as for gold, there are usually mechanical, chemical, or metallurgical processes followed by automatic grading or refining into standard purities. Because of the very great variety in which diamonds occur, they are handled as individual commodities from the moment they are discovered. Except for the very small and imperfect material, every stone is given a classification and value before it is marketed.

Sorting begins at the diggings or mine. In small outfits, the digger himself classifies the stones he finds, merely by deciding how much money he expects to get from a diamond buyer. He may know nothing of sorting, not even enough to argue with the buyer, but the buyer will have a knowledge of sorting and be able to 'make a price' in competition with other buyers.

Larger mines will do a certain amount of sorting to arrive at values. They may only divide crystals into gem and industrial, or separate them into a dozen or so classifications.

Classifications vary a lot from mine to mine, and depend on the categories at the sorting offices described in detail later. In general, a mine's classifications will include good quality crystals, known as close goods, probably categories depending upon irregular crystallization, on spotted stones, on colour, and perhaps on categories of size. Very small crystals that pass through a fine sieve are separated and known as sand.

Central Sorting Office

The main channels for the distribution of gem diamond crystals were described in Chapter Seven. There are many others, including one for gem diamonds from the Russian mines, and a Tanzanian government sorting office in London for pricing and sale of crystals from the Williamson and other mines to the Diamond Trading Company.

Parcels of stones from the mines in the Republic of South Africa and from South West Africa, each normally containing a month's production, are sent to a Central Sorting Office in Kimberley. Parcels from each mine are kept separate in order to preserve the identity of the mine. The diamonds are cleaned in acid, weighed, and counted.

The initial sorting is into broad gem and industrial categories. The two groups go to separate sorting offices in Johannesburg.

Some stones, although satisfactory in other respects, are too small for making into gems. Others are so awkwardly shaped or twinned or of such bad colour or bad quality that they have to be categorized as industrial. There are always

Fig. 8.2. *Rough diamond of gem quality being sorted into size, shape, quality, and colour at the London offices of De Beers Central Selling Organization before being valued and offered to buyers at the monthly sights.*

borderline cases and commercial demand determines whether these are preserved as gems or are consumed as industrials.

During the sorting of the gem crystals another group appears, known as near-gem, which is sold to Industrial Distributors, in London, for eventual sorting into the top industrial grades. This group contains crystals of marginal colour and quality (clarity) which go to either the gem or industrial market, according to which is paying the best prices.

Gem Crystal Sorters

Sorters are highly trained men and women who are able to identify, almost instantly, subtle differences in crystals. The sorters sit at benches in the Central Sorting Offices at Kimberley under south-facing windows the length of very long rooms. The benches are covered with fresh white paper. When the diamonds reach London they are resorted in similarly arranged rooms, but under windows facing north, in the Diamond Trading Company's office in London, near Hatton Garden (Fig. 8.2). In London there is an extra problem of the short daylight hours in winter months during which diamonds can be sorted.

Sizes and Mêlée

First of all, gem crystals are divided into two broad categories of size. One group, known as sizes, are all crystals weighing over a certain amount, which depends on the market. Usually it is about a carat. At the time of writing, sizes are stones over 1·2 carat. Crystals under this weight are known as mêlée. Separate groups of sorters deal with sizes and with mêlée. Sizes are sorted into a greater number of categories because of their higher values.

Sorting Sizes

Sizes are divided into about eleven different size groups, by sieving, not by weighing. These are distributed to sorters for separating into groups of different crystal forms, colours, and qualities. Categories of sorting have been changed from time to time in relation to demand. The basic ones are given here for completeness although at times certain categories are telescoped into each other.

Sorters first deal with the shapes of crystals (Fig. 8.3). These are, in descending order of value:

1. *Stones:* Unbroken crystals of regular formation.
2. *Shapes:* Unbroken crystals of less regularity.
3. *Cleavages:* Irregularly-shaped or broken crystals.
4. *Macles:** Twinned crystals of roughly triangular shape.
5. *Flats:* Diamond crystals of irregular shape with flat parallel sides like pieces of broken glass.

Brilliant-cut gems can be fashioned from all except the last category. Those made from suitable *macles* tend to be shallow, however. Baguettes and other small cuts are made from *flats*.

While he deals with crystals by shape, the sorter is also making divisions into quality, which is the name used by sorters for clarity. When he receives his pile of crystals, he first goes through it and picks out the pure regular octahedra known as *stones*. Then he picks out any other unbroken octahedra which may be irregular in form and have varying degrees of inclusion. Any pure ones will be irregular in form and, unless very distorted, will go into his first pile of *stones*. The remainder, including those with fairly obvious inclusions which are called spotted goods, will become his pile of *shapes*. At the time of writing these categories are grouped together.

* Spelt macle or maccle.

Stone

Irregular shape

Cleavage

Stone

Fig. 8.3. Categories of shape into which layer gem rough is sorted. The more ideal forms are shown in the drawings and actual examples in the photographs. Some groups have been telescoped. Mêlée (stones under about a carat) are sorted into fewer shapes and qualities.

Macle

Flat

Shape

Macle

Cleavage

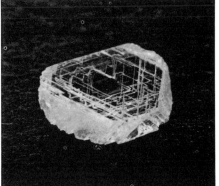

Flat

The next class, *cleavages*, is normally the biggest. The crystals in it are not all cleavages in a crystallographic sense, as they include all diamonds that were imperfectly formed or were fractured, as well as those that were split along a cleavage plane at some stage of their existence. *Cleavages* can contain very large stones of the very highest quality. For example, the Cullinan would have been graded as a *cleavage* had it reached the sorting rooms. *Cleavages* range in form from near *stones* or *shapes* with distorted or broken faces to irregular lumps of diamond with no recognizable crystallographic features.

The next category of *macles*, is easily identifiable. The macle is a rotation twinned octahedron with a triangular form and usually a seam as explained in Chapter Seventeen. It is usually quite flat but often thick enough for cutting into a brilliant.

The final category of *flats* covers tabular crystals too thin for making brilliants. As this is being written, *flats* and *macles* are also lumped together at the Central Sorting Office.

The sorter now goes back to his groups of *stones* and removes from them all the crystals that have a definitely lower value. These include frosted crystals, which have one or more faces with a ground glass appearance. The difficulty with them is that they are harder to grade accurately. Oxidized stones were once removed, but are no longer. These have an orange tinge, as they contain iron oxide, and are usually from alluvial deposits. Finally, brown tinted stones are separated. Greens, which are very pale, used to be separated but are now left in the main categories. Figs. 8.4 and 8.5 show a variety of rough diamonds.

Sorting for Quality

Now the sorter returns to the remaining stones to divide them into groups of different qualities. It is not as simple as it seems, because what he is really doing is to separate them according to their value to a cutter. For example, an octahedral crystal with a heavy inclusion near one point of the octahedron will be as good as a clean crystal because the corners are bruted away during cutting, but one with an inclusion near the centre will be of low value because so much material will be lost during cutting. A substantial amount may be lost from an octahedron when a central flaw has to be sawn out. Each inclusion, according to size and darkness, as well as position, and each feather or cleavage mark within the stone, as well as any twinning, has to be examined carefully to determine the quality.

The sorter picks up the crystal between thumb and first finger and twists it in all directions by a kind of rolling action while examining it closely, and places it in a grading category. A 6X hand lens is often used to study the inclusions. Breathing on the stone to dull its natural lustre sometimes helps to see into it.

Ten grades of quality are employed for crystals, numbered from 1–10. For *stones* and *shapes*, only the first five – although this may be extended to seven if demand is strong – are regarded as the gem group. The remainder, from 5, 6 or 7 to 10 are the near-gem quality and merge into industrials. For *cleavage, macles*, and *flats* the gem group normally spans qualities from 1–4, but this may also be extended to seven when the market is lively.

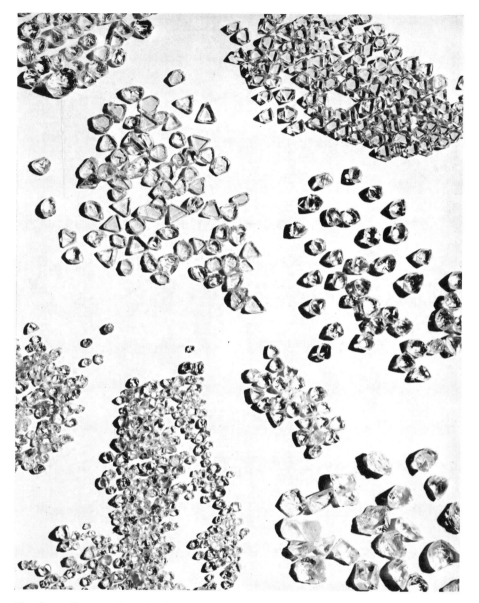

Fig. 8.4. *Some sorted rough. Top right is a pile of stones, all well-formed octahedra. Macles can be seen in the second pile down on the left. At bottom right there are cleavages.*

The sorter starts with what appear to be the cleanest stones and works down the scale of qualities making a row of piles of different sized crystals for each quality. As a fairly general guide, quality 1 is clean; 2 has a few small spots or a white spot near the edge; 3 has a larger single white spot or a crack near the edge; 5 has quite heavy inclusions, cracks or spots.

Fig. 8.5. *Gem and industrial rough. At top left is a macle and beside it an octahedron. The large darker stone in the centre is irregular (and Type II material). The tongs hold a form of star twin which is useless as gem material.*

Sorting for Colour

Next he deals with colour. Browns have already been separated. He removes any full-bodied yellow stones known as golden fancies, and any other full-bodied colours, such as the very rare deep blues, pinks, and ambers, which are called fancies. Numbers of large golden fancies come from the Dutoitspan Mine. When they are under 2·5 carats, they are classified as industrials and when over, as gems.

The remaining crystals will be varying tints of white, from the extremely rare true blue-white down to pale yellow. Colours are divided into ten categories named 1st, 2nd, 3rd, and so on to 10th. A crystal from 1st to 6th colour (or to 7th according to the state of the market) is in the gem group provided that it is also in the correct purity quality. Crystals below the first six or seven colour categories are the near-gem group and considered as industrials.

Shapes of first colour and quality used to be called ex. collection, i.e. extra collection. Such crystals are, of course, very rare. Stones of second colour and purity were called collection. The remaining colours were numbered from one to eight and the next two at the bottom of the scale were named Capes and Second Capes, which are spotted yellow stones.

Having dealt with *stones* the sorter starts on the other categories and divides them into groups according to their colour and degree of spottiness. Generally, the lower the quality of the stones, the smaller the number of other grades into which they are divided.

Yellow stones are sorted into qualities and grades of colour. Brown ones are sorted into qualities and five grades of colour: (1) Finest light brown, (2) Fine light brown, (3) Light brown, (4) Brown, (5) Dark brown.

Sorting Mêlée

The smaller crystals are similarly divided into types of crystals. The categories are:

1. *Stones:* Same as larger *stones* and *shapes.*
2. *Chips:* Same as larger *cleavages.*
3. *Macles* and *flats.*

There are many variations in the details of sorting which change from time to time.

The Sorting Bench

As mentioned earlier, the sorter receives his *stones* in size groups. He retains these and at the end of a sorting session has in front of him, on the white paper covered bench, 'grids' of piles with the largest and finest crystals at the top left and the poorest and smallest at the bottom right, as shown in Fig. 8.2. Each rectangle of piles is made for a single colour. Each vertical row contains crystals of the same quality and each row to the right is of a lower quality. In each horizontal row are stones of the same size group. Sizes are in descending order from the top. The rectangles of piles contain crystals of the same colour category, with the best to the left.

Normally there are six colour categories and each of these six rectangles could contain up to five vertical rows of purity and say eleven horizontal rows of five sizes. A much simpler system is used for *cleavages* and *macles* and *flats* and a still simpler one for mêlée.

Formula for Valuation

When the crystals have been sorted, an official known as the Chief Valuator examines them and puts a price on them. This is obviously a task that calls for a very high degree of judgement and considerable experience. As a starting-point for evaluation, the various diamond producers have agreed amongst themselves a formula by which the basic value of a particular classification of diamonds can be calculated, for guidance. After arriving at a basic figure, the valuator adjusts it according to his assessment of what recovery of polished stone is possible from a particular crystal, i.e. how much flaws and their positions will influence the cutting. In practice, price books based on the formula are used up to 10 carats and stones are sorted against a sample parcel, but the valuator deals individually with stones of over 10 carats.

It is not easy to price a diamond crystal for the colour it will be when cut because the colour in diamonds is not always uniform. A crystal of poor quality may be improved by removing the small area which is the only part poorly coloured, and was previously suffusing the stone. A diamond crystal may be coated with a 'skin' of bad colour and be of excellent colour inside. Colour may also occur in spots or layers; some octahedra have colour only in the corners or along the edges.

Another of the difficulties of the valuator of rough diamonds is that the colour of a crystal 'improves' in relation to how much is lost in cutting. A good octahedron from which a high recovery is possible will 'improve' less than a poorly formed stone from which the recovery is lower. The phenomenon of colour saturation is well known. A deeply coloured liquid in a narrow bottle will look quite pale. Glass which is, say, dark red, will appear white if powdered small enough.

Sorting Industrials

Near-gem crystals are sorted into three categories of crystals:

1. *Stones.*
2. *Shapes* (which include macles).
3. *Cleavages.*

These categories include crystals down to a certain size, separated by passing them through a wire sieve. They are divided themselves also by sieves into two categories of size. Near-gem crystals are then graded for quality and for colour.

In sorting for quality, different criteria apply than for gem sorting. For example, good points (corners) on an octahedron are more important than internal flaws, unless the flaws are very bad, because the corners are used as cutting tools.

There are three grades of colour in the *stone* and *shape* categories: Grey, yellow, and brown; and three in the *cleavages*: Grey, coloured, and brown.

Diamonds that are not near-gem are classified into *drilling* and *boart*. Drilling also includes the small stones rejected from the near-gem categories. It is used for mounting in the heads of rock drills and sold in sieving sizes. There are four main categories: (1) Drill rounds, (2) Cast setting (for use when metal is cast round the diamonds), (3) Mixed drilling (very small stones), and (4) Dust.

Crushing boart is the lowest quality of diamond of any kind. It varies enormously in its appearance and characteristics. It can be a hard black cokey mass, sugary and greeny-yellow like Congo boart, or black in large broken octahedral crystals like much mine boart.

Gem Crystal Sorting by the D.T.C.

After sorting, diamonds are sold by the Diamond Producers Association, to the Diamond Trading Company (D.T.C.) and sent to their sorting office in London, where they are joined by crystals coming from many other sources. In London, the whole process of sorting is repeated in even more detail for repricing and preparation of parcels of stones to suit particular buyers. At times the D.T.C. has sorted crystals into more than 2,500 categories.

The D.T.C. Sorting Office retains parcels of selected stones in each classification for use as standards of quality and colour. From time to time, sorted crystals are compared with the standard to make sure that there is no drift in quality and that different sorters are applying the same standards. A similar system is applied in Kimberley.

Weighing Rough

When all the diamond crystals have been re-sorted, the Diamond Trading Company mixes those of the same categories from different sources, and at this point they are weighed. Up to this stage they have been divided only into general weight categories, except for stones above about 15 carat, which are sold separately. Normally, crystals are counted into groups of a hundred of approximately the same size and weight together. For example, a hundred stones might be offered as weighing 100 carats. Not every stone would weigh exactly a carat. Some might be 0·9 carat and others 1·1 carat.

Weighing is always carried out to one-tenth of a carat and shown to one place of decimals thus: 3·4 ct., 14·7 ct., 8·0 ct., 0·9 ct. After diamonds are polished, the trade weighs them to a hundredth of a carat, shown thus: 0·34 ct., 2·06 ct., 3·10 ct., and so on.

CHAPTER NINE

The History of Diamond Cutting

There was little or no incentive to polish and shape diamonds during the centuries that they were regarded as talismans. Those set in rings were usually natural octahedra and perhaps, in many cases, glassies with flat, highly reflective faces. The Indian lapidary work 'Agastimata', probably written in the fourteenth century, is the earliest record of the fact that diamonds can be finished by using other diamonds, but the author gave a warning that a diamond polished on a wheel would lose its magical powers.

Cleaving, Grinding, and Bruting

Cleaving is a rapid way of shaping a diamond, but only octahedral forms can be produced. Grinding and polishing with diamond dust is slower but much more flexible, because many different shapes or patterns of facets are possible. The diamond grinding wheel called the scaife was in use in the fourteenth century and if diamonds were ground before its introduction, the operation was probably carried out in the same way as other gemstones were ground at an early date, as shown in Fig. 9.1 from the book of Presbyter Theophilus of about the tenth century. A table facet was rubbed on gems other than diamond by using a sandstone, a lead table, and finally a goat skin with brick dust moistened by saliva.

It is most likely that grinding and polishing (which is a refined degree of grinding) were practised before the mechanics of cleaving were discovered. It has been suggested that the first diamond polishers polished the faces of octa-

Fig. 9.1. *A gem polisher, shown in a book by Presbyter Theophilus, produced in about the tenth century.*

Fig. 9.2. *Coat of arms of a Nuremberg diamond polisher. The date is unknown.*

hedral crystals to make 'point-cut' stones (Fig. 1.7.). True octahedral faces are impossible to grind and polish, however, so this cut was probably made by an alternative method. The first reference to cleaving appears to have been made by Tavernier when writing of tabular crystals found in the Indian Raolconda mines. He commented that Indians were more skilful than Europeans at cleaving.

A major step in diamond shaping was the invention of bruting, usually described in the past simply as cutting (hence 'cutting and polishing' described the whole operation), which probably occurred in the late fourteenth or early fifteenth century. In bruting, a whole piece of diamond set in a stick, instead of diamond powder, is used as a tool to shape another diamond before facetting it.

Sawing is a specialized form of grinding used to divide diamond crystals and probably followed bruting as a manufacturing method.

Origins in Venice

It is surmised from examining existing records that the polishing of diamond faces in Europe originated in Venice some time after 1330. From Venice the art spread to Bruges, in Flanders, and then to Paris. In the fifteenth century it appeared in other towns, notably Antwerp. A report of a court case of 1465, involving the Dukes of Burgundy, refers to four diamond polishers from Bruges, described as *diamantslypers*, who were called as expert witnesses. Guillebert de Metz, in his description of Paris of 1477, refers to the district of La Courarie as the home of the workers of diamonds and other stones. A diamond worker named Herman, a Flemish name, is mentioned.

There is a record of a Wouter Pauwels, *diamantslyper*, in Antwerp in 1482 and of diamond polishers in Lyons in 1497. In a bankruptcy case at Augsburg in 1538 it was reported that a diamond of 11·5 carats had been reduced to 5 carats after being worked on. This strongly suggests that the diamond had been bruted before being facetted by grinding and polishing.

The earliest reference to cutting, presumably bruting, is in 1550 in Antwerp as a document of this date includes the name *diamantsnyder*. *Slypen* appears to have meant grinding and polishing and *snyden* to have meant cutting, i.e. bruting. A guild charter was granted in 1582 to diamanten robynsnyden in Antwerp. A Nuremberg polisher's coat of arms is shown in Fig. 9.2. The date is unknown. Nuremberg flourished as an early centre of clock, watch and jewellery making at the same time as the nearby town of Augsburg.

There are, however, several earlier references to shaped diamonds. In 1420, the Duke of Burgundy owned 'un dyamant taillé à plusieurs faces'.

Trade Routes and Cutting Centres

There were two main overland trade routes by which diamonds from the Indian mines reached Venice through the Mediterranean. The southern one was from Bombay and the ports of Malabar by sea to Aden and then overland to Ethiopia and Egypt and to Cairo and Alexandria. The northern route was from the gem trading centre of Ormus to Arabia (Aleppo), Persia, Armenia, and Turkey.

When the Portuguese discovered the direct sea route to India, Antwerp grew rapidly as a diamond centre, being supplied with rough through Lisbon as well as Venice, which had supplied alone until then. Venice still remained an important supplier of rough, particularly to Flanders, throughout the sixteenth century and continued as a more important finishing centre than Antwerp in the first half of the seventeenth century. A population of 186 diamond cutters worked in Venice in 1636.

In 1585, there were Spanish attacks on Antwerp and many craftsmen fled elsewhere. Some diamond cutters settled in Amsterdam, where Willem Vermaet was cutting in 1586, and there is a marriage entry dated 1589 of a diamond cutter, Pieter Goos, who had apparently come from Antwerp. A large section of the Amsterdam trade appeared to have moved from Lisbon after 1579, however, when the Inquisition gained power in Portugal.

It was because of religious persecution in the latter part of the sixteenth century in a number of countries including Spain, Portugal, Germany, and Poland, that many craftsmen including a large number of Jews took their skills elsewhere. Many found homes in the Netherlands, where there was no barrier to them until they tried to join a craft guild. As diamond cutters were relatively new as a craft, they had no guild, so the immigrants were attracted to diamond cutting. During the eighteenth century there was an attempt to form a guild that excluded Jews.

Near the beginning of the seventeenth century, the Dutch began buying rough direct from India and by mid-century had taken most of the trade from the Portuguese. By the end of the century, Amsterdam had become established as the main centre for the supply of rough and Antwerp as the cutting centre.

Lisbon was a cutting centre at an early date after the Portuguese began trading directly with India and it was perhaps around the same time that cutting centres were established in Spain, at Valencia, Barcelona, and Madrid.

Late in the seventeenth century London emerged as an important cutting centre, ranking third after Amsterdam and Antwerp. The British were gaining strong interests in India and the discovery of diamond deposits in Brazil in the eighteenth century, which were under the control of the Portuguese who had close links with the British, helped not only Lisbon but London as a trading centre for rough. Amsterdam flourished and reached its peak in the eighteenth century as a cutting centre, while Antwerp declined. It was in the eighteenth century that trading in rough became much more separated from cutting and, in the nineteenth century, the South African discoveries accelerated the separation of the two activities, and the influence of London as a market.

London became and has remained the centre of supply of rough. The principle cutting centres today are in Belgium (Antwerp), India (Bombay), Israel (Tel Aviv), South Africa (Johannesburg, Kimberley, Cape Town), the U.S.A. (New York), Puerto Rico (San Juan, etc.), West Germany (Idar-Oberstein, Brucken, Hanau, Odenwald), the U.K. (London, Brighton), Holland (Amsterdam), France (St. Cloud, in Jura), Portugal (Lisbon), and Sierra Leone. The U.S.S.R. has a big and still growing cutting industry at Sverdlovsk in the Urals, and perhaps at Peterhof, near Leningrad, and Kolyvanskaya, in the Altai.

Fig. 9.3. The first known drawing of a diamond polisher (diamantslyper) by Jan Luiken, made in Holland in 1695. A woman provides the power to drive the scaife (grinding wheel).

There are also cutters working in Australia, Brazil, Japan, Guyana, Italy, Venezuela, Tanzania, Indonesia, and some other Eastern countries. Each centre tends to specialize in a particular class of work. For example, Antwerp handles cleavages, macles, and chips; stones and shapes tend to go to the U.S.A.; and Amsterdam, Israel, and West Germany all specialize in mêleé (small stones). India also cuts 'smalls'.

Cellini's Description

The first known description of diamond cutting (bruting) and polishing was given in 1568 by the celebrated Italian goldsmith, Benvenuto Cellini, who wrote:

'One diamond is rubbed against another until by mutual abrasion both take a form which the skilled polisher wishes to achieve. With the powder which falls from the diamond the last operation for the completion of the cut is made. For this purpose the stones are fixed into small lead or tin cups, and with a special clamping device, held against a steel wheel which is provided with oil and diamond dust. This wheel must have the thickness of a finger and the size of the palm of the hand; it must consist of the finest well-hardened steel and be fixed to a mill-stone so that through the rotation of the latter it also comes into rapid movement. At the same time 4 to 6 diamonds can be attached to the wheel. A weight placed on the clamping device can increase the friction of the stone against the moving wheel. In this way, the polishing is completed.'

Cellini's description could have been written today. In almost any diamond workshop in any part of the world will be found solder dops in which the stone is held as it is polished on the top surface of the horizontal scaife. Today's scaife is larger, however.

Cellini did not describe how the scaife was driven, but it was undoubtedly by hand. In 1604, A Boetius De Boot described and illustrated a treadle-driven horizontal shaft with a point at the end, treated with diamond dust, for gem engraving, but early diamond polishing scaifes appear to have been driven by hand, despite the invention of a horse-driven diamond mill, claimed as early as 1550 by a Nuremberg man, H. Lobsinger. The first known drawing of diamond workers, made in Holland in 1695, shows a lever that was hand-driven (Fig. 9.3).

Horse-drive became general in the first quarter of the nineteenth century. By mid-nineteenth century, the Industrial Revolution was responsible for the introduction of steam engines into diamond factories to drive a number of scaifes through shafts and belts. In this century, the coming of electric power

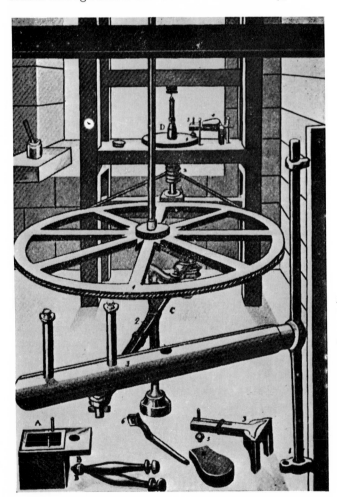

Fig. 9.4. *Diamond polisher's equipment shown in A. Felibien's book of 1676. The beam across the picture is moved to and fro by the handles to turn the large wheel and drive the scaife under the window. In the foreground left are the tools used for cleaving and bruting and on the right a tang, a weight and, centre, a spanner. On the shelf, left background, is a pestle and mortar for making diamond powder.*

resulted in scaifes being driven by individual electric motors. They are always driven anti-clockwise.

Incidentally, some diamond factories are still set up with the polishers sitting at long benches with their backs to the light. This is a tradition carried over from the days of hand-drive when the flywheel took up most of the room.

Polisher's Equipment

The earliest reliable record of a diamond polisher's equipment is that published in 1676, by A. Felibien, a French architect. One of his illustrations (Fig. 9.4) shows the scaife and the dop tang (a kind of very squat three-legged stool) on the far bench. The diamond to be polished was fixed in a solder dop and was fitted to the tang to provide one of the legs. The polisher sat with his back to the window at the far end. The scaife was driven by the big cartwheel type of flywheel, turned by a crank attached to the thick horizontal arm in the foreground. The upright handles were grasped by an assistant (usually one of the polisher's family) to move the arm backwards and forwards.

Cleaving Diamond

On the left at the bottom of the drawing are a cleaver's box and lying beside it, two holders, or cleaver's sticks. The origin of cleaving is unknown. De Boot believed a cleaver could split a diamond with his fingernail and a certain amount of know-how! The diamond is cleaved with a blade and a mallet as described in Chapter Eleven (Figs. 9.5 and 9.6).

Cleaving has not changed from the early days until now, either in its technique or in the tools employed. The mystery clung to it longer than other fabricating practices, largely because nothing was known of crystallography, and the diamond cutter developed his own rules-of-thumb.

Even J. Mawe in 1823 referred to the fact that cleavers kept their art a secret. Despite this, the English physicist, Robert Boyle, had given a correct explanation of octahedral cleaving in relation to the diamond cutters' grain in 1672 in his 'Essay about the Origin and Virtue of Gems'. (He also mentioned trigons – triangular pits – on octahedral faces.)

Fig. 9.5. *The bruter (cutter) at work, from Mawes' book of 1823. The box receives powder produced. On the right is a charcoal fire to soften the cement for fixing diamonds in the sticks. This method is also used to produce a notch or kerf (Fig. 9.11) for the cleaving blade.*

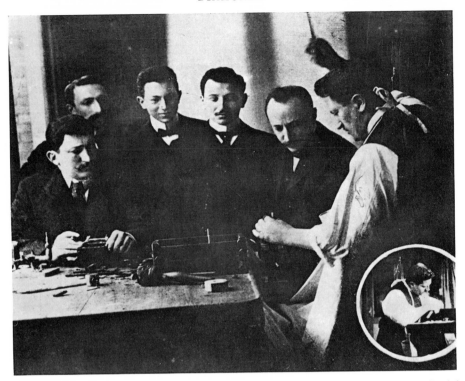

Fig. 9.6. *Joseph Asscher cleaving the huge Cullinan diamond on February 10th, 1907. Special tools were made for the task.*

Bruting (Cutting) Diamonds

The process of rounding the corners of a diamond is known as bruting. In the past it was a form of hand grinding carried out with the same tools as cleaving. A stone called a sharp, cemented in the end of one stick, was used to rub the corners off a stone cemented in the other stick, by holding one stick in each hand as shown in Fig. 9.5, which is taken from Mawe's treatise. The vigorous rubbing action was carried on over the cleaving box to catch the chips of diamond.

Very considerable force was needed when bruting by hand and the crystals could be only approximately rounded. The two vertical steel pegs that can be seen projecting upwards from the edge of the cleaver's box in Fig. 11.10 are to give purchase when bruting. The bruter wore leather gloves but still suffered from damage to his hands.

The old method of bruting by hand over the cleaver's box persisted until the end of the nineteenth century. In 1891, D. Rodrigues took out a British patent for a bruting machine driven by power, and it was his type of machines that eventually came into use. Grodzinski recorded having seen a machine-bruted diamond made in 1826, however.

Diamond Powder

Chips and other pieces of diamond unsuitable for making into gems were crushed into powder with pestle and mortar, which may be seen in Fig. 9.4 on the small

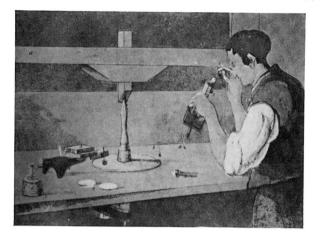

Fig. 9.7. *A polishing bench in John Mawe's book with a weighted tang being used on the scaife (spelt skive in the book) and another with its diamond being inspected. On the left is a pestle and mortar for making diamond dust and beside it glasses of olive oil and diamond powder.*

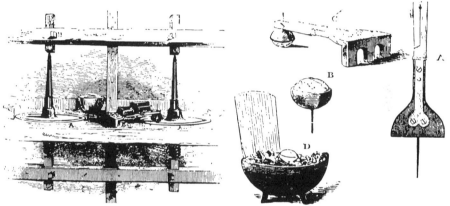

Fig. 9.8. *Diamond polishing equipment in mid-nineteenth century. The scaife spindles are running in blocks of the hard wood, lignum vitae (as in Fig. 9.7.). Top right is a tang with dop fitted and right a tang showing the tail. The brazier in the centre was to melt the solder in the dop, which holds the diamond being polished.*

table on the left beside the bench in the window. It was necessary to hammer the pestle to break up larger diamond chips.

Producing diamond dust for grinding and polishing by this method is surprisingly efficient. The dust will pass through present-day commercial sieves. Over nine-tenths of the powder is under one micron (under a fifty-thousandth of an inch) and the largest grains are only about twenty microns. Unsieved powder is still used today by diamond polishers, although many now use graded synthetic diamond powder. Diamond is the only material that can be polished by ungraded powder. Industrial users prefer to have it sieved and graded, because any larger grains in a powder will scratch metals being polished.

Tang and Dop

The tang and dop for grinding and polishing are seen in more detail in the foreground on the right in Felibien's drawing (Fig. 9.4). The tang is, in modern engineer's language, the tool holder. When using metal-cutting lathes, the operator always held the tool by hand until Maudslay invented the fixed tool holder (saddle) at the beginning of the nineteenth century, yet the fixed tool holder for diamond cutting was in use from the fifteenth century (Fig. 9.7).

The dop which held the diamond was originally a cup on a thick copper stalk, and often still is today. The diamond to be cut is fixed in a fairly large bulk of plumber's solder in the cup. The solder was softened in a gas flame and the diamond embedded in it, so that the only part exposed was that to be ground and polished. The solder was worked, while soft, into a cone shape, with the diamond at the point, by a worker known as a vesteller. He used his thumb on the hot solder to smooth it, and consequently developed a really tough skin because the solder melts at about $215°$ C ($420°$ F). There are still a few vestellers in the diamond cutting trade. Originally a coke brazier was used. (Fig. 9.8).

A weight was sometimes placed on top of the tang, as mentioned by Cellini, to increase the grinding pressure. Such a weight is seen in the foreground of the illustration Fig. 9.4., with the spanner used for tightening the clamp for the dop. An early workshop is shown in Fig. 9.9.

Mechanical Dops

In the second half of the twentieth century, the mechanical dop employing clamps instead of solder to hold the diamond became more common, and quadrants to set the angles were incorporated in some tangs. De Boot had suggested such quadrant devices, and also showed an invention of his own for polishing sixteen diamonds at the same time, in his book of 1604 (Fig. 9.10).

The clamp of the mechanical dop allows the stone to be turned easily and

Fig. 9.9.   *Another polisher's workshop of later nineteenth century. The pins fixed on the benches (left) are to prevent tangs from being swept off the rotating scaifes. The tang is placed between the pins.*

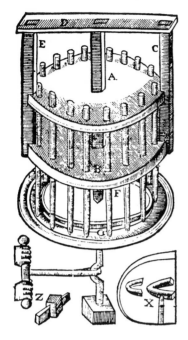

Fig. 9.11. *A diamond on which a kerf (notch) has been rubbed preparatory to cleaving.*

Fig. 9.10. *De Boot's invention of 1604 for polishing sixteen diamonds at the same time.*

quickly to position it for grinding another facet, whereas turning a stone in a solder dop is a lengthy performance, but the advantages are not all on one side. It is easier to lose a stone from a mechanical dop and also the stone becomes hotter because air does not conduct away the heat generated by polishing as quickly as solder does.

Today, for small stones, there are automatic dops which change their positions to grind facets semi-automatically. One version will place forty-eight facets on the girdle of a diamond without attention in about two minutes. The traditional methods are always used for larger and more important stones, however.

Sawing Diamonds

Sawing was used to remove flawed parts, which it is impossible or uneconomic to remove by cleaving, or to reduce the size of a crystal. John Mawe described the saw in 1823. 'It was', he wrote, 'made of a fine wire of brass or iron, attached to the two ends of a piece of cane or whalebone, the teeth being formed by the particles of diamond powder, which became embedded in the wire, as soon as it is applied to the line.'

The bow saw was the ancient Chinese tool for sawing jade using crushed garnet as an abrasive. The line referred to by Mawe was a notch cut in the edge of a stone by rubbing with a sharp – as when preparing a stone for cleaving (Fig. 9.11). The notch or kerf was filled with oil and diamond dust.

The sawing direction seems always to have been 'in the cube plane', as when cutting off the point of an octahedron to form a table stone. The process was very laborious and it is recorded that it took a year to cut the 410-carat Regent Diamond in half. Mawe wrote, 'If the stone be large, the labour of eight to ten months is sometimes required to complete the operation.'

Circular saws for cutting gems were referred to by Felibien in 1676, the saw blade being vertical as modern practice, but it was apparently not until much later, about 1900, that the method was applied to diamonds. The first reference to a circular diamond saw is dated 1874.

L. Claremont wrote in 1906, 'There is in use in Amsterdam an instrument in the form of a circular saw, for the purpose of dividing diamonds. It consists of a small, thin metal disc, with an edge prepared with diamond powder. . . . With this machine it is possible to cut through a diamond in any direction. The process, however, sometimes takes as long as two or three weeks.'

Claremont was wrong about being able to saw in any direction. It is impossible to saw in an octahedral direction because the diamond will cleave instead. Diamond was at first always sawn in the cubic direction and it was not until the 1930s that it was sawn in the dodecahedral direction as well. Today, sawing is the usual practice with octahedral crystals. Banks of sawing machines are tended by a single sawyer.

Centuries ago, diamond polishers used to carry round with them their scaifes, and tangs and dops, and set them up where they worked. Even today there are highly-skilled polishers who will only use their own scaifes and not those supplied by the firm for which they work. There is still very much individuality about these craftsmen, who are temperamental and still regard their craft as a highly personal art.

REFERENCES

Treatises on Goldsmithing and Sculpture, by Benvenuto Cellini (Florence, 1568).
Gemmarum et Lapidum Historia, by A. Boetius de Boot (1604).
Essay about the Origin and Virtue of Gems, by R. Boyle (London, 1672).
Des Principes de l'Architecture, de la Sculpture, de la Peinture et des Autres Arts qui en Dependent, by A. Felibien (Paris, 1676).
Treatise on Diamond and Precious Stones, by J. Mawe (London, 2nd ed., 1823).
Diamond Technology, by P. Grodzinski (London, 2nd ed., 1953).
Industrial Diamond Review. 'Special Supplement on History of Diamond Polishing', by Grodzinski and Feldhaus (London, 1953).
A History of Jewellery 1100–1870, by Joan Evans (London, 1953).
The History of Diamond Production and the Diamond Trade, by Godehard Lenzen (London, 1970).

CHAPTER TEN

The History of Cuts

About 1490, Bartolomeo de Pasti wrote a book of commerce which referred to two types of diamond, *diamanti*, which were shipped to Antwerp, and *diamanti in punto*, which went to Lisbon and Paris. *Diamanti* were no doubt rough sent for cutting. *Diamanti in punto* were pointed stones, which may have been octahedral rough called glassies or point-cut stones.

The Point Cut
Pointed diamonds in old jewellery have angles appreciably below those of the natural octahedron and must have been fashioned into point cuts. The point cut is believed to be the earliest diamond cut (Fig. 1.7). Macles – flat, triangular octahedral twins with specular faces top and bottom – were also set in jewellery.

Pointed stones appeared in diamond jewellery of the Middle Ages, and remained popular into the Renaissance period. The first true cut for diamond was the table cut, introduced into Europe some time before 1538, perhaps with the invention of bruting, but maybe earlier if the flat table facet was produced by grinding.

The Table Cut
The table cut was an octahedron with its top point flattened to a square facet called the table, as shown in Fig. 1.8. Sometimes the lower point was also ground to make a smaller facet, the collet or culet. Many early table stones had a facet on the bottom about half the size of the table facet on the top and were known as Indian-cut as they came from the Orient. Most were re-cut in Europe. The table cut was produced by bruting and polishing.

Cutting was dominated by the table stone throughout the sixteenth century and into the beginning of the seventeenth, because classical influences remained and the golden mean of Pythagoras, who mingled geometry with magic, was exemplified by the cut. Although the golden mean was the ratio 1:1·618, it was based on the square; the table stone from the top presented one square within another. Many coloured stones were also table cut for what seemed to be the same reasons.

Point stones were still common during the period, but they were gradually being re-cut as table stones. De Boot of Bruges, writing in 1600, described in detail the procedure for manufacturing a table-cut stone out of a pointed stone.

The Rose Cut
A rose-cut stone has a flat back and a domed and faceted front. The form may be as old as the table cut because the Koh-i-Nûr, which was cut no later than

1530, was a form of rose cut, as was the Great Mogul (Fig. 10.1). Cellini described, in 1568, methods of cutting the rose and faceted stones as well as table-cut and pointed stones.

The shape of the original diamond crystal largely determines the shape into which it will be cut. The rose was found to be more suitable for flatter and thinner rough. The name of the 'modern' rose cut, from the seventeenth century, derived from the fact that it is supposed to look like an opening rose bud. It can show considerable life, but is invariably deficient in fire.

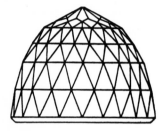

Fig. 10.1. *The Great Mogul diamond, from the Kollur Mines in India, which is said to have weighed 787½ carats in the rough and 280 carats when cut.*

Rose-like cuts were already in wide use in the first half of the fifteenth century. They were of various shapes, triangular being the most common, with each face divided into three facets. The term rosette stood for an early arrangement of diamonds of pear-shaped outline arranged in a circle like petals of a flower.

Both Amsterdam and Antwerp specialized in rose cuts, particularly in the eighteenth and nineteenth centuries. The Dutch rose is more pointed than most other rose cuts. The facets are in groups of six, the upper or central ones being known as the crown or star facets, and the surrounding outer groups of six, the teeth. The height is usually half the diameter of the stone and the diameter of the base of the crown about three-quarters of the diameter. The base of the crown is usually three-fifths of the total height from the base (Fig. 10.6).

The Antwerp rose, also called the Brabant rose, was not as common as the Dutch rose. It is not as high and the base is more steeply inclined, while the crown is less so (Fig. 10.6).

Most rose-cut diamonds were round, but some were of oval and pear-shaped outline. There were, of course, other variations of the rose in the arrangement of the facets. The double rose had some popularity in the nineteenth century and the earlier part of this century for ear-rings and watch-chain pendants before the wrist watch became popular. The stone is faceted in a dome on both sides. The double rose cut is old, because at least two historic diamonds, the Florentine and the Sancy, were cut in this way.

Diamonds faceted all over, called briolettes, pendeloques and beads are a form of rose cutting. Both are shown in Fig. 10.8. They were often pierced along their lengths for use as earrings or beads.

Faceted Octahedra
The table stone lent itself to modification by adding facets. The first elaboration was to grind and polish the four edges of the table and the pavilion to provide

four extra narrow facets on the top and four on the bottom to improve brilliance and lustre. This modification is shown in Fig. 10.3. Further modifications into more complex pattern of facets were similarly possible by grinding facets on edges, as shown in the same illustration.

It seems likely that from about 1500 to about 1650, the table cut was the most popular, but there were point-cut stones in use, too, although many were being re-cut to table stones and, for the more fashionable wearer, some table cuts were being modified by adding extra facets. Modifications were also being made to the outline of the stone, when seen in plan, by rounding the corners by bruting before faceting, and later by rounding the sides. Up to this point, the octahedral origin of the cut stone was clearly discernible. Although the outline was changed, the angles of the table and the pavilion to the girdle remained not very different from those of the original crystal, about 55°.

The Mazarin Cut

One of the early facetted cuts has become known as the Mazarin cut, having been named after Cardinal Mazarin of France, who was one of Tavernier's best customers. The Cardinal's diamonds included the famous Sancy and the Mirror of Portugal. He left them in his Will to the French Crown on condition that they were to be known as The Mazarin Diamonds.

The cut was cushion-shaped in outline with seventeen facets above the girdle, including the table, and seventeen facets below, including the culet. The cut was not invented by the Cardinal, but was, according to H. Tillander, introduced before his era, in about 1620. (Fig. 10.3). Mr. Tillander says the cut is rare and, as far as he has discovered, is not included in the Mazarin diamonds, most of which were table-cut.

Early cuts had a large culet, by modern standards, as it was needed as a reflecting facet to increase brilliance. In the early twentieth century, the lower part of the stone, the pavilion, was made shallower to improve internal reflection and more or less eliminate the culet.

The various versions of faceted cuts may have evolved into what became known as the brilliant cut, but this is in doubt.

The Brilliant Cut

There was no single inventor of the brilliant cut although it is often credited to a seventeenth-century Venetian lapidary named Vincenzio Perruzzi, after whom one faceted cut is named. Research by H. Tillander has shown that the Perruzzi family came from Florence and that there is no record of a member named Vincenzio.

Facetted diamonds based on the octahedron with rounded corners or cushion outlines, as well as the more modern conical shapes with round outlines, were all called brilliant-cut diamonds and referred to colloquially as brilliants.

An increase in the cutting of brilliants occurred about mid-seventeenth century, and the eighteenth saw a spate of re-cutting to modernize old cuts. This was partly due to the awakening of interest in technical innovation and partly due to the waning interest in the invariable classical form of the table stone. Rough stones were often rounded by the immensely laborious process of hand bruting if they were of octahedral form. Many cutters, however, according to Tillander, found that rough of approximately rhombic dodecahedral form lent itself naturally to the fashioning of brilliant-cut stones. As there were insufficient crystals of dodecahedral shape, someone named Perruzzi may have invented a similar design from octahedral rough.

The discovery of the Brazilian deposits gave great impetus to the brilliant cut in a form known as the triple cut, shown in Fig. 10.4, and today usually referred to as old-mine cut. The girdle outline is cushion-shaped and there are thirty-three facets on the crown and twenty-five on the pavilion, making fifty-eight in all, the same as the modern brilliant. Another name for these stones is old-miners.

Even as late as 1750, the English jeweller David Jeffries thought the brilliant cut to be a whim of fashion and that the rose cut would outlive it, but over the next two centuries large numbers of old roses were re-cut to brilliant form with 'dreadful sacrifice of weight', as C. W. King put it in 1870.

Smaller and less valuable stones were double cut instead of being triple cut. The double cut was an older style with a square table and sixteen other facets on the top with duplicate facets on the bottom, except that the culet was much smaller than the table, making a total of thirty-four. There was an English double-cut brilliant that had the triangular corner facets reversed so that the table became octagonal and the centre of an eight-rayed star, while the pavilion remained similar to that of the double cut except for the loss of four corner facets (Fig. 10.3).

The outline of the girdle of a stone depended much more on the form of the crystal before it was cut in earlier days than today because the problems of manufacture were greater. Most girdle outlines became cushion-shaped, as already mentioned, but some were almost or quite round and others of rounded triangular shape, when the facets were grouped in threes instead of fours. Other crystals lent themselves to the manufacture of oval or pear-shaped brilliants.

Most historical diamonds were cut in modifications of the brilliant form, although the original cut of some was different. The retention of weight has been an important consideration when cutting or re-cutting, however, so that the full brilliance has not always been achieved.

In the nineteenth century, more rounded brilliants appeared and with these and cushion shapes, English cutters tended to make thinner girdles than Dutch cutters, an indication of origin. The thin girdles have often become chipped. Round brilliants of the time, with small tables and large culets by modern standards and greater overall depth to the stone, are known in England as Victorian cut.

The Modern Brilliant

The modern brilliant cut came about with the publication of the ideal dimensions in a theoretical treatise on the subject by Marcel Tolkowsky in 1914. The angles of the pavilion to the girdle and the angle of the crown had been largely determined by the octahedral crystal angles although some cutters had previously been experimenting and discovered that they could increase brilliance by reducing these angles.

Making brilliants to Tolkowsky's ideal cut involved much more work on the rough material and encouraged the introduction of machine bruting to round the crystals and machine sawing to shape material. Not all brilliant cut-diamonds were cut to the ideal proportions by any means, but Tolkowsky's work had a very important influence on the cutting of larger and higher quality material. Lower quality rough was cut to retain maximum weight, as it is today.

The brilliant cut with the round girdle became almost universal. The culet was small, but still very noticeable through the table, and the facets below the girdle reached about half-way down the pavilion, as shown in Fig. 10.4. After the Second World War, there were further small modifications. The lower girdle facets became gradually longer some extending to eight-tenths the distance down the pavilion, and the table tended to become larger, resulting in a shallower crown.

A modern form of the ideal cut is shown in Fig. 10.2. The names of the facets of the brilliant originate from cutting procedures and can be quite complex, particularly of those around the girdle, which have been simplified to upper and lower girdle facets in the diagram.

Variations of the Brilliant

The brilliant cut is applied to shapes other than the conical or standard brilliant. They include the boat-shaped marquise or navette cut, the pear-shaped pendeloque cut, the oval brilliant cut, and the heart-shaped brilliant cut. They are shown in Fig. 10.5.

It has been pointed out that for a gem such as diamond, depending for some of its beauty on colour dispersion, the number of facets should be increased with the size of stone. S. Rosch suggested that no facets should be longer than 3 mm. or shorter than $\frac{1}{2}$ mm., from which it follows that stones of over 10 carats should have more than fifty-eight facets, and those of under $\frac{1}{8}$th carat (about twelve points) should have fewer facets to give maximum brilliance.

In fact most small stones today are made as eight-cuts (single-cuts), or Swiss-cuts, with fewer facets as shown in Fig. 10.7. For larger stones there are several modifications of the brilliant cut with more facets, including the Jubilee with eighty-eight, the King with eighty-six, and the Cairo star cut with seventy-four, as shown in Fig. 10.5.

Facetted Girdles

The girdle of a brilliant-cut diamond is normally left in its bruted state, which is matt, so that it reflects very little light internally. The loss is very small if the girdle is of normal width. A few cutters concerned with high quality do facet or polish the girdles of stones, however. Louis H. Roselar in the U.S.A. placed forty small facets around the girdle. A. Monnickendam in England polishes the girdle in a circle without facets by a special technique.

Patents on facetted girdles have now expired and some other cutters add them to the standard brilliant-cut. In one version, known as the Royal 144, forty extra facets are placed on the girdle, and forty-eight more on as 'wreath' of extra cross, skill and kite facets on the pavilion near the girdle which is claimed to add to the stone's brilliance. Small facets are today often cut very rapidly by automatic processes.

Girdles of polished stones that are not round, including pendeloque, emerald, and square cuts, are ground and polished. The girdle of marquise stones can be bruted or ground and polished.

In 1960, a London cutter, A Nagy, introduced an unusual and economic cut for flat crystals to give a large superficial area of diamond. It was at first called the Princess cut and is now the profile cut. The shape, shown in Fig. 10.8, is based on a cut originally developed for diamond tools used for dressing grinding wheels. It comprises a series of V-grooves on the back of the stone at the angle shown in the diagram. The cut is lively, but lacks fire.

Step and Square Cuts

A step or trap cut may have pointed or bevelled corners. When such cuts are bevelled, they are often called emerald cuts. Diamonds cut in these forms naturally lose brilliance and lustre because the cuts are not ideal from the point of view of beauty. The proportions of both can vary from square or almost square to a long oblong, depending on the shape of the original crystal. Steps cuts are often made from octahedra that are elongated in one direction, as shown in Fig. 10.8. When the shape is very elongated in relation to its width, the cut stone is called a baguette after the long French loaf.

It is possible that the earliest baguette diamonds were produced in India by cleavage in a dodecahedral direction from an octahedral crystal to give long, boat-shaped chips.

The most common fault in an emerald or square-cut stone is a window, a facet through which one can see, looking at the stone from the table. The number of steps is unimportant, but to avoid windows, the pavilion facets should be cut at greater than the critical angle of 24° 26'. This is sometimes difficult, if not impossible, particularly with the end pavilion facets of an elongated octahedron crystal.

As the pavilion of a step or square-cut stone is deeper than that of a brilliant-cut stone, the crown should be shallower, in order to make the overall depth about the same as an equivalent brilliant. Brilliance is lost when a stone is over deep. A rule of thumb is that the width of the bottom pavilion facets should together be about equal to the width of the table.

Similar considerations apply to diamonds cut in triangle, kite, and other shapes, but when such shapes are favoured it is often because of particular shape and flatness of the rough, so that it is difficult or impossible to apply sound optical principles to the cut.

Diamond Cuts

The various ways in which diamonds can be shaped and facetted may be divided into four main groups, each containing variations on a basic cut. They are listed in the following table.

BRILLIANT CUT
Possible Chronological Development

Point cut (corrected octahedron with 8 polished faces)
Many fancy shapes
Table cut (9 to 10 facets)
Tablet cut
English square cut (17 + 13 = 30 facets)
Mazarin cut and variations (17 + 17 = 34 facets)
Perruzzi cut (33 + 25 = 58 facets)
Rounded single cut (9 + 9 = 18 facets)

English star cut (17 + 9 = 26 facets)
Old mine or cushion cut (33 + 25 = 58 facets) and variations with same number of more facets
Old European round brilliant cut (33 + 25 = 58 facets)
English round cut brilliant cut (33 + 25 = 58 facets)
Full cut or modern brilliant cut (33 + 25 = 58 facets)

Note: *Only the full brilliant cut under chronological development, is now made. It outnumbers all other cuts by a vast majority.*

Variations on the Brilliant Cut with more Facets

Jubilee or twentieth century cut (40 + 40 = 80 facets)
King cut (49 + 37 = 86 facets)
Cairo Star cut (74 facets)

Magna cut (61 + 41 = 102 facets)
Royal 144 (33 + 73 + 48 on girdle = 154 facets)

Note: *There are many other cuts with more facets but few are used. The Royal 144 is the only one for smaller stones.*

Modern Shaped Variations of the Brilliant Cut

Oval brilliant cut (33 + 25 = 58 facets)
Marquise or navette cut (33 + 25 = 58 facets)

Heart-shaped brilliant cut (37 + 28 = 65 facets)
Pendeloque or pear-shaped brilliant cut (33 + 25 = 58 facets)
Trilliant cut (25 + 19 = 44 facets)

Note: *33 + 25 = 58 facets, etc., means that there are 33 facets on the top of the stone, and 25 under it, totalling 58. Both table and culet are counted as facets.*

Round Cuts for Small Stones

Single or eight cut (9 + 9 = 18 facets)
Swiss cut (17 + 17 = 34 facets)

French cut (9 + 9 = 18 facets)
Split brilliant (21 + 21 = 42 facets)

ROSE CUT

Triangular rose
Full Dutch rose or Holland rose (24 + 1 = 25 facets)
Double-Dutch rose or Double Holland rose (36 + 1 = 37 facets)
Pear-shaped rose (24 + 1 = 25 facets)
Boat-shaped rose (24 + 1 = 25 facets)

Double rose (24 + 24 = 48 facets
Half brilliant (33 + 1 = 34 facets)
Twelve-facet rose, Antwerp-rose or Brabant rose (12 + 1 = 13 facets)
Six-facet rose (6 + 1 = 7 facets)
Three-facet rose (3 + 1 = 4 facets)

Note: *Larger rose cuts are not now made except perhaps for a special purpose such as restoration of a piece of antique jewellery, but many roses up to 30 or 40 points still come from Amsterdam.*

STEP CUT

Emerald cut (square or oblong in shape with truncated corners)

Square cut or bevel cut (square in shape with pointed corners)

Baguette (long oblong with pointed corners)

Tapered baguette

Spade baguette or bullet cut

Pentagon

Triangle

Kite

Hexagon

Long hexagon

Octagon

Long octagon

Trapeze

Lozenge

Trap brilliant and many others, mainly for smaller diamonds used as surrounds

Note: *The numbers of facets are not given for step-cut stones because they vary with the size of the stone. Larger emerald cuts are relatively common, but most step cuts are for smaller, thinner rough.*

BEAD CUT

Bead   Briolette   Rondelle   Note: *All are rare.*

Miscellaneous: Princess or profile cut.

Principles of Diamond Design

As the most prized diamonds are colourless, their beauty depends entirely upon their optical properties other than colour – high refractive index, high degree of clarity, colour dispersion, reflectivity, and lustre. To make the most of optical effects, the designer is obviously confined by optical laws.

The quality of light reflected from the surface of a material is known as its lustre. In diamond, this quality is unique and is known as adamantine lustre. The only other gems approaching it in lustre are zircon and demantoid garnet.

Lustre depends not only on the light reflected from the surface, but on rays that have been partly absorbed before being reflected back. Materials of high transparency, such as diamond and glass, would not be expected to be very reflective, and most are not, but diamond is an exception. The surface will reflect about 17 per cent of the light falling directly on it, compared with about 5 per cent of light falling on a transparent paste (glass) gem.

Changing intensities of light reflected are important in lustre. If a diamond were cut out of a flat plate and seen by a stationary observer in motionless surroundings, it would appear to have little lustre. Cut in rose or brilliant style and seen in moving candlelight, it would have a high lustre.

Brilliance, Life and Fire

The best forms of cut for diamond were not evolved with lustre mainly in mind, because other effects were thought more important, but they do in fact result in a high degree of lustre. The criterion with diamond was to produce the maximum brilliance. Brilliance depends on two factors – life and fire. Life is the amount of light which, after falling on the stone from the front, is reflected back to the

PARTS AND FACETS OF THE BRILLIANT CUT

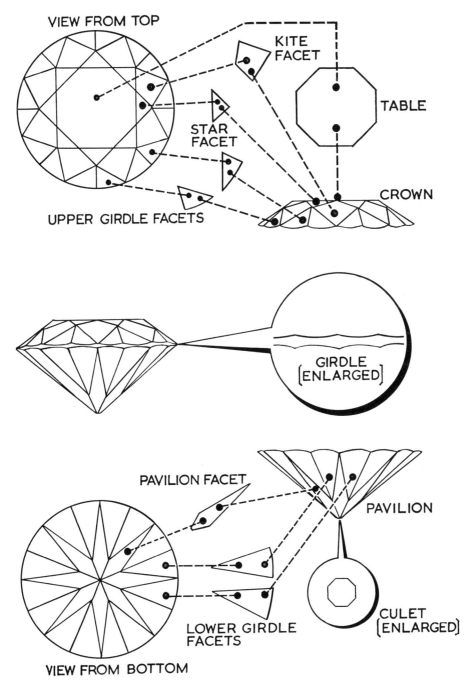

Fig. 10.2. *Parts of the brilliant cut diamond. The names of the facets have been simplified from the old cutters' terms and are generally accepted.*

DEVELOPMENT OF THE BRILLIANT OR FULL CUT

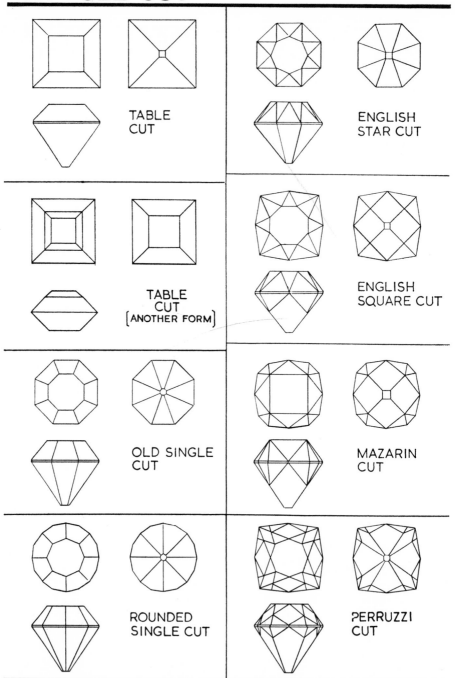

TABLE CUT

ENGLISH STAR CUT

TABLE CUT [ANOTHER FORM]

ENGLISH SQUARE CUT

OLD SINGLE CUT

MAZARIN CUT

ROUNDED SINGLE CUT

PERRUZZI CUT

Fig. 10.3.

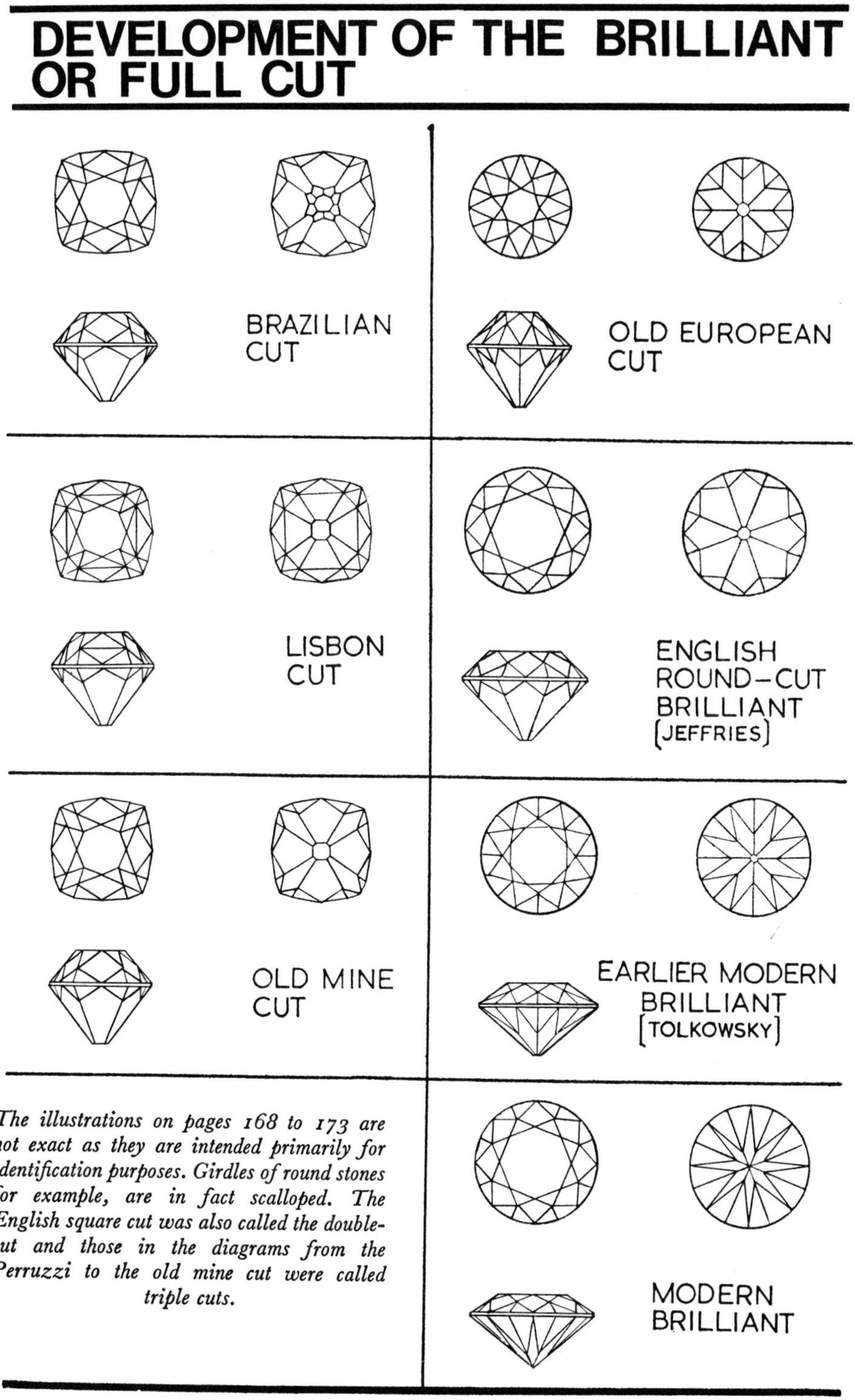

DEVELOPMENT OF THE BRILLIANT OR FULL CUT

BRAZILIAN
CUT

OLD EUROPEAN
CUT

LISBON
CUT

ENGLISH
ROUND–CUT
BRILLIANT
[JEFFRIES]

OLD MINE
CUT

EARLIER MODERN
BRILLIANT
[TOLKOWSKY]

The illustrations on pages 168 to 173 are not exact as they are intended primarily for identification purposes. Girdles of round stones for example, are in fact scalloped. The English square cut was also called the double-cut and those in the diagrams from the Perruzzi to the old mine cut were called triple cuts.

MODERN
BRILLIANT

Fig. 10.4.

SOME VARIATIONS OF THE BRILLIANT CUT

OVAL BRILLIANT

PEAR — SHAPED BRILLIANT

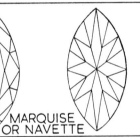

MARQUISE OR NAVETTE

SEMINAVETTE

HEART — SHAPED BRILLIANT

 JUBILEE CUT

 KING CUT

MAGNA CUT

 ROYAL 144

Fig. 10.5.

ROSE CUTS

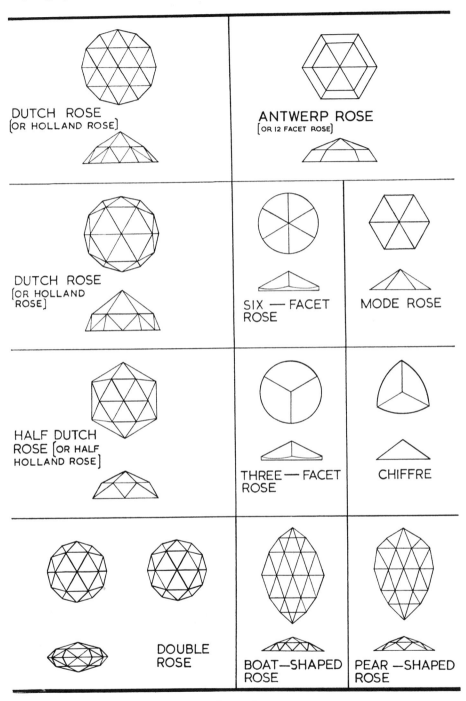

DUTCH ROSE
(OR HOLLAND ROSE)

ANTWERP ROSE
[OR 12 FACET ROSE]

DUTCH ROSE
[OR HOLLAND
ROSE]

SIX — FACET
ROSE

MODE ROSE

HALF DUTCH
ROSE [OR HALF
HOLLAND ROSE]

THREE — FACET
ROSE

CHIFFRE

DOUBLE
ROSE

BOAT—SHAPED
ROSE

PEAR —SHAPED
ROSE

Fig. 10.6.

CUTS FOR SMALL STONES

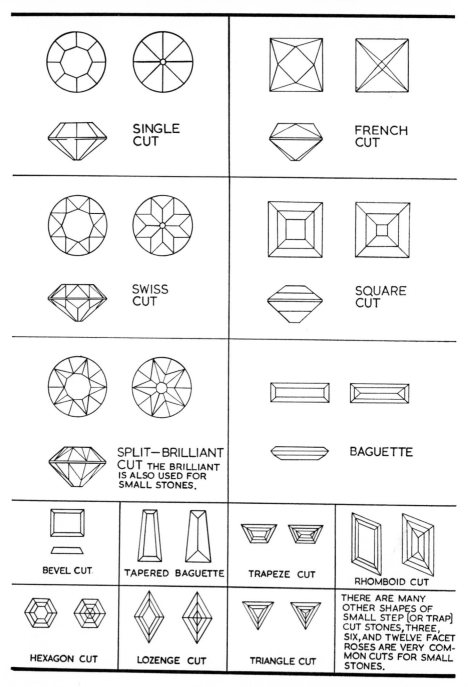

SINGLE CUT

FRENCH CUT

SWISS CUT

SQUARE CUT

SPLIT—BRILLIANT CUT THE BRILLIANT IS ALSO USED FOR SMALL STONES.

BAGUETTE

BEVEL CUT.

TAPERED BAGUETTE

TRAPEZE CUT

RHOMBOID CUT

HEXAGON CUT

LOZENGE CUT

TRIANGLE CUT

THERE ARE MANY OTHER SHAPES OF SMALL STEP [OR TRAP] CUT STONES, THREE, SIX, AND TWELVE FACET ROSES ARE VERY COMMON CUTS FOR SMALL STONES.

Fig. 10.7. *The single-cut is also called the eight cut.*

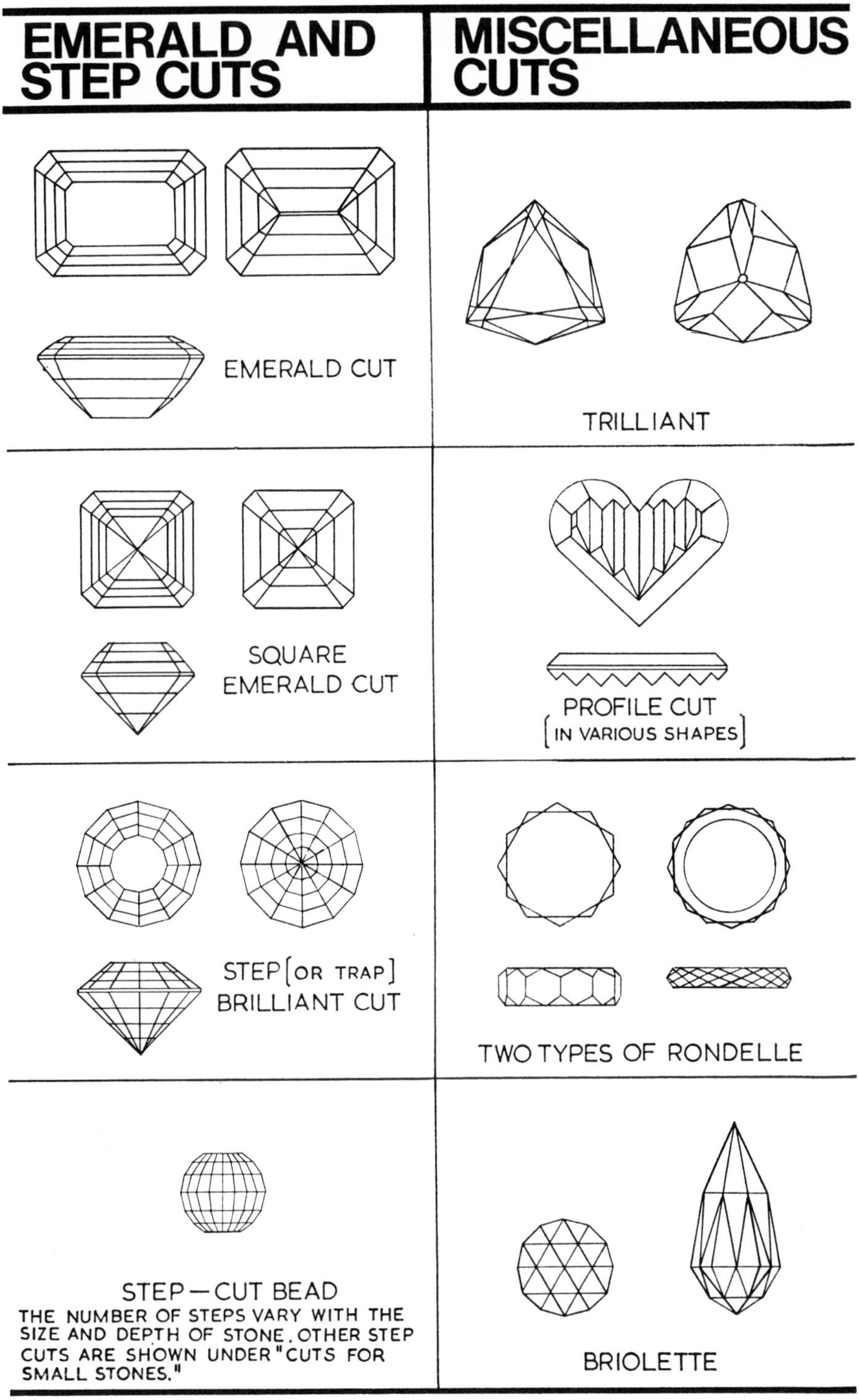

EMERALD AND STEP CUTS	MISCELLANEOUS CUTS
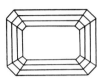 EMERALD CUT	TRILLIANT
SQUARE EMERALD CUT	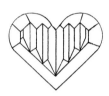 PROFILE CUT [IN VARIOUS SHAPES]
STEP [OR TRAP] BRILLIANT CUT	TWO TYPES OF RONDELLE
STEP — CUT BEAD THE NUMBER OF STEPS VARY WITH THE SIZE AND DEPTH OF STONE. OTHER STEP CUTS ARE SHOWN UNDER "CUTS FOR SMALL STONES."	 BRIOLETTE

Fig. 10.8.

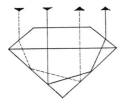
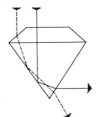
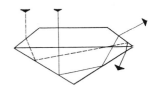

Fig. 10.9. *How light is returned by an ideally-proportioned brilliant cut diamond, but lost through the back when the stone is too deep or too shallow.*

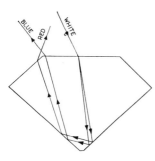

Fig. 10.10. *White light dispersed and refracted to produce fire.*

viewer. Fire is the amount of colour flashing caused by the stone splitting white light into the spectrum colours.

The amount of light entering a diamond may be up to about 83 per cent, since about 17 per cent is reflected from the surface, so that there is much more potential brilliancy from light which enters the stone than from light reflected from the surface.

The problem of the designer is to make sure that light entering the stone is not lost through the sides and back, but is reflected inside the stone and sent back to the eyes of the viewer. The most important factor to him is the critical angle of diamond, the angle at which total internal reflection of light occurs. It depends on refractive index and for diamond it is 24° 26'.

In a cut diamond designed with angles to take fullest advantage of total internal reflection, the back facets will act like mirrors inside the stone and most light entering the stone from the front will therefore be reflected back out of the front, to give maximum life to the stone (Fig. 10.9).

The fire produced by a stone depends on the colour dispersion of the material and on the amount by which the white light entering the stone is refracted (Fig. 10.10). The more it is bent, the more the fire. On the other hand, the life of a stone is decreased the more the light is refracted. It is impossible therefore, to obtain maximum life and maximum fire at the same time.

The object in cutting is to obtain an optimum balance of life and fire, which occurs when life multiplied by fire is a maximum. This quality, called brilliance, is an extremely important factor in evaluating the quality of a diamond. A stone with maximum brilliancy is instantly recognizable to anyone who handles diamonds because of its almost 'sharp' or 'hard' appearance.

Diamond Design: the Rose Cut

A natural portrait diamond has two parallel surfaces. Light striking one will be refracted and pass through the other, being refracted again as shown in Fig.

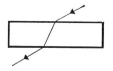 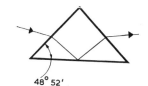 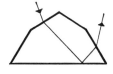

Fig. 10.11. *Light passing through a portrait stone.* Fig. 10–12. (centre) *Light internally reflected from the back of a theoretical rose-cut stone.* Fig. 10.13. *Light internally reflected more towards the front of a rose-cut stone.*

10.11. It will therefore be possible to see clearly through the stone. If the top is angled and the bottom left flat as in Fig. 10.12, the result is the basic rose cut.

It can be shown by simple geometry that if each lower angle is twice the critical angle, i.e. 48° 52′, the rose cut is excellent for reflecting all light back through the front, i.e. it has excellent life. However, this simple solution has a big disadvantage owing to the fact that the light leaves the stone at the same angle as it enters. It is not refracted and therefore no fire results.

To obtain some fire from rose cuts, it is necessary to 'break' the angles, as shown in Fig. 10.13, so that light entering at one angle leaves at another angle, and provides a small display of spectrum colour, although at the expense of life. Fundamentally, the rose cut is wrong, and is rarely if ever cut at steep enough angles because it is much better to use suitable material for brilliant cuts.

The Brilliant Cut

Turn the rose cut upside down and it becomes the basic brilliant cut in Fig. 10.14. By calculation it can be shown that for light entering the top to be reflected out again as shown, the angle of the facet causing the first reflection must be more than 48° 52′ and that for the facet causing the second must be less than 42° 43′, which is impossible in a symmetrical stone, so a compromise has to be found.

It was calculated by Marcel Tolkowsky in 1919 that the best compromise angle is 40° 45′ as it provides the greatest refraction, and therefore most vivid fire, with least loss of life, i.e. the greatest brilliance. A greater angle would give better reflection but would not compensate for the loss of fire.

Although most light is reflected back as shown by ray 1, in the basic cone-shaped brilliant cut of Fig. 10.15, some can still be lost round the edges as shown by ray 2. The loss can be corrected by inclined facets which refract the light instead of reflecting it (and also increase dispersion) as shown in Fig. 10.15. Tolkowsky calculated the best angle for these bezel facets to be 34° 30′.

As twice reflected oblique rays may be lost at the edge of the bezel, small facets need to be added at an angle of about 42° to refract them. These are the half facets or halves, also called the upper girdle facets. Similarly, facets about 2° steeper than the pavilion, said Tolkowsky, should be added near the girdle at the back to avoid losses from light which might be reflected from the facets round the bezel. They are the halves on the pavilion, or lower girdle facets.

Other facets are normally added around the table of the stone, known as the star facets, at about 15° to the horizontal. They tend to decrease the light leakage

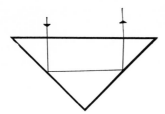

Fig. 10.14. *Light entering and internally reflected out of a theoretical brilliant-cut stone.* Fig. 10.15. *(right) Light that might escape from the edges is allowed to escape from the front if the edges are bevelled.*

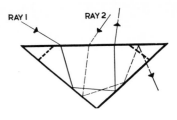

through the back and improve the distribution of light. They decrease dispersion, however, but compensate by increasing the number of rays that are dispersed.

Certain other basic conditions are required for maximum brilliance from a brilliant-cut diamond. They are: maximum clarity and no trace of colour in the stone, absolute symmetry in the placing of facets which must be an even number around the stone, and the highest quality of polishing.

European and American Cuts

Later calculations have differed from Tolkowsky's.

In 1926, S. Rosch calculated by graphical methods the angles which would fulfil conditions of maximum brilliance for diamond. They were never accepted by the trade. In 1940 Dr. W. Fr. Eppler gave figures for a practical ideal cut, known as the Eppler fine cut.

The main apparent difference between Tolkowsky's calculations and later ones are in the size and the depth of the table. Americans have adhered to the earlier figures. Tolkowsky-proportioned diamonds are sometimes, therefore, said to be American-cut. Eppler-proportioned brilliants have been called European-cut.

In 1970; the Scandinavian countries published a standard proposal for Europe, known as Scan D.N., giving standards of nomenclature and grading. It suggests ideal proportions with a slightly larger table than other 'ideal' cuts, more in accordance with cutting practice and derived from the Eppler fine cut.

For comparison, here are the relative proportions as percentages of the diameter of the stone and degrees in the case of angles.

	Tolkowsky	*Eppler*	*Scan. D.N.*
Diameter of girdle	100%	100%	100%
Diameter of table	53%	56%	57·5%
Thickness of crown	16·2%	14·4%	14·6%
Thickness of pavilion	43·1%	43·2%	43·1%
Depth, table to culet*	59·3%	58·5%	57·7%
Angle of crown facets	34° 30′		34° 30′
Angle of pavilion facets	40° 45′		40° 45′
Angle of upper girdle facets	42°		
Angle of lower girdle facets	41° 30′		

* To this must be added the 1 to 3% for the girdle (*a* in the diagrams) to give total depth.

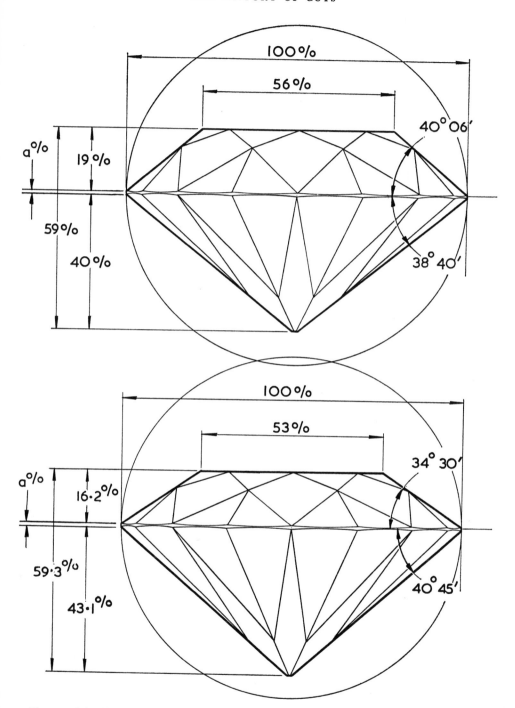

Fig. 10.16 (top).   *One of a number of theoretical calculations for an ideal brilliant cut diamond.*
Fig. 10.17 (lower drawing).   *The angles of the ideal brilliant cut calculated by M. Tolkow-sky, as subsequently revised in the U.S.A.*

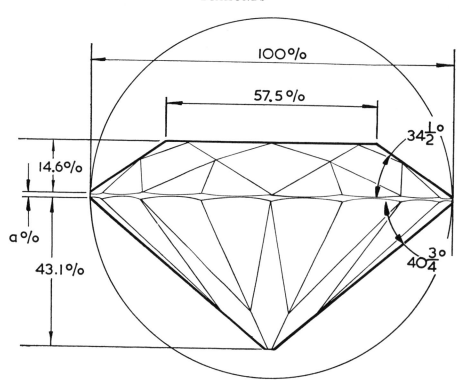

Fig. 10.18. *Angles for the brilliant cut in the Scandinavian standard, SCAN D.N.*

Modified Tolkowsky proportions and some other theoretical ones are shown in Figs. 10.16 and 10.17. Fig. 10.18 shows the proportions in Scan D.N.

A study by Dr. W. R. Eulitz has emphasized the need for reasonable accuracy in the pavilion angles particularly. He calculated the angles of emergent rays of light for three different brilliants with pavilion angles of 35°, 41°, and 48°. The results are shown in Fig. 10.19.

The top illustration with a pavilion angle of 41° is of a good brilliant cut. When the angle is too shallow, as on the right, there is a blank area in the middle of the stone which makes it dark and results in what is known as a fish-eye (See also Fig. 14.6). When the pavilion angle is too great and the stone is deep, as on the left, the bezel reflections are poor and the stone has little or no fire (See also Fig. 14.5).

In practice, even high quality diamonds are not always cut to precise angles for a variety of reasons. The crown angles will be found to vary from 29° to 35° in whole stones and from 29° to 30° in sawn stones. It is not even necessary to be absolutely exact in all the dimensions, and a difference of, say, 5 per cent in the diameter of the table will make no appreciable difference to the brilliance. The table diameter is measured from opposite corners of facets, not between two sides.

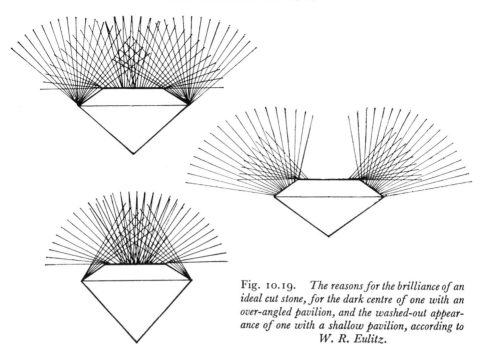

Fig. 10.19.   *The reasons for the brilliance of an ideal cut stone, for the dark centre of one with an over-angled pavilion, and the washed-out appearance of one with a shallow pavilion, according to W. R. Eulitz.*

Variation from the Ideal

When the proportions of a brilliant-cut stone are far from ideal, there are almost invariably good reasons for this. A cutter can concentrate on:

1. Obtaining the maximum weight of cut stone from the crystal, or
2. Arriving at the ideal proportions for maximum quality of cut.

In each case he is influenced by the price likely to be obtained for the cut stone. If the crystal itself is not of the highest quality in colour and clarity, the cutter may well try to obtain the maximum weight to optimize his profit. If the crystal is of high quality, he will try for more ideal proportions. Frequently a compromise is sought.

REFERENCES

Diamond Design, by Marcel Tolkowsky (London, 1919).
Figures given in *Zentralblatt für Mineralogie* by Dr. W. Fr. Eppler (1940).
'Faceted Gemstones: Cutting for Maximum Brilliance', by O. Le M. Knight *The Journal of Gemmology*, London, Jan. 1960.
'The Optics of Brilliant-Cut Diamonds', by W. R. Eulitz. *Gems & Gemology*, Los Angeles, Vol. XII. No. 9, 1968.
'Lecture to Fellows of the Gemmological Association of Great Britain', by H. Tillander of Helsinki (London, April 1965) and private communication.
Precious Stones, by Max Bauer (Reprint edition, London, 1970).
The History of Diamond Production and the Diamond Trade, by Godehard Lenzen (London, 1970).

CHAPTER ELEVEN

Diamond Manufacture

Only diamond will cut diamond and the problem involved has been dramatized by likening it to sharpening a pencil with a piece of wood. The diamond cutter and polisher is known in the trade as a diamond manufacturer, because he manufactures polished goods from rough goods, but the only true manufacturer of diamonds is the maker of synthetic diamonds. Diamond cutting can mean almost any diamond manufacturing process and is not a very appropriate term. Here it will be used in a general sense and avoided for particular operations in favour of the following terms:

Cleaving: Splitting a diamond along a cleavage plane.
Sawing: Dividing a crystal by diamond saw.
Bruting: Removing part of a crystal by rubbing with another crystal.
Grinding: Making a flat surface by the abrasive action of a rotating wheel or lap prepared with diamond powder.
Polishing: Preparation of the final high-quality surface by a similar method to grinding.

The Designer

The designer in a diamond factory – he has different names in different places or none at all – has perhaps the most important task of all. Usually the owner of a cutting works is also the chief designer. He studies each crystal and decides how it should be cut to produce the optimum value in polished goods. With clean regular octahedra this is relatively simple. With large irregular stones without crystal faces, it can be very difficult. In extreme cases, as with the Cullinan, the crystal may be studied for weeks before a decision is made. The grain against which to polish is easily determined once the stone is cleaved or sawn.

The designer has to bear in mind the weight of the crystal and its quality. Into how many polished diamonds should it be cut? Usually this is the minimum number, because the price per carat rises steeply with the size. Should the polished stones be cut to exact angles, or would cutting them to gain maximum weight per polished stone at a lower carat price produce more profit? What is the demand at the moment for different sizes and qualities of polished goods? Any decisions are affected by this important consideration. Whether lower qualities of rough are made into gemstones or tool tips is determined very largely by demand.

During his preparatory examination, the designer has also to consider the crystal classification – whether the crystal is a stone, a shape, a cleavage, a macle, or a flat – whether or not it is coated, and the actual shape of the crystal. The

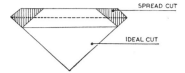
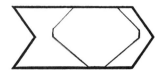

Fig. 11.1. *How a brilliant cut is spread to gain weight and increase diameter which results in an overdepth pavilion. A stone can be cut with correct angles, as here, but with a correct depth of pavilion and a table which is too shallow.* Fig. 11.2. (right) *How a brilliant can be cut from a macle.*

shape will determine how the crystal can be cut and what shape it will be when cut.

A simple example is that a well-shaped octahedron will be fashioned into one brilliant cut stone if small and two if larger, but an elongated octahedron may be cut into a brilliant-cut oval or marquise or an emerald-cut diamond, if of high quality. A large irregular stone might be divided to make polished stones of different cuts.

The cut is the shape of the finished diamond and the pattern of its facets. The brilliant-cut is the standard for diamond and all others are lumped together under the name of fancy cuts.

The Make

The nearness of the finished brilliant cut to the ideal proportions (see page 176) is known as its make. A stone which is near the ideal is said to be of good make or fine make. One that has been cut to gain in weight, to spread the diameter so that it weighs less than it should, is out of round, has the pavilion out of centre, has too thick a girdle, or has facets at incorrect angles, is of poor or bad make.

The diamond cutter works to the market. If he is cutting medium and lower quality goods, he will make the best return he can on his rough, which often means cutting to recover as much weight as possible while producing an acceptable make. The commonest way of doing so is to increase the diameter of the stone by sacrificing some crown height and adding to the width of the table. An octahedron is sawn in half through the girdle (see Fig. 11.12), and each half becomes a spread stone. The amount of weight gained by spreading the stone instead of cutting it to ideal proportions is shown in Fig. 11.1. As much as 10 per cent can be saved in this way.

Even high quality goods are sometimes spread, especially when spreading takes the stone over a carat or another favoured unit in weight. Thus a cutter can offer a carat stone, say, at considerably less than an 80-pointer which would have resulted had the proportions been nearer ideal.

Increasing pavilion angles also costs weight. A thick girdle will add a considerable percentage to the weight. Considerable weight, in fact, can be saved by leaving a stone thick.

Macles that are cut in brilliant style are often too thin to provide the full depth without too much loss of material Weight is therefore made up by increasing the girdle width and the culet size, as well as by spreading the table (Fig. 11.2).

Thin macles and flats are made into baguettes and other cuts that are thin.

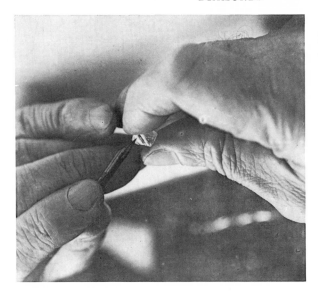

Fig. 11.3. *Marking a stone with Indian ink to show how it is to be sawn.*

When the rough is too flattened to be made into a reasonable brilliant-cut yet too thick to be wasted on minor cuts, it is made into a pear-shaped or marquise-cut diamond, in which the pavilions may be much shallower than the brilliant-cut gems.

Reducing Flaws

With all these possibilities in mind, the diamond designer first studies the stone from outside. For example, he will decide where the girdle of the cut stone should be. The thinnest side will then become the table and the thickest side will become the bottom. It is preferable to keep inclusions to the top, as any in the bottom will be reflected several times and therefore appear even worse than they are.

Then, having made a first decision, he examines the stone carefully inside, usually rolling it between thumb and first finger and looking inside through an 8 × or 10 × hand lens. The designer then imagines himself to be inside the stone, decides just where the flaws are, which must be removed, and which may be left in the polished stone. Again the decision is often a nice balance to produce an optimum value.

The internal examination may determine whether a fancy cut would be more satisfactory than a brilliant one and what the make should be. Some diamond designers will examine a stone in polarized light to discover the strain in it from the extinction pattern (Fig. 18.12). This will isolate the stones which would be risky to saw or cut in any other way.

Before a final decision is made, the rough is often 'opened' from various angles, by grinding facets or even cleaving thin pieces off opposite faces. These windows enable the interior to be studied much more accurately.

Finally, the designer must decide on the method of manufacture. The three general methods in fact determine the broad commercial classifications of crystals, as shown below:

1. *Makeables:* Whole stones which are ground without preliminary work. (macles, cleavages, chips, etc.).
2. *Sawn:* (Stones, shapes, mêlée, chips, smalls, etc.).
3. *Cleaved:* (Cleavages, macles, chips, etc.).

Having made his decisions, the designer takes a pen and Indian ink and marks the crystal with fine lines to show where it is to be sawn or where it is to be cleaved. A good operator will divide the Indian ink line down the centre when sawing or cleaving a precisely-marked stone. It is usually only necessary to mark whole stones with a dot to show the position of the table (Fig. 11.3).

Grain

The diamond cutter relates all his work to what he calls the grain of the diamond; thus he 'saws grain' and polishes 'against the grain'. The grain is represented by the lines forming a triangle seen on octahedral faces (Fig. 11.4), the straight lines on dodecahedral faces (Fig. 11.5), and those in a 'square' on cube faces, represented in Fig. 11.6 as the top of an octahedral crystal, where the lines on the octahedral faces show the directions of grain on the cube face. The faces are also shown diagramatically in Fig. 11.28. The grain is related to the crystal axes and structure (see Chapter Eighteen) and exists inside the crystal, too, where sometimes it can be seen through a lens or microscope as fine parallel lines.

Fig. 11.6. (right) *Grain from the cube direction of an octahedron.*

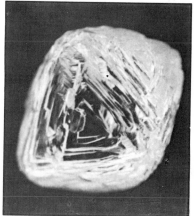

Fig. 11.5. *Grain on dodecahedral faces.*

Fig. 11.4. *Grain on an octahedral face*

Cleaving

The cleaver in cutter's parlance, follows the grain. That is, he cleaves in an octahedral direction, which is parallel to any of the faces when the crystal itself is an octahedron. In any shape of crystal there are four directions of cleaving (Fig. 11.7). Cleaving a rhombic dodecahedral crystal truncates a three-pointed corner.

The cleaver has several special sticks about eight inches long and a cleaver's box. Even today these are often the personal possessions of the cleaver. The box is fixed to the bench. It is rectangular and also has hollows to hold loose crystals as shown in Fig. 11.8 and 11.9.

The diamond to be cleaved is cemented to the end of one of the special sticks with a cleaver cement, which may vary a lot in composition but is basically a mixture of shellac and rosin with brick dust, finely powdered glass or similar material. (One old recipe for diamond cement includes a glass of 'good' brandy

Fig. 11.7. *The part of an octahedron removed by cleaving. Each of the eight faces can be cleaved off i.e. there are four cleaving directions.*

Fig. 11.8. *Rubbing a kerf before cleaving. The actual kerf is shown in Fig. 9.11. The box catches the powder that results.*

CLEAVED
OCTAHEDRON

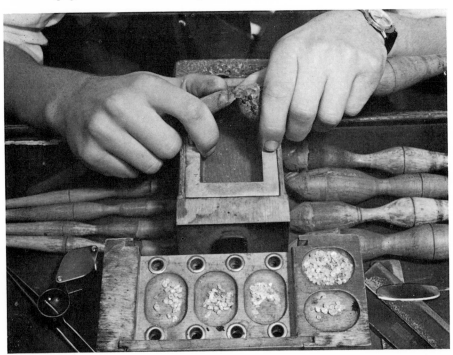

Fig. 11.9.   *A Hatton Garden, London, cleaver studies the kerf before cleaving.*

or rum!) The cement of course must be slightly elastic as the diamond has to be parted without flying out of the cement.

Another diamond is cemented into the end of another stick. This stone is usually a chip with a cleavage edge and is used to make a nick called a kerf in the edge of the diamond to be cleaved, as shown in Fig. 9.11. The cleaver rubs one diamond against the other (Fig. 11.8) so that the kerf is produced on the Indian ink line made by the designer. The chippings removed fall in the box.

Next, the stick holding the diamond to be cleaved is fixed upright in a tapered hole in the bench or cleaver's box. The cleaver rests a special knife-blade in the kerf and gives the blade a sharp tap with the handle end of a cleaver's stick. Some use a short iron bar. The stone will split along the cleavage plane. The cleaving action is shown in Fig. 11.10. The knife is a rather thick steel blade about 4 inches by 2 inches in size. The edge is thin but not sharp and rests in the kerf without touching the bottom so that it acts like a wedge. The slightly curved sides are polished for a short distance from the cutting edge.

A cleaver needs a knowledge of diamond structure (grain directions), a good eye and a steady hand. He also needs an even temperament because so much depends on that simple little action of tapping the blade. It is possible to shatter a very valuable crystal by bad cleaving. Cleaving is so exacting that at one time it was commonplace to send stones to a group of specialist cleavers in Amsterdam.

Cleaving may be useful for opening a window in a stone, removing a flaw, or reducing a large crystal to smaller pieces. It was commonly used for making rose cuts, which have flat backs. As it can be carried out only in four directions, it is of no help in splitting an octahedron in two for the manufacture of brilliant-cut diamonds. This cut has to be made parallel to the cube face, as indicated in Fig. 11.12.

Cleaving has a place in making industrial diamond tools. One example is to cleave irregular rough in four directions to make octahedra which are then polished by a tumbling process. These artificially-made octahedra are used for setting in the crowns of drills.

Sawing

The sawyer 'saws grain'; that is, he cuts in a non-cleaving direction. There are two normal directions of sawing, one in the cube direction and the other in the dodecahedral, to use the crystallographer's terms. The sawyer calls these

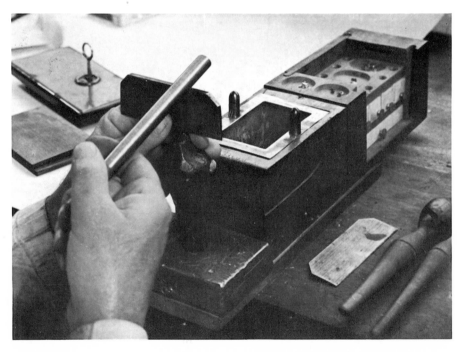

Fig. 11.10.   *The stone is cleaved by placing a special blade in the kerf and tapping it with a rod.*

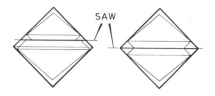

TWO BRILLIANTS FROM ONE
OCTAHEDRON - TWO METHODS

Fig. 11.12. *Two ways of sawing an octahedron to produce two brilliants. The first is known as a bishops' head.*

Fig. 11.11. *A particularly fine octahedron sawn in two by A. Monnickendam Ltd to make two emerald cut stones of identical weight.*

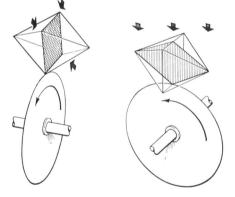

Fig. 11.14. *Flaw sawn out of the middle of an octahedron. The slightly curved lines are the saw marks and the straight lines at right angles to them are grain.*

Fig. 11.13. *(left) Sawing in a cube plane (four point) from a corner and sawing in a dodecahedron plane (two point) from an edge.*

four-point sawing and two-point sawing. The first is through or parallel to an imaginary plane through the four points of the octahedron. The second is through or parallel to an imaginary plane through two points of the octahedron. Fig. 11.13 should make this clear. It is almost impossible to saw diamonds in another direction, even if only a few degrees different.

When a medium sized or larger octahedral crystal classified as a stone is being sawn, it is usual to divide it across the natural girdle in the manner shown in Fig. 11.12, so that it will produce two brilliant-cut stones of approximately equal size, or sometimes, when it is more economic, two of different size, called a bishop's head (Fig. 11.12). The wastage occasioned by manufacturing from the awkward shapes that were the only ones possible to produce by cleaving, is largely eliminated by sawing (Fig. 11.15 and 11.16).

Sawing is also employed to remove flaws. Fig. 11.14 shows how the centre of an octahedron containing a bad feather can be sawn out, leaving two pieces to

Fig. 11 15   *Banks of sawing machines in the works of A. Monnickendam Ltd at Brighton, England. One man attends to a bank of machines.*

Fig. 11.16.   *Adjusting a machine to saw an octahedral crystal in a cube plane. The Indian ink mark made by the designer can be seen. On the right edge is a long screw that acts as a stop. It is adjusted so that the diamond is cut in a number of stages.*

be shaped into brilliant-cut stones. Windows are usually polished on the girdles of rough crystals before sawing, in order to locate any flaws, spots, and naats.

Diamonds are sawn in a machine by a very thin disc made from a special bronze. The diameter of the disc is between 3 and 4 inches and the thickness only 0·06 to 0·15 mm. A driving belt turns the sawing blade at speeds from 4,500 to 6,500 revolutions a minute, according to the needs of the sawyer.

The blade, which has a central hole with two or four slots to prevent it from dishing, is clamped between two thick flanges (Fig. 11.17) in the machine. When mounted, it is made to cut true to within half a thousandth of an inch by running the machine and holding the edge of sharp chisel (usually made from a hacksaw blade) to the edge of the wheel. Sometimes a new wheel will have some side whip. This is eliminated by massaging the sides of the blade with a hardwood stick, working outwards towards the rim.

Next, a new blade has to be dressed with the diamond powder which is responsible for the cutting action. Any diamond powder will have grains lying in all directions, from hardest to softest. Therefore, there will always be some grains in a hard direction that will cut a diamond in a soft direction.

Diamond powder of less than 325 mesh, under about 0·04-mm. or 0·0016-inch grain size is prepared by moistening it with a few drops of olive oil until it becomes a paste and letting it stand for at least two days. From ten to twenty drops of oil to a carat of powder is the right proportion. Some paste is applied to the surface of a hardened steel roller (Fig. 11.18) and the roller held by hand against the rotating disc, as shown in Fig. 11.19. The roller is moved slowly from side to side across the edge of the disc and sometimes the sawyer will slow down the disc by braking it with his thumb.

The sawing disc will rotate the roller and diamond powder will be forced into the pores of the metal at the edge of the disc.

The diamond to be sawn is mounted in a holder at the end of an arm of the machine so that the diamond rests on the top of the sawing disc, as shown in Fig. 11.20. The diamond is held by a clamp or by a cement of plaster of Paris and fish glue in a dop. The holder can be adjusted to any position to present the diamond at the correct angle to the sawing disc.

The pressure of the diamond against the edge of the disc is provided by gravity but is adjustable because different stones need different pressures. A weight at the end of the arm provides the pressure (Fig. 11.20) and there is also an adjustable stop, to be seen about half way along the arm in the same figure. This stop is adjusted progressively to control the depth of cut. It also prevents the stone dropping after it is sawn through.

To start a cut, the diamond is mounted so that it is sawn across a diagonal (if in the four-point sawing direction), but is set a few degrees off the grain so that it will be on the grain when the cut reaches the centre of the stone, and therefore the greatest bulk. This is necessary because of the swinging action of the arm holding the diamond. The marks of sawing across a diagonal are shown in Fig. 11.14.

A wide blade is sometimes used to start the cut and a thinner one after the cut has been established. At the half-way stage through the widest part of the stone, the blade is usually recharged.

Fig. 11.17. *The phosphor bronze wheel, in its spindle, used for sawing.*

Fig. 11.18. *The roller used to apply diamond dust in oil to the edge of the sawing wheel.*

Fig. 11.19. *Applying diamond powder to the edge of the wheel.*

Sawing wears down the diameter of discs, which means the rate of revolutions has to be increased to keep the cutting speed the same. A single disc will cut about half a dozen 1-carat stones before becoming too small for further use.

The sawyer keeps a very close watch on stones being sawn, examining them from time to time with a lens. He normally looks after a bank of sawing machines. He has particularly to watch for any changes of hardness through an area of different crystallization. These naats sometimes have rope formation or spider's web formation in a stone and will turn the blade and spoil the cut.

Fig. 11–20.
*Complete
sawing
machine
with the
spherical
weight at the
back which is
adjusted to
provide the
required
gravity feed.
The stop is
also clearly
visible.*

If the blade runs into a naat, sometimes it can be sawn by changing the direction of rotation, which is done by crossing the driving belt. The same method is used to avoid splitting when a blade runs into a natural cleavage in the crystal. Sometimes the blade will wander towards an easy direction, i.e. towards a cleavage plane. When this happens, the sawyer turns the stone round and begins a cut from the opposite side.

Special diamond-impregnated sintered bronze discs have been developed to overcome many of the problems of sawing through naats, but most diamond factories stick to the old methods. With increased demand and competition however, there is a slow process of change.

Sawing is still a very slow operation compared with cleaving. To saw through a quarter-of-a-carat octahedron takes about forty minutes. A carat stone may take from well over two hours to a day according to the difficulty of sawing. Australian stones are so full of naats that they cannot be sawn.

It takes about a tenth of a carat of diamond powder to saw through a one carat stone and the loss in weight of the crystal which is sawn is about 3 per cent of its weight.

Bruting

The bruter works on sawn, cleaved, or whole stones. He shapes them into circular outlines in such a way that he removes what flats he can and yet retains as much as possible of the original crystal.

The lathe or bruting machine is like a small wood-working lathe and will not only produce a round girdle on a stone but can be used to make a flat surface such as the table of a brilliant. The tables of gem diamonds are normally produced by grinding, but bruting is used for the tables of industrial die stones.

The diamond to be bruted is cemented into a dop which is mounted in the chuck of the bruting machine (Fig. 11.21). Another diamond, selected as the cutting-tool tip, is cemented to a similar dop at the end of a stick about two feet long. The bruter holds this stick under his arm and applies the diamond at the end of it to the diamond which is rotated in the lathe. There is a holder for the stick at the front of the lathe and also a pan to catch the diamond dust, as may be seen from Fig. 11.21.

The diamond being bruted has to be centralized so that the minimum amount of chips are removed to make it round. For example, if one corner projects more than the others, more of this will have to be removed otherwise there will be excessive wastage. It is also necessary at times to bring flaws or inclusions in a

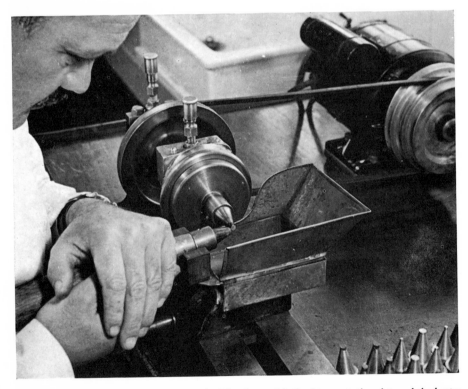

Fig. 11.21.   *The bruter or cutter at work. The diamond is fixed to a rotating dop and the bruter turns it round by using as a tool another diamond cemented to the end of a long stick.*

stone to an eccentric position so that these are removed in an early part of the bruting operation.

The bruter has to obtain more 'rondist' on the side where the flaws are, i.e. a wider girdle there.

The bruter – still frequently called the cutter in many workshops – has to be very skilful in making sure that he ends with a round diamond and not an oval one when engaged in such operations. The bruter, like all diamond workers, has at all times to keep losses as low as possible, and will often brute a stone so that there is a small part of the original skin – natural surface of the crystal – left. It indicates that he has extracted the maximum possible diameter from the crystal. Such an indication, known as a natural or a naif (Fig. 13.31), is not infrequently seen on the girdle of a polished stone. Normally there will only be one on a stone, but two, three, or four on a particularly symmetrical crystal, are possible.

Usually the diamond used as the tool is one of those to be bruted. The corners are used progressively to remove the corners of the stone in the lathe. When the stone being bruted is finished, that in the stick is mounted in the lathe and a new one cemented to the end of the stick.

The bruter's service is needed again during the grinding and polishing stage.

Grinding and Polishing

The final stage in the preparation of a gem diamond is to grind the facets and to

Fig. 11.22.   *Vesteller mounting a diamond in a solder dop ready for polishing facets on it. A gas flame is used here and a piece of metal instead of the vesteller's thumb.*

polish them. Although grinding and polishing are carried out by an almost identical operation, they are separated because the first is a coarser process than the second.

The equipment comprises a power-driven horizontal grinding wheel, a scaife, and a holder for the diamond, a tang (Fig. 11.23). A few works still employ solder dops, as described in Chapter Nine, but the great majority have changed to mechanical dops, one of which is shown in Fig. 11.25 The diamond is held in a clamp which is screwed tight to hold it in the position required. Whether a solder or a mechanical dop is employed, it has a copper stem, which can be bent to obtain the exact angle needed to grind a particular facet.

The Scaife

The scaife is made of a cast-iron disc from 10 to 12 inches in diameter and about an inch thick when new. The thickness is reduced as the surface is from time to time trimmed to get rid of grooves caused by the grinding process. Through

Fig. 11.23.   *Polishers benches at the Monnickendam works where traditional methods are still employed to cut high quality stones.*

Fig. 11.24. *Three diamonds being polished at the same time in mechanical dops. All the tangs are weighted. The scaife is of the traditional pattern. In the foreground, left, is the kind of folding lens favoured by diamond polishers.*

the centre of the traditional scaife is a steel axle with pointed ends, so that the whole is like a big top, as shown in Figs. 11.23 and 11.24.

The points of the axle run in conical holes to two *lignum vitae* or other hardwood blocks, above and below the scaife and are lubricated with tallow or grease. Since 1940, some scaifes have been made without top axles, as can be seen in Fig. 11.25. The scaife is driven by a belt or directly by an electric motor at a speed of about 2,500 r.p.m. It is mounted in a bench so that the bench surface is approximately at the same level as the surface of the scaife. Also mounted on the bench are two pegs or stops. These are placed so that the tang is held in position with the diamond resting on the scaife and is not swept aside by its rotation. One of the pins rests against the side of the tang itself and the other against a rod projecting from the back of the tang like a tail.

The scaife has to run absolutely true and free of vibration for accurate diamond grinding and polishing. It is balanced by small lead weights, held underneath in a groove near the spindle by a thin cord wound round. The cast iron surface is turned in a lathe and lapped to be as flat as possible. Then it is scored as shown in Fig. 11.26 to retain diamond paste. The scoring is done by hand with a stick of the hard material, silicon carbide.

Diamond paste is made with diamond ground in a pestle and mortar and mixed with a few drops of olive oil in the same way as described for sawing.

Fig. 11.25. *A modern scaife with ball-bearing mounting instead of a top pivot, in use in Belgium. The mechanical dop is also of modern adjustable design.*

There is not the same necessity to grade the diamond powder accurately when cutting diamond as there is when cutting softer materials by diamond powder. Diamond polishers often have their own 'formulae' for making paste, using the white of an egg, spittle, detergent, and other such media. The paste is applied with the thumb, as a rule.

The scaife surface is usually divided into three areas by the polisher (Fig. 11.27).

1. The testing ring, used to find the correct starting point of a facet, by judgement and some trial and error. It is usually prepared with dry diamond powder.
2. The running ring (also called the loopkring) on which the facet is ground to size.
3. The polishing ring (also known as the soetkring) for polishing the facets to as perfect as possible surfaces by removing the grooves – the running lines – caused by grinding.

The testing ring and running ring are towards the centre and the polishing ring, which has the biggest area, towards the edge of the scaife. The polisher will gradually 'use up' the surface of the scaife, abandoning a grinding or polishing ring as it ceases to cut or produce a good finish. A good polisher will use a scaife for six to eight weeks before the surface needs renewal. Paste is worked into the surfaces by actually polishing a facet.

Fig. 11.27. *The three rings on the scaive can be seen here. The inner one is for testing, the centre one for grinding, and the outer one for polishing.*

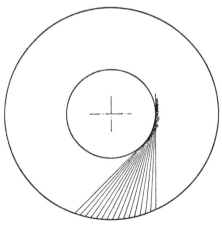

Fig. 11.26. *Scoring a scaife to hold diamond paste.*

A polisher will usually grind from two or four diamonds at the same time on a scaife, but in some works even more.

Four-, Three- and Two-point Stones

The diamond polisher has to decide upon a plan of action before he starts work on a stone. This will first of all depend upon relation of the crystal structure to the final brilliant-cut. The polisher puts it another way; how he cuts the stone will depend upon whether it is a four-pointer, a three-pointer, or a two-pointer.

These expressions are explained in relation to structure in Fig. 11.28. A three-pointer stone is also called a was – pronounced 'vaas'.

To the polisher, a four-point stone is one in which the table originally had four corners. It may be a whole stone or part of a sawn octahedron. The saw marks across the table indicate that it is a four-point stone and also indicate the direction to the grain.

A three-point stone has a table which was originally an octahedron face with three corners. It may be a whole stone, a macle, or a cleaved stone as in Fig. 11.28.

A two-point stone has a table in a rhombic dodecahedral direction, that is, it is along one of the straight edges of an octahedral crystal and therefore has only two corners. It will almost certainly be a stone sawn in this direction.

The three possibilities and the directions of grain are shown in the three illustrations. The polisher would not only look for sawing lines but also at grain lines on any naturals left by the bruter to establish the best direction for grinding and polishing. When he has established the possible directions, he will try them on the testing ring to discover which polishes best. Although two opposite directions are equally possible, usually one polishes much better than the other.

Practical Cutting

The best indication to the polisher that the direction is good is the sound. A diamond that is running well makes little sound, like a faint ringing note. The more off the best grain direction, the louder the sound, although very occasionally a stone will produce quite a loud note when it is running well.

The facet surface is also an important indication. The more the stone is forced by running in an unsatisfactory direction, the less perfect the finish.

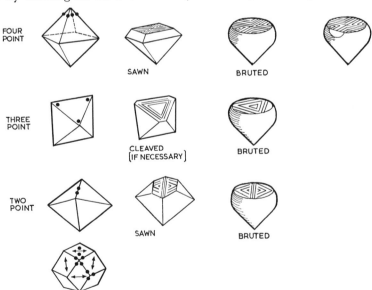

Fig. 11.28. *Diamond cutter's and polisher's names for directions in an octahedral and* (bottom) *a dodecahedral stone.*

198

Forcing with the grain will make the facet greyish and even tear the scaife and the facet surface.

Often a lead weight is placed on the tang to obtain the best grinding pressure, but increasing the pressure or speed indefinitely does not produce faster and faster cutting. There is a point when the facet begins to burn or graphitize.

Each facet is made at the correct angle by studying the tang upside down and by bending the copper stalk of the dop holding the diamond and by turning it in its clamp when necessary.

A quite exceptional degree of accuracy is achieved by diamond polishers measuring by eye alone. Once the basic facets are put on, they work by aligning edges and reflections of edges. P. Grodzinski measured the angles between facets on a brilliant-cut stone and found them to be within a few minutes of a degree.

Compass of the Tang

As diamonds can only be ground in certain directions, the diamond grinder and polisher uses a jargon of his own to describe the direction of cutting once the stone is adjusted in the dop in a tang. It is a kind of compass direction, as shown in Fig. 11.29, which is the simplest of several notations. The tang is 'read' by taking it off the anti-clockwise running scaife and holding it with the diamond pointing to the eyes. The stone can now be turned so that the point of a facet being cut is left out, right, or whichever direction is appropriate. The actual directions in which brilliant facets are cut is shown in Fig. 11.33.

Modern diamond-bonded wheels used for cutting diamonds for diamond tools have not been found suitable for polishing gems as they do not give the high finish obtainable by using the traditional scaife.

In practice, making brilliant cuts from bruted stones is not divided strictly into grinding and polishing, but into cross-cutting and brillianteering.

Work of the Cross-Cutter

The cross-cutter puts on the first eighteen facets. These are the table, the culet, four corners and four bezels on the top, and four corners and four pavilions on

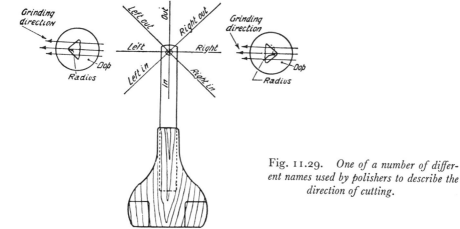

Fig. 11.29. *One of a number of different names used by polishers to describe the direction of cutting.*

the bottom. The order in which this is done differs from factory to factory, but a common sequence is shown in Fig. 11.31 to 11.32.

The table is ground first. The next step is to grind the first facet. This is most important and critical of the whole process, because the entire symmetry, life fire and ultimate quality of the final gem depends upon the accuracy with which this facet is ground.

The first facet is normally a corner at the top of the stone, which should be at the correct angle to the plane through the girdle. It is also extremely important to grind the facet to the right size. Although the cross-cutter will use a gauge, much depends upon the accuracy of his judgement and his skill and experience.

When satisfied, he will grind the corner opposite, and then the third and fourth (Fig. 11.30). He then proceeds to polish the bottom facets. It is of the greatest importance that these facets are at an angle of not more than 41° and not less than 40° in order to obtain the maximum brilliance. They must meet in a point (which will become the culet) in the exact centre of the diamond.

The bottom facets must be perfectly aligned under the top facets to obtain a perfectly even girdle. Also if one facet either on the top or bottom is not the same depth in the girdle this will give the appearance of a seesaw edge. If the angles of the bottom facets are over 41° the diamond will have a blackish appearance in the centre. If the angles are under 40° the stone will appear 'watery' and the girdle will be reflected through the table.

There are now four facets on the bottom of the stone and four facets on the top. Viewed through the table, the culet should be in the exact centre of the now square table. The cross-worker examines a reflection of the bottom facets in the table. It should be quite square and of a certain size.

Four more facets are now cut on the top of the stone, usually in sequence opposite each other. There are now eight, which are known as the eights (Fig. 11.31). The sizes of the facets must be accurately ground so that when completed they are all the same size and make the table a perfect octagon.

The stone now has eight facets on the top and four on the bottom. It is turned over again and four more facets, called the pavilions, added to the bottom by grinding on the edges of the four original facets as shown in Fig. 11.31. At this stage the stone has eight facets and culet at the bottom and eight facets and table at the top.

Rondisting

Before further grinding or polishing, the stone is returned to the bruter for further work on the girdle which is now thinner and can be made perfectly round in an operation called rondisting.

Polishing

The cross-cutter has the stone back to polish the facets he has ground. He does this on the outer polishing ring on the scaife. Grinding leaves a series of curved grooves on facets which have to be removed before the adamantine polish is achieved, but it usually takes only a few seconds to polish a facet, by swinging the dop quickly in an arc to and fro across the polishing ring. Each facet is

Fig. 11.30. *An octahedral crystal in the rough, sawn* (centre) *sawn as a bishop's head and* (right) *with the lower half bruted.*

Fig. 11.31. *Work of the cross-cutter. The table of the stone is ground first,* then a top facet (on the left-hand diagram). *The eights have been completed in the centre. The illustration on the right has the sixteen main facets plus the table and culet.*

Fig. 11.32. *The brillianteerer puts on the remaining facets either in groups or in sequence.*

polished in sequence and examined frequently under a magnifying eyeglass to make sure that the polishing is effective and even.

The Work of the Brillianteerer

Brillianteering is the final stage in making a brilliant-cut diamond by adding the remaining twenty-four facets to the top or crown and the remaining sixteen facets to the bottom or pavilion.

Starting on the top of the stone, the brillianteerer will place and polish a star-facet as accurately as he can. This is a key operation and demands a high degree of skill and judgement because the facet is cut quickly and has to be inspected every few seconds to make sure that the angle of the dop is exact.

The star-facets are those surrounding the table so as to form an eight-pointed star. Each is placed at the junction of the edge between two eights with the table, as shown in Fig. 11.32. It is ground so that it extends half-way down the edge of the eights. It is usual with mechanical dops, in which the diamond can easily be adjusted, to complete all the star-facets before grinding the rest of the facets in sequence on the top of the stone. With solder dops, to avoid too much work moving the diamond, it was usual to complete what polishers call a set,

Fig. 11.33. *The actual grinding directions in four-point, three-point, and two-point stones.*

which comprises two stars and four girdle facets as shown in the illustration in Fig. 11.34.

The upper girdle facets, also known as halves, number 16 and each connects the outer point of a star-facet to a point on the girdle midway between the eights, as can be seen in the top diagram of Fig. 10.2. After a set is finished, the original eight has become a kite-shape and is sometimes known as a kite facet. (See Fig. 10.2.)

The stone is next turned over to complete the bottom facets. All sixteen of these are halves or lower girdle facets, around the girdle. At one time they were cut to form points about half-way down the edges between eights, but the modern fashion is to make these facets much longer. In most makes today, they extend about thirteen-sixteenths (about 80 per cent) of the distance from girdle to culet, with the exception of when a stone is flat in the bottom because the facets are at an angle less than 40°.

Closed Culets

On earlier made stones it was the practice to leave a relatively large culet. Today the culet is sometimes missing, which illustrates the extreme skill of the cutter. It is best to have a very small culet, however, as it has a practical function. It minimises damage to the point. A sharp point or short edge, called a closed culet, is more easily fractured. Too large a culet can be too readily seen through the table, marring the brilliance.

Final Finishing

Top quality diamonds are given a final check visually and 'repair' work, known as making-over, carried out if necessary. This comprises polishing very tiny facets (that do not affect the quality of make) to remove any remaining minute defects.

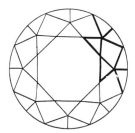

Fig. 11.34. *Facets are placed in sets like this when using a solder dop, today usually on top grade stones only. With mechanical dops, facets of the same kind are placed in sequence.*

Modern polished diamonds are sometimes given an acid bath after cutting to remove any oil and debris that have entered any tiny fractures and cleavages that reach the surface of the stone. Acidizing can have an important effect on quality and there are specialists in the process.

REFERENCES

Diamond Technology, by P. Grodzinski (London, 1953).
Basic Notes of Diamond Polishing, by Jules J. Canes (S. Africa, 1964).
'Diamonds are Different', paper by D. M. Rainier, Diamond Research Laboratory (Johannesburg, 1968).

CHAPTER TWELVE

Grading Polished Stones for Colour

Grading a cut stone for colour means deciding the amount by which it deviates from the whitest possible (truly colourless) i.e., how much off-colour it is. Nature provides a continuous darkening in the tints from white to yellow, from white to brown, from white to green, and (in the industrial category) from white to grey. There are no natural divisions in any of these groups. Divisions are determined by demand and the ability of the human eye to separate one tint from an adjacent one that is very slightly lighter or darker.

The white to yellow group, the most important and largest in gem diamonds, may be divided into, say, three categories, or fifty. Many people will be able to grade a pile of cut stones into three colour groups, but very few indeed will be able to separate them into fifty that gradually increase in yellowish tinge. Everybody, however, will have the same difficulty with stones that fall between two adjacent groups, and this will always be so.

Picking Prices

In the colour categories of any commercial firm there are always some stones that could arguably be graded higher or lower. That is why firms that work on broader divisions of colour and quality impose a higher price per carat on a customer who wants to pick out stones himself from a category instead of accepting what he is offered.

The picking price is between the price for the particular category and that for the next higher category. Of course, a customer electing to pay a picking price must know what he is doing. He could pick a stone that merges into the next lower category and thus pay too much for it.

Conditions for Grading

Since a body, or fundamental, colour of a diamond must be judged in white light, it follows that the white light must not be reflected from coloured surfaces in a room. The ideal room for judging colour should therefore have dead-white walls. Also the stones must be seen against a dead-white background. White paper or white blotting-paper is normally used, but white paint is used in grading instruments and white plastics materials are also suitable, provided that they are not strongly fluorescent.

A second, and very important consideration is that any fluorescence in the stone must be suppressed. A visible blue fluorescence can be caused in a yellowish diamond when ultra-violet light, which is invisible, falls on it. If the diamond is examined in sunlight, even reflected light, which contains ultra-violet light, the blue fluorescence will tend to cancel the yellowish body colour because the colours are nearly complementary, and the stone will appear to be whiter than it is. These stones are often mistakenly called 'blue-white'. Similarly a stone that fluoresces yellow will appear worse in white light containing ultra-violet.

It is therefore important to grade stones in white light that is relatively free of ultra-violet and the orthodox method is to use daylight from a north-facing window in the northern hemisphere and from a south-facing one in the southern, i.e. with one's back to the sun. Morning and evening light have an excess of red because of refraction through the atmosphere when the sun is low. Also there must be sufficient intensity of light. These restrictions mean that in the winter in London, for example, it is only possible to grade between the hours of about 10 a.m. and 2 p.m.

Standard Lighting

To provide a standard light for colour grading and to eliminate the nuisance of being only able to grade during a few hours of daylight, the Gemological Institute of America introduced the Diamondlite. A standard artificial white light free of ultra-violet and equivalent to north daylight, is contained in a metal box with an open front. The inside of the box is painted dead-white. This eliminates reflections from surroundings and also limits the confusing effects of dispersion of colour, enabling the stone under test to be compared with master stones. The instrument also incorporates an ultra-violet tube for detecting fluorescence in diamonds and a magnifier for examining small stones. The

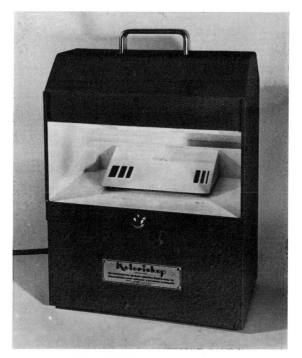

Fig. 12.1. *The Koloriscop, a specially designed standard light box for judging the whiteness of diamonds. A stone can just be seen in the tray.*

Americans provide a special colour-grading lamp for use in conjunction with their diamond-grading microscope.

A standard light box for diamond colour-grading is also made in Europe under patents held by Dr. E. Gübelin, of Switzerland. It is called the Koloriscop (Fig. 12.1) and has a stronger source of light than the G.I.A. version, which makes it more convenient for use in daylight. The brighter light, however, tends to accentuate colour difference.

Each instrument has the important advantage of providing a standard light in which to judge colour, but it must be remembered that diamonds are rarely seen in such ideal conditions in wear because there is some ultra-violet in most daylight.

Judging Colour in Daylight

The stone should be removed from its paper packet, especially if this has a blue lining paper, which is intended to 'improve' the colour.

The most convenient method of judging the colour of loose polished diamonds in daylight is that traditionally used by diamond sorters. The only 'equipment' required is a piece of white paper. It must be white or slightly grey, but it should have no tinge of colour. Comparison of different sheets of 'white' paper will soon show that the whiteness varies as much as the whiteness of diamond. Special

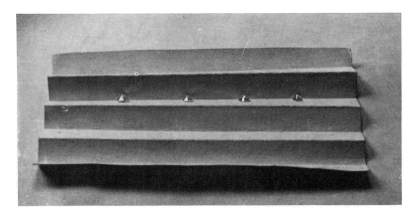

Fig. 12.2. *Diamonds placed table down in fluted white paper so that the colours may be judged by looking through the sides of the pavilions.*

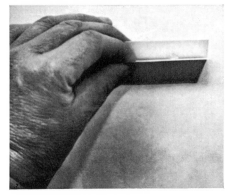

Fig. 12.3. *A thin V-shaped card which is effective for colour judgement.*

paper is available from trade sources, but there is no problem in finding ordinary blotting paper suitable for all but the finest grading.

It is difficult to judge the body colour of a polished diamond by looking at the table of the stone because the spectrum colours caused by fire confuse the eye. The stone must be examined through the side of the pavilion.

Cut the paper into a rectangle about three by four inches (say 10 by 13 cm.) and fold it into a concertina shape as shown in Fig. 12.2. A diamond for grading is placed in a fold with the table down on the side nearest the grader so that the colour of the side of the pavilion may be seen. (Stones are similarly examined in the standard light boxes previously described, being placed in a groove in a metal or plastic holder.) The folded paper is held or placed on a table, so that light from the north falls on it. A small piece of selected thin white card with a single fold, such as that marketed in West Germany for the purpose, is also very effective for grading when used as shown in Fig. 12.3.

The best way to gauge the colour of a stone is to compare it with a similar one of known colour grade, a comparison stone. It should be reasonably easy after some practice to decide which of the two stones has a lighter tint or whether they are nearly the same. Using one or more standard stones for colour grading is the safest method because one's judgement does not vary much.

Professional diamond graders do not constantly use standard stones, however, because they become quick and accurate without them. Nevertheless, even the most skilled grader can experience a drift in colour judgement, especially after a long grading session, and he will from time to time make a comparison with one or more stones that have been agreed as standard colours by his company.

Very few diamonds are truly colourless and the professional grader can distinguish a range of extremely faint tinges of colour in stones that to anyone else are all absolutely colourless. Practice enables most people to start seeing yellow tinges; that is, when the stone begins to 'draw colour'. Few notice the very slight brown tinges and often it is only the skilled grader who is able to see at once the slight green tinges. In polished stone grading, faint tinges of brown are usually treated as comparable depths of yellow because scales are based on ranges from white to yellow.

Learning to Grade

Stones that just begin to draw colour are the mental standard used by anyone, including the skilled grader, when not using a standard stone by which to judge. If a stone is placed by itself – without a comparison stone – in the paper concertina, the first thing to determine is whether it draws colour, whether it has any body colour at all, even the very, very faintest tinge. Anyone judging stones must know the grade of the stone in which he personally can just see a tinge of colour.

The way to begin is to examine as many stones as possible and compare them with each other and with stones that have already been reliably graded. Then take a single polished stone, study it in the folded paper and determine whether it draws colour. Then make the following decisions.

No draw:	Decide if the colour is	Fine White
	or	White.
Just Draws:	Decide if the colour is	Commercial White.
	or	Top Silver Cape.
Obviously draws:	Decide if the colour is	Silver Cape
	or	one of the lower categories.

The grading shown above is one of the scales used in the U.K. It does not matter what names, numbers, or letters are used, the principle of grading without standard stones is the same. For example Top Crystal is the key colour that just draws in the Scandinavian standard colour grading scale.

Comparison Stones

Without doubt, the use of standard comparison stones is the most reliable method of grading. It is essential to most people when grading the top range of colour. One comparison stone is better than none. The colour grade chosen should be determined by the purpose of grading. Suppose a retailer wants to buy loose stones only above white grading. His standard stone should be of white grade. Three standard stones is a practical number to carry on one's person and five or seven are nearer the ideal. The stones should be selected so that they are one, two, or more steps apart in the colour scale, according to the accuracy needed (See special colour plate).

In use, the stones are placed in a standard viewing box or the folded paper concertina in grade order with about an inch between each. The stone under test is moved from gap to gap until it is seen to fit into the colour graduation, when it can, of course, be given a category.

The standard stone method is taught in the U.S.A., Switzerland and Germany. A system exists for standard stones to be graded by a central authority.

Unfortunately grading is not as simple as it may now appear by the previous description, because the size or bulk of the stone causes an illusory difference in colour. If, say, a Silver Cape stone is recut to a quarter of its weight, it will appear to improve in colour to, say, Top Silver Cape, because of the loss in bulk. A mental allowance has, therefore, to be made for size when grading. A 3-carat stone with a tinge of yellow will be graded much higher than a ½-carat stone with a tinge of yellow. It is not necessary to grade stones of under about 0·50 ct. as finely as larger ones simply because the values are lower.

Another problem for cutters and dealers who buy stones in quantity is that stones of better or worse colour become 'hidden' in a parcel or pile of stones because of colour saturation. It is only possible to check such a parcel by examining the stones one by one away from the others.

Grading Mounted Stones

It is impossible to grade mounted diamonds accurately because the setting and any surrounding stones affect the colour and also because one often has to look at the table when spectrum colours can confuse the eye.

When the setting is yellow gold, the diamond inevitably reflects or transmits some yellow from the metal. A fine stone is therefore depreciated by mounting it in yellow gold. Platinum is by far the best metal for mounts as it is not only white but much more hard wearing than gold. In the past, and currently with fine stones, it was normal practice to make the mount itself out of platinum whatever the rest of the ring or other jewel was made of. The price of platinum has risen so steeply, however, that white gold is often substituted for platinum today and well designed claws of white gold are usually quite satisfactory. One compromise is to have platinum claws on white gold.

When a diamond is mounted close to a blue stone, suffusion causes its colour to 'improve'. That is one reason why blue sapphires surrounded by diamonds are so popular. Diamonds set with yellow, brown, or green stones, naturally tend to suffer as far as their colour is concerned.

If daylight is being used, it is best to use a comparison stone held in a prong type holder by the side of the ring as shown in Fig. 12.4 or 12.5.

Colour Grading System

Names used in colour grading fall into three main categories: those based on the names of mines or areas from which the bulk of such rough originated, such as Wesselton and Cape; those used by the cutters, such as Fine White and Commercial White; and those based on neutral numbers and letters.

The traditional scale is in the first category as on page 210. For retail purposes, the traditional names are preferable. Top Crystal or Crystal is not so derogatory as Commercial White for the same colour. To call a colour number three sounds the same as calling it third rate, and who can visualize a colour called E?

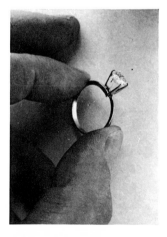

Fig. 12.5. *Another form of clip holder is shaped like a ring and useful for visualizing a stone when set.*

Fig. 12.4. *A prong holder is useful for comparing a loose stone of known colour against one of unknown colour set in a ring.*

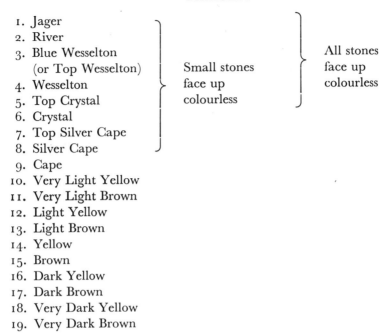

1. Jager
2. River
3. Blue Wesselton
   (or Top Wesselton)
4. Wesselton
5. Top Crystal
6. Crystal
7. Top Silver Cape
8. Silver Cape

Small stones
face up
colourless

All stones
face up
colourless

9. Cape
10. Very Light Yellow
11. Very Light Brown
12. Light Yellow
13. Light Brown
14. Yellow
15. Brown
16. Dark Yellow
17. Dark Brown
18. Very Dark Yellow
19. Very Dark Brown

In lay terms, all of these from River to about Light Yellow are shades of White. Without guidance and practice, the layman would see no colour in the first dozen grades. Large or small stones in the first five or six grades will face up without colour. That is, only a skilled eye is likely to detect a trace of colour when the diamond is seen from the front. Small stones in the next grades down to Silver Cape will also face up colourless, but larger ones will show a tinge of colour to the trained eye. (See frontispiece.) Mounted stones below that grade will become increasingly evidently coloured, even to the untrained eye.

It remains a fact, of course, that stones in the top grades cannot be accurately classified even by the most skilled sorter, if they are mounted.

'Blue-White'

Jager, number one in the traditional colour scale, is abnormal and is usually omitted from current scales. It refers to a particular type of white stone from the Jagersfontein Mine that is very slightly bluish owing to its strong blue fluorescence. The term blue-white arose from such stones. Jagers are very few indeed and it is incorrect to call other stones blue-white. The term has been very much abused. There were even firms in the USA that called their lowest grade blue-white! It is probably true to say that 99 per cent of the diamonds sold retail as blue-white are not only *not* blue-white, but are not even in the top five colour grades.

In the Code of Trading issued by the National Association of Goldsmiths of Great Britain and Ireland, Rule 40 states: It is an unfair trade practice to use the term 'blue-white', or any other term, expression, or representation of similar import, as descriptive of any diamond which under daylight or its equivalent, shows any colour other than a trace of blue.

Small mounted stones appear colourless

Mounted stones appear colourless

Mounted stones appear increasingly tinted

Mounted stones appear yellow

A.G.S	G.I.A	SCAND.D.N under 0.50ct	SCAND.D.N 0.50ct and over	U.K
0	D / E	RAREST WHITE	RIVER	FINEST WHITE (BLUE-WHITE*)
1	F		TOP WESSELTON	FINE WHITE
2	G	WHITE		
	H		WESSELTON	WHITE
3	I	TINTED WHITE	TOP CRYSTAL	COMMERCIAL WHITE
4	J		CRYSTAL	TOP SILVER CAPE
5	K			
6	L		TOP CAPE	SILVERCAPE
	M		CAPE	LIGHT CAPE
7	N	YELLOWISH		
	O			
8	P		LIGHT YELLOW	CAPE
	Q			
	R			
9–10	S–X	YELLOW	YELLOW	DARK CAPE

Fig. 12.6. *Approximate comparison scales of colour. Blue white is marked with an asterisk because it truly applies to the rare Jager colour but is commonly and incorrectly used for River stones all over the world. See facing page.*

This is identical to Rule 28 in Rules for the Jewelry Industry published by the Federal Trade Commission in the U.S.A. from which it was derived. Members of the American Gem Society are forbidden use of the term 'blue-white' in advertising because the term has been misused so widely.

'Over-Blue' Stones

There is another class of stone with a strong blue fluorescence that comes from the Premier Mine and does not appear in the colour scale. The blue fluorescence is so strong that it masks the body colour of light yellow so effectively, the stone appears to be over-blue, even slightly oily blue, in daylight. These stones are known as Premiers or Premier over-blues.

Scan. D.N.

In 1970, the Scandinavian countries (Denmark, Finland, Norway, and Sweden) issued their Scandinavian Diamond Nomenclature and Grading Standards, known as Scan. D.N., in seven languages. The standards contain definitions, colour standards, clarity standards in great detail, and standards of cut. Colours are defined in terms of readings by a special German colour photometer, originally developed for the textile trade but modified for work on diamonds. Colours are named from the traditional scale but with different names for small stones because there is no commercial reason for grading them so accurately. Scan D.N. appears to be more practical than other proposals. The colour scales, shown with the American official scales and a British one for comparison are illustrated in Fig. 12.6. The American scales, referred to again later, are also based on readings of a different instrument, a colorimeter, which is no longer made and is to be replaced by one of another type.

Ranges of Grade

Colour grading systems for polished diamonds vary considerably even among cutters and dealers in the same country, but very gradually a broad degree of standardization is emerging through the activities of certain professional gem organizations, related instructional classes, and international trading in diamonds.

For the individual business, the grading scale used must depend on the class of goods bought or sold. A cutter who polishes only a certain quality of goods has no need of an elaborate system extending far beyond the quality of the roughs he buys. One who deals only in low qualities requires three or four broad categories. One who deals in top goods must have more fine classifications, but they need extend only over the top end of the colour scale. Few firms employ more than a dozen classifications.

Some concerns use the traditional named colours, but many have devised systems of their own which are too numerous and confusing to detail.

Practice in the Trade

In the cutting trade certain terms have become generally accepted although exact interpretations of what is meant by them may vary, and there are also variations in some of the expressions. They are:

Finest White (also called Blue White)
Fine White
White
Commercial White
Top Silver Cape   Finest Light Brown
Silver Cape   Fine Light Brown
Light Cape
Cape   Light Brown
Dark Cape   Dark Brown

Where this scale fits in relation to the traditional scale depends entirely on the interpretation of the manufacturer or dealer. How it should fit into other scales is shown in Fig. 12.6.

The position of the brown grades shows approximately where they stand in price. Very light brown in the traditional scale has been upgraded to Finest or Fine Light Brown and made roughly equivalent to yellow tints. Very light tints of brown are less easily seen than those of yellow, especially with the stone face-up. There are bigger steps in the lower end of the scale.

Commercial considerations must affect any such scale since it exists for commercial purposes, i.e. it determines the price. The U.K. has always been a very big market for the middle qualities of stones because of the diamond engagement ring tradition, hence a compression of the scale into the middle range by dealers. In any case, it is pointless usually to attempt fine grading for colour or other considerations for stones under about half a carat.

Commercial Scales

Many commercial scales are based on numbers or letters of the alphabet, which is reasonable, but even so have become confusing because of upgrading, so that a scale that originally began with A may now begin with AAA, and one that originally started at 1 or 0 may now start at 000. The reason may be the quite legitimate expansion of the firm's business into a higher grade than it previously dealt in so that its best now becomes its second or third best and other categories are added without upsetting the existing ones.

One of the best known individual letter system is that of the British firm of A. Monnickendam Limited because it exports most of its production and deals in top qualities. For colour, the scale is AA, A, AAB, AB, B, BC, C, D, which covers the top of the traditional colour scale down to Silver Cape. Figures are used for purity grades. What is most important is the consistency in grading that they have maintained.

Some diamond dealers have their own grading systems but sell according to the particular systems and standards employed by their individual customers, so that a stone may be sold as a certain grade to one person and at another grade to another person, although the price will remain the same. The merchant will probably have a third grade for his office standard.

One fact is certain, that if say Fine White stones are bought from a dozen firms, their colours may actually range over several grades in the colour scale. The reason is not because of dishonesty in trading. It is mainly because each category must spread over a range of colour, and, particularly in lower grades, some firms use broader colour scales than others. Also, there is no universally accepted grading scale, and each firm has its own standard. The judging of colour is in any case a personal, subjective judgement and some people are better able to do it than others. The instruments in use for measuring colour are by no means perfect.

American Standards
The term Commercial White has been very much abused by applying it, particularly in the U.S.A., to goods of lower quality and therefore the American Gem Society forbids its use if it misleads the public.

The Americans have gone furthest towards a universal colour standard. There are in fact two scales in use. One is technically based on the A.G.S. colorimeter, an instrument which is available only to American Gem Society members. The A.G.S. system has eleven grades from Colourless to Yellow signified as 0, 1, 2, 3, 4, 5, 6, 7, 8, 9, 10. The steps are broader than in the traditional scale, roughly equal to two steps in the scale on page 212.

The other U.S.A. standard is that devised by the Gemological Institute of America in which the steps are smaller than in the traditional scale and are indicated from colourless to yellow as: D, E, F, G, H, I, J, K, L, M, N, O, P, Q, R, S, T, U, V, W, X. The top grade was coded as D to avoid any confusion with the various A, B and C systems employed by dealers. The bottom end goes beyond colours normally encountered in the gem diamonds, which end at Q or R.

The G.I.A. encourages use of its system by courses of training for members, by designing and selling colour grading instruments, and by running two Gem Trade Laboratories which will grade diamonds and issue certificates. One is in New York and the other in Los Angeles.

Members of the trade (at a trade fee) and members of the public (at a retail fee) may have stones graded. There is also a lower fee for diamond students. A certificate is issued for the stone giving not only colour grade but weight, measurements, shape and cut, fluorescence, purity grade, proportion grade (i.e. percentage variation from ideal cut), and details of flaws in finish.

Despite these meritorious efforts to standardize colour grading, the problem is far from solved largely because there still remain four problems in one, each of which has to be tackled separately.

They are: (1) Standardizing the terminology, (2) Standardizing the conditions under which stones are graded, (3) Standardizing the comparison stones, i.e., the named colours, and (4) Overcoming the forces of conservatism and the economic circumstances that perpetuate present systems.

On the other hand, there are some diamond cutters and dealers who handle diamonds in large numbers, dividing them into parcels of broad ranges of middle qualities, who have a genuine grievance. They say that, owing to the propaganda about grading, their customers complain about individual stones in a parcel.

Their prices, however, have been determined by economic rapid and broad grading. If stones were sold with individual gradings, the prices would be much higher.

The solution will probably come about through operation of the market in such a way that the trade in all countries is forced to accept a common system just as cutters have to accept basic grading of rough diamonds from the mines.

CHAPTER THIRTEEN

Clarity Grading of Polished Stones

The clarity or purity of a polished diamond affects its quality and therefore its price, because any inclusion, cleavage, crack, or other natural feature inside or defect on the surface will interfere with the passage of light through the stone and affect its brilliance or appearance to some extent. Even normally invisible defects, such as twinning, can act as light sinks, absorbing some of the light entering the stone. The term clarity is preferred to purity, because purity suggests there are only two types of diamond, pure and impure.

Grades of Clarity

Diamonds are graded according to the degree of clarity, the finest being called flawless, clean, pure, perfect, or similar name. There are other names for levels of decreasing clarity.

Diamonds which just fail to be of the highest clarity are internationally referred to by dealers as VVS. This originally meant very, very slightly imperfect. The word imperfect is unsuitable when referring to natural inclusions and by general agreement among the leading trade and gemmological organizations of most countries the meaning has been replaced by very, very small inclusion.

Next down the scale of clarity is VS, meaning very small inclusions, then SI, small inclusions. After that, clarity grades are called First piqué, Second piqué, and so on. Piqué is French for pricked, referring to the inclusions. It is often written as PK.

Some cutters and dealers have lower grades which they call spotted and which may also contain two or more categories. A number have a bottom category which they find profitable to cut and sell although it does not fit into their normal scale of clarity. These goods they call rejection.

As with colour, scales of clarity vary in different countries and from cutter to cutter. They also depend upon the class of goods being graded. Owing to the steeper rise in price according to quality, top quality stones will obviously be graded on a much finer clarity scale than stones that are of lower quality in clarity and colour.

Equipment for Grading

Very little equipment is needed for grading diamonds. As with colour, however, a refined instrument is also available for those who prefer more sophisticated methods. The basic tools of the grader are a pair of diamond tongs, a piece of chamois leather, and a good hand lens of 10 × magnification. (Fig. 13.1). At times, a shaded spot lamp is also required.

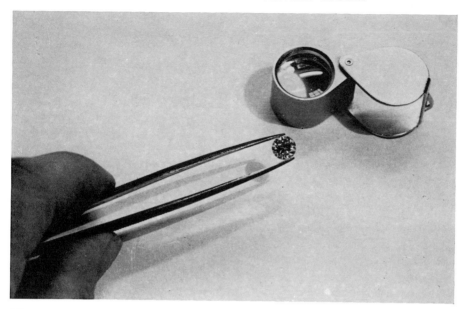

Fig. 13.1. *The basic tools for clarity grading: diamond tongs and a 10 × corrected hand lens.*

Cleaning Stones

It is easy to be misled by specks of dirt and tiny hairs on the surface of a diamond if one is not a professional grader. It is therefore essential to clean a stone before attempting to grade it for clarity.

The grader should wipe the stone with a small piece of clean chamois leather and afterwards it should not be fingered, but handled only with stone tongs. Some graders dip stones in carbon tetrachloride before wiping them with a chamois leather, to make sure they are absolutely clean. A camel hair paint brush is also useful for removing dust.

Standard Magnification

Since it is relatively easy to find inclusions or other features in most diamonds with a sufficiently high-powered microscope, and clarity grading is for commercial purposes only, the degree of magnification must be specified. This is internationally agreed to be by a ten-times magnifying lens, which has been corrected for chromatic and spherical aberration. The magnification should not be greater, or the stone might be downgraded. Neither should the magnification be lower, otherwise the stone might wrongly be upgraded.

It is also essential that a stone be examined under adequate illumination and by a trained eye. The traditional way of grading for clarity is to use a 10 × hand lens (most top graders seem to prefer the Zeiss) in daylight against a corrected white paper background. Grading can be done efficiently also by artificial light, preferably using a heavily-shaded spot lamp as shown in Fig. 13.2.

Diamond Tongs

The usual stone tongs employed by most gemmologists are too coarse for holding diamonds. Special diamond tongs with fine non-slip tips are available. They are blunter than watchmakers' tweezers, have fine milling inside the tips, and usually are not so strongly sprung. Some tongs incorporate slides to hold the stone in the clamped position, but usually these will be found less convenient as skill in handling improves.

Most people hold the stone in tongs in the left hand and the lens in the right hand. It is therefore most convenient to be able to pick up the diamond left-handed, but many people find it easier to pick up a stone with the tongs in the right hand and then transfer them to the left. A stone is most conveniently picked up by tongs if it is standing on its table on a firm surface. Picked up from the paper, it is likely to be held out of square and may fly from the tongs. The tips of the tongs should be just past the centre line of the stone.

Stones should be examined in a comfortable position where there is no danger of losing a stone if it is accidentally dropped.

A lamp, if used, should have an opaque shade and should be positioned in front of the grader as shown in Fig. 13.2. The stone should be held so that light from the side of the lamp reaches it. This provides almost dark field illumination and makes it easier to find inclusions. A little experimenting will provide the best position.

Fig. 13.2 *How the stone should be held in relation to the shaded lamp, so that inclusions can be seen. Stones can also be clarity graded, of course, in suitable daylight.*

Fig. 13.3. *There are many effective ways of holding the stone and lens, but the lens must always be near the eye and the hands touching to hold the stone steady and adjust the focus. Here is one way and another is shown in* Fig. 13.4 *below, taken at the Tel Aviv Diamond Bourse. Still another method is shown in* Fig. 14.17.

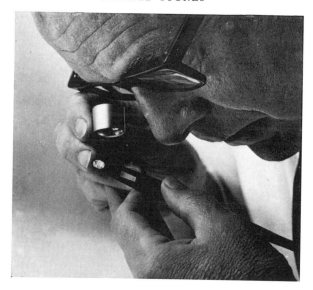

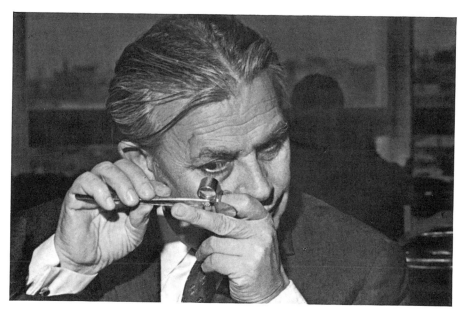

Focusing the Diamond

To keep the stone in focus, rest a finger of the hand holding the lens on the other hand so that both hands are steady together, and stretching or relaxing the finger will provide fine focusing. The method is shown in the illustration, Fig. 13.3 and an alternative in 13.4.

One method of examining a stone internally, is to look into it from the pavilion side. Inclusions will often be reflected a dozen or many more times by facets, which increases the chances considerably of finding them. Having noted any that show up through the pavilion, turn the stone over and examine it systematically through the table, first searching the volume under the table and then going round the volume under the other facets clockwise to make sure none of the stone is missed.

Afterwards – or before, if this is preferred – a similarly systematic study of the surface of the stone, both above and below the girdle and around the girdle itself, should be made. Turn the stone so that light is reflected from the surfaces of the facets, which will show up any naats, polishing lines, missing or extra facets, or damage.

It will be necessary to put down the stone and pick it up again after turning it about 90° in order to make sure that no inclusions or other features were concealed by the tongs. Several rotations will also be necessary when examining the girdle.

The Gemolite Microscope

The Gemological Institute of America advises the clarity grading of diamonds by a binocular microscope magnifying to ten times, preferably with dark field illumination. It supplies such a microscope, rather confusingly named the Gemolite, which provides either dark field or light field illumination and has a special universal holder for the stone (Fig. 13.5).

There is wide field binocular magnification and also a zoom lens, so that a particular inclusion, say, may be examined at a higher magnification. The Gemolite is an excellent instrument and makes the mechanics of grading much easier, but it is expensive in the U.K., and is, of course, not portable. Japanese and German instruments for grading have also been placed on the market.

A standard grading light is available for attachment to the Gemolite so that clarity and colour grading may be carried out with the aid of the instrument.

The zoom feature has led to a practice in certain places of noting the location of very small inclusions at $50 \times$ magnification and then seeing if they can be found by $10 \times$ magnification. Not all the trade accepts this practice.

A Basic Grading System

Anyone, particularly a retailer, handling diamonds, should acquire the habit of looking at them, whether set or unset, with the naked eye to see if inclusions are visible. It is very easy *not* to see inclusions unless the act of looking for them is deliberate.

This first inspection by naked eye is the first act of grading into an upper or a lower class. When inclusions can be seen by the naked eye, the stone falls into the piqué grades or below.

The beginner can look at grading in this way:

Top Grades: Flawless, VVS, and VS can only be identified with a $10 \times$ lens
   If there is any mark under the table, the stone cannot generally be in these grades.

Middle Grade: SI can be identified with a watchmakers' eyeglass.

Lower Grades: Piqué and spotted stones can be identified with practice by the naked eye, but should be graded through a lens, each lower grade becoming more obvious.

Dark-coloured spots downgrade a stone more than light-coloured ones. A spot in the pavilion will often be reflected several times in a stone and this will downgrade it more than a spot in the crown which is not multiplied by reflection.

Unfair Descriptions

There are some expressions that are regarded as unethical in grading polished diamonds, because they are misleading. They include eye-clean, commercially perfect, and 'our very best quality'.

Clean is a term commonly used in the U.K. and exception is not normally

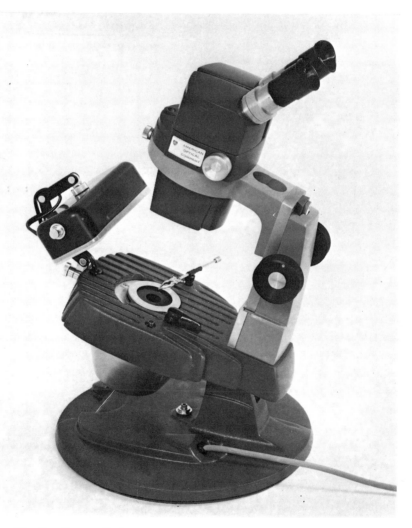

Fig. 13.5.   *The Gemolite, an effective 10 × binocular microscope for diamond grading supplied by the Gemological Institute of America. The diamond is held in the removable clip seen on the stage, under which is dark ground illumination. Over the stage is a colour grading lamp. A zoom lens is incorporated and there are other fittings including a special eyepiece for proportion grading.*

taken to it. It was so abused in the U.S.A., however, that it has been prohibited as a clarity description of diamond by the American Gem Society. The Federal Trade Commission in the U.S.A. allows its use only if the diamond meets the Commission's definition of perfect.

Commercial Grading

There are not as many different grading systems for clarity or purity as there are for colour, but there are many different interpretations of the scales that do exist by different cutters and dealers, and many different names for scales using numbers and letters.

If a diamond is bought from a reputable dealer, it will be a certain price per carat. If another diamond of the same size and quality is bought from another reputable dealer, the price will be in the same region. Comparison of how the different dealers describe the stones may reveal a considerable difference however. One stone might well be described as 'Fine white, clean', and the other as 'Commercial white, slight piqué'. There is no universally accepted standard of grading.

The same problem occurs with clarity as with colour grading, i.e. that Nature does not provide convenient steps into which one can classify inclusions. For example, a spot under the table would grade the stone lower than one at the edge, but suppose the spot is between the table and the edge, at what point is the stone downgraded? The grader is always having to make borderline decisions like this, and the more divisions into grades the more borderline cases occur.

It is obvious therefore that disputable classifications occur and that within any category there are better and less good qualities, so that a picking price is usually charged as described on page 204.

Grading Scales

The N.A.G.* Code of Trading requires a stone described as Internally Flawless to be completely transparent and free from internal inclusions when examined by a skilled observer with normal or corrected to normal vision in daylight or its equivalent with a ten-power lens corrected for chromatic and spherical aberration. To be claimed as Flawless it must also be free from surface marks.

The broad scale of clarity used by the Gemological Institute of America is given opposite and compared with one commonly employed in the U.K. In most gem diamond classes in Europe, the American scale or a version of it is used, but the diamond trade employs its own grading systems.

The Scandinavians have included in their recommended scale a grade between Flawless and VVS to accommodate stones with slight marks on the surface only that can be made Flawless. The grade is called Internally Flawless, and has been included opposite.

The Americans and Scandinavians have divided each of the VVS, VS, and SI grades into two for larger stones, of over half a carat. It is very difficult to grade small stones into such fine categories, and also rather fruitless as far as

---

* National Association of Goldsmiths, London, E.C.2.

price is concerned. As the size increases, however, from about half a carat upwards it becomes less and less difficult to make these finer gradings.

In general, grading of such accuracy is only necessary with larger stones of higher quality and value. Even then, the market is likely to operate more powerfully as an influence on price of exceptional goods than the grading system, to judge by the range of price asked for and obtained in private and auction sales.

The scales shown are roughly equivalent:

A Scale Commonly Used in the U.K.	Scandinavian Diamond Nomenclature	Gemological Institute of America Scale
Flawless (clean)	FL	FL
	IF (Internally Flawless)	
VVS	VVS$_1$	VVS$_1$
	VVS$_2$	VVS$_2$
VS	VS$_1$	VS$_1$
	VS$_2$	VS$_2$
SI	SI$_1$	SI$_1$
	SI$_2$	SI$_2$
1st Piqué	1st Piqué	I$_1$ (Imperfect)
2nd Piqué		
3rd Piqué	2nd Piqué	I$_2$
Spotted	3rd Piqué	I$_3$
Heavy Spotted		
Rejection		

Grading Examples

Examples of inclusions and blemishes in polished diamonds and how they are graded are shown in Figs. 13.7 to 13.24. These refer to stones of half a carat and over.

Clarity grading depends upon:
1. Inclusions within the stone.
2. Surface damage.
4. Certain minor imperfections of make.

The third category requires some explanation, because make – the nearness of the cutting to the ideal proportions – is a separate consideration when estimating the quality of a cut stone. Sometimes a cutter will add a very tiny extra facet (Fig. 13.6) at a junction of facets to remove a tiny part of the original crystal skin or a tiny flaw in the crystal. The facet will not affect the make, because it makes no difference to main angles or proportions. Very small extra facets do not down-grade the diamond in the clarity scale, although larger ones do so.

The size of the polished diamond must also be considered when grading for clarity. It is obviously a waste of time grading small diamonds with great accuracy because there is not enough price difference to make it worth while. It must never be forgotten that the purpose of all grading is commercial. Generally,

223

Fig. 13.6. *Very small extra facet on the front of a stone, the result of removing a tiny blemish.*

stones below 0·50 ct. will be graded into fewer classifications than larger ones because their values are less.

Criteria for Grading

Some examples of the maximum allowable blemishes are shown below as a general guide. The grades given are commonly used in the U.K. but the Scandinavian IF has been included.

Maximum Allowable Blemishes Only Just Visible with 10 × Lens

Flawless	Internal growth lines that show no colour from the front of the stone. Minor natural (skin left after bruting) on girdle. Minor roughness of girdle. Very small extra facet not visible from front which does not flatten girdle.
VVS (IF – Internally Flawless)	As above with the addition of minor nicks or pits not in the table, girdle roughness, and slight facet abrasion, all of which may be removed by simple diamond polishing.

Very difficult to find with 10 × Lens

VVS	Internal very tiny spot or group of externally small spots outside the table. Very tiny crystal under facet edge, tiny feather not visible from the top of the stone. Externally, minor naturals on the girdle, minor pits and scratches not in the table. Slightly rough facet edges. Slight bearding of the girdle not visible from the front. Very slight abrasion of the culet. Slightly larger extra facet.

Difficult to find with 10 × Lens

VS   Internal growth lines that show slight colour from the front. Small cleavages not under the table. Small colourless crystals not under the table. Surface scratches. Indented naturals on the girdle. Some general abrasion. Bearding of girdle. Abraded culet. Slightly larger extra facet.

Just Visible with Watchmaker's Eyeglass

SI   Group of pinpoints not under centre of table. Fissure under a facet edge. Colourless crystals outside table. Slight cloudy areas. Rough culet. Nick in girdle. Slightly larger extra facet.

Only Just Visible to the Naked Eye

1st Piqué   Slight visible cloud (fluorescent) under table. Dark crystal not under table. Colourless reflecting crystal under table. Cleavage visible from the front. Small cracks from girdle. Externally, small indentation of table. Rough girdle. Larger extra facets.

More Easily Visible to Naked Eye

2nd to 3rd Piqué   Internal butterfly not under table. Group of dark spots under table. Dark cloud under table. Feather under table. Longish coloured cleavage not under table. Externally more scratches and abrasion. More abraded culet. Larger extra facets.

Easily Visible to Naked Eye

Spotted   Internal butterfly under table. Fair sized dark inclusion or group of spots under table. Coloured cleavage reaching under table. Cloudy areas reaching under table. Externally, scratch on table, more abrasion. Larger indented naturals.

Very Easily Visible to Naked Eye

Heavy Spotted   Internal large or very numerous dark spots under table. Large areas of colourless crystals under table. Coloured cleavage under table. Externally, deeper scratches on table. Broken culet. Natural near girdle. Flat on girdle. Large extra facets.

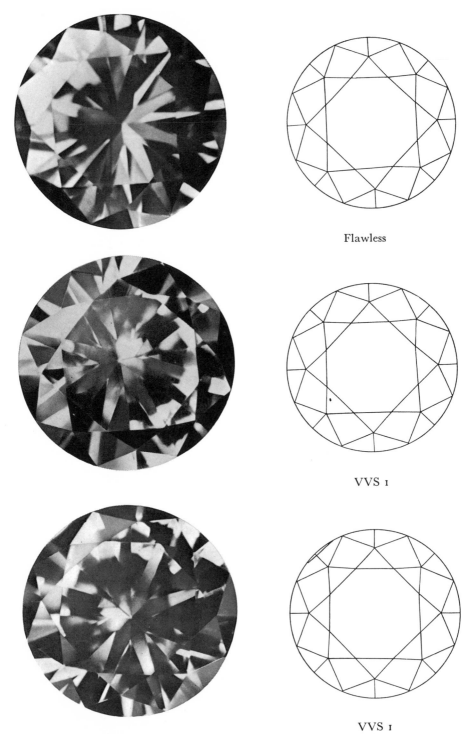

Flawless

VVS 1

VVS 1

Fig. 13.7. to 13.24.   *Examples of clarity grading.*

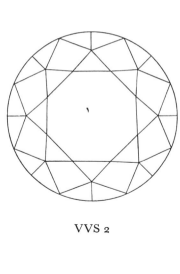

VVS 2

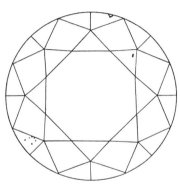

VVS 2

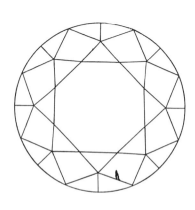

VS1

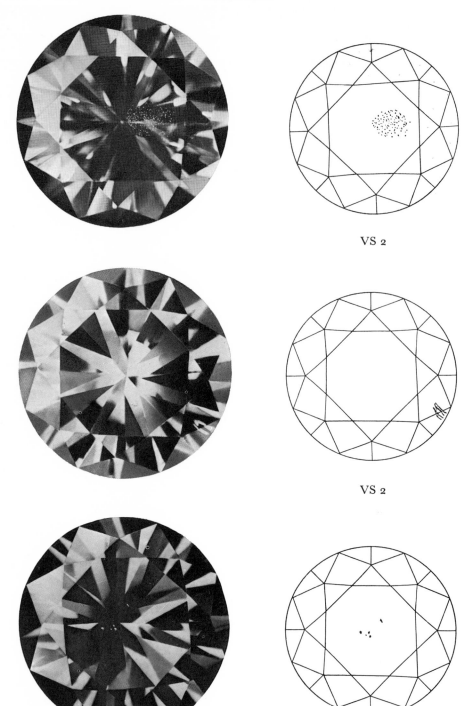

VS 2

VS 2

SI

1st piqué

1st piqué

2nd piqué

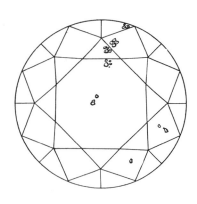

2nd piqué

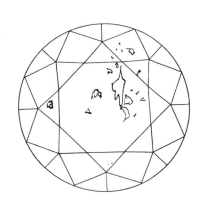

3rd piqué

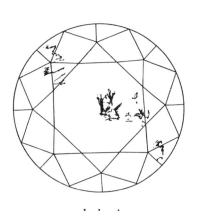

3rd piqué

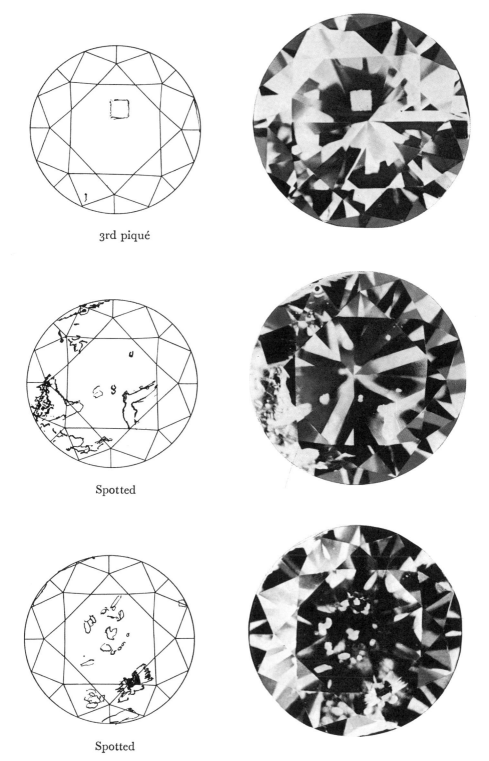

3rd piqué

Spotted

Spotted

Heavy spotted

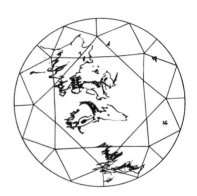

Heavy spotted

Heavy spotted

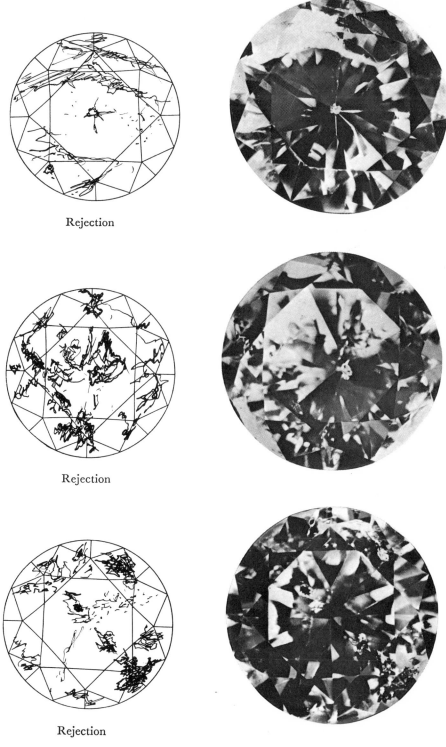

Rejection

Rejection

Rejection

Fig. 13.25. *A feather* (top right) *and butterfly* (above, centre), *as seen through a 10 × lens.*

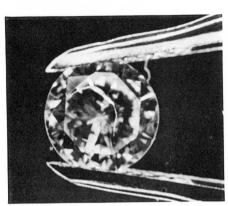

Fig. 13.26 *Crack under the table.*

Fig. 13.27. *Cracks inside the pavilion.*

'Carbon Spots'

An inclusion that diminishes quality may vary from the tiniest spot which is black or white and only just possible to find with a 10 × lens, to masses of coke-like inclusions and cleavages that can instantly be seen with the naked eye.

For fine grading of top quality larger stones, it is very important to study inclusions by light from the sides of the stone to give a dark field effect or to use if possible proper dark field illumination, otherwise it is impossible to know whether some inclusions are transparent or opaque. All look black if light is passed through the stone (transmitted light). From this fact arose the incorrect belief that all inclusions were black 'carbon spots'. Very few, if any, are carbon and only a few are truly black.

Types of Internal Blemishes

Inclusions and other blemishes usually fall into the following categories:

1. *Solid inclusion,* which may be black or white and vary from a pin point to a large mass.
2. *Bubble,* which is transparent and roundish and may be very tiny to fairly large.

234

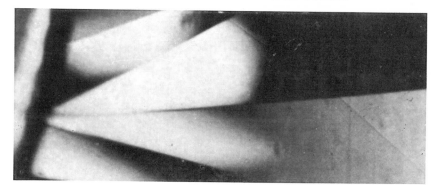

Fig. 13.28.   *Naats showing as a result of polishing.*

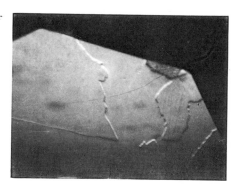

Fig. 13.29.   *Naats on the surface of a polished stone.*

3. *Cloud*, which is a group of very tiny transparent bubbles or inclusions too small to be seen individually but gives a clouded appearance.
4. *Feather*, or *glets* (the Dutch name), a cleavage crack that looks like a feather when viewed flat on (Fig. 13.25).
5. *Butterfly*, an inclusion with cleavage cracks around it, that from some directions look like the wings of a butterfly (Fig. 13.25).
6. *Crack*, a fracture in a non-cleavage direction (Fig. 13.26).
7. *Knot* or *naat* (the Dutch name), twinning which although usually visible externally may also be visible if internal, if the twinned area is a different colour from the rest of the diamond. It is usually a minor feature, but may be more serious Figs. 13.28 and 13.29.
8. *Fezels*, shallow, white, whispy inclusions in a twinning plane, similar to those in Fig. 17.37.

External Features

For a diamond to be regarded as flawless, it must be free of external blemishes as well as being clean internally. There is one exception to this rule. As already mentioned, a small natural on the girdle is not regarded as an external flaw by some top graders, unless the girdle is polished. It does not cause loss in brilliancy if it does not flatten the girdle and is no wider than the girdle.

The main external blemishes are:

Fig. 13.30. *Bearding around a girdle which may be slight enough to be almost invisible, or fairly obvious.*

1. *Scratches.*
2. *Chips* and *nicks.*
3. *Pits* or *cavities.*
4. *Flats* on the girdle.
5. *Naats* on the surface.
6. *Polishing lines.*
7. *Burn marks* caused during polishing.
8. *Naturals* or *naif* (the Dutch name) near the girdle (Figs. 13.31 and 13.32).
9. *Bearded girdle* (Fig. 13-30).

Surface Damage on Cut Diamonds

Abrasions and scratches on the surfaces of cut diamonds are caused by contact with other diamonds. Under a lens, the defects look like white lines. Although a scratch on a facet may appear straight and sharp, magnification will show the edges to be rough. Normally such scratches are very shallow. Sometimes the edges of facets have become abraded by rough contact with other diamonds and

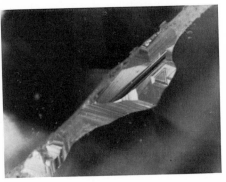

Fig. 13.31. *Natural on a girdle large enough to be a blemish.* Right: *Magnified view of a natural.*

236

may also be nicked. The culet may also be damaged by abrasion or by chipping.

As carrying two or more cut stones loose in a diamond paper caues sthe damage described, the stones are often referred to as paper worn or paper marked. Cut stones should always be carried in separate papers. If they are small, several can be carried between a folded piece of lint in the paper. Using lint is a sensible protection for all valuable stones.

Chips usually occur on girdles, but may be seen on facet edges. They are often conchoidal fractures caused by light blows. Impact from a hard pointed article can cause cleavage marks on the surface of a stone. These marks are normally square or hexagonal (according to whether the piece removed was in the direction of the cubic or dodecahedral plane). Damage to a stone caused by impact usually shows signs of both fracture and cleavage, which occur together in a roughly stepped formation.

A fissure in the surface of a stone will have been caused by a cleavage crack extending to the surface.

Naats usually show as pits in the surface. A pit, or in more extreme cases, a cavity, may have been caused by a naat being pulled out of the surface while polishing. A naat on the surface will stand up as a slightly raised plane with straight edges because of its different hardness when the stone was being polished. (Fig. 13.29), just like a knot in a piece of sandpapered wood.

Other Surface Features

Polishing lines are seen as a series of close parallel lines on the surface of a facet and may be the result of a facet having been ground and by accident not polished, by careless polishing, or by the facet having been forced by trying to grind it in a hard direction, i.e. with the grain. (Fig. 13.33). One result in this case will be burn marks.

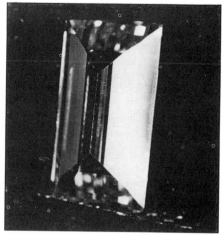

Fig. 13.32. *Exceptionally large natural on the pavilion.*

Fig. 13.33. *Polishing lines on a facet.*

Bearded girdles are more strictly an internal fault, but are included with the external ones because they are, like most external faults, induced in some way. They are in fact caused by over zealous bruting during the manufacturing process, which causes a series of fine hair-like cracks extending a short distance radially into the stone from the girdle, as shown in Fig. 13.30. Such fuzzy girdles also lack the normal waxy finish because bruting has been carried out too rapidly.

CHAPTER FOURTEEN

Grading Polished Diamonds for Cut Weighing and Weight Estimating

Brilliant-cut Proportions

An accurately proportioned stone, as shown in Fig. 10.18, will attract the highest price per carat. When the diamond is cut to gain weight, or spread to make it look larger than it is, it may be too deep or too shallow above or below the girdle, or the table may be too wide in proportion to the total diameter of the stone. The price per carat will be lower.

At the bottom of the price scale are the badly-cut stones, which may be unsymmetrical, out-of-round, have irregular tables, or misplaced facets, the table out of square, the culet not central, too large a culet, etc. Some examples are shown in Figs. 14 and 14.2. Visual inspection of the outside of the diamond with a 10 × lens will instantly show whether a stone is really badly cut and often examination with the naked eye is sufficient.

The Make

Some cutters stake their reputations on always guaranteeing a good make, i.e. they always stick to certain proportions. Makes vary considerably and it is possible to identify the origin of some brilliant cuts by their make. The diamond trade all over the world makes its estimate of the quality of the make of a stone simply by eye, using a lens.

If the stone is unmounted, it is easy to examine for proportion. If mounted, a little guesswork is inevitable as damage or bad cutting could be concealed by the claws or mounting, but it is still relatively easy to estimate the quality of the make, unlike estimating the colour.

The general proportions of a brilliant-cut stone are based on the full diameter across the girdle. From this can be estimated (1) The diameter of the table as a percentage of the full diameter, (2) The height of the crown, (3) The depth of the pavilion, and (4) The thickness of the girdle. These proportions are listed exactly in Chapter Ten.

Spread Table

When the table is spread, i.e. made too large in relation to the diameter of the stone, the thickness of the crown is necessarily reduced, as indicated in Fig. 14.1, although the angles may well remain absolutely correct. A shallow crown and wide table mean smaller crown facets and less display of prismatic colours because the crown facets are mostly responsible for such fire. Although a shallow table may suggest that the cutter has lost weight, in fact he has gained it, by

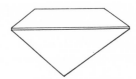

Fig. 14.1. *Sloping table; out-of-centre culet; and overdepth pavilion with correct angles; thin crown (spread stone).*

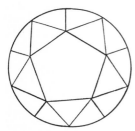
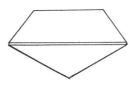
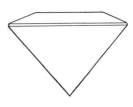

Fig. 14.2. *Assymetrical cutting; crown deep with shallow pavilion; and pavilion overdepth with wrong angles; thin crown.*

making the diamond of larger diameter than would be possible with ideal proportions (Fig. 11.1).

When the crown is thin, the pavilion appears to be over-depth, but in relation to the diameter of the stone, it is quite likely to be reasonably correct. An over-deep pavilion is caused by the pavilion angles being made too great, more than the ideal of about 40° and nearer the 55° of a natural octahedral crystal.

A simple way of gauging the table size in relation to the diameter of the stone has been suggested. The table with the star facets comprises two squares superimposed on each other at 90° as shown in Fig. 14.3. It is said that, if the sides are square, the table is about 60 per cent, and if they are concave or convex, the table is less than or greater than 60 per cent. This is only true, however, if the bezel facets reach half way up the bezel.

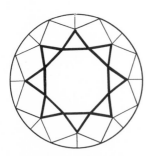
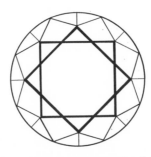

Fig. 14.3. *If the star facets reach half way across the bezel (centre diagram) a stone with a 60 per cent table appears as shown. Those with smaller and larger tables are as on the left and right.*

Fig. 14.4. *Reflec-tion of the table in the table of an ac-curately angled bril-liant.*

Fig. 14.5. *Fish eye stone with shallow pavilion.*

Fig. 14.6. *Dark-centred or lumpy stone with an over-angled pavilion.*

Judging Pavilion Depths

To be able to judge by eye whether or not the pavilion of a stone is over or under depth is not difficult to acquire with practice because it can be done by using reflections in the table, looking direct at the table.

In the centre of the table of a correctly-proportioned stone, viewed by eye or through a lens, it should be possible to see a bright image of the table, caused by reflections from the pavilion facets. The depth of the pavilion of this stone is just about 43 per cent of the diameter of the diamond. If the table is about the correct proportion the reflection of it (Fig. 14.4) should be from a third to a half the width of the table itself.

Fig. 14.5 illustrates a diamond which is too shallow below the girdle. A circular reflection will be seen near the edges of the table. It is a reflection of the girdle of the stone and in the diamond trade is known as a fisheye, or cod's eye.

If the pavilion is too deep, the stone is known as lumpy. In such stones, there are large black reflections in the centre of the table as shown in Fig. 14.6, and the stones are described in the trade as dark-centred or black-centred. The deeper the pavilion over the ideal 40 per cent, the blacker will be this reflection.

Facet Proportions

Next look at the pavilion from the side. Modern practice is for the lower girdle facets to be made long, to the proportions shown in Fig. 10.4. When the round brilliant-cut was introduced before the First World War and until after the Second World War, the lower bezel facets were usually no more than half the length of the pavilion, as shown in Fig. 10.4.

Girdle and Culet

The girdle should not be knife-edged, which encourages chipping, in its thinnest parts, neither should it be too thick. (Figs. 14.7 and 14.8). Practice makes estimation of girdle proportion relatively simple. Ideal proportions for different sizes of stones used in the U.S.A., are given on page 244. One cannot measure these without an optical instrument, and there is little point in doing so when judgement by eye is effective. The girdle should be as shown in Fig. 10.18, and the thickness is about the same for stones from about fifteen points up, however big. It should, of course, be even all round and not thicker one side than the other.

There may be small naturals on the girdle, but these are not considered as cutting flaws unless they extend over a facet.

The culet should also be examined directly or through the table if it is not accessible. Too big a culet mars the appearance of the modern brilliant cut from the front. A closed culet, i.e. where the pavilion comes to a point, is likely to lead to breakage of the point, which also mars the appearance. The ideal is for the culet to be just identifiable as having a very, very small facet. On old styles of make, it was common for the culet to be large.

Fig. 14.7. *A very thick girdle, made to save weight.*

Polish

All the facets should be highly polished. Colour interference, like oil on a puddle of rain, can sometimes be noticed under a lens on a well-finished facet. Very occasionally a stone is seen where the brillianteerer has missed finishing a facet. (Fig. 14.9.) The facets should also be correctly shaped.

Occasionally extra facets are added to remove a poor part or damaged part of the crystal. When extra facets are relatively large, they downgrade the make, but when very small they are acceptable as already noted.

The Proportionscope

In 1967, the Gemological Institute of America introduced an optical comparator for rapid checking of the proportions of a brilliant. It is called the Proportionscope and will handle stones from about 0·18 to 1·30 and from about 1·21 to over 8 carats on one or other of its two screens. A magnified shadow of the stone is thrown on a line diagram of the correct proportions on the screen, as shown in Fig. 14.10. A scaled eye-piece and stone holder are also available for the Gemolite. They are much lower in price and in some respects superior to the Proportionscope.

The ideal proportions are modified from the earlier Tolkowsky figures. Some tolerances are permitted, for example, the correct table proportion is 53 per cent, but tables from 53 to 57 per cent are allowed. Similarly although 16·2 per cent is considered ideal for the height of the crown, the range acceptable is 15·1 to 16·5. For the pavilion depth, ideal 43·1, a figure between 42·9 and 43·3 is permitted before quality and therefore price begins to suffer.

It is notable that a stone cut to acceptable European proportions would be downgraded by the Proportionscope.

The G.I.A. gives these percentages of stone diameter as reasonable for the girdle:

Fig 14.8. *A thin girdle which is liable to chipping.*

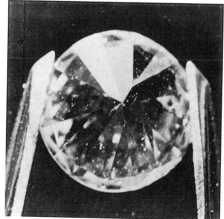

Fig. 14.9. *Some lower girdle facets have been missed when cutting this stone.*

Up to 0·40 carat	.	.	.	up to 3·00 per cent.
0·41 to 0·80 carat	.		.	2·0 to 2·5 per cent.
0·81 to 1·50 carat	.	.		1·5 to 1·75 per cent.
1·51 to 3·00 carat	.	.	.	1·25 to 1·75 per cent.
3·10 carats upwards	.	.	.	1·0 to 1·5 per cent.

Make and Price

Up to now the quality of cut has been the least important factor in deciding price, compared with the weight, colour and clarity. The importance of good proportion in relation to price per carat depends to a considerable extent on the market. In some countries, more than others, buyers are very conscious of make in larger fine diamonds. At present, the U.S.A. is the most proportion-conscious market. Good make has a much bigger influence on the price of top-quality stones than on lower-quality ones in any market.

Fig. 14.10. *The G.I.A. Proportionscope with the shadow of a diamond under test on the scaled screen.*

244

It is difficult to state exactly what the relationship is. If a stone of fine quality is cut to correct proportions, and another of equal quality is cut to poor proportions, with a deep pavilion and thin crown, say, the price difference could be calculated by estimating the weight that would be lost by recutting the poorly made stone, then mentally repricing it at the lower price per carat, because of its reduced weight, and adding the cost of cutting. This estimated value could be as low as 60 per cent of that of the well-made stone of the same top quality.

As a very general rule of thumb, it can be said that the price of a stone of very fine colour, which is flawless and of excellent make, would fall to about 90 per cent if the cut were just good, i.e. if some of the proportions were just off the ideal, causing the stone to lose some brilliance. If the cut were only fair, as for example when the table is too large, the price could be down to 80 per cent. A poorly-cut stone which is lumpy or a fisheye, would bring the price down to 60 per cent or less.

Weights of Diamond

The previous chapters plus the first part of this one have described the estimation of three factors in gauging the value of a diamond, the colour, the clarity, and the cut. The fourth, the carat weight, is the final factor, and is often the most important.

Early Measures

One of the first owners of the Koh-i-Nûr diamond, Sultan Barbar, gave its weight as about eight *mishkals* and described the *mishkal* as equalling 40 *ratis*. Other records give different values for the *rati*. The Indians had another weight between the two, the *mangeli*, which seems to have been much nearer the *rati* than the *mishkal*.

Before the days of standardized weights, merchants had to rely on natural objects that were fairly common. Dried seeds were most favoured for small weights, especially if they did not much vary in weight from seed to seed. The dried grain of wheat, simply known as the grain, was common, and so was the dried seed of the Carob tree, called the carat.

The Grain

The grain was employed at an early time for measuring the weight of pearls and also of diamonds. It was lighter than the carat, and is now considered to be 50 milligrams or a quarter of a metric carat. The grain became the unit of comparison between the Avoirdupois general system of weights and the Troy system for precious metals in the United Kingdom. One ounce Troy is 480 grains and one ounce Avoir equals $437\frac{1}{2}$ grains. A gram equals 15·432349 grains.

Grains are not now a legal weight for gemstones in the U.K., but the pearl trade still refers to weights in grains and the diamond trade occasionally refers to grains as a general indication of size, in the expressions a grainer, a three-grainer, a six-grainer and so on, for diamonds of about 0·25, 0·75, and 1·50 carat and so on.

245

The Carat Weight

Diamonds (and other gemstones) are normally measured by the very old unit of weight, the carat. In the U.K. in 1969 it became legal only for gemstones' weights to be described in carats. The carat weight was originally the seed of a tree that is common in the Middle East, the locust tree or Carob tree (*ceratonia siliqua*). Its fruit is an almost black bean (Fig. 14.11). Inside the pod is a sweet syrup and many small seeds. The ancient pearl merchants of the Middle East discovered that the seeds when dried were exceedingly uniform in weight and adopted them as units of weight for pearls.

The word carat comes from the Greek name for the tree, *keration*, meaning little horn, which its bean pod resembles. Incidentally, it was the syrup from these locust beans that John the Baptist probably ate in the Wilderness, not the flying grasshoppers called locusts.

As commerce in gems increased, various countries standardized the carat in relation to their own units of weight, which varied. A London carat was therefore different from a Venice carat and both were different from a Madras carat. Early in the twentieth century, various countries agreed to accept an international standard metric carat, which was one-fifth or 0·2 of a gram, and to express weights in decimals instead of the old fractions of 64ths, when a weight was shown as, say, $12\frac{36}{64}$ carat. This is the system used for diamonds and other gems.

The weight of a polished diamond of one and a quarter carats is expressed as: 1·25 ct. When a stone is less than a carat the weight is shown correctly in this way: 0·25 ct., 0·30 ct., 0·05 ct. To avoid confusion, a zero should be placed before the point and two digits are always shown after it. It is common practice

Fig. 14.11.   *Carob beans and their seeds, originally used as 'carat' weights.*

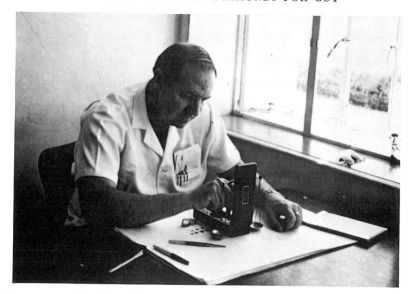

Fig. 14.12.   *Mr. Trevor Urry, a South African licenced diamond buyer, using portable scales in his Maseru office.* See also Fig. 7.6.

to call the hundredths 'points' so the three weights just given are referred to as twenty-five points, thirty points, and five points.

When polished stones are much smaller than a carat in weight, they are commonly referred to as so many to the carat, instead of being so many points each. Since there are always small variations from stone to stone, it is more accurate to refer to a parcel of small stones in the first way. Polished stones may therefore be, say, five to the carat, or even as small as four hundred to the carat.

Weighing Loose Stones

The only problem in weighing loose stones today is that of accuracy. The traditional diamond scales are a simple form of pan balance as shown in Fig. 14.12, which folds up and is packed with the weights in a small wooden box. They are used by holding them by hand in the air or by mounting them on the opened box. Such scales have been in use for centuries and are still used today by merchants in many parts of the world and particularly by diamond buyers at the mines, where accuracy in weighing crystals is not as important as in weighing polished stones. Diamond scales are of most value to the dealer who has to travel to places where there is no Diamond Club or Diamond Bourse and a more accurate balance is not available. With them, it is very difficult to be accurate to a hundredth of a carat.

Many jewellers and gemmologists employ a simple chemical balance of the type shown in Fig. 14.13 for weighing gems. With great care it is possible to be accurate to about a point.

Diamond merchants use a more sophisticated balance which can be operated

Fig. 14.13. *Chemical balance used by jewellers for weighing gems.*

Fig. 14.14. *The Oertling diamond balance.*

Fig. 14.15. *Plastics hole gauges must be used with caution. The stone in the 1 carat holes is actually 0.88 ct. Fig. 16.14 (below) is a metal gauge.*

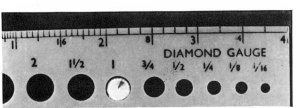

from outside its enclosing case and indicates the points on an illuminated scale. An example is the Oertling diamond balance in Fig. 14.14. The stone is placed in the left-hand pan. If it is less than a carat, the weight is shown on the illuminated scale in the centre of the base. If it is between 1 and 100 carats, the extra units are added by weights that are dropped on the beam by an outside control, or added to, the right-hand pan. The scales indicate to 0·01 carat and are easily zeroed.

The Mettler diamond balance is one of the most sophisticated, needing no weights.

Estimating Weight by Hole Gauge

When a diamond is mounted, there are problems in making an accurate evaluation of its weight. The only way is to measure the stone, visually inspect it for proportion, and make an estimate of its weight from its dimensions. The simple diamond hole gauge (Fig. 14.15) is most commonly employed for this purpose to give an instant reading of the weight. In the hands of extremely few highly experienced jewellers it is surprisingly accurate. In the hands of most people, it is frequently as much as 20 per cent wrong.

For brilliant-cut diamonds, the gauge holes correspond to the diameters of ideally-cut diamonds of increasing weights. The gauge takes no account of the fact that some diamonds are lumpy and that others are fisheyes. Allowance has to be made from experience. It is often difficult, owing to the setting of a stone, to make an accurate gauging, i.e. to match the hole exactly to the outside diameter of the diamond.

The hole gauge has its uses as a rough guide, but valuations of costly stones should never be made on its evidence. A high quality diamond may be worth £800 a carat, which is £8 a point. With a ring gauge one can be 20 points out, a difference in the valuation of more than £160 if the estimate of weight is too

Fig. 14.17. *One plate from a diamond sieve is in the foreground. Sieve plates fit into a barrel.*
See Fig. 8.1.

high, and much more than £160 if the estimation of weight is too low, because
the price per carat varies with the size of the stone.

The Sieve
A form of hole gauge, a steel plate with a grid of accurate holes in it, is used by
diamond manufacturers and dealers for sorting quantities of polished stones. It
is used as a sieve in conjunction with other gauges with smaller and larger holes,
to divide stones into plus and minus size (and therefore weight) groups (Fig.
14.17).

The Moe Gauge
A simple caliper gauge, known as the Moe gauge, is made to take into account
the depth as well as the diameter of a diamond of which the weight is being

estimated (Fig. 14.18). After these dimensions have been taken, a table is referred to and the weight obtained. The Moe gauge is a big improvement on the ring gauge, but some models available are not easy to read accurately as the scale is stamped in the metal for cheapness, which nullifies some of the advantage. It is possible to estimate weights within, say, 5 per cent using a well-made Moe gauge, or closer with experience. The tables are easier to use than those for the Leveridge gauge.

The Leveridge Gauge

One of the more accurate diamond gauges is the A. D. Leveridge mm. diamond gauge and estimator, invented in 1937 by an American of that name and now made for his company in Switzerland. The gauge, shown in Fig. 14.19, is a precision instrument and shows sizes in millimetres on a dial. It has jaws to

Fig. 14.18. *A version of the Moe gauge for mounted diamonds.*

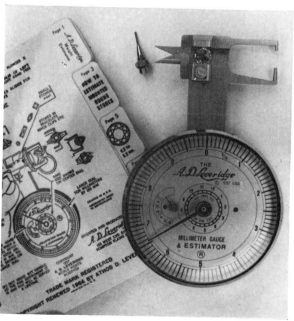

Fig. 14.19. *The Leveridge gauge and tables for mounted stones. A loose stone is between two of the jaws. The pointed piece is to fit to the caliper jaws for deep set stones.*

measure the dimensions of stones in almost every type of setting likely to be encountered. The tables provided with the gauge are calculated for diamonds of almost all cuts. Moreover, they can also be used for other gems by a simple calculation to allow for the different specific gravities.

The tables provided are calculated for mêlée of 0·25 carat down to 0·02 ct. brilliant cut, and from 30 to 240 stones a carat eight-cut, both of which are gauged for diameter only. For larger brilliant-cut stones from 17 points to 7·50 carats, there are tables by diameter, each with a series of depths for stones with thick and thin girdles. Similar tables are provided for other cuts. It is possible to gauge within about 2 per cent of the true weight of larger stones and also to make allowance for ovality. Other tables give weights for gauged marquise, pear, emerald, and square cuts, even baguettes.

More accurate gauges of other makes measuring to 0·01 m.m. are also available.

An unusual gauge shows actual colourless brilliant-cut synthetic spinels of equivalent diamond weights, for direct comparison with diamonds that are set and perhaps cannot be gauged another way (Fig. 14.20). It is particularly useful for demonstrating the visual appearance of a diamond of a particular weight without the problem of obtaining the diamond.

Weight by Calculation

P. Grodzinski suggested a formula that gives the weight of a brilliant-cut diamond in relation to its diameter (d) in millimetres to an accuracy of 5 per cent.

$$\frac{d^3}{6·42} = \text{weight in carats.}$$

B. W. Anderson gives a more accurate formula that includes depth, for the use of those with a millimetre gauge but no tables. Measure the diameter (d) and height (h) in *centimetres* and:

$$6hd^2 = \text{weight in carats.}$$

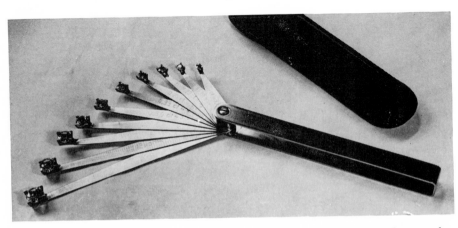

Fig. 14.20. *A comparison gauge for mounted stones. Brilliant cut synthetic spinels are made to the dimensions of different weights of diamond.*

Leveridge also gives a formula, for larger round brilliant cuts over 12 mm in diameter, that takes into account the height (h) as well as the radius (r) in millimetres:

$$0.0245 \, hr^2 = \text{weight in carats.}$$

This table is based on one calculated by P. Grodzinski. The diameters and depths are shown to two places of decimals as, in practice, it is just possible to estimate to a tenth of a millimetre with a good millimetre dial gauge. Grodzinski's formula for diameter only, tends to exaggerate the weights of larger stones.

APPROXIMATE SIZES OF BRILLIANT-CUT DIAMONDS

Average diameter in mm.	Weight of brilliant in carats	Average height in mm.
1·38	0·01	0·78
1·74	0·02	0·98
2·37	0·05	1·33
2·98	0·10	1·67
4·04	0·25	2·26
5·09	0·50	2·85
5·83	0·75	3·27
6·42	1·00	3·60
6·91	1·25	3·88
7·35	1·50	4·12
7·74	1·75	4·33
8·09	2·00	4·54
8·71	2·50	4·88
9·25	3·00	5·19
9·76	3·50	5·47
10·19	4·00	5·72
10·60	4·50	5·95
10·98	5·00	6·16
11·33	5·50	6·37
11·67	6·00	6·55

Small Diamonds

Small diamonds of below about 2mm. diameter (30 per carat) are often eight-cut instead of brilliant cut when the quality is lower. The weights of these can be calculated by Grodzinski's formula with 5 per cent added.

Weight of Crystals

B. W. Anderson gives a formula for estimating the weight of octahedral diamond crystals which is useful to prospectors and buyers in the field with only a millimetre gauge available. If the side(s) of a regular octahedron is measured in centimetres:

$$8.29s^3 = \text{weight in carats.}$$

SIZES AND WEIGHTS OF MELEE

Eight-Cut		Brilliant-Cut	
Stones per carat	Diameter in mm.	Stones per carat	Weight in carat
240	0·9	—	—
200	1·0	—	—
155	1·1	—	—
125	1·2	—	—
100	1·3	—	—
85	1·4	100	0·01
73	1·5	80	—
58	1·6	60	—
48	1·7	50	0·02
40	1·8	40	—
33	1·9	36	—
30	2·0	33	0·33
	2·1	29	—
	2·2	25	0·04
	2·3	22	—
	2·4	20	0·05
	2·5	18	—
	2·6	16	0·06
	2·7	14	0·07
	2·8	12	0·08
	2·9	11	0·09
	3·0		0·10
	3·1		0·11
	3·2		0·12+
	3·3		0·14
	3·4		0·15
	3·5		0·16
	3·6		0·17
	3·7		0·18
	3·8		0·20
	3·9		0·22
	4·0		0·25

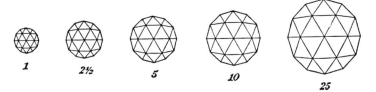

1   2½   5   10   25

Fig. 14.21.   *Approximate sizes of Dutch rose cut diamonds.*

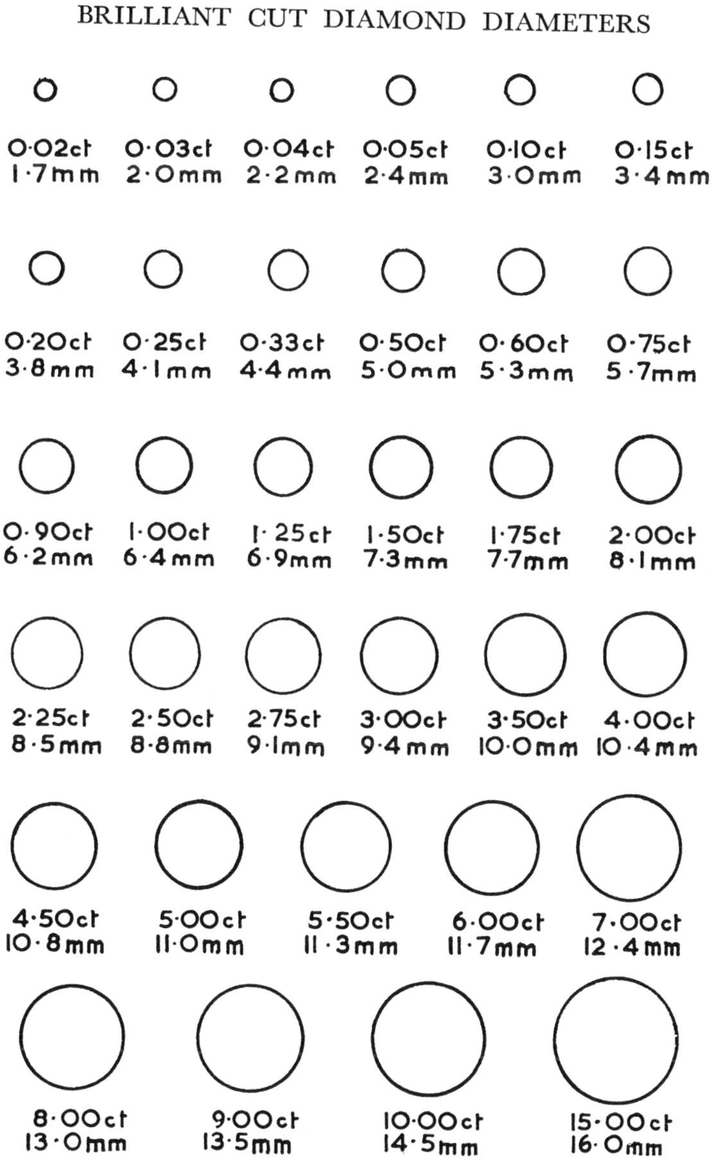

BRILLIANT CUT DIAMOND DIAMETERS

OLD MINERS							

Ct.

Ct.							
0·25		O·02ct 1·7mm	O·03ct 2·0mm	O·04ct 2·2mm	O·05ct 2·4mm	O·10ct 3·0mm	O·15ct 3·4mm
0·50							
0·75							
1·00		O·20ct 3·8mm	O·25ct 4·1mm	O·33ct 4·4mm	O·50ct 5·0mm	O·60ct 5·3mm	O·75ct 5·7mm
1·25							
1·50		O·90ct 6·2mm	1·00ct 6·4mm	1·25ct 6·9mm	1·50ct 7·3mm	1·75ct 7·7mm	2·00ct 8·1mm
1·75							
2·00		2·25ct 8·5mm	2·50ct 8·8mm	2·75ct 9·1mm	3·00ct 9·4mm	3·50ct 10·0mm	4·00ct 10·4mm
2·25							
2·50		4·50ct 10·8mm	5·00ct 11·0mm	5·50ct 11·3mm	6·00ct 11·7mm	7·00ct 12·4mm	
2·75							
3·00		8·00ct 13·0mm	9·00ct 13·5mm	10·00ct 14·5mm	15·00ct 16·0mm		

Fig. 14.22. *The* inside *diameter of the circles give approximate diamond diameters.*

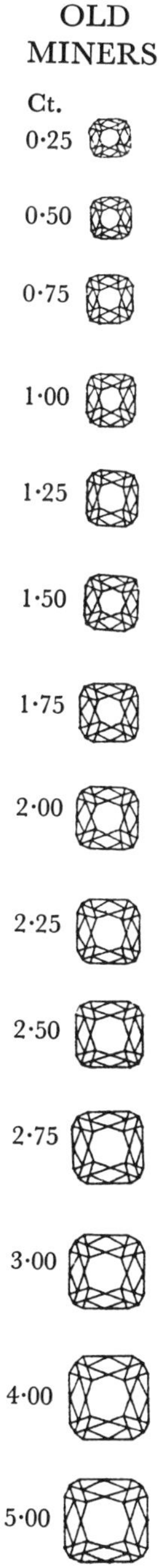

4·00	
5·00	

Fig. 14.23. *Approximate sizes of old mine cut stones.*

SIZES IN CARATS

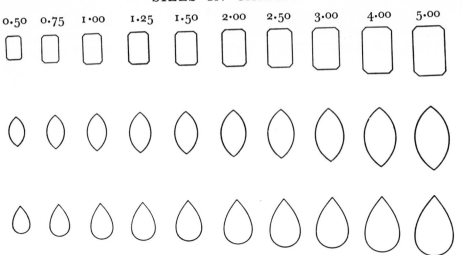

Fig. 14.24. *Approximate sizes of emerald, marquise, and pear-shaped diamonds.*

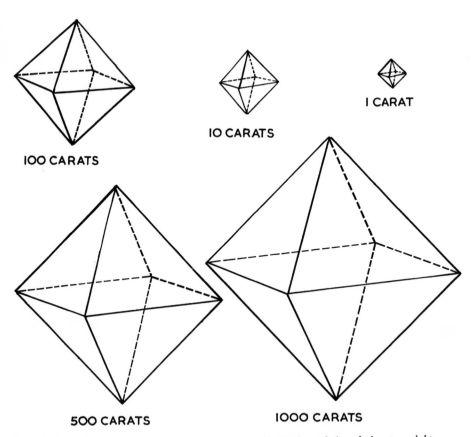

Fig. 14.25. *Approximate sizes of octahedral diamond rough in relation to weight.*

Sizes and Weights

Approximate sizes of various cuts of stone and of octahedral crystals are given in Figs. 14.21 to 14.25.

REFERENCES

'Diamond Proportion Grading and the New Proportionscope', by Richard T. Liddicoat, Jr. *Gems and Gemology*, Spring 1967 (C.I.A., Los Angeles).
Diamanten-Fibel, by Verena Theisen (Essen, 1968).

CHAPTER FIFTEEN

Prices of Diamonds: Valuations

A general rule for pricing rough diamond used by merchants for many centuries still gives a guide. David Jeffries wrote in 1750: 'The . . . rule is that the proportional increase, or value of diamonds, is as the square of their weight, whether rough or manufactured.'

He went on to explain that a parcel of rough of various qualities, all suitable for cutting, would be priced at so much a carat for the whole parcel. Price of the individual crystals could then be worked out from the rule. For example, suppose the average price were £100 a carat (Jeffries suggested £2 a carat!). A 2-carat crystal would therefore be priced at £100 times the square of the weight, i.e. (£100 × 2^2) = £400, which is £200 per carat. A 3 carat crystal would be worth (£100 × 3^2) = £900, which is £300 a carat.

Today, the price of 80 per cent of the world's rough is to a much more complex formula (see page 145), so the old rule has only very general application.

Prices more than Doubled by Cutting

When a stone is manufactured, at least half the weight is lost, so this, apart from costs of cutting immediately at least doubles the price of a polished stone compared with the rough crystal from which it was made. As a very general rule, then, it can be said that, if the 2-carat crystal in the example of the previous paragraph were cut, it would produce a 1-carat diamond of approximate value £400, which is £400 a carat compared with £200 a carat for the rough. When cut, the 3-carat stone would be worth about £900 a carat according to the squaring rule.

Because mining and recovery methods have improved, fewer large diamonds are being found, modern cuts reduce the percentage of recovery from crystals, more poorly-shaped crystals are cut, demand has changed, and many other things have changed since Jeffries' days, the squaring rule has to be modified. In general, it still applies to top qualities up to about three carats, but qualities increase in price much less in relation to increasing weight.

Quality and Price

The figures opposite are for polished stones of low and high quality for the year 1970, and were supplied by diamond manufacturers in the U.K. and Belgium. Beside each of the actual figures has been inserted in italics the price calculated by the squaring rule from the quarter carat price:

| WEIGHT | LOW QUALITY | | HIGH QUALITY | |
	Market Price	Calculated Price	Market Price	Calculated Price
ct.	£	£	£	£
0·25	16	16	38	38
0·50	58	64	128	152
1·00	240	256	670	608
2·00	900	1,024	2,440	2,432

The price of diamonds, since they are controlled from source, follows reasonably predictable trends, so that it is possible to chart prices. A cutter's prices depend upon the price he pays for his rough, his overheads and other costs, and the usual business considerations. He is able then to compile a price list at which to sell various sizes and qualities. This may be different from a similar list produced by another cutter. It is sometimes forgotten by retailers that there is not an absolutely fixed price for diamonds. Cutters compete with each other like other merchants in price and quality.

Method of Estimating

If one is a buyer of diamonds or diamond jewellery, or a valuer, it is necessary to be able to arrive at reasonably accurate prices, often over a very wide range of goods. Anyone not handling diamonds so regularly that he has a mental picture of the price structure, can adopt the method to be described. Its rules are three:

1. Weigh the stone or make an accurate estimation of weight by a gauge, preferably a Leveridge gauge.
2. Evaluate the quality of the stone as explained elsewhere in this book. (By colour, clarity, and cut).
3. Refer to a chart of prices.

The chart of prices is the usual stumbling block. There are some diamond merchants who issue lists to their customers. A current price list obviously can be made the basis of a chart. Some trade associations from time to time provide members with average prices for different qualities of stones. Actual buying and selling provides the most useful information of all.

There are obviously many ways of compiling a personal chart of prices for reference because there are four variables – weight, colour, clarity and cut. Weight is the most important and must have its own columns. Cut may be omitted and all prices assumed to be of good cut, mental allowance being made for lower qualities of cut. Colour and quality have to be separated to some extent but can be grouped, so that one arrives at a chart with weights along one co-ordinate and quality along the other, as in Fig. 15.1.

The steps in weight and the closeness of grading depends upon the uses to which the chart is to be put and the market in which the user is operating. Some users may need only the middle grades on a broad scale, others require fine differences in top-quality stones only. It is fairly obvious that the higher the

PRICE PER CARAT

	0·25	0·50	0·75	1·00	1·25	1·50	2·00
River	£	£	£	£	£	£	£
Flawless	—	—	—	—	—	—	—
VVS	—	—	—	—	—	—	—
VS	—	—	—	—	—	—	—
1st PK	—	—	—	—	—	—	—
Wesselton							
Flawless	—	—	—	—	—	—	—
VVS	—	—	—	—	—	—	—
VS	—	—	—	—	—	—	—
1st PK	—	—	—	—	—	—	—
Crystal							
Flawless	—	—	—	—	—	—	—
VVS	—	—	—	—	—	—	—
VS	—	—	—	—	—	—	—
1st PK	—	—	—	—	—	—	—

Fig. 15.1.   *A means of keeping a note of known prices and extrapolating them.*

quality, the finer the shades of difference in price between different weights and qualities.

Having drawn out the columns of the chart in a pocket notebook, the prices can be filled in in the appropriate places when they are discovered. Obviously there will be variations, but a pattern will begin to emerge and it will be possible to estimate missing ones by extrapolation. Also any excessively high (or low) price will at once show up for what it is because it does not fit into the grid.

Prices of stones over, say, 2 carats, are more subject to fluctuation of price because the demand is more variable, whereas stones of say under a carat are bought in quantity by jewellery manufacturers which tends to keep prices more stable. The chart will therefore be a more accurate guide on lower than on higher weights.

Prices per Carat

The prices in the chart are given in prices per carat, which is the normal way of indicating price in the diamond trade. For example, a parcel containing a stone may be marked '0·55 ct. £200 pc.' This means a price of $55/100 \times £200 = £110$ for the stone.

A few dealers mark parcels with the actual price in such a way: '0·55 ct. £110 for the stone'.

Using the grid in Fig. 15.1, then, one must remember that £80 under the

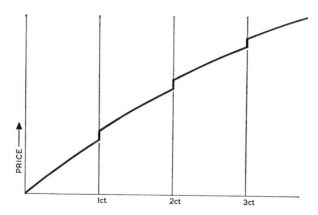

Fig. 15.2. *How diamond prices per carat rise in steps.*

column 0·25 ct. does *not* mean that a quarter-carat stone of that quality is valued at £80. It is valued at £80 *per carat,* or £20 for the stone.

Market Fluctuations

The chart should be kept up to date because prices keep creeping upwards. The major price changes come when there is an increase in the price of rough or the selling pattern is changed. If De Beers announce an increase of 5 per cent in the price of rough, however, that does not mean all prices in the chart can be increased by 5 per cent. The increase is an average one to cutters, and is most likely to increase the price of higher quality goods at the expense of lower qualities.

It should also be noted that there may be 'humps' in the grid caused by demands for particular sizes and qualities. At a particular time, for example, there may be very strong demand for stones around twenty points which causes a price hump at this level.

There are price humps at carat levels also, known as carat premiums, which are an artificial feature of demand caused by the 'magic' of owning a diamond of 1 carat, 2, 3, 4 carats or whatever it may be, rather than one of just under a carat, just under two carats, etc. The graph in Fig. 15.2 shows how the price jumps at each carat level and also applies to a lesser extent in quarter carat, and half-carat steps. The factor is a nuisance in the market and was for some years aggravated by an extensive advertising campaign to the public in several countries which illustrated diamonds in these steps of size.

As polished stones increase in size, they do not continue to increase in price at the same rate. Buyers become fewer and less willing to pay the increased rate per carat.

Ultimately a polished stone could become so big that no buyer could afford or want to afford it. Crystals of this size are only cut for special purposes or people. Ordinarily, large crystals are cut into a number of stones of sizes that provide the optimum increase in value.

Influence of Quality on Price

Colour and clarity have roughly the same influence on price, but the actual amount depends on public taste. In some countries there is a stronger demand for better colours, with clarity a secondary consideration. In others, the public prefers a stone to be flawless even if the colour suffers a little.

It is difficult to show the influence of make or accuracy of cutting on value in the same way because make can be improved by re-cutting, but colour can not; neither usually, can clarity. A low-quality stone may therefore fall to 20 per cent of its top value if it is badly cut, whereas a fine quality stone may fall only to 80 per cent of its value through poor cutting, if it can be recut without losing much material. Another factor is that a top-quality stone is not likely to be badly cut, but a low-quality one could have been 'swindled' to gain maximum weight.

These facts have prompted the Scandinavians to suggest a special category of grading for stones that are flawless except for superficial defects in finish, that can be removed by repolishing with the removal only of a very small amount of material.

Diamonds and Investment

In general it is the policy of those whose actions determine the prices of diamonds to keep these prices as stable as possible. A free market in diamond would destroy its stability of price. If it is regarded as a currency, its purchasing power has probably remained steadier than that of any other currency, including gold. Certainly it has remained more stable than any of the paper currencies.

The implications of keeping the average price of diamonds stable is rarely fully realized, even by the trade. A stable average price means that as the cost of living goes up, so does the average price of diamonds. It means too, that diamonds, regarded as a currency, will purchase about the same now as they did last year, five years ago, or twenty years ago.

It means that if a diamond would have purchased a plot of land fifty years ago, it should still buy the same plot of land today, all else being equal. Compare this with the real value in purchasing power of most countries' paper money which has plummetted in almost every country in the world.

Comparison of diamonds with gold as currency also shows a more realistic situation for the diamond. Gold prices have been manipulated because they are still tied to the values of paper currencies, and because international settlements are still made by gold bullion.

Portability and Durability

Diamonds regarded as a currency have not only remained more stable than other currencies, but have the same advantages in that they are portable and durable and can be exchanged all over the world for the local currency or for goods. In addition, they have a high intrinsic value, unlike paper money or other demonetized currency.

If there were only one quality of diamond as there is only one quality of pound notes, the validity of what has just been written would be easily appreciated. In fact there are thousands of qualities of diamond and wide variations of carat price in relation to the size of a stone. The average price per carat of diamond is somewhere among extremes of price in various direction.

It is human nature to seek the best, rarest, most beautiful, and to pay for it with effort, or money (the result of effort), despite what some theorists would like us to believe. Therefore, rarer stones – those of top quality and larger size – are more sought after than smaller ones of poorer quality. The result is that larger stones of higher quality are of much higher price than smaller, low-quality ones. As the size increases or the quality improves, so does the rate of increase of price. Furthermore, the difference increases with time. This indicates that high-quality larger stones are more likely to be a profitable investment.

Prices and Inflation

Since the average price remains approximately in step with the cost of living, it follows that prices of low-quality diamonds must go down in purchasing power.

This can be expressed in another way. The average price of diamonds advances roughly in step with world inflation which is increasing at say 3 to 5 per cent a year. Therefore the average price of diamonds is rising at this rate, and the purchasing power of money is going down at the same rate. Larger top-quality diamonds increase in price above the average rate, say at 10 to 20 per cent.

Best Sizes and Qualities

It is now possible to answer the question, 'Are diamonds a good investment?' The answer is, 'Yes, if they are of top quality and are large enough.' In practice this means the best stones to invest in are from about one to three carats in weight and of River, VVS quality or better. Larger stones may appreciate more but are sometimes more difficult to sell.

Being able readily to sell is an important factor in investment. A good investment of any kind may turn out to be a poor one if it is not possible to turn it into cash in an emergency.

Another factor in some countries, including the U.K., is liability to capital gains tax.

Medium Qualities and Investment

In retail shops, the question 'Is it a good investment?' is often asked by a customer who is interested in buying diamond-set jewellery. Jewellery should never be bought as an investment, only for its beauty, but the customer must be answered and the answer could in this case be given in terms of purchasing power.

'A woman was left a fine solitaire diamond ring which became her favourite possession. One day, however, she fell for a £1,500 sports car. The dealer persuaded her to part with her ring, which he decided to keep for himself in exchange for the sports car. In five years' time, the woman took back the sports car to sell it and found it to be worth £350. But the ring, now being worn by the dealer's wife, would still have purchased a brand new sports car.'

The point is that diamonds will hold their value against currency and withstand devaluation, inflation, runs on currency, and the uncertainties caused by unstable government. Stocks and shares which often produce substantial profits, are not as stable as they can tumble in value overnight. They cannot be transferred elsewhere or cashed easily. Their value is in most cases utterly dependent on the actions of the government and the economy concerned.

Stability of Values

To some extent, diamond production, and therefore diamond prices are also dependent on government, but the actions of a single government are not so effective in upsetting values because of the international marketing arrangements. For example, prices have remained relatively unaffected by the 'wind of change' in Africa, when African governments took over, the revolution in the Congo, various pressures on the South African Government, big pipe finds in the U.S.S.R., and the manufacture of synthetic diamonds.

If diamond prices can withstand such upheavals, they can probably withstand anything except world recession or a return to the free-for-all days.

True Investment Values

It must never be forgotten that the value of gem diamonds depends entirely on the value of them in jewellery. It would be very dangerous if the stability of the market were threatened by diamond investment operators with no interest in jewellery, but powerful enough to influence prices, as has happened in the art world.

Finally, it should be evident that diamonds are not a substitute for investment of other kinds, but more a supplementary investment with special aspects of security in troubled times. They are no substitutes for industrial shares, property, insurance and land. But they are a valuable means of diversifying investments, and are also not liable to the wide fluctuations in value that occur with paintings and some other works of art bought for investment.

Price Structures

The layman is generally ignorant of the fact that all wealth originates in producing things and trading in them. Agriculture, mining for materials to manufacture into articles people need or want, and distributing them to people who require them, all of these activities create increased money values. Every merchant must make a profit on a transaction to stay in business – to pay his employees and his overheads after replacing the item he has sold.

The diamond merchant and the jeweller, like every other trader, has to make a profit on every transaction. Yet a surprisingly high number of customers imagine that they can sell back diamonds and diamond jewellery at the same prices as they paid. Even if it is explained that the trader cannot afford to lose his profit, they fail to see that he has to make one on the buying transaction as well as the original selling transaction. This applies right along the line and accounts for the value of everything.

A diamond is worth nothing if picked up in the desert by a native tribesman with no access to the civilized world. It is worth more to someone who knows it only as a pretty pebble and wants it for an ornament or a toy and is therefore prepared to exchange it for a tin of tobacco. It is worth more still to someone who has discovered that it can be used for inscribing other stones, or to someone who covets it because no one else has one. A price structure is beginning to emerge.

There is the first cost of finding the place where diamonds occur, then in mining them, in carrying out manufacturing processes, and last but not least in distributing them to the people who want or need them. At each transaction there must be a profit to pay for staff, buildings, equipment and other items. If there were no profits in industry and commerce, there would be no money to buy the products of industry and commerce. In the process, various non-producers, notably governments, but also lawyers, doctors and others, take large parts of the profits in return for services which, however valuable, do not add to the wealth of the country, but do add to costs and therefore prices.

In the case of diamonds, the first cost is for prospecting and mining. It is high because of the low rate of recovery. The government in whose territory the mines are situated usually takes a percentage of the value; for example, the South African Government receives 5 per cent of the value of exported diamond rough. Some governments take a profit at source.

Price Margins
At the sights, when De Beers sell rough to about 200 selected dealers and cutters, sales are negotiated through authorized brokers who receive a fee of 1 per cent. Some goods that are in demand elsewhere are sold by dealers who may add from 5 to 10 per cent brokerage. In 1969, cutters and dealers were buying rough at an average price of about £100 a carat. Less than half the rough was recovered as polished goods, so the average price of these was about £250 a carat.

After that, the jewellery manufacturer has to mark-up his products about 25 per cent, to pay his craftsmen's wages and his overheads. In the U.K., at the last stage of retailing diamond jewellery the government steps in and demands a part of the value in tax, before the retailer can legally sell the jewellery. The retailer has therefore to add his own mark-up and the government's (which can be the higher).

Mark-up is usually confused with net profit in the public mind, and often in the minds of otherwise highly intelligent people. From mark-up a gross profit results, out of which, rent, wages, insurance, taxes, rates, etc., have to be paid, leaving the individual trader with, he hopes, enough to live on.

Synthetic Diamonds and Prices
The question is often asked, 'Won't diamond prices fall if gem diamonds are made in the factory?' The answer is that natural gem diamond prices are *not* likely to be affected by synthetic gem diamonds if they are made commercially in quantity.

The reason for the price of natural stones not being affected – or perhaps even being enhanced – arises from two factors. The first has already been referred to – human nature, which demands the best of the natural gems. (In the jewellers' shops of Gorky Street in Moscow, people queue for diamond jewellery, which is produced in some quantity since the big diamond finds in Russia, so the kind of economy makes no difference.) The second factor is the ability to distinguish between natural and synthetic gems. Its importance is not fully realized even by many people in the gem trade.

While it is possible to prove categorically that this stone is natural and that one is synthetic, a price difference will remain between them.

The less perfect a gem material, the more likely will be opportunities for finding some difference between the natural and the synthetic. Diamond is such a perfect mineral and is very occasionally so pure that the eventual polished synthetic gem diamond, may prove to be difficult to identify, but early tests on the first gem diamonds synthesised in 1970 suggest that positive identification will not be difficult if undertaken by a properly-equipped gem laboratory.

The whole of the gem jewellery trade affected by synthetic stones depends utterly on the ultimate deterrent of a gemmological laboratory's ability to detect synthetic stones to prevent them from being sold as natural. It can only be ignorance that makes a number of important jewellers selling expensive gems indifferent even to the existence of an efficient laboratory.

Making a Valuation

Appraisal of diamonds and diamond jewellery can be carried out more accurately than of coloured gemstones and jewellery. The reason is two-fold.

1. Diamond prices are relatively stable and price changes are notified.
2. Standards of quality are universally acknowledged and the quality of a stone can be ascertained.

The value in cash of anything, however, depends upon the circumstances of the sale. When an appraisal is given, therefore, it is assumed that the price quoted would be that obtainable on an open market. Nevertheless it is still necessary to know which market would be involved. In the U.K. there are three general groups of sale:

1. *For probate.* Where it is assumed that the articles will have to be sold in a given time and usually in a single lot.
2. *For resale.* A valuation for resale may be higher than for probate because it is assumed that the owner can wait for the best market conditions. It is also assumed that the item will be sold in isolation, whereas when many items are sold for probate they are usually offered as a single lot.
3. *For insurance.* When a customer wants a valuation for insurance, he is asking what the replacement value of the jewellery or diamond would be at that time to him. In other words, he wants an estimated retail price for an identical new article.

One more form of 'valuation' is probably peculiar to the jewellery trade and causes considerable damage to honest reputations and generates much bad feeling. It is initiated by a customer who buys an article from one shop and then goes to another shop for valuation as reassurance that the price paid in the first shop was fair.

A jeweller asked to price new goods should make it quite clear that he is valuing for insurance. He should be very cautious if he is asked to make an offer. To be offered new goods for sale is always suspicious when so much jewellery is being stolen.

Unfortunately there are a few unscrupulous traders in all countries who will deliberately undervalue goods bought from their competitors in order to discredit competitors, a practice called 'poisoning' in the trade. A retailer faced with a customer who bought from him an article that has been poisoned by a competitor should offer the customer the full price of an identical article bought at the lower price quoted by the competitor.

There are simple people about who think that if they buy a diamond today for, say £250, they can sell it tomorrow for the same price, yet do not expect to do the same with a motor-car. A buyer of a diamond will have to wait until any rise in value swallows the original retailer's margin and the selling margin before he can even get his money back.

Some retailers, quite legitimately, offer to buy back diamond jewellery at a future date against the sale of a more expensive article. They will often make a loss in buying because the original price included purchase tax, but they are prepared to lose some profit to keep the customer.

Methodical Appraisal

In the U.K. the engagement ring tradition ensures large sales of diamond rings. If a trader knows this kind of stock, it is not difficult for him to make a quick valuation which is usually quite accurate. The reason is that such rings fall only in a fairly narrow band of quality. Large numbers of diamonds set in them, for example, are Top Silver Cape, second piqué. As soon as the size is known, the insurance value is quickly estimated. After estimating the price of the diamond, the value of the jewellery in which it is set is arrived at in stages. The mental process is as follows:

1. Gauge (or weigh) diamond and calculate price.
2. Add estimated cost of mount.
3. Add purchase tax and retail margin.

When the diamond is sizeable and of higher quality, a more sophisticated approach is necessary. The principle is to obtain the weight of the stone, to ascertain its quality, and to refer to a current table of prices, as explained earlier in this chapter. Accurate weight estimation is extremely important.

Valuation of Other Cuts

Some difficulty arises with cuts other than full brilliants. In general, for modern fancy cuts such as marquise, about 10 per cent should be added to the brilliant price. Modern square- and emerald-cuts are about that much less.

Valuations for resale or probate of fancy cuts is a more difficult task as the factor of ready saleability has to be taken into account. In this case, a fancy cut can depreciate the price of a stone or jewellery. For example, some earlier emerald-cut stones are almost unsaleable except for re-cutting. This gives the clue to estimating the value of unfashionable and old cuts of stone, including old mine-cut and Victorian-cut stones, of which there are many still in existence.

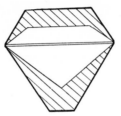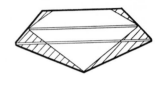

Fig. 15.3. *Estimating re-cut weights of old mine and of shallow stones.*

Valuing Stones of Old-fashioned Cut

To estimate the value of an old mine or similar cut, gauge or weigh the stone, then estimate how much weight could be recovered if it were re-cut as a modern brilliant. The estimating process is as follows:

1. Gauge (or weigh) diamond.
2. Estimate weight if re-cut in brilliant style (usually from 40 to 60 per cent).
3. Calculate price of brilliant-cut.
4. Deduct price of re-cutting.

The same principle of estimating the re-cut value and deducting the cutting charges may be employed with all badly cut stones.

If a Leveridge or Moe gauge with tables is available, estimating recut sizes is simple. Decide whether the stone is over or under depth. If over, take the smallest diameter and look it up in the table against a normal depth and if under, take the height with normal diameter. Each will give an approximate recut weight (Fig. 15.3).

Re-cutting prices depend upon the size of the diamond and are charged at a rate per carat, but naturally vary according to any difficulties encountered. It must be emphasized that this is for re-cutting an already polished stone. Cutting a crystal obviously costs much more.

Rose-cut diamonds pose a different question for valuation as only the larger ones are suitable for re-cutting as brilliants. The loss in weight in this case will be very much more. There is, however, a small demand in the antique jewellery trade for rose-cuts for replacement of lost stones. Prices offered are below the equivalent prices of brilliants, but it is impossible to give a guide because demand fluctuates considerably.

REFERENCE

'A treatise on Diamonds and Pearls; in which their Importance is considered; and plain rules and exhibited for ascertaining the value of both; also the true method of manufacturing diamonds', by Richard Jeffries, Jeweller (London 1750).

CHAPTER SIXTEEN

Origin and Geological Distribution

All diamonds were found in the gravels or conglomerates of active or extinct rivers until about a century ago when they were discovered in great pipes or plugs of rock that penetrated deeply into the Earth. It was supposed that the rock, subsequently called kimberlite, was solidified lava and the tapered pipes of it were the roots of extinct volcanoes. The supposition is now known to be incorrect. Kimberlite pipes are not in fact long funnels that go down to the mantle under the earth's crust. They are more like the heads of tulips or forked carrots – great cavities filled with kimberlite – that were fed from a number of narrow vents from the Earth's mantle. See Fig. 16.1.

Any diamonds are closely contained in the kimberlite rock, but are not attached to it. As single diamond crystals are found with faces bounding all sides, they did not grow attached to a matrix like many gem crystals such as beryl and quartz.

Eclogite Not Parent Rock

For the first part of the twentieth century, it was believed that the birthplace of diamond was the rock eclogite. Professor T. G. Bonney's pronouncement that diamond crystallized in it, made this ultra-basic rock world famous. He supposed that the rock was disrupted to release the diamonds, which became accidental inclusions in kimberlite. Some diamonds had been found in eclogite, which is a constituent of kimberlite. Eclogite occurs as large boulders from deep in pipes. It is an aggregate of green pyroxene, red garnet, bluish kyanite, and white mica, which is very pretty when slabbed and polished.

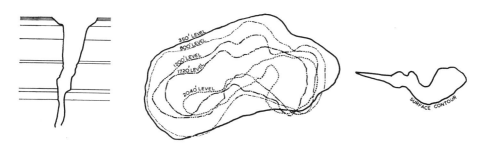

Fig. 16.1.   *Examples of a diamond pipe in section, contours of a pipe at different depths, and the surface contour of a fissure.*

Current Theory

It is still not certain how diamonds originated. Knowledge gained by making synthetic diamond helped in evolving one of the most recent theories, that diamonds were formed in the Earth's mantle at depths of not less than 200 kilometres (about 120 miles), and were forced to the surface by an explosive drive of carbon dioxide gas.

The material of the mantle is probably the ultra-basic rock, peridotite. (Ultrabasic means that it contains no quartz. Basic rocks are heavy and have a low content of quartz. At the opposite end of the scale are the acid rocks which are light in weight and in colour and do contain quartz.)

Peridotite may contain some iron from the Earth's core and when this is present in amounts from 7 to 12 per cent, in the form of iron oxide (FeO), conditions are right for the genesis of diamond from carbon by slow precipitation. The peridotite must be molten, as diamond forms at pressures and temperatures between about 0·5 million pounds a square inch at 700° C. and 1·3 million pounds a square inch at 2,500°C.

It is believed that such conditions remained stable for long periods during crystallization because a pressure of carbon dioxide gas from below equalled the pressure of the Earth above. During their growth, and for millennia before kimberlite pipe formation, most natural diamonds must have been maintained at temperatures high enough and long enough to allow for the migration of nitrogen atoms in the crystals and their condensation into platelets, as described in Chapter Eighteen.

Eventually the gas pressure built up, driving the diamond-bearing rock to the surface and also preventing the diamonds from reverting to graphite *en route*. It is clear that the diamond-bearing rock – kimberlite – is not lava, as lava erupts at a temperature of 1,000 to 1,200° C and any diamonds in it would vaporize. Some kimberlite has been found to contain pieces of coal and log and even human bones that must have dropped at least a mile down from the surface. It is inconceivable, therefore, that the kimberlite came to the Earth's surface as lava.

The possibility of the series of events described is supported by several observable facts. One is that the rocks in which most diamonds appear contain from 7 to 12 per cent iron oxide, although most of the FeO has been converted to haematite (Fe_2O_3). Oxidized diamonds, i.e. coloured brown or orange by iron oxide, are not uncommon. Another fact is that the minerals associated with diamond have been found to contain minute cavity inclusions of carbon dioxide.

The current theory was anticipated in 1897 by Sir William Crookes who described kimberlite as 'a geological plum-pudding of heterogeneous character, agreeing, however, in one particular. The appearance of shale and fragments of other rocks shows that the melange has suffered no great heat in its present condition, and that it has been erupted from great depths by the agency of water vapour or some similar gas.'

The Possible Course of Events

To sum up, it seems that diamonds crystallized from carbon over long periods of time in great reservoirs of molten magma in certain favourable parts of the Earth's mantle of peridotite. Various accompanying minerals possibly crystallized also in the same magma, which, perhaps while in a plastic or semi-plastic state, was driven upwards by explosive pressures of gasses from great depths, to pierce the Earth's crust in a multitude of relatively small fissures and pipes, and to solidify.

On the way, the magma became altered by chemical change and also picked up many other rocks and minerals, to become kimberlite. During this forceful process, constituent minerals were released, some were broken or altered and retrapped or suffered other changes.

Although most irregular diamonds were formed irregularly, diamonds that are broken, chipped or cleaved when mined must have been damaged *en route*. A. F. Williams records the finding of a large diamond, shaped like a man's finger, in the De Beers mine. It was in two separate pieces with cleaved surfaces that fitted exactly together. Yet the two pieces had been recovered in two quite distinct parts of the pipe which were mined separately.

Pipes are referred to as primary sources of diamond, but are not truly so, because the diamond was transported from its original source deep in the Earth. The age of pipes in South Africa is estimated at about 120 million years.

Kimberlite Pipes

Kimberlite pipes tend to occur in groups, and there are often fissures in the area as well. Only in a very general sense are pipes tulip-shaped. On the surface, most are of an irregular oval contour, more or less level with the surface. But kidney-shapes occur, as do dumb-bell shapes as well as pipes of very irregular section. Also, the top of the pipe may be level with surrounding country, project above the surface, or be a shallow depression, as the Premier and Wesselton were.

The pipe area usually decreases with depth and eventually becomes a number of fissures. This may occur several thousands of feet down. Pipes are not normally uniform in section as they often have hollows or protuberances in the sides. They vary considerably in size. The smaller ones are under 100 feet across. The largest in Africa are the Premier in Pretoria, the Finsch, the Williamson mine in Tanzania, and AK1 in Botswana, which is nearly a mile across the greatest width.

Pipes, fissures and dykes of kimberlite are relatively numerous, but only a few of them are diamondiferous and even fewer have diamonds in sufficient quantities to be payable. See Fig 16.1.

It is estimated that there are about 900 pipes and fissures located in Southern Africa, alone. There are many in the South West African Protectorate, but not one is diamondiferous although the very many diamonds found along the Sperrgebiet coast must have come from pipes. There is another group of pipes south of them in South African territory. This group is also not diamondiferous and in fact is not truly kimberlitic. To the south of the rich pipes in Kimberley are other groups that are very poor in diamonds. Some of the fissure deposits in South Africa are still worked privately for diamonds.

Kimberlite

Kimberlite is related in origin to peridotite and to eclogite. It varies very considerably in composition and in general appearance from pipe to pipe and even in the same pipe. Sometimes it is a very finely granular and compact material. At others it is a conglomerate of huge boulders of different rocks, sometimes feet across. When it contains diamonds, the diamonds also vary in crystal habit, colour, quality, and in other ways, from pipe to pipe.

The colour changes with depth. In the Finsch pipe, for instance, the yellow ground becomes progressively less weathered with depth, changing gradually to blue ground, until at about 300 feet down, the kimberlite is hard and unaltered. The weathering of kimberlite into blue ground and yellow ground is fairly consistent throughout pipes.

There is a third form of kimberlite named hardebank by the diggers because it did not disintegrate even when exposed to the elements for fifty years or more. Hardebank appears to be a form of kimberlite that cooled rapidly when it formed. It is found in parts of some pipes where blue ground grades into hardebank, as can be readily seen by the change in colour, but there is no definite line of contact between the two forms of kimberlite. It is most evident in the small fissure and dyke formations of a number of small mines in South Africa.

Composition of Kimberlite

Although the composition of kimberlite varies from mine to mine, the most abundant of the primary minerals forming it is olivine, a mineral that is subject to many alterations, one of which is to serpentine. Other minerals are ilmenite, phlogopite, perovskite, magnetite, and apatite. There are also traces of nickel. Nickel was one of the first catalysts used in making synthetic diamond.

Secondary minerals in kimberlite may include serpentine, calcite, chlorite, talc, magnetite, limonite, siderite, phlogopite, perovskite, amphibole, haematite, leucoxine and pyrites. The principal minerals that may have been transported by the rock are pyrope garnet, chrome diopside, chrome spinel, enstatite, ilmenite, magnetite, rutile, hornblende, augite, and of course diamond.

Among diamonds that occur in pipes are perfectly formed crystals only a fraction of a millimetre in size, which have to be recovered by special techniques. The presence of micro-diamonds suggests that kimberlite includes the magma in which diamonds were originally formed.

Some kimberlite also carries shales, sandstones, conglomerates, etc., which are accidental inclusions and are probably from the country rock surrounding the pipe, or might have been carried from veins of other minerals penetrated by the kimberlite magma. There are reports of very strange inclusions, including coal, fossilized branches of wood, old blackened ostrich eggs, and human skeletons, including a headless one, the head having been discovered 50 feet away at half the depth. A whole undamaged ant-hill was also found about fifty feet below the surface of one pipe.

'Cape Rubies' and 'Tanganyika Rubies'

Garnets are usually scattered throughout the kimberlite and vary in size from specks to crystals about half an inch across, although occasionally large pieces occur over six inches across. In the earlier days of diamond digging in the Cape, diggers used to sell the many garnets they recovered with diamonds as 'Cape rubies'. Those from Tanzania are still mis-called 'Tanganyika rubies'.

Nodules of chrome-diopside often occur in a shell of kimberlite in the kimberlite mass. This also happens to garnets, olivines, and other minerals, too. In a number of mines there are occurrences of large numbers of these nodules packed together ranging in size from marbles to cannon balls and cemented together by decomposed kimberlite.

Mica and Iron Ores

Phlogopite is a form of mica and appears commonly in kimberlite both as a primary mineral and a transported one. It occurs in sizes up to six inches. The flash of smaller mica inclusions is readily seen in a lump of kimberlite. Often the phlogopite crystals are like the pages of a book buried in the kimberlite. Biotite is another form of mica, but is much less common in kimberlite.

Magnetite is a magnetic iron ore commonly found in masses of small cubic or octahedral crystals, when it has been transported, but it also occurs as scattered particles when broken down to serpentine. It is easily extracted from crushed blue ground by magnets. It is opaque and black to pale brown. Some of it occurs in large lumps corroded round the outside.

Ilmenite, another iron ore, is found in kimberlite in large corroded lumps, and also scattered through the rock in small opaque specks.

Zircon, Corundum, and Other Minerals

Zircon is quite common in kimberlite and, being dense, is recovered in the concentrate of other heavy minerals including diamond. The zircon crystals are almost invariably broken and irregular. Corundum – ruby and sapphire – also turns up in the concentrate, but in quite good crystals because it is hard and tough enough to survive attrition.

Apatite is found in specks and rarely in larger crystals or broken lumps of crystal. Calcite is a common constituent impregnating kimberlite and is also found as very large included nodules, sometimes two feet across. It also appears in well-formed crystals.

Graphite and Quartz

Graphite, which might be thought a common constituent of kimberlite, is rare. Impure graphite in large nodules has been very occasionally found destroyed because of its softness.

Although kimberlite containing quartz and chalcedony is very rare, when it does occur, it is rich in quartz. At least this appears to be true of the South African mines. Some Brazilian diamonds are said to contain quartz as inclusions. The presence of quartz in kimberlite has not yet been satisfactorily explained, but silicated water was responsible in the specimens from South Africa.

Concentration of Heavy Minerals

If blue ground is crushed, many of the minerals it contains are released as separate pieces or crystals, which can be concentrated into a heavier group.

The average specific gravity of blue ground is around 2·8, but many of the constituent minerals are much denser. These include magnetite at 5·0, zircon about 4·7, ilmenite 4·5, rutile 4·2, garnet about 4·0, corundum 4·0, spinel 3·6, diamond 3·5, epidote 3·3, olivine 3·3, and apatite 3·2.

Diamond Yields from Pipe Mines

The deeper a pipe mine is mined, the smaller the yield of diamonds, and the smaller average size of diamond. In South Africa, for example, the Bultfontein mine yielded 0·42 carats a load (1,600 lb. of blue ground) at the upper levels and 0·31 at about the 1,000-feet level.

The decrease in yield was particularly sudden in the Premier mine. Only 0·19 carats per load was recovered from the ground between 410- and 510-feet levels, but the blue ground at the top gave from 0·80 to 1.29 carats a load. This suggests that the very top of the mine which was eroded away by weathering must have been very rich indeed. Over twenty-seven million carats came from the first 500 feet of blue ground so it is probable that more than this amount was eroded away.

The reason for decreasing richness down a pipe is not known, but it seems to be a rule that yield decreases with depth. Certainly a number of mines have ceased to pay as they were worked deeper.

Diamonds from underground in pipe mines probably account for much less than 10 per cent of all those mined. It is difficult to estimate how much diamond is produced from both open-cast and deep working of pipes, but it may be in the region of twenty per cent of the world total, which means that about 80 per cent comes from alluvial sources, although the Russian pipe mines have probably altered the proportion.

Alluvial Deposits

It is assumed that all alluvial diamonds were released from pipes or similar extrusions. The pipes must have been upstream of the river beds where diamonds are found, although river courses may have changed, perhaps very considerably, over millions of years. It is possible that pipes occur under what is now the sea bed, although none has been discovered.

The original kimberlite at the tops of pipes undoubtedly weathered very rapidly compared with other rocks, to free any treasury of diamonds it may have contained. Weathering takes place at all times, but it was much more violent

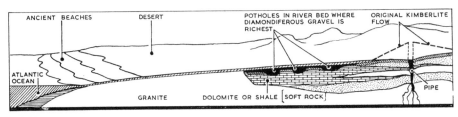

Fig. 16.2. *How diamonds were carried from the heads of pipes down rivers to the sea.*

millions of years ago during long periods of torrential rains and greater extremes of heat and cold. Diamonds and other minerals and rocks released would have been carried quickly away by rushing waters.

Water carried the diamond-bearing gravels and other detritus short or long distances, sometimes hundreds of miles towards and even into the sea, before depositing the gravels as beds or terraces (Fig. 16.2.).

Formation of Terraces

Rocks are broken up by contraction and expansion, the winter and summer temperatures causing cracks between the mineral grains, and are then washed away by rains. They are also eroded by chemical processes when acted upon by water, carbon dioxide, and oxygen.

A river will build terraces as a result of several natural processes. It may be fast flowing and carrying much detritus near its source. Then it reaches a plain and floods, so that it slows down and deposits detritus, which builds up so much that the river has to cut new channels through it, leaving some parts to dry out (Fig. 16.3).

A river may carry an excess of detritus because of excessive rainfall, and deposit it as terraces when the flow returns to normal, or excessive rain may bring with it so much detritus that it never reaches a river and is left well inland in terraces.

When a river reaches the sea, the meeting of the waters causes it to become deeper at the mouth. This slows the flow of water and detritus carried this far is deposited. The result is that the lowering of the bed tends to move gradually upstream. Terraces of silt and gravel are therefore built up gradually across the river from the mouth. If the supply of detritus fails, the river will run much faster, not having to shift a great weight of rocks, gravels and sands, and will

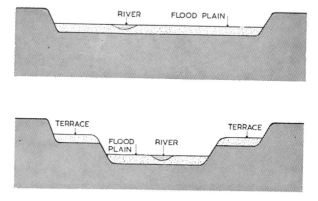

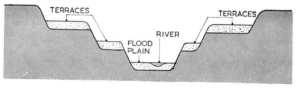

Fig. 16.3. *How a river forms terraces.*

275

tend to straighten its course. The terraces will be left to dry out, and probably to become covered with sand and earth.

Diamond terraces found in the areas around and at the mouths of rivers, such as the Orange River and others on the same coast, were deposited by such an action.

Marine Terraces

If the finer and larger crystals were in fact at the tops of pipes, many of the best stones were carried to alluvial deposits. Certainly the alluvial deposits along the South West African coast have produced the greatest number of fine gem crystals and continue to do so.

So much diamondiferous gravel was brought down to the sea on this South West African coast that huge quantities were deposited in the sea itself. The Orange and other rivers would have been torrents when this happened. Now they are dried out for most of the year.

A longshore current up the coast, caused by the prevailing SSW wind, took the gravels up the coast for distances of 100 miles or more. The action of the tides and waves tended to concentrate diamonds in areas at the edge of the sea in beaches. Over a long period of time, the sea advanced and receded a number of times, leaving four wave-cut rock platforms, each with a deposit of diamondiferous gravel just like a modern shingle beach except that it is covered with up to about fifty feet of sand (Fig. 16.4).

These marine terraces overlaid the river terraces near the northern bank of the Orange River mouth. The gravel include pebbles of various agates, and other forms of quartz, including jasper, that are attractive when tumble-polished.

In areas farther north up the coast, near Luderitz, high winds that still today cause walking sands (moving drifts), concentrated diamonds in old valleys and blew the sand away so that millions of pounds worth of fine stones were left exposed in this wild inhospitable area for anyone to find and pick up. At the beginning of the century, most of them were found and picked up by prospectors from Germany.

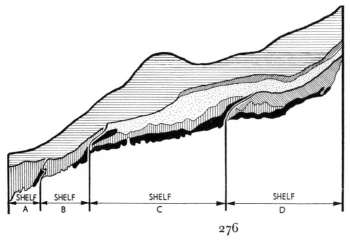

Fig. 16.4. *Various shelves or terraces in a marine deposit. The gravel is shown black. Above it are other deposits topped by sand.*

Diamondiferous Gravels

Ancient gravels are not like the gravels of present river-beds, which were formed when the level of the country was reduced by general erosion, after the deposition of terraces.

Alluvial gravels are usually a well-defined band – although not a strata – of boulders from local sources mixed with small pebbles. The pebbles are mainly of chert, quartz, quartzite, jasper, chalcedony, and banded ironstone. There is usually fine silt, rather than sand with the pebbles. The gravels may be any distance from a few inches to many feet below the surface, and the bands or widths from a few inches to several feet.

Marine terraces have layers of boulders, pebbles and grit, all rounded by the action of the sea, which often lie on a bedrock of shale, covered by sand. The range of sizes is greater than in alluvial deposits. There is sand with the gravels, as well as on top of them, and often oyster and mussel shells. The pebbles are mainly of quartz with some banded ironstone. Pebbles of chalcedony, epidote, felspar, garnet, and jasper are also found.

Diamonds are still found in the beds of some very active, torrential rivers, such as some in Guyana, South America, where pockets in the bedrock trap diamonds and other heavy minerals and also cause whirlpools. The conditions are presumably similar in some ways to what those in South Africa were many thousands of years ago.

Water-worn Crystals

In alluvial sources, the forces of Nature have acted as a sorting plant. As diamonds are relatively heavy, they tend to sift to the bottom of layers of sand and gravel during movement. Also larger diamonds settle more rapidly than small ones. The small crystals were therefore more likely to have been carried on towards the sea and carried there more rapidly so that they suffered much less from wear. Any small crystals that travelled slowly for one reason or another would have become water-worn, through being jostled for aeons of time in the gravels. The same action must have broken up flawed and previously fractured stones and spilt up porous crystalline diamonds. This may be why there is a very high proportion of gem diamonds along the South West Africa coast.

Sharp-edged octahedral crystals (glassies) are found in alluvial deposits, such as those in Sierra Leone, that are probably a long way from the original pipes, yet the crystals show no evidence of wear during their long journey with river detritus. It is possible that sharp-edged diamonds are found in all alluvial diggings. Perhaps they travelled originally with much softer materials. It is unlikely that they were ever jostled together. Diamonds will wear each other quickly, as dealers who carry cut stones together in gem parcels soon find out.

Other Sources of Diamond

In the Witwatersrand in South Africa, diamonds are found in a conglomerate that is older than the kimberlite pipes, according to A. F. Williams, which indicates that there was also an older form of 'primary' deposit. Diamonds are found in hard conglomerates, almost like concrete, in dry diggings and also in

277

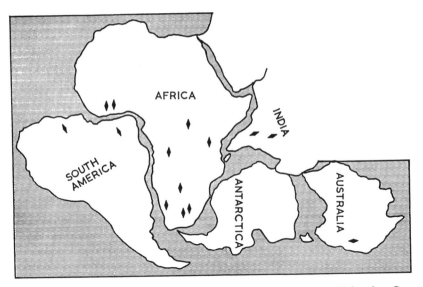

Fig. 16.5. *Dr. M. W. McElhinny, of the Australian National University, Canberra, has, through combined palaeomagnetic measurements, produced a new map showing the original position of continents before drift. Here diamond deposits have been added to his map, which suggests there may be some in the Antarctic.*

marine deposits, but the conglomerates are in these cases merely gravel that has become concreted through natural action after the gravels were laid.

A few diamonds are found in gold mines. In 1968, it was stated that those from South Africa's gold mines totalled thirty-eight and all were now in museums. They all appear to be ordinary Type I crystals, but are greenish in colour. After studying them, the Diamond Research Laboratory at Johannesburg decided that they must have suffered irradiation by charged particles and at some stage of their existence became annealed at a temperature of not more than 500° C.

It is believed that the main land masses originally fitted together, which suggests a relationship among diamond deposits, as shown in Fig. 16.5.

REFERENCES

'The Parent Rock of the Diamond in South Africa', by T. G. Bonney. *Geological Magazine*, 1899. p. 309.
The Genesis of the Diamond, by Alpheus F. Williams (London, 1932).
'The Genesis of Diamond Deposits', by George C. Kennedy and Bert E. Nodlie. *Economic Geology*, August 1968.

CHAPTER SEVENTEEN

Diamond Crystals

The Octahedron (111)

The octahedron is the normal habit of diamond, although from some sources another form of crystals may be more common. The most regular crystals have flat, smooth faces and straight edges and are known in the trade as glassies (Fig. 17.1). They come from various mines, both pipe and alluvial. Some Russian crystals are even 'glassier' than those from Sierra Leone, and sharper at the edges.

Glassies in general tend to draw colour, i.e. they do not include the finest whites, which usually are in other crystallizations including worn octahedra. When the colour of a gem diamond is poorer, the clarity often tends to be better, according to sorters, and there is a good proportion of high clarity stones among glassies.

Glassies are commonly distorted by one or two faces not having developed to the same extent as the others, probably because the face was starved during crystallation. The face of an octahedron becomes smaller in area as it grows. The underdeveloped face is therefore larger than the others, as shown in Fig. 17.2. Sometimes the flattening is so extreme that the crystals become tabular (see later). Distorted octahedra are shown in Fig. 17.11.

Octahedra with rounded edges and corners are the most common of this form of diamond crystal and are found in many different sources, both pipe and alluvial. Examined from the side, the edges will be seen as curved or humped, as shown in Fig. 17.3. Again, few such crystals are perfect so that the opposite

Fig. 17.1. *A glassie.*

Fig. 17.2. *Developed* (left and right) *and undeveloped* (centre) *faces of an octahedron.*

Fig. 17.3. *Rounded octahedral crystal containing a naat (interpenetrant twin crystal).*　　Fig. 17.4. *A cubic crystal.*

pairs of faces are rarely equidistant. The faces are usually domed, sometimes have traces of other possible crystal forms and invariably have trigon markings even if these are not immediately evident.

Some have grooved instead of rounded edges. (See negative crystals, later.)

The Hexahedron or Cube (100)

Cubic crystals are relatively common, but are almost entirely confined to low quality (industrial) stones. Cubes of chrome yellow colour are occasionally found in gem quality. The edges of cubes are rounded as shown in the photograph, Fig. 17.4, and may sometimes be fairly clearly defined as dodecahedral faces. Faces of cubes are frequently domed. They are never smooth but are covered with growth or etch features. These may be terraced steps aligned to the edges of the cube, or pyramidal depressions aligned with the diagonals across faces.

Sometimes a pyramidal depression occurs in the centre of a face. (See negative crystals, later.)

Isolated cube faces occur frequently on crystals of combined form in gem as well as industrial qualities.

The Rhombic Dodecahedron (110)

As the edges of an octahedron (111) become more developed, as seen in Fig. 18.4, the rhombic dodecahedron (110) crystal appears. It can also derive from the edge of the cube (100) developing (study Fig. 18.4). In each case the original octahedron or cube faces become smaller and smaller and eventually disappear. (Fig. 17.6).

True dodecahedron crystals are rare (Fig. 17.5), but crystals of intermediate form tending towards spheres are common. These often have hexakis hexahedroid* faces. One is shown in Fig. 17.7. The dodecahedron edges are nearly always sharper than the octahedron edges.

* As many forms of crystal have rounded sides and edges, the suffix 'oid' is sometimes used to describe these, as suggested by J. R. Sutton in *Diamond* (1928). Hence octahedroid, dodecahedroid, and hexahedroid (rounded cubic form), etc.

Fig. 17.5. *Rhombic dodecahedral crystal*   Fig. 17.6. *Combination dodecahedral and octahedral form.*

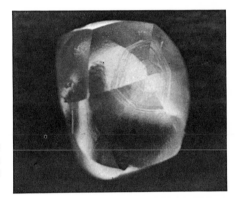

Fig. 17.7. (*right*) *A combination form. The rhombic dodecahedral face at the top has a seam across it, which is the beginning of a tetrakis hexahedron.*

Crystals of near dodecahedron form occur not infrequently in yellow colours and are often of high clarity. As the colour denies their use as gemstones, they are much sought after for industrial use in wire drawing and are known as die stones. A hole is drilled through a die stone and is employed to reduce and control the diameter of wire during its manufacture. It is obvious that purity of the crystal is important in die stones. The direction in which a die stone is drilled affects its wear because hardness is directional. If a die stone is drilled at right angles to a (111) face, the hole will eventually wear triangular. If it is drilled at right angles to a (100) face, it will wear square.

The Tetrakis Hexahedron
A dodecahedral face can be recognized by its rhomb or boat shape and occurs commonly in crystals or mixed form. There is often a fine ridge or seam across the short diagonal, which is the beginning of the formation of a tetrakis hexahedron (Fig. 17.7.). A tetrakis hexahedron is like a cube with a four-sided pyramid on each face and is rare, if it exists, in a pure form. (See Fig. 17.4.)

281

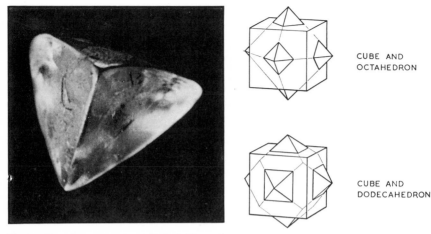

Fig. 17.8. *An apparent tetrahedral diamond and* (below) *its relationship to the octahedron.*

Fig. 17.9. *Relationship of the three basic shapes of diamond crystal.*

Triakis and Hexakis Octahedra

Triakis and hexakis octahedra also probably do not occur as whole crystals, but the forms are quite common as faces on octahedroid and dodecahedroid crystals.

The Tetrahedron

Sutton says the tetrahedral form 'is not frequent, and even then probably illusory. Its symmetry always is either masked by curvature or it is in combination with some other form.' He reported that an excellent tetrahedron with plane faces was recovered at Wesselton, but examination showed every face to be cleavage. A. F. Williams wrote, 'in all the years I have examined diamond, I have never found a diamond having the form of a tetrahedron'.

It is probable that the true tetrahedral diamond crystal does not exist. The nearest approach to tetrahedral form is probably the distorted octahedron, an example of which with curved faces is shown in Fig. 17.8. Tetrahedral crystals of certain minerals show pyro-electricity and also piezo-electricity. That is, they develop positive and negative polarity when heated and also when squeezed. A tetrahedral diamond crystal should show similar effects.

Irregular Crystals

Crystals of no form or a hardly recognizable one, are the most common of all. There is no recognizable exterior form, but when the crystal directions have been

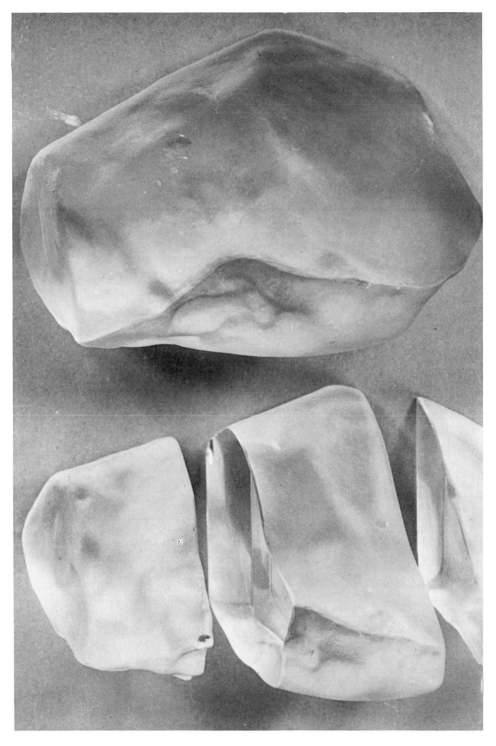

Fig. 17.10. *The 3,106 carat irregular Cullinan, shown full size, and* (below) *how it was first cleaved.*

identified the gem cutter can often make a high recovery. Some have one or more cleavage faces. The famous Cullinan was such a stone and was cleaved into workable sizes and shapes as shown in Fig. 17.10.

Shapeless industrial stones are sometimes cleaved into octahedra and polished all over by a tumbling process, which makes them more useful for setting in tools and drills. Except to the experienced eye, which recognizes a peculiarity on the surface lustre, these rounded octahedra look like natural ones.

Tabular Habit

Very thin crystals occur when parallel faces on an octahedron are hardly developed while the others are very strongly developed. Usually such crystals are hexagonal in outline as if a slice were taken out of the octahedron parallel to the undeveloped faces (Fig. 17.11). Sometimes one face is hexagonal and the other triangular. Those of cuttable thickness are known as flats. The thicknesses of tabular crystals varies considerably from crystal to crystal. Some are as thin as a post card. In the past, such crystals have been used to glaze miniature paintings and are called portrait stones or lasques. Today they are very occasionally cut square or rectangular and fitted as 'glasses' in very expensive watches. They are, of course, scratchproof. (Synthetic colourless sapphire is commonly used for scratchless watch crystals.)

Cushion, Bolster and Round Crystals

Combinations of forms based on octahedral and dodecahedral crystals are sometimes of flattened cushion form. Not infrequently the crystal is elongated or of bolster form. Usually there are some recognizable faces. Sometimes crystals are almost perfectly round. (Round stones known as ballas are not single crystals.)

Cushion and bolster-shaped crystals often have smooth rounded faces, some of recognizable form, such as octahedra, triakis and hexakis octahedra, and rhombic dodecahedra (Fig. 17.12 to 17.14).

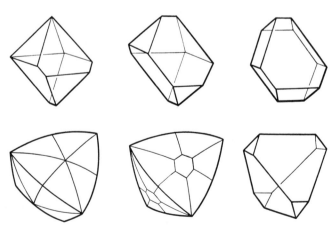

Fig. 17.11. *Distorted octahedra. That at top right has become tabular.*

Dog's Tooth and Nail Crystals

The extreme rhombic dodecahedral forms with certain faces over-developed become long thin crystals which are curved slightly and have one end blunt and the other pointed, like a dog's tooth (Fig. 17.13). Very occasionally there is a head at the blunt end, giving the crystal the appearance of a horse-shoe nail.

Multiple Crystals

Diamonds are commonly found which are two or more crystals joined together. They can be large or small crystals, of various crystal form or more, and can be locked together in various ways, some more intimately than others. The extremes are two crystals (twins) and masses of tiny crystals (aggregates).

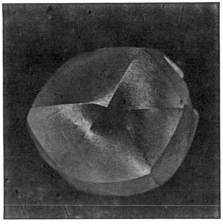

Fig. 17.13. (below)   *Dog's-tooth crystal.*

Fig. 17.12.   *A cushion-shaped stone.*

DISTORTED HEXAKIS OCTAHEDRON

Fig. 17.14.   *Other forms of distorted crystals.*

DISTORTED DODECAHEDRA

285

Twinning

True twinning occurs when a material of crystal structure has changed the orientation of its structure during growth. This naturally changes the outward forms of the crystal. It also alters physical properties, particularly the hardness.

The result of a change in orientation of the atomic structure is a composite or double crystal, with some of its edges and/or faces parallel, but others reversed. Twin crystals are of two types, and interpenetrant and contact. Both are common in diamond.

Interpenetrant Twins

An interpenetrant twin occurs when two crystals appear to have grown within the same space but with different crystal orientations. One appears to penetrate the other Fig. 17.15.

Occasionally a diamond is found to contain another diamond crystal which is of quite separate formation; the inside one is an included crystal and not an interpenetrant twin and the atomic structures of the containing and the included crystal in this case are entirely separate. There are usually strain cracks in the large crystal around the smaller one (Fig. 17.16).

An interpenetrant octahedral twin is shown in Fig. 17.17. A corner of one crystal can be seen poking through an octahedral face of the other. Interpenetrant twins occur occasionally in octahedra and also in cubes (Fig. 17.15).

Interpenetrant tetrahedra twins are found on rare occasions. They have a centre of symmetry, unlike the tetrahedron, thus falling within the most symmetrical crystal class, 32. The crystals are eight-pointed, as shown in Fig. 17.20.

Star-Twins

Extremely rare is the dodecahedron interpenetrant twin, which is star-shaped with six points alternatively above and below the central plane (Fig. 17.19). About fifteen miles from Virginia in the Orange Free State, South Africa, is a

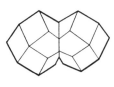

Fig. 17.15. *Forms of twinning in diamond.* Top row: *interpenetrant cubes, contact twin dodecahedra, and interpenetrant octahedra.* Bottom row, left and centre: *parallel growth in octahedra and lamellar twinning in an octahedron.*

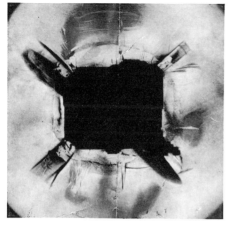

Fig. 17.16. (top) *Strain cracks around a diamond inclusion in a diamond.*

Fig. 17.17. (top right) *Twin octahedra. Note the trigons.*

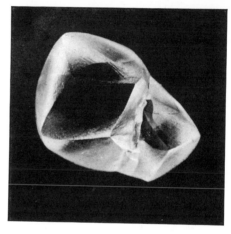

Fig. 17.18. (right) *Twin dodecahedra.*

small mine which produced an exceptional number of star-shaped diamonds and the company working it was called Star Diamonds (Pty) Ltd. Most stones were of very good colour.

Star twins of various mixed forms also occur. Three are shown in Figs. 17.21 to 17.23. Stars can also occur through contact twinning as indicated later. Another form of star is the result of cyclical twinning and is extremely rare. There are apparently six points, but one will be found to comprise two smaller points.

Contact Twins

Contact twins are like crystals that have grown side by side, but with different orientation. One part of the crystal appears to have been rotated through 180° around an axis – the twinning axis. It can also be regarded as being rotated on a plane. Another name is in fact rotation twins.

If rotation occurs through 180° on a cube (100) plane of an octahedral crystal, another octahedral crystal will grow on it parallel to the original one, as shown in Fig. 17.15. The twinning crystals will have their axes and faces parallel to each other, but will not usually be of the same size. Often, too, they are displaced as shown in Fig. 17.15.

Contact twins of this type often comprise more than two individuals and are known as parallel growths. Some parallel growths are truly so, as in alum, but true parallel growth is not common in diamond. The twinning crystals are usually only approximately parallel. Diamond aggregates of approximate parallel growth occur frequently.

Fig. 17.19. *More forms of twin. An example of that on the left is shown in* Fig. 17.21; *that in the centre is a star twin; an example of the tetrahedral twin on the right is shown in* Fig. 17.20.

Fig. 17.20. *Interpenetrant twin tetrahedra.*

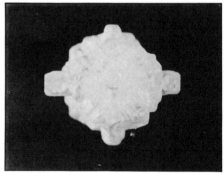

Fig. 17.22. *Extremely rare mixed twin.*

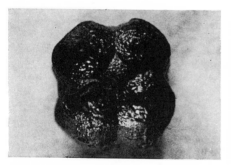

Fig. 17.21. *A mixed twin that occurs very occasionally.*

Fig. 17.23. *Extremely rare star form.*

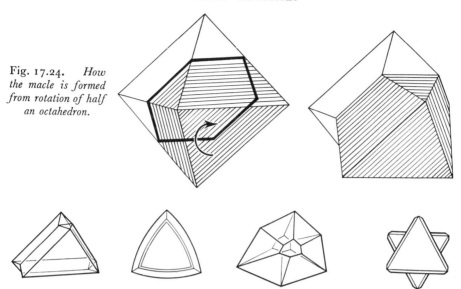

Fig. 17.24. *How the macle is formed from rotation of half an octahedron.*

Fig. 17.25. *Forms of macle. From the left: with re-entrant angles, triangle, with hexakis hexahedral faces, and partly rotated to form a star.*

Macles

Contact twins occur very commonly in diamond with one crystal rotated through 180° on an octahedral plane. This, unlike rotation on a cube plane, radically alters the appearance of the crystal. The change is so unexpected it is difficult to visualize without the help of a model and has in fact been made the basis of a puzzle. Fig. 17.24 attempts to show how such a twin occurs.

The resulting twinned octahedron is universally known as a macle or maccle (French for twin) in the diamond trade. The plane of rotation of a macle is a hexagon, as shown in Fig. 17.24. The resultant twin crystal is triangular and tends to be tabular in habit. Macles often have a re-entrant angle, as shown in Figs. 8.3 and 17.25, which is an indication that the crystal is definitely a twin and not an untwinned tabular crystal, known as a flat.

The twinning or composition plane is usually called the seam in the diamond trade. It is rarely a flat plane, which introduces problems for the diamond cutter. The majority of macles also seem to be flawed at the edges by feathery lines running inwards from and at right angles to the edges, parallel to dodecahedron faces, as shown in Fig. 17.26. When the faces are flat they are often highly specular.

Triangles

Macles also occur with rounded faces, sometimes showing triakis or hexakis octahedroid features. The rounded faces form sharp points to the crystals, masking the re-entrant angles, and the crystals are usually called triangles. Careful examination will usually indicate whether or not these triangles are twinned. Many have large feathers or cracks in them. One is shown in Fig. 17.26.

Sometimes crystals are found in which the two parts of the macle appear to have slipped or moved slightly in relation to each other, towards one of the edges. On other occasions, the rotation has been through a little less than 180°. Very rarely, half of the macle rotates to produce a crystal of six-pointed star shape. (Fig. 17.25.)

Macled cubes have been reported from Brazil. A macled tetrahedron, if such exists, would be identical in shape to an octahedron.

Repeated and False Twinning

Twinning on a plane can reverse repeatedly. This gives rise to a series of crystal layers, or lamellae, of different orientation, each being rotated by 180° in relation to the next layer. The lamellae may be quite thick or extremely thin. Such polysynthetic twinning or lamellar twinning, as it is also known, is common in diamond. (Fig. 17.15.)

Lines and ruts caused during growth or by etching through the corrosive forces of nature during a long period of time can be like parallel twinning in appearance and are then known as false twinning.

Crystal Aggregates

The growth of several diamond crystals together as an aggregate is common. There may be only two, three, four or so crystals locked together, or as many as hundreds. The sizes may be large or minute.

Again, the aggregate may be irregular, with no relationship between the orientation of the crystals, or regular, when different axes, edges, or faces are parallel to each other. Diamond aggregates are nearly always irregular. Many are formed of large masses of small crystals in haphazard order.

If there are no outward faces or edges to define separate crystals, a mass may still be made up of thousands of tiny crystals of diamond of different

Fig. 17.26.　*Two macles. They are commonly flawed as on the right.*

orientation, but the mass is then more cryptocrystalline mass than a crystal aggregate.

Growth Features

The growth of diamond occurs in layers. Crystal faces are often marked by lines which, on examination, are seen to be shallow steps or terraces. They are usually close to and parallel to the edges of octahedron faces. Sometimes the triangular terraces appear on an octahedron face in repeated flakes or lamellae. On other crystals there may be more prominent pyramids. Stepped crystal development of this type on a cube face is square. The striations on dodecahedral faces are parallel to the long axis. These and the lines on other faces are one outward expression of what the cutter calls grain.

Shallow depressions such as trigons in the octahedral faces and the squares in cubic crystals are similar phenomena. All are believed to be growth features. Accelerated growth produces an elevated projection and decelerated growth produces a depression which is orientated oppositely to the face.

Secondary face development occasionally results in hexagonal terraces near the centre of an octahedron face as shown in Fig. 17.27.

Negative Crystals

Some octahedral crystals have quite deep grooves along the edges, because these were negatively developed, and even holes in the corners. They are sometimes referred to as negative crystals (Fig. 17.28). A similar growth occurs with cubes, when four-sided hollow pyramids appear on the faces. The corners of the hollow pyramids point to the sides of the crystal, and the sides of the hollows may be terraced in steps – in the form called a hopper or skeleton cube – may be columnar and straight, or basin-shaped.

Negative growth is believed to be caused when conditions of growth favour the edges rather than the faces of a crystal or faces rather than edges.

Fig. 17.27. *Secondary face development.*

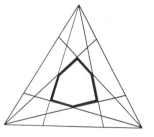

Fig. 17.28. *So-called negative growth, causing grooves along the edges.*

Trigons

Almost every, if not every, natural octahedral face has triangular markings on it, known as trigons. Some trigons are easily recognizable by the naked eye and a face with visible trigons probably invariably has thousands of faint ones as well, when viewed under high magnification. Some may be as shallow as ten angstrom units. The triangles are equilateral with straight edges (Fig. 17.29). They are orientated oppositely to the face – their corners point to the edges of the face – and they are always aligned strictly with each other.

Trigons appear to be of at least three types – pyramidal pits which go down to a sharp point, pyramidal pits with flat bottoms, and flat-bottomed pits with steep almost vertical sides.

Professor S. Tolansky, who has made a special study of diamond surfaces by his multiple beam interferometry methods, examined one portrait stone which had no apparent trigons on its surfaces. Under an effective magnification of half a million times, he found well over a million shallow trigons on each of the two sides. The area of each side was only about one square centimetre.

Etch Features

By etching diamond with a hot oxidizing agent, Tolansky has produced surface features on various faces. These are triangular on octahedron faces. boat-shaped

Fig. 17.29. *Trigons on an octahedral face. They are orientated in an opposite direction.*

Fig. 17.30. *Continued etching of an octahedral face cause the triangular pits to overlap and appear to be rectangular.*

on dodecahedron faces, and square in outline on cube faces. All are orientated with the face. The etched triangles of an octahedron face are aligned with the edges of the face, for example, compared with trigons which are orientated in an opposite direction.

As etching proceeds, in each case the edges of the pits become curved. They afford clear evidence, he says, that in each crystal, growth has proceeded by a layer formation, the layers being parallel to the octahedron faces (Fig. 17.30).

Fracture and Cleavage

It is because growth of the diamond has proceeded in places parallel to the octahedral planes that diamond will cleave in these planes, leaving flat faces. Diamond is often found in nature with one or more cleaved faces. It will also fracture in other directions and again diamonds are found in nature with concoidal fractures which show a shell-like rippled form. There is often a combination of these.

A cleaved surface is extremely flat by ordinary standards. It may vary by less than a millionth of an inch in unevenness. Although the octahedral cleavage of diamond is said to be perfect, however, it is very rarely so when examined by interferometric methods. The cleaved surface when highly magnified is often found to be broken in almost conchoidal form. It has been shown by Tolanksy that this is the characteristic cleavage of the most common diamond, Type I.

On the other hand, the cleavage of Type II stones is almost perfect. There are almost flat regions separated by steps which are only a few angstrom units high. It has been suggested that Type II stones consist of a mosaic of separate 'blocks' each being of a more perfect crystalline unit than Type I. This would, perhaps account for the steps.

There is also possible dodecahedral cleavage in diamond, since this direction gives the next looser bonding of the atomic planes. Some of the chips used in early Indian jewellery are said to be dodecahedral.

Naats

Sometimes a small volume of twinned crystals occurs within another. The most used name for this is the Dutch one, naat. In a strict sense, the naat is the junction of the two crystals of different orientation. The seam of a macle is therefore a naat.

Naats are visible when they reach the surface of a crystal. They are sometimes, but not always visible inside the stone. The small volume of cross-twinned material which is an intimate part of the crystal structure may have a different tinge of colour from the body of the crystal.

Coated Crystals

Many diamond crystals are coated when mined. The surface is more opaque than and often a different colour from the material inside. The name is a misnomer because the coating is inferior quality diamond near the surface. The depth of coating varies considerably, from very thin to a substantial part of the stone.

Coated stones come from various mines and the Congo provides a high proportion of industrial quality. An example with an octahedral face cleaved off it, is shown in Fig. 17.31. The nature of the coating gives an indication of the area where the crystal was found.

At times a coating of bad colour conceals diamond of magnificent gem colour and quality. This is particularly true of certain Brazilian stones which appear, when mined, to be light green to brown, according to the thickness of the coat, but can be collection colour once the coat is removed. On the other hand, some are brown stones all through. Venezuela stones sometimes have a shiny coat of sea-green colour under which the diamond is of top quality.

Under a coating may be a diamond of fine quality but fancy colour. A Monnickendam refers to a stone of about five carats in the rough, which was 'coated with a dirty-looking layer of skin'. When cut it proved to be a magnificent ruby red. He also points out that coated stones are not necessarily the same or better under the coating. They can be worse. Octahedra from Namaqualand may appear whitish in the rough and Silver Cape in colour when cut and are a source of worry to master cutters. They do not appear to be coated, but 'one infers that they have a transparent coat of such a nature that the yellowish tint in the stone is neutralized'.

Close examination of a coating will show it to be part of the diamond which contains many small inclusions which make the coating, or appear to make it, a different colour from the rest of the stone. Under the microscope, the inclusions

Fig. 17.31. *A face has been cleaved off this octahedron to show the 'coating'.*

are often like many small flakes of foreign material close to the surface, and the coating colour may be grey, greenish, brown or black. The surface may be shiny or dull, frosted or drusy.

Green coatings are believed to be 'skins' of induced colour caused by the crystals having been in the vicinity of radio-active materials such as uranium.

It is normally a highly speculative financial operation to buy a coated crystal which has not been opened. Opening comprises polishing windows (facets) opposite each other, through the coating. Then some appraisal of the purity and colour may be made. The coating that remains will still prevent close judgement of colour, however. Sometimes, when stones are octahedra, opposite faces are cleaved off to open the stone.

Accidental Coatings

On very rare occasions a cut diamond acquires a coating by accident that depreciates its colour. One such case was reported by Robert Crowningshield, Director of the G.I.A. Gem Trade Laboratory in New York, in 1966. An engagement ring with a stone of less than half a carat had become gradually yellow over eighteen months. Examination showed a brownish-yellowish coating that would not wash off. After treatment with hot acid, the original fine white colour was restored. The coating was apparently caused by the local iron-rich water.

Skin

Cutters sometimes refer to a skin on octahedral faces. This is in fact a physical effect caused by sudden changes in hardness when the direction of grinding is changed, as described on page 307.

Inclusions in Diamonds

Most diamonds contain small crystals of other minerals that crystallized with the formation of diamond in the original magma. The most common of these syngenetic inclusions are olivine and garnet. Others include brown chrome spinel, chrome enstatite or green chrome diopside, and diamond itself. Sometimes syngenetic inclusions suffer pseudomorphic changes, to become such minerals as serpentine, biotite, phlogopite, and chlorite.

Certain inclusions are formed by a mineral penetrating the diamond crystal from outside, through cleavage fractures and fissures. Various iron oxides penetrate diamond in this way. Oxidized diamonds are relatively common. Sometimes polished diamonds are seen with oxidized fissures in them, the brown colour of the oxide suffusing the stone. Some inclusions are shown in Figs. 17.32 to 17.37.

The rare inclusions of graphite in diamond are thought to be the result of the graphitization of diamond caused by stress in the crystal.

Industrial Crystals

Although this book is primarily concerned with gem diamonds, a brief classification of industrial stones is included for completeness. The borderline between classification of whole crystals as gems or as industrials depends upon the economic circumstances at the time.

Normally about 80 per cent of production is for industrial use. The diamonds are consumed, eventually disappearing. Of the remaining 20 per cent used as gems, over half the weight is lost in cutting, so somewhat less than 10 per cent of all diamonds are not consumed.

Stones considered to be industrial are those that do not meet the current demand for gems in quality, or are too small, badly crystallized, crypto-crystalline, or awkwardly twinned from the cutter's point of view. A stone may be almost perfect as a crystal and flawless in purity, but if it is of yellow or brown colour unsuitable for gem use, it becomes an industrial. Similarly, a fine octahedral crystal of collection colour may be classified as industrial because it has bad inclusions.

All diamonds can be classified into the following general groups:

1. Gem diamonds.
2. Industrial stones,
     (a) shaped diamonds,
     (b) rough diamonds.
3. Diamond boart.

The most preferred gem crystals are those of good octahedral shape which are as pure and white as possible. The most preferred shape of crystal for shaped diamonds for industrial use are the dodecahedron and similar rounded crystals. The purity must be as high as possible, but the colour is not so critical, although hardness or durability appear to be related to colour (page 308).

Shaped diamonds include die-stones, which are drilled with a shaped hole for wire manufacture, shaped tips for metal-cutting and finishing tools, tips of hardness indenters for measuring hardness, record player needles, truing diamonds for shaping grinding wheels and tips of rock drills.

Octahedra are better for tools used for truing grinding wheels. Triangles are also classified separately for industrial use, particularly tool-tips.

Fig. 17.32. *Group of various guest crystals (well developed diamonds and garnets as well as reabsorbed olivines and diopsides) forming an interesting assembly of the diamond's para-genesis. All are twin formations of the host.*

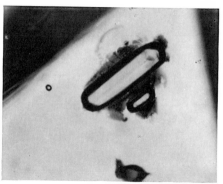

Fig. 17.33. *Pair of pseudo tetragonal olivine crystals that settled on an octahedral face lying parallel to the edge of the octahedral face. Olivine crystals are of syngenetic origin with diamond.*

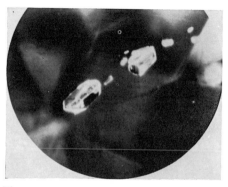

Fig. 17.34. *Idiomorphous partly-resorbed oli-vine crystals aligned parallel to a former edge of an octahedron face of the host diamond when it was still in the juvenile phase.*

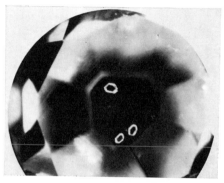

Fig. 17.35. *Very small olivine crystals of well-formed shapes.*

Photographs by E. Gübelin.

Fig. 17.36. *Straight flat cleavage fissure running diagonally through table of a brilliant-cut diamond. Such a fissure forms a zone of weakness in the host, easily causing its breakage.*

Fig. 17.37. *Irregular tension cracks diverg-ing from a common centre. Such cracks are very dangerous for the diamond as they may cause it to break easily.*

Fig. 17.38. *Hail-stone boart, cut across the middle to show the layers.*

The second class of industrial stones under 2b above, is that of irregular crystals used for glaziers' diamonds, stone saws, rock drill bits, etc.

Boart

Boart is the name given to minutely crystallized grey to black diamond masses which are useless either as gem or industrial diamonds. Boart is crushed and powdered for grinding and polishing purposes. The word appears to be derived from one meaning bastard. Boart can be classified into several varieties.

Hailstone boart is of particular interest as it is different from other types, being made up of alternate layers of diamond and a grey to black cement-like material in appearance. The diamond comprises shells of clouded material and the other substance is like a porous paste. When the outer layer is diamond, the shape is octahedroid or dodecahedroid; when it is paste, the boart is shapeless. The core is either diamond or the other material (Fig. 17.38).

Diamond material known as ballas or shot boart has a spherical form, and ranges in colour from milky white to steely grey (Figs. 17.39 and 17.40). It does not show crystalline faces or edges, appears to have no definite lines of cleavage, and does not have inclusions like common boart. The ball shape derives from a stalk-like formation of diamond crystals or irregular growths of multiple crystals. The random directions of greatest hardness give it great durability. It is an intermediate form between carbons and true diamond.

Carbonado or Carbons

Carbons are a crypto-crystalline material composed of diamond graphite, and amorphous carbon – diamond in various transitional stages, in fact. They are commonly called carbonado, the Brazilian name. Carbonado occurs in some quantity and in sizes weighing as much as two ounces in the State of Bahia and in stream beds in the State of Minas Gerais, in Brazil.

Fig. 17.39. *Ballas.*

Fig. 17.40. *Twin ballas.*

So-called black diamond is carbonado or heavily-included diamond. It does not have the rarity and high intrinsic value sometimes attributed to it in fiction, although there are at least two famous and therefore highly-valued black diamonds, one of which is shown in Fig. 1.14.

REFERENCES

The Genesis of the Diamond, by Alpheus F. Williams (London, 1932).
Diamond, by J. R. Sutton (London, 1928).
Microstructures of Diamond Surfaces, by S. Tolansky (London, 1955).
The Magic of Diamonds, by A. Monnickendam (London, 1955).

CHAPTER EIGHTEEN

Physical Properties of Diamond

Chemically, diamond is carbon in an exceptionally pure form. The only foreign element commonly present is nitrogen, which may amount to as much as 0·23 per cent. Any other foreign elements will be only parts in a million.

The carbon atom is unique in having four electrons in an outer shell which can hold up to eight. It therefore occupies a position half-way between the electro-positive and electro-negative elements, yet is not chemically neutral. Two carbon atoms can link together by sharing an electron from one, which fills a hole in the shell of the other. As there are four electrons and four holes to each atom, each atom can link with four others; i.e. it has a valency of four.

Such bonds are called covalent and can hold atoms together so that they form geometrical structures known as atomic crystals. The lattices are always strong and rigid and the resulting substances are hard solids with high melting-points. The most exceptional atomic crystal is that of diamond; it has the following structural form:

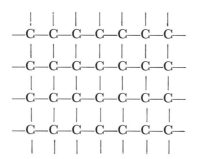

Single molecules of such substances do not exist. Diamond can therefore be described as a giant saturated molecule of carbon.

The four bonds to each atom are not of course flat, as in the structural formula shown, but are at 109·5° to each other as shown in Fig. 18.1. Each atom is at the geometric centre of four others which are at the corners of an imaginary tetrahedron. Every bond is the same, 1·544 angstrom units long.

The linking of a number of carbon atoms in this way into a three dimensional diamond lattice can be seen in Fig. 18.3. One layer is shown shaded to draw attention to the puckered hexagonal rings of atoms that result from the structure. This is in fact one octahedral direction in the crystal, the others being in the planes of a tetrahedron, as shown in Fig. 18.3.

In graphite, the only other crystalline form of carbon, the atoms form also into hexagonal rings, but the rings are flat and in thin plates or scales as shown in Fig. 18.2. Within a scale or layer, the atoms are closely linked with atomic

Fig. 18.1. *Tetrahedral bonds of the carbon atoms.*

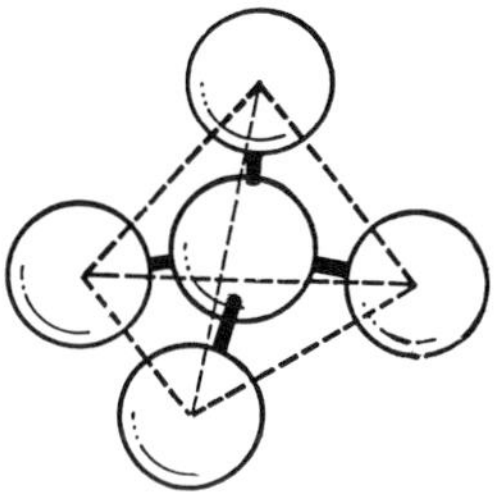

Fig. 18.2. (left). *Structure of graphite.* Fig. 18.3. (right). *Structure of diamond. Two of the three cleavage directions are shown.*

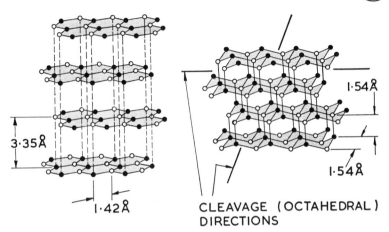

1·54Å

3·35Å

1·42Å

1·54Å

CLEAVAGE (OCTAHEDRAL)
DIRECTIONS

bonds of 1·42 angstrom units – more powerful even than diamond. Atomic forces between the layers are feeble, however, the bond being 3·35 angstrom units, and they sheer easily, giving the substance a greasy feel.

The melting-point of graphite is in the region of 3500° C and that of diamond is thought to be as high as 3700° C owing to its atomic structure. Behaviour under heat is described in Chapter Nineteen.

As there are no free electrons or holes in a perfect diamond crystal lattice, diamond has high resistance to the passage of electricity. Graphite, owing to the loose bonding between scales, has free electrons which provide the ability to pass an electric current. The lattice of diamond is exceptionally strong, which results in its extreme hardness and resistance to deformation, but it is not particularly dense.

Many other physical properties can be related to the atomic lattice of diamond. The very high thermal conductivity, for example. The high refractivity of light is probably due to the long chains of carbon atoms that extend in all directions.

Crystallography

Most minerals are crystalline, having regular internal structures, but not all form into single crystals, in which the external form reflects the internal lattice. Sometimes the substance is made up of many zones that have crystallized, but in different directions to each other, so that the whole is crystalline and without external form. Diamonds occur both in single crystals and also in formless crystalline masses.

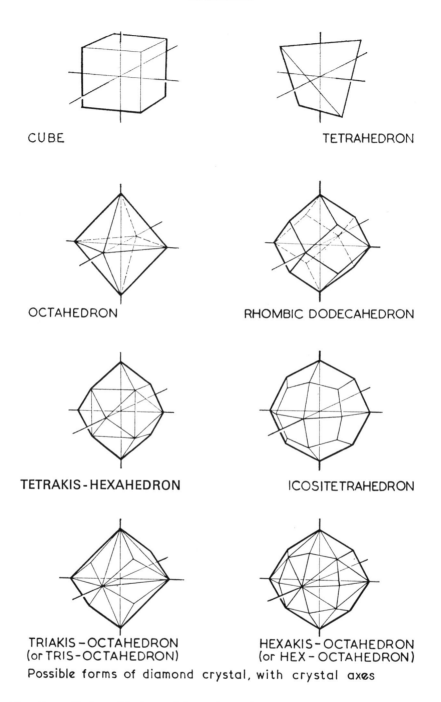

CUBE

TETRAHEDRON

OCTAHEDRON

RHOMBIC DODECAHEDRON

TETRAKIS-HEXAHEDRON

ICOSITETRAHEDRON

TRIAKIS-OCTAHEDRON
(or TRIS-OCTAHEDRON)

HEXAKIS-OCTAHEDRON
(or HEX-OCTAHEDRON)

Possible forms of diamond crystal, with crystal axes

Fig. 18.4. *Ideal possible forms of diamond crystal. The natural habit is the octahedron.*

Crystals are divided into seven main systems of symmetry and diamond falls into most symmetrical of them, the cubic, also called the regular or iso-metric system. As well as these systems it is possible to build up thirty-two crystal classes in ascending order of symmetry. The cubic system, being the most symmetrical, includes the last five classes, from 28 to 32.

It has not been definitely established whether diamond belongs in the most symmetrical, Class 32, or in the next down, Class 31. Investigations of its atomic lattice by X-ray techniques appear to favour Class 32, the most perfect. If diamond should belong to Class 31, another form of crystal is possible, the tetrahedron, which does not have a centre of symmetry.

The possible forms in Class 32 are as follows and are shown in ideal shapes in Fig. 18.4.

Hexahedron, or cube	6 faces	(100)
Octahedron	8 faces	(111)
Rhombic dodecahedron	12 faces	(110)
Tetrakis hexahedron	24 faces	
Icositetrahedron	24 faces	
Triakis octahedron	24 faces	
Hexakis octahedron	48 faces	

In the diagrams, crystal axes are shown, from which faces are identified. A face is often indicated by a kind of shorthand indicating the axes which the face intercepts and known as the Miller indices. With brackets these indices indicate the whole form, as included in the list above. A plane in any shape of diamond can be identified by its crystal name, as shown in Figs. 18.7 and 18.8.

It is conventional in crystallography to represent a crystal by a space lattice that is a model of the unit cells of the same shape that make up the crystal. A cubic crystal is thus shown as an assemblage of skeleton cubelets. The basic unit of diamond is not a single, but a double cell. It is represented by two inter-penetrating face-centred cubes, as shown in Fig. 18.5. Perhaps a simpler way of visualising it is as a face-centred cube (with atoms in the corners and centres of the faces). Inside this are four other atoms located at the centres of four of the eight smaller cubes that make up the cell.

Crystal Dynamics

It must not be thought that crystal lattices are formal structures of hard balls of atoms joined by rod-like forces, as suggested by models and the diagrams here. It is true that atoms appear to behave like spheres in contact, but they are better imagined as closely jammed together, and in movement.

Dame Kathleen Lonsdale has described the image in these words: 'The space lattice is quite imaginary; there is no actual framework. The atomic model is quite imaginary; the crystal is much more like a quivering jelly full of vibrating pips.' In diamond, vibration is considerable even at room temperature, and at over 700°C becomes so violent that the atoms jump into the more stable atomic arrangement of graphite.

Trace Elements

Although relatively so pure, diamond usually includes a few atoms of other elements in its lattice. Among these are nitrogen and aluminium, which have

303

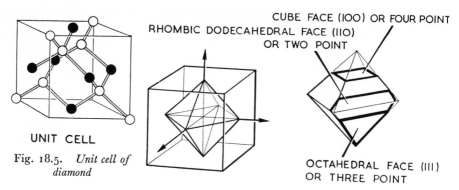

UNIT CELL

Fig. 18.5. *Unit cell of diamond*

CUBE FACE (100) OR FOUR POINT

RHOMBIC DODECAHEDRAL FACE (110) OR TWO POINT

OCTAHEDRAL FACE (111) OR THREE POINT

Fig. 18.6. (left) *Relation of octahedron crystal axes to cube crystal axes.* Fig. 18.7. (right) *Different faces or directions in an octahedral crystal.*

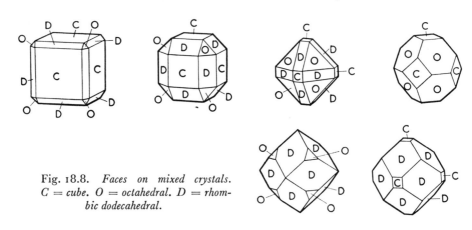

Fig. 18.8. *Faces on mixed crystals. C = cube. O = octahedral. D = rhombic dodecahedral.*

decisive effects on the physical properties as explained later, silicon, calcium, iron, copper, magnesium, barium, chromium, silver, titanium, strontium, sodium, and even lead. Diamonds from different areas include different trace elements.

Without foreign atoms, the structure could be perfect, like that in Fig. 18.3, all through, but foreign atoms have different bonding which upsets the regular arrangement. The result is a mosaic structure of crystallites which are staggered or warped like bricks in a badly-constructed wall. They can even be in spiral formation.

Cleavage

When a crystal model of diamond is viewed from certain directions, the atoms are seen to be in layers. These directions are the cubic, the octahedral, and the rhombic dodecahedral. It will also be noticed that the density of the bonds between atoms is higher between layers in certain directions that between layers in others. In the octahedral direction, there are alternate layers with more and fewer bonds, i.e. every other layer is less strongly bonded.

A layer with more bonds is shown shaded in Fig. 18.3. It has three to every one in the same area of the next layer. When diamond is cleaved in an octahedral direction, it splits between two such closely bonded layers breaking only one bond in each tetrahedral group, so that the resulting cleaved surfaces are 'perfect'. Although octahedral cleavage is usually the most common, Sir C. V. Raman has reported finding rare dodecahedral and even cubic cleavage on some very small pieces of diamond.

Valency bonds per unit area are also a general indication of hardness in different directions experienced by the cutter when grinding and polishing diamond.

Hardness

Hardness is difficult to define in an absolute sense. Hardness scales depend on the relative hardness of one substance in relation to others. One of the earliest scales, devised by the mineralogist Mohs, was 'scratch' based on the fact that any mineral in a numbered scale will scratch those of lower numbers and be scratched by those of higher numbers:

1. Talc; 2. gypsum; 3. calcite; 4. fluorspar; 5. apatite; 6. feldspar; 7. quartz; 8. topaz; 9. corundum; 10. diamond.

On the scale, a fingernail would be about $2\frac{1}{2}$ and a steel file about $6\frac{1}{2}$. The scale is by no means linear. For example, the hardness gap between 9 and 10 is much greater than that between 1 and 9. There are no natural minerals in the gap from 9 to 10, only manufactured hard materials such as the carbides of tungsten, silicon, and boron.

Scratch tests have been refined into abrasion tests. A micro-abrasion technique currently used for measuring the directional or vectorial hardness of diamond was devised in 1949 by P. Grodzinski and W. Stern. A small 110° double cone shaped grinding wheel charged with diamond dust is rotated at high speed and applied to the surface under test for a certain time. The depth of cut it makes, measured by an optical interference technique, is a measure of the hardness of the surface.

Another method of testing hardness is to measure the deformation of a material under a given load. For most materials, the load is applied to a shaped diamond indenter which penetrates the test surface. Different results are obtained by different methods and different apparatus using the same method. Some comparisons are shown below based on figures by B. W. Anderson, which were recalculated using corundum to a base of 1,000:

Mohs' Scale	Mineral	Grinding (Rosiwal)	Sand-blasting (Eppler)	Indentation (Knoop)
10	Diamond	90,000	18,530	5,180
9	Corundum	1,000	1,000	1,000
8	Topaz	195	154	766
7	Quartz	175	170	483

Polishing Gems

When gems and most other materials are polished, the surface is not abraded, but is made to flow. It is locally melted on the high spots so that the polished surface becomes a series of flakes that have flowed. The surface layer is in a vitreous amorphous state about a thousandth of a millimetre deep, rather like a coating of varnish that is harder than the original surface, and is called a Beilby layer after its discoverer. An experienced lapidary can feel when the surface slips as he is polishing a gem. It is said that, to obtain the best surface when re-polishing a gem other than diamond, the original polished layer should first be removed by grinding it away.

Diamond is believed not to behave in this way. The surface is abraded and does not form a Beilby layer. The abrasion of diamond is still little understood despite the long history of cutting. M. Seal has experimented with rubbing one diamond very slowly (at a rate of one centimetre a second) against another. This produced wear and a debris that did not appear to be diamond; it was of hexagonal structure. He thinks that diamond grinding is not entirely a mechanical or thermal process but may be linked with conversion of diamond to another substance.

Directional Hardness

Diamond is not isotropic in hardness. The relative hardness in different directions has been studied by E. M. Wilks and J. Wilks, who give this order from softest to hardest:

1. Dodecahedron parallel to crystal axis.
2. Cube parallel to crystal axis.
3. Octahedron towards dodecahedron.
4. Octahedron towards cube.
5. Dodecahedron 90° to axis.
6. Cube 45° to axis.

The difference in hardness from hardest to softest varies from something under ten times to as much as 100 times. The only two really practical grinding (polishing) directions are the first two, which are shown diagrammatically in Fig. 18.9.

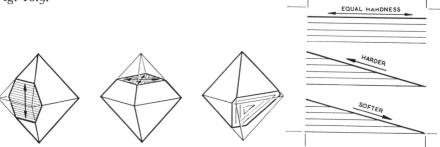

Fig. 18.9. *Possible grinding directions in an octahedral crystal on the dodecahedral and cube faces. The true octahedral face cannot be ground. Here the grinding face is shown tilted, in a direction that permits grinding.*

Fig. 18.10. *Polishing 'against the lattice' is harder than polishing with it.*

The third 'softest' direction, on the octahedral face or was, is very difficult to grind and perhaps impossible on the true (111) face. Cutters always lift the point of the face slightly so that the face is tilted towards the dodecahedral direction (Fig. 18.9).

Fig. 18.11 shows the polished cube face of a gem diamond by phase contrast photography. Superimposed over the polish lines are rectilinear patterns. Such a picture is unique for any polished diamond, according to E. M. Wilks, and is more marked on poorer quality diamonds.

Although opposite grinding directions on dodecahedral and cube faces should theoretically be of equal abrasion hardness, the polisher will usually find one way very much harder than the opposite. This difference has also been investigated by Wilks and Wilks, who found it was caused by crystal faces being out of alignment with the atomic lattice. On one diamond a difference of three times the hardness was found in opposite directions. Misorientation of the face in relation to the crystal lattice may be only a few minutes of a degree or as much as two or more degrees. The difference in hardness arises from polishing 'against the lattice' as in Fig. 18.10.

For the four-fold hardness symmetry of the cube face to be evident, the face must be at least within thirty minutes of the true crystallographic plane. An octahedral face, which has two-fold hardness symmetry, is very much more sensitive to accurate orientation, and because of this, is believed by some cutters to have a hard skin. The real reason is that slight misorientation of the face to the crystal lattice can make the change in hardness very abrupt when turning the stone on the scaive.

Four-point corners of natural octahedral crystals are used as industrial cutting tools. These are softer when reground and the reason is that the cutter cannot

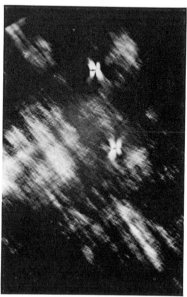

Fig. 18.11. *Polished lines (diagonal) and recti-linear pattern on a cube face.*

Fig. 18.12. *Anomalous double re-fraction in a brown diamond.*

grind an octahedral face and has to tilt the stone very slightly in a dodecahedral, i.e. a softer, direction.

Hardness and Colour

The tilt of the natural surface of a diamond in relation to its crystal lattice, is related to the colour of the crystal. In white crystals, the surfaces may be aligned or misaligned with the true octahedron faces without bias in a particular direction. Brown stones, on the other hand, tend to have faces slightly tilted towards the cube plane. Yellow stones tend to have relatively larger tilts towards the dodecahedral plane. As brown stones incline towards a harder direction than yellow ones, they stand up to wear better than yellow ones.

Density and Optical Properties

The specific gravity of diamond is very constant and is usually given as 3·52. The exact figure depends upon the impurities in the stone and Anderson confirms a range of densities from 3·514 to 3·518 previously arrived at by Crookes as accurate for larger stones of good quality. Carbonado may have a density as low as 2·9 dependent upon the impurities it contains.

As diamond is optically isotropic, it is normally considered to be singly refracting, but the presence of two types of material causes bi-refringence in many stones. Between crossed polaroids such stones show anomalous double-refraction (Fig. 18.12). Anomalous D.R. also occurs in crystals under strain and some cutters determine whether a stone may safely be cut by examining the extinction patterns.

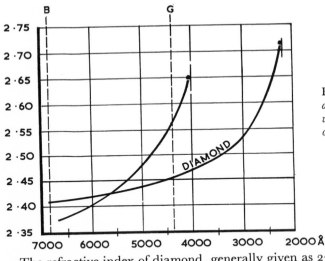

Fig. 18.13. *Refractive index of diamond for different wavelengths of light. The other line shows the R.I. of strontium titanate.*

The refractive index of diamond, generally given as 2·42, is more accurately 2·4175 in sodium light and is the highest of all natural gemstones. Dispersion between the B and G Fraunhofer lines, i.e. the difference in refractive index over the visible spectrum, is 0·044. The figure is low in relation to diamond's refractive index, despite the usual statement that diamond has a 'high' dispersion. If the curve for refractive indices is plotted from the deep red to the ultra-violet, it will be found flatter in the visible range, which accounts for the relatively low dispersion from B to G (Fig. 18.13).

Transparency and lustre were dealt with in Chapter Ten.

Type Classification

In 1934, a study by R. Robertson, J. J. Fox, and A. E. Martin showed that diamonds fell broadly into two categories, which they called Type one and Type two. They showed sharp differences in their transparency to ultra-violet light and in their infra-red absorption spectra. Type I diamonds absorbed ultra-violet strongly from about 3300 Å onwards and showed absorption bands at 7·8, 8·3, and 9·1 μ in the infra-red. Type II stones transmitted ultra-violet light down to about 2200 Å and showed no absorption bands in the infra-red.

Further research pinpointed other differences which can be summarized as shown in the table:

	Type I	Type II
Infra-red absorption	Between 8 and 10 μ Bands at 4 to 5 μ	None between 8 and 10 μ Bands at 4 to 5 μ
Ultra-violet absorption	Complete beyond 3300 Å	Transparent to 2200 Å
X-ray diffraction	Shows extra spots and streaks	Normal
Birefringence	Present	Absent
Photoconductivity	Poor	Good
Thermal conductivity	Very good	Extremely good
Electrical conductivity	None	Very few are semi-conductors
Luminescence	Present	Present with differences
Cleavage	Relatively uneven	Relatively perfect

Birefringence

It was thought that only about one in a thousand diamonds was Type II, but investigation of large numbers of stones by Tolansky has shown that almost all diamonds incorporate both Type I and Type II material. In any diamond it is usually Type I or Type II that predominates, which determines the final classification.

Tolansky's method was to examine birefringence in about 2,000 diamond crystals of about a carat each, including octahedra, dodecahedra, triangular twins, Cape dies (yellow dodecahedral industrial stones), and chips, all of which showed birefringence in some degree. His conclusion was that the chances of finding a non-birefringent diamond appears to be remote. There is clearly now a very strong case for believing that almost all diamonds are birefringent.

Crystal Habit and Type

Type II diamonds are the purer and approximate more to the ideal diamond crystallographically. Type I stones are less pure and much more common. J. F. H. Custers has pointed out that nearly all larger diamonds are Type II. They include the biggest ever found, the Cullinan. Almost all large diamonds do not have a definite crystal form. The Cullinan, for example, was a cleavage.

It appeared that, when diamonds were formed, certain impurities were necessary in the crystal structure to cause crystallization into a definite form and that these impurities also gave rise to physical property defects. Stones of good crystal form, such as octahedra, are therefore certain to be Type I. Type II stones tend not to show symmetrical crystal faces, and this is perhaps why they include larger stones not restricted in growth by crystal form.

Stones containing both types of material, in layers or mosaics, are under physical as well as optical strain which may explain why many fractured crystals are recovered from mines.

Nitrogen in the Structure

The impurity that causes diamond to divide into two types was found in 1959 by W. Kaiser and W. Bond to be nitrogen. Type I diamonds can be broadly defined as those with nitrogen in their structure and Type II diamonds as those without.

Nitrogen has a valency of five compared with oxygen's four which means that the presence of nitrogen alone would free electrons and make the diamond conduct electricity. Almost all diamonds contain some aluminium atoms, however, which have a valency of three and mop up free electrons, so that current cannot pass.

Type IIb Diamonds

Custers proposed in 1952 and 1959 that Type II stones should be divided into Type IIa and Type IIb on the basis of differences in luminescence and photo-conductivity. Type IIb stones are a very small proportion of Type II, possibly about one in a thousand. Unlike other diamonds, they are electrical semi-con-ducters, i.e. they are neither good conductors nor good insulators. The reason is the presence of aluminium and the absence of nitrogen. The missing bonds (holes) in the lattice make the passage of electrons possible.

Type IIb includes all natural blue stones, the only current source of which is the Premier Mine. The famous Hope blue diamond is also Type IIb and this almost certainly came from the old Kollur Mine in India.

Types and Colour

Nitrogen and aluminium in the lattice of a diamond are responsible for many of the optical properties of diamond. When the concentration of nitrogen is low

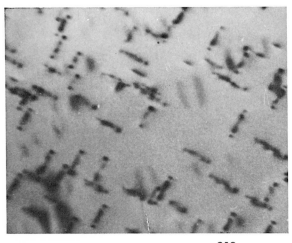

Fig. 18.14. *Nitrogen plate-lets in the atomic lattice of Type Ia diamond, photo-graphed by the Diamond Re-search Laboratory, Johannes-burg.*

(in the order of one part in a million) and the nitrogen atoms are dispersed through the crystal lattice, the diamond absorbs light in the blue region. This upsets the colour balance and results in a yellowish body colour. Greater concentrations of nitrogen introduce a green tinge.

All Type I diamonds contain relatively substantial amounts of nitrogen and it would therefore appear that none could be of gem colour, which is contrary to the facts. The explanation was discovered by scientific workers at the Diamond Research Laboratory in Johannesburg. If the concentration of nitrogen is greater than one part in 1,000, the nitrogen atoms will have migrated in most cases into local concentrations of platelets, as shown in the electron microscope picture, Fig. 18.14. They are more stable thermo-dynamically in this form.

Nitrogen atoms dispersed at random throughout a crystal require a long and stable period of high pressure and temperature to detach themselves from where they are anchored and gradually move through the carbon atom lattice towards other nitrogen atoms to form platelets. It is assumed that such conditions existed for millions of years during the formation of diamonds deep in the Earth.

When nitrogen is concentrated in platelets, it has a different effect on light. Instead of absorbing in the blue part of the visible band, giving the stone a yellow to green colour, the absorption is shifted into the ultra-violet. Visible light is therefore unaffected, and the stone can have a white body colour, up to the finest gem colour according to the absorption of the particular stone.

Some natural Type I stones contain only dispersed nitrogen, but they are few in number, about one in 1,000. They were given the designation Type Ib by Diamond Research Laboratory workers in 1965. Type Ib stones are paramagnetic.

Type IIa stones contain no appreciable nitrogen and are always of good gem colour, i.e. they are colourless. Although almost all very big diamonds found fit this category and were, when found, without crystal form, there are some of inferior colour for some reason, including the 601-carat Lesotho diamond discovered in 1968, which is formless but has a brownish tinge.

Synthetic Diamonds

Because synthetic diamonds are made almost instantaneously and do not remain at high temperatures and pressures for long periods of time, there is no opportunity for any nitrogen atoms trapped in the lattice to migrate into groups, Consequently synthetic diamonds are normally Type Ib, of a yellowish to green colour, and paramagnetic.

If nitrogen is specifically excluded during growth, synthetic diamonds become Type II and are colourless.

Summary of Types

All natural diamonds can be divided into the following categories, but many are mixtures of categories merging into one another.

Type Ia: Diamonds containing nitrogen in platelets. They comprise the majority of all natural diamonds.

Type Ib: Diamonds containing dispersed nitrogen, and number about
             0·1 per cent of Type I.

Type IIa: Diamonds without significant nitrogen. They are a small minority
             of all natural diamonds.

Type IIb: Diamonds with aluminium but without nitrogen. A very small
             percentage of Type II, including all natural blues.

Type III: A proposed classification for meteoric diamonds, which were
             established by Kathleen Lonsdale as having a hexagonal struc-
             ture, and have been given the name Lonsdaleite.

Photographic Method of Separation

If there is occasion to separate Type I from Type II stones, a simple method is
immersion-contact photography. A camera is not needed. The diamonds are
placed on photographic paper in water and exposed for a few seconds to short-
wave ultra-violet light for a short time, using a short-wave ultra-violet lamp with
a Chance No. 7 (OXY) filter over the lamp and exposing in the dark. If printing
paper is used and afterwards developed, the Type II stones, which transmit
ultra-violet light, appear dark and the other white against the black background.

Spectra of Diamonds

When examined by a spectroscope, most diamonds are found to have characteristic absorption spectra. The predominant band is in the violet at 4155 Å,
which is the 'arrow head' of a series of less powerful bands (Fig. 18.15). Dispersed nitrogen in the lattice is responsible for this 4155 system, which causes
light absorption mainly in the ultra-violet region but encroaches on the blue
end of the visible spectrum, thus affecting the body colour of the stone.

If the 4155 system is entirely absent, the diamond is of the very finest quality
in whiteness. If it is present, but only very faintly, then the diamond is a top
White, but just misses being of the finest colour. As the 4155 system becomes
more evident, so the diamond becomes more yellow – from White, to Commercial White, Top Silver Cape, Silver Cape, Cape, and so on. Anderson has
shown that the intensity and width of the main band increases in step with the
depth of colour and that other bands appear as the colour deepens.

Cape and Brown Series

Diamonds with the spectrum just described are Type Ia and are called Cape
series stones.

Some diamonds have another characteristic spectrum based on a line at
5040 Å, which is also the hinge of a series of bands with remarkable mirror-
image symmetry (Fig. 18.15). These are diamonds known as the brown series,
which have body colours in increasing shades of brown to amber and also a
greenish colour. They include stones with a relatively large amount of dispersed
nitrogen and fewer platelets, i.e. Type Ia, which merge into Type Ib.

When the colour of a diamond has been altered artificially by irradiation
(see Chapter Nineteen), the structural damage to the atomic lattice causes a
colour change that is also detectable in the spectrum. The most diagnostic line

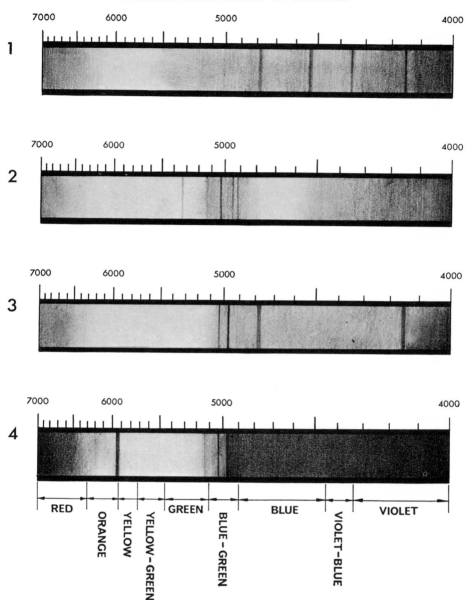

Fig. 18.15. *Spectra of some diamonds, after R. Crowningshield. 1, pale yellow (Cape spectrum); 2, brown; 3, treated yellow, yellow-green, light brown, and some blue; 4, treated yellow-brown, yellow, and black. The red of the spectrum is shown on the left in the traditional manner employed by gemmologists.*

is at 5940 line in the yellow. It is narrow and not easy to detect, but G. R. Crowningshield and B. W. Anderson have both seen it in large numbers of treated golden yellow stones. The 5940 line does occur in nature, but is very rare indeed.

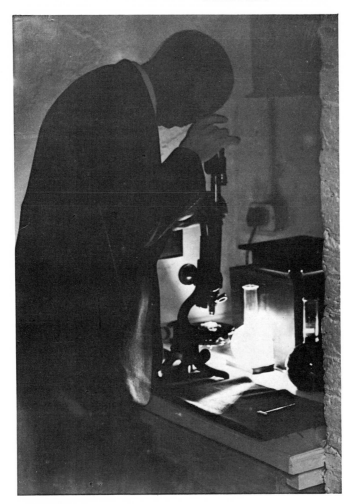

Fig. 18.16. *Examining the spectrum of a diamond with spectroscope on the top of a microscope without the ocular. Light passed through a flask of copper sulphate solution is passed also through the diamond on the stage.*

Using the Spectroscope

The hand spectroscope usually favoured by gemmologists can be employed with light reflected off or transmitted through the stone. It is difficult to transmit light through a brilliant-cut diamond, so the best way is to hold the stone sideways in a clip or by a blob of plasticine so that light is transmitted through the girdle.

As the principal lines are in the blue end of the spectrum Anderson suggests making them more visible by using light which has passed through a flask of blue copper sulphate solution (Fig. 18.16).

Luminescence under Ultra-Violet Light

Luminescence is the visible glow of light produced in certain substances when rubbed, scratched, subjected to chemical change, or irradiated in some way by invisible electromagnetic radiations, such as sunlight, ultra-violet rays, cathode rays, and X-rays. The gemmologist is most concerned with fluorescence, when the substance glows when irradiated, and phosphorescence, any after-glow on removal.

The gemmologist must use a convenient source of irradiation and normally employs long-wave ultra-violet light of 3650 Å from a mercury vapour lamp with a Wood's glass filter over it.

Quite brilliant blue fluorescence occurs in some stones under ultra-violet light in the dark, gradually building up in brightness. If such a stone, set or unset, is removed quickly from under the ultra-violet lamp and masked by cupping it in the hands, it may be seen to have a yellow-green after-glow. This after-glow is a positive test for diamond and its intensity is in step with the brightness of the blue fluorescence.

The most common fluorescence in diamonds is blue or mauve, ranging from bright sky blue to weak and rather dark violet. Others have green, yellow, or orange glows. Quite often the glow is patchy or in bands related to the crystal form. Intensities vary considerably from stone to stone. A suggestion was made in 1943 by Anderson that diamonds could be classified into three groups on the basis of their main fluorescent colours is still valid:

Blue fluorescing diamonds: The most common, Cape series stones with the 4155 absorption band system and certain fluorescent bands.

Yellow-green fluorescing diamonds which belong to the Brown series with the 5040 absorption band system and certain fluorescent bands.

Yellow fluorescing diamonds including true canary yellow diamonds, with no visible absorption or fluorescent bands at normal temperatures.

Some pink diamonds from India fluoresce and phosphoresce with a strong orange colour, and the Hope blue diamond has strong red fluorescence. Most natural blue stones are inert, however, although they give a bluish after-glow.

Type II stones in general do not fluoresce.

The ultra-violet light in sunlight will cause some diamonds to fluoresce blue in daylight, and some have an after-glow in darkness, but this effect is slight and has been much exaggerated in past reports. The fluorescence cannot be separated by the eye, but being blue, will mask any yellow tinge in a stone. A diamond may therefore appear to be of a higher quality in colour when seen in sunlight or light from the direction of the sun, even if masked by clouds. The same applies in any artificial light that contains a high proportion of ultra-violet.

The blue fluorescence of a few stones is evident to the naked eye in daylight and gives the stone a bluish milky, or even oily, appearance. These are the over-blues, also known as Premiers. There are also a few stones that have a yellow-green fluorescence strong enough just to be evident in daylight that gives the diamond the colour of Vaseline.

Identification Records

Robert Webster has suggested a practical application for the unpredictable response of diamonds to long-wave ultra-violet in the identification of jewellery set with many diamonds. If the fluorescing jewellery is photographed, a picture similar to that in Fig. 18.17 is obtained. The picture is unique and even an otherwise identical piece would give a different pattern. The jewellery is first photographed in white light and then in filtered ultra-violet light with an Ilford Q or Wratten 2B filter over the camera lens.

Fluorescent Spectra

The light from a fluorescing diamond can be examined with a spectroscope with the slit quite wide. The strong blue fluorescence that is quite common will be seen to be strongly banded, a means of identifying diamond.

Other Luminescent Effects

Diamonds under X-rays will usually show the most consistent luminescent effect, a rather uniform bluish white glow. Cathode rays give most brilliant fluorescent effects and some diamonds have been found to glow different colours on different faces.

A diamond made to fluoresce blue under ultra-violet light will phosphoresce

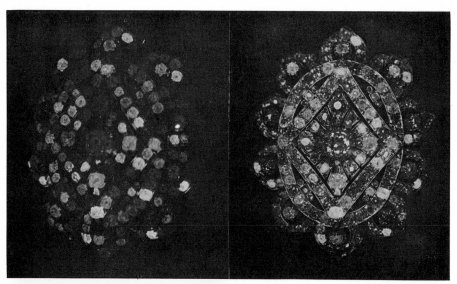

Fig. 18.17. *A means of photographing the fluorescence of diamond jewellery for identification purposes, suggested by R. Webster.*

Fig. 18.18. *Fluorescent cubic crystal.*

yellow-green at the same time, but the yellow-green will be masked by the strong blue emission. If the ultra-violet light is cut off, the stone will have yellow-green after-glow because the blue emission remains 'frozen' in the stone. It may later be released by heating the stone to about 200° C, when it will glow blue. This effect is called thermo-phosphorescence.

Diamond will luminesce if rubbed, exhibiting triboluminescence. C. F. Kunz stated that the luminescence could be produced by rubbing the stone on various materials including wood, wool and certain metals. He found that it was most evident when the diamond was rubbed on wood across the grain!

Conduction of Heat

Diamonds feel cold to the touch because of their high thermal conductivity, which is the highest of any known material. Diamond conducts heat so rapidly that it can be plunged red hot into liquid nitrogen without being harmed, whereas most non-metallic minerals would shatter. Its high thermal conductivity is a principal reason why diamond is such an effective material for tipping tools.

The thermal conductivity of diamonds depends upon waves called phonons through the lattice, which means that lattice defects affect it. Type IIa stones are in fact between three and five times more thermally conductive than the less perfect Type I. They are used industrially as heat sinks to conduct heat away from delicate apparatus.

The thermal expansion of diamond is extremely low, being almost zero at 39° C. In general it is about 80 per cent that of invar, the nickel steel used for the pendulum rods of high precision clocks.

Electrical Behaviour

Although Type I stones and Type IIa stones are classed generally as extremely good insulators, there are a few Type IIa stones with lower resistances, nearer Type IIb. Diamond is exceptional in conducting heat and resisting electricity. Usually heat and electrical conductivity go together.

Type IIb stones can be used as p-type transistors, but the conductivity varies from stone to stone. The semi-conductors silicon and germanium have the same form of crystal structure as diamond.

Diamonds are photoconductive, retaining their high resistivity only in the dark and in light with no ultra-violet content. When ultra-violet light falls on them, their resistance drops. Type IIb stones are photoconductive to gamma rays. When gamma rays fall on such a crystal any current of electricity through it is amplified, so it may be used like a geiger tube, for counting radiation.

If a D.C. voltage is applied across a Type IIb stone, at first the current will be small, perhaps a few milliamps. After a few minutes, it will rise to several ampères and the stone will become red hot and eventually vaporize if the current is not cut off. This does not seem to occur if A.C. current is used, but the diamond scintillates with blue light.

Two other especial properties of diamond is its lower compressibility than any other material, and its very low coefficient of friction.

CHAPTER NINETEEN

Synthetic Diamonds: Artificial Coloration

In 1673, the English physicist, Robert Boyle, discovered that diamond disappeared in acrid vapours when heated to a high temperature and some years later a diamond was caused to vanish at a public demonstration in Florence by heating it with a burning glass. In 1772, Lavoisier showed the vapours to be carbon dioxide and we now know that diamond begins to burn and convert to carbon monoxide and dioxide in air at a temperature between about 700° and 900° C depending on the quality of the stone.

Diamond jewellery accidentally dropped into a fire or overheated during repair by the jeweller's blowtorch, usually suffers superficial damage which shows as dulling or clouding of the polished surfaces to a leaden colour. Repolishing usually restores the finish. In extremely hot fires, as for example may occur after an air crash, some stones may be damaged beyond repair.

Soldering Diamond Jewellery

The traditional and usually effective means of avoiding damage to a stone set in jewellery being hard gold soldered is first to coat the diamond with a paste made of boracic acid powder and water. This dries as a coating that will prevent air from reaching the stone. As no oxygen can reach the stone, it cannot therefore burn and will stand a much higher temperature without damage. Diamond jewellery is only repaired with the stones in place when it is uneconomic to unset and reset them, as would be done with more valuable stones.

The modern way to avoid damage is to use resistance or microwave welding, which is so rapid that a negligible amount of heat travels through the metal and reaches the stone when altering the size of the shank and even when replacing a claw with the stone in position, if microwave welding is employed.

Conversion to Graphite

Diamond heated in the absence of oxygen, such as in a vacuum or in an inert atmosphere, will not burn and will eventually convert to graphite. The process begins to take place at between 800° and 1700° C, depending on the quality of the diamond. At first only a thin layer of the surface is affected. At a temperature of approximately 1700° C, a second process begins and conversion to graphite is rapid and right through the stone, which eventually disintegrates into a pile of graphite powder.

Diamonds can be damaged or converted to graphite by forms of heating other than a fire or furnace, such as intense radioactivity and by passing a current of electricity through a stone that is a semi-conductor. Too rapid cutting or attempting to cut in a hard direction will also cause some conversion (burning), which appears as areas of small dark spots. It is more common on whole stones than on sawn stones. Diamond powder collecting on the clamps of mechanical dops will also at times cause abrasion and even burning of the stone during polishing because the high frequency vibration causes the clamps to act as ultrasonic drills.

Diamond is a thermodynamically unstable form of carbon at normal temperature and pressure. In simple terms, the rate of transition of diamond to graphite at room temperature is zero. At a temperature around 1700°C transition is rapid – taking only a few minutes.

Attempts to make Diamond

For centuries, interested experimenters in alchemy or natural history tried to make diamond without knowing it to be carbon. The information that diamonds were discovered in river gravels gave no hint of their composition, but it was certainly known to some at the beginning of the nineteenth century that carbonaceous materials, heat and pressure, were needed to produce diamonds. It was from that time that some attempts at synthesizing can be regarded as scientific.

When diamonds were found in pipes around 1870, the kimberlite was regarded as the magma in which the diamonds were formed and a number of efforts were made by amateurs and scientists to produce diamonds from melts of kimberlite.

Meteoric diamonds

In 1880, diamonds were detected in a nickel-iron meteorite that had fallen in Siberia. In 1893, meteoric iron from the giant crater of Canyon Diablo in Arizona, U.S.A., was also found to contain them. In both, the proportion of diamond to meteorite was much higher than the proportion of diamond to kimberlite in pipes. These discoveries gave fresh ideas to would-be diamond makers.

There are two diametrically opposed theories about the origin of diamonds in meteorites. The first is that they were formed from carbon by the heat of the meteorite after it passed through the Earth's atmosphere and the shock of the impact. The other is that they were already contained in the meteorite, because some studies suggest that meteoric diamonds were formed under static high pressure.

The Canyon Diablo meteorite iron contains polycrystalline cubes of diamond and also cubo-octahedra. Some of the diamond is of hexagonal crystallographic structure. As the Canyon Diablo region contains graphite and the micro-diamonds were found in the iron round the rim, it seems likely that the shock and heat of impact of the giant meteorite formed diamonds in the crater.

Studies of meteoric diamonds led Professor S. Tolansky to speculate that the moon may be a source of diamond.

Transition of Graphite to Diamond

Despite the disarming similarity between crystalline carbon as graphite and as diamond, changing the stable graphite into the unstable diamond proved far from easy.

Graphite is a hexagonal structure of carbon in flat hexagonal rings in planes, with loose bonds between planes, which give it its soft, flaky texture. Diamond is a cubic structure or puckered hexagonal rings with no loose bonds. Graphite's more open structure gives it a density of 2·2 grammes a cubic centimetre. Diamond is denser, weighing 3·5 grammes per c.c.

The problem is to squeeze the graphite until its hexagonal rings of carbon atoms become puckered and take up the smaller cubic atomic structure, and then to prevent the atoms from springing back to the hexagonal structure of graphite after the pressure is removed. High temperature is applied during the squeeze to keep the atoms moving to that they will be encouraged to take up the new bonds.

The two structures are shown in Fig. 18.2 and 18.3.

Notorious Attempts to make Diamond

Some earlier diamond-makers were more concerned with making money. One was Henri Lemoine of Paris, who began a series of experiments in 1905. He managed to obtain an interview in London with Sir Julius Wernher, the South African financier who founded Wernher, Beit and Co., and who was also a life governor of De Beers Consolidated Mines, to ask for financial backing. He claimed to be able to make gem diamonds on a commercial scale by a secret process which he offered Sir Julius in exchange for royalty payments on the diamonds he made.

Lemoine persuaded Sir Julius to visit a laboratory he had hired in London to carry out a demonstration. He prepared certain ingredients in a crucible which he put in an electric furnace for half an hour. Then he withdrew it, stirred the contents, and produced twenty-five small, well crystallized diamonds of good colour. Sir Julius advanced enough money for Lemoine to set up a laboratory in Paris, where for three years he continued experiments, sending sample diamonds at intervals to Sir Julius.

Eventually even Sir Julius became suspicious, especially as there was no difference between Lemoine's 'synthetic diamonds' and crystals recovered from the Jagersfontein mine in the Orange Free State. After an investigation, Lemoine was charged with fraud and arrested. He was tried and sentenced to six years' imprisonment.

A much more mysterious affair took place as late as 1952, when a large group of West German scientists under Dr Herman Meincke, claimed to have synthesized diamond. A series of tests in the presence of two solicitors produced twenty small stones of up to 2·8 milligrams each. They were real diamonds, but were fractures of crystals exactly similar to industrial boart. In a further test attended by the public prosecutor and three detectives, crystals were produced but they were not diamond. Legal action followed.

Early synthesis experiments: Hannay

Of the serious early attempts, only one withstood testing. It was by James Ballantyne Hannay, a Glasgow chemist (1855–1931), who had been searching for a solvent for alkali metals such as sodium and potassium. He found that even an inert substance like paraffin would decompose when heated under pressure with hydrogen gas and one of the alkali metals. The hydrogen combined with the metal and the carbon from the paraffin was freed. This gave him the idea that carbon could be made to re-crystallize as diamond.

To obtain the high pressure necessary, he had thick coiled tubes of wrought iron made by the same methods as gun barrels but open only at one end. A tube was filled with the reaction material and sealed with a blacksmith's weld. It was then placed in a large reverbatory furnace for several hours.

After a long series of eighty experiments, only three were successful. In most cases the tubes exploded or leaked. On several occasions, the furnace was wrecked. In the three successful experiments, he used a four milligram of lithium and a mixture of 10 per cent rectified bone oil and 90 per cent paraffin spirit. After being fired, the tubes were found to contain much gas, a little liquid, and a smooth mass of solid material covering the walls. Pulverizing the mass yielded some tiny transparent crystals.

Hannay decided these were diamonds and submitted some to M. H. N. Story-Maskelyne, F.R.S., Keeper of Minerals at the British Museum, who announced in a letter to *The Times* on 20th February, 1880, that there was no doubt that Hannay had produced diamonds. Later that year, Hannay presented a detailed paper to the Royal Society.

Of all the early claimants to have synthesized diamonds, J. B. Hannay was unique because his material still exists, but attempts to repeat his experiments have failed.

In 1943, the crystallographers F. A. Bannister and Kathleen Lonsdale borrowed the twelve surviving Hannay crystals from the British Museum and submitted them to tests not available to Hannay. They found that eleven were diamonds, but one was not.

Since the authenticity of the Hannay diamonds still remained in doubt, Michael Seal, a diamond research worker, obtained permission from the British Museum to examine the crystals by electron microscope. Some of the structures seen on the surfaces resembled neither those of natural or synthetic diamonds. On many of the surfaces small solid particles were found that on analysis turned out to be compounds of silica. In his paper, Hannay had commented that a few grains of silica had been mixed with the carbon. Seal tends to favour the view that Hannay made synthetic diamonds, although this cannot be proven.

Moissan's Experiments

About ten years after Hannay's work, F. F. Henri Moissan (1852–1907) carried out a large number of experiments in France. The discovery of tiny diamonds in the Canyon Diablo meteorite suggested to him that, if he selected a metal that would expand on solidifying, an outer skin would be formed as it cooled and extremely high pressures would be produced at the centre. This should produce temperatures and pressures sufficient to form diamond from carbon.

He examined the solubility of carbon in the metals aluminium, chromium, iron, magnesium, manganese, platinum, silver and uranium, and also in silicon. His most successful results were when dissolving carbon in pure iron in a carbon crucible in an electric furnace. The molten mass of iron with absorbed carbon was plunged into water to form a rigid crust, then allowed to cool in air.

Afterwards he found that cooling in molten lead was more effective. After the whole was solidified, it was placed in an acid bath and slowly eaten away to release any crystals it contained.

The particles that resulted were found by Moissan to scratch ruby, and to have a specific gravity of between 3 and 3·5. He examined them under the microscope and also measured the amount of carbon dioxide they gave off when burned in oxygen. As a result he pronounced them to be diamond.

Moissan's reports to the Académie des Sciences in 1893 and 1894 caused considerable controversy and many attempts were made by others to reproduce his experiments. In England, Sir William Crookes produced the required pressures by exploding cordite in closed steel tubes and claimed to have produced diamonds. Sir Charles Parsons, also in England, reported to the Royal Society in 1918 that he had repeated both Hannay's and Moissan's experiments with improved apparatus and had also employed some ingenious techniques of his own. He had no success with Hannay's apparatus but claimed it with Moissan's method. Later he withdrew this claim.

M. Seal and A. R. Bobrowsky have repeated Moissan's work in recent times and submitted the particles produced to X-ray tests. They followed Moissan's own instructions with success in four of twelve runs, producing about twenty crystals in each of the four. The crystals, examined through a microscope and photographed resembled Moissan's published drawings and in some the similarity was quite striking.

Submitted to individual X-ray diffraction tests by special techniques, crystals tested turned out to be of silicon carbide, amorphous material or alumina. Seal concluded that, although Moissan was well aware of the presence of these materials, 'it is tempting to suggest that Moissan's product was also silicon carbide or alumina'.

First Repeatable Synthesis: A.S.E.A.

Unqualified success was not achieved until 1953, when the Swedish company Allmana Avenska, Elektriska Aktiebolaget, known as A.S.E.A., made crystals of under a millimeter in size under the direction of B. von Platen. A.S.E.A. apparently thought they were the only concern working seriously on the problem and their intention was to make gem quality stones. It seems that they did not realize the potential of the industrial market. Consequently, they did not announce their success until 1955, when the Americans had also had success.

The Swedish technique employed pressures of between 80,000 and 90,000 atmospheres at a maximum temperature of about 2760°C. The major problem is generating the high pressures because even a vessel made of carboloy (tungsten carbide cemented with cobalt), which has the highest compressive strength, will fail at about 65,000 atmospheres. It was found, however, that pressures much above the yield point can be maintained if the vessel is surrounded by massive supports.

The supports have to be arranged so that the pressure increases towards the centre. This was done by using six four-sided pyramids arranged with their points together in the form of a cube. The points were removed to form a hollow spherical chamber of about 400 cubic centimetres. If the area outside is, say, fifteen times greater than the area of the chamber inside, pressure per square centimetre applied on the outside will be magnified fifteen times inside. In the Swedish experiments an outside pressure of about 5,800 atmospheres was boosted to about 97,000 atmospheres.

Pressure was applied to the six pyramids by six pistons and the whole assembly was placed in a tube 53 cm. (about 22 in.) in diameter strengthened with steel bands. Water was pumped into the tube until its pressure was 5,800 atmospheres. This forced the pistons and pyramids together.

In the hollow centre was placed a hollow sphere of soapstone containing thermite; in this was another hollow sphere, of tantalum and in the centre of this sphere a reagent, comprising iron carbide and graphite. Thermite is a mixture of magnesium and barium peroxide, which produces a very high temperature when ignited. The 5 mm. thick shell of soapstone was to insulate the thermite from a copper holder in which the whole sample was contained, as it was ignited electrically. The diameter of the whole sample was about 7 mm. (about 3 in.).

After cooling, the sample was removed and cut in half. Diamonds were found in the centre of the iron carbide. Later, electrical means of heating and metal-graphite mixtures were found more effective. A factory was set up at Robertfors, in the north of Sweden, manufacturing industrial diamond at a rate which had reached about two million carats a year in 1964.

In 1967 A.S.E.A., made an agreement with De Beers, referred to later.

American Synthesis: G.E.

Experiments were meanwhile being conducted by the company General Electric in the U.S.A., using similar principles of boosting pressure and dissolving carbon in molten metals. At first they used a mixture of iron sulphide and heated it while in contact with carbon and tantalum metal. Tantalum was found to act as a catalyst. Subsequently it was discovered that nickel and cobalt were satisfactory catalysts, as was iron.

G.E.'s first experiment produced smaller amounts of diamonds than the A.S.E.A., method, but in 1955 they were able to announce that they had made synthetic diamonds and were able to repeat the process so that commercial production of synthetic diamond was possible. They were, of course, unaware of the work that had been successful in Sweden owing to the secrecy of A.S.E.A. G.E. applied for, and obtained, world patents.

The theoretical basis of the success rested on the work of Nobel Prize winner, P. W. Bridgman, and the group mainly responsible for the practical synthesis comprised Francis Bundy, H. Tracy Hall, Herbert Stroud, and Robert Wentorf. Their largest crystals weighed about one thousandth of a carat and were not more than a millimetre long.

It was discovered by G.E. that the mineral pyrophyllite had a unique property that was valuable for diamond synthesis. Pyrophyllite is a soft, slate-like material. It is a hydrous aluminium silicate which is in the same family as the material used for slate pencils, as talc, and as the steatite or soapstone used in the Swedish method. When subjected to extreme pressures, its melting point rises from 2400° to 4800°F (1360° to 2720°C).

The success of the G.E. production depends to a great extent on a high-pressure apparatus known as the belt, which is versatile and will stand up to much abuse as well as being simple and having a good capacity. The belt is a ring made of tungsten carbide. The hole in the centre is shaped to form a cylinder which is flared at each end. Two tapered pistons are driven into the opposite ends of the central hole as shown in Fig. 19.1. Pressure is applied to the pistons by a large hydraulic press.

To make diamond, a short cylinder of pyrophyllite is filled with the reaction material – graphite or other form of carbon, with tantalum or nickel – and placed in the hole in the belt. Pressure is then applied and a current of electricity passed through the centre to provide the temperature. The pyrophyllite acts as a gasket to seal the gaps. It flows under very high pressure and allows the pistons to advance and compress the carbon and metal.

The pyrophyllite also prevents leakage of current and heat when the electrical current is passed through. Pressures employed are over 100,000 atmospheres (about 1·5 million pounds a square inch) and temperatures over 2,000° C, with transient peaks in the range of 3,000° C. Diamonds are recovered by using acids on the hard black mass of material that results.

The belt was one of the designs of Bridgman and Tracy Hall. Another method used in diamond production is a tetrahedral structure of hydraulic rams employing trahedrally-shaped pieces of pyrophyllite to hold the carbon and metal.

South African Success: De Beers

In 1959, De Beers Consolidated Mines announced that they also had evolved a commercial process for making diamond. The decision to carry out research was made in 1955 within a month of the G.E. announcement, in co-operation with the Belgian Congo mining company the Société Minière du Becéka. Becéka produced most of the world's natural industrial diamond grit until disturbances occurred in the Congo after the granting of independence.

The successful De Beers team was J. H. Custers, H. B. Dyer, B. W. Senior, and P. T. Wedepohl, of the Adamant Research Laboratory, Johannesburg. By coincidence, the first South African synthetic diamonds were made on the same day in September 1958, as the lifting of a secrecy order imposed by the U.S. Government on the G.E. method.

The South African team also used a belt system, developed from work published by Bridgman and others, and their first diamond was 0·4 by 0·25 millimetre and comprised six equal sized particles closely cemented together. Continuous production was next achieved and a patent applied for. Later, there was a patent dispute between G.E., and De Beers which was eventually settled to the advantage of both.

A synthetic diamond factory, Ultra High Pressure Units, was set up at Springs, in the Johannesburg area, with seventy-five high-voltage presses. The pyrophyllite cylinders in which the diamonds are made are about $2\frac{1}{2}$ by $\frac{3}{4}$ inches with tapered rings over each end as shown in Fig. 19.1. The reaction material comprises a series of alternate discs of carbon and nickel. The operating cycle is only two or three minutes.

The nickel discs melt, expand, and percolate the carbon discs, on the edges

324

of which diamonds form. The masses of hard material removed from the presses go to a chemical cleaning section where they are crushed and boiled in various acid baths which dissolve non-diamond materials. Diamonds recovered, a substantial amount per cycle, are cleaned, dried and sent to the sorting department (Fig. 19.2).

Sorting into sizes is carried out through a cascade of six or seven vibrating sieves. The upper one traps the largest grit and the lower ones successively smaller sizes.

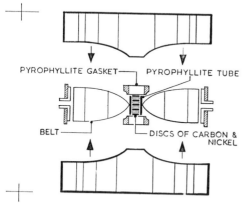

PYROPHYLLITE GASKET

PYROPHYLLITE TUBE

BELT

DISCS OF CARBON & NICKEL

Fig. 19.1. *Principle of diamond synthesis using the belt (a tungsten carbide ring) between the jaws of a hydraulic press. An electrical current produces the heat.*

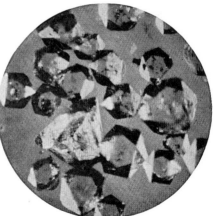

Fig. 19.2. *Some synthetic diamond crystals. They are magnified, being only of grit size.*

Sorting into different shapes is done by an ingenious electrically vibrated sorting table designed by Diamond Abrasive Products. The table is triangular and fixed at a sloping angle. Along one side is a series of twelve to fourteen traps like 'billiard table' pockets. From the opposite corner a glass container feeds diamond particles on to the surface. These swarm over the table like demented ants and finish in one or other of the pockets. Blocky particles move in a downward direction and needle-shaped ones in an upwards direction.

The particles are marked in about twenty-five categories of size and shape for industrial abrasive uses. In 1963 Ultra High Pressure Units opened a synthetic diamond factory in Shannon, Eire, and in 1967 an agreement was made with the Swedish concern A.S.E.A., to combine production.

The price of synthetic grit was at first nearly twice as much as natural grit, but by 1965, had fallen below that of natural grit. Synthetic grit will not do all that natural will and each has its industrial applications. World production in 1969 was estimated to be 40 million carats of synthetic grit compared with 44 million carats of all natural diamonds.

Direct Synthesis by Explosion

Attempts have continued to be made to synthesize diamond directly from graphite, despite the success of the static pressure/temperature techniques which have become commonplace. In 1959, J. van Tilburg took out a patent for a method using explosives, and interested N. V. Asscher, the famous diamond cutters. About the same time, work was going on along similar lines in Poulter Laboratory of the Stanford Research Institute in the U.S.A.

Natural diamonds were submitted to shock tests. Although blackened and cracked, they survived as diamonds and were not converted to graphite. Further work yielded practical methods of explosive loading of graphite for conversion of rather less than 10 per cent to diamond and a patent was issued in 1966 to De Carli and the Allied Chemical Corporation.

Direct conversion of graphite to diamond by a non-explosive technique had, however, been accomplished by F. P. Bundy of G.E. in 1962. Bundy submitted a graphite specimen to a static pressure of about 130,000 atmospheres, then discharged a large electrolytic condenser across it, which raised the temperature to about 3,000° C, when the centre of the specimen abruptly collapsed.

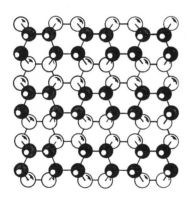

Fig. 19.3. *Structure of hexagonal diamond.*

On examination it was found to contain a cemented mass of fine crystalline diamond. It was estimated that the reaction took about two or three thousandths of a second.

Many other firms and individuals have carried out experiments involving different methods, some apparently with success.

Hexagonal Crystals

Small quantities of diamonds made by explosive methods are hexagonal instead of cubic in crystal structure, similar to some diamonds found in meteorites. Its structure is shown in Fig. 19.3. The American Du Pont company claims to be able to make hexagonal diamonds also by a static method.

Explosion-synthesized diamonds are normally polycrystalline and are therefore very hard, like carbonado, but are coarser and contain a high proportion of metallic inclusions.

Growing from Seed Crystals

A chemical engineering group at Case Western Reserve University, Cleveland, U.S.A., has grown diamonds on seed crystals at a temperature of 1,050°C (1,922°F) and a pressure of only 735 pounds a square inch (5 atmospheres).

The seed crystals are extremely small, about 0·00025 mm. across. The method is to mount one in a transparent quartz tube and pass methane gas (marsh gas) through the tube. The gas decomposes and carbon atoms are deposited on the seed crystal, which grows, but at an extremely slow rate. It can be seen all the time through the tube. It is thought that the technique may eventually produce gem quality crystals.

Synthetic Gem Diamonds

Production of white, clear synthetic gem quality diamonds in a laboratory was first announced by General Electric in the U.S.A., in 1970. Some crystals they made weighed over a carat. (Fig. 19.4.) They were described as having cost many times more than gem quality rough from Africa. The men responsible were Dr. Herbert M. Strong and Dr. Robert H. Wentorf. The best crystals were classified as equal to natural rough that was white and had very small flaws and inclusions.

A special pressure chamber (Fig. 19.5) is used with the belt type of apparatus. A small mass of synthetic diamond crystals is placed in the centre of the chamber and on each side of it a bath of catalyst metal, such as iron or nickel, which becomes molten at operating so that there are free carbon atoms in the bath. The central part of the chamber is maintained at a higher temperature than the ends. More carbon is dissolved at the hot part in the centre than the cooler ends can hold in solution, so that carbon atoms wandering in the bath tend to come out of solution and crystallize at the ends. They would normally crystallize as graphite, but diamond seed crystals are provided at each end on to which the carbon atoms move slowly from the central synthetic diamond mass to the seeds at the ends until the diamond mass is used up. Rate of growth is about 2 to 3 milligrams an hour.

The greater the difference in temperature between the centre and ends of the pressure chamber, the faster the seed crystals grow. Usually a difference of 50° to 60°F (28° to 33°C) is enough. Typical figures are 2600° and 2650°F (1427° and 1455°C). These temperatures are held for several days at a pressure of about 60,000 atmospheres. The best crystals grow at the bottom of the molten bath because dirt and stray diamond crystals float upwards and stay out of the way of the growing crystal. Impurities can be added to achieve unique features of colour, electrical properties, hardness, internal structure, and so on. Crystals first produced were tabular in habit.

Identification of Synthetic Gem Diamonds

Early examination by the Gemological Institute of America's New York laboratory of a number of synthetic gem diamond crystals in a variety of colours showed that the near-colourless and blue ones were highly electro-conductive

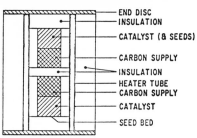

END DISC
INSULATION

CATALYST (8 SEEDS)

CARBON SUPPLY

INSULATION
HEATER TUBE
CARBON SUPPLY

CATALYST

SEED BED

Fig. 19.4. Some General Electric synthetic gem diamond crystals compared with a pencil. They are tabular in habit, being truncated octahedra with modified cube faces. Sizes are from 0·60 tp 1·10 ct.

Fig. 19.5. Diagram of the pressure vessel used in synthetic gem diamond production.

and highly fluorescent and phosphorescent. Natural diamonds are not conductive unless they are Type IIb, most or all of which are blue. Conductivity in colourless and slightly yellow diamonds indicates their synthetic origin. Blue synthetics were much more conductive than natural ones. The objective of G.E. research is in fact to produce semi-conductors.

A canary yellow synthetic diamond was not conductive and could not be identified from the natural stone by this means. Dr. Strong reports, however, that synthetic and natural material have different distributions of nitrogen impurities that can be identified by X-ray Lauegrams.

Under 10× magnification, dark blue stones showed an unusual whiteish cross, caused by a concentration of white 'dust'. White dust-like inclusions could be seen in all crystals under higher magnification.

Features of Synthetic Crystals
G.E., in America have released certain information about the growth of crystals in their process and a number of research workers have studied De Beers as well as G.E. diamonds.

Diamond crystals produced synthetically are often more regular than those found in nature. The irregularities of natural crystals are probably the result of constriction by surrounding rocks when they grew and lack of carbon in the solution. Laboratory experiments suggest that natural diamonds may have been partly dissolved after their original formation.

When synthetic crystals are grown at the lowest possible range of temperatures and pressures, the cube is the most common crystal form. Growth occurs in roughly square-shaped layers parallel to the cube faces. The layers start in the centre of the faces and creep outwards so that each face is smooth but in a series of very fine steps towards the raised centre. Natural cubes are rough on the surface and pitted.

At higher temperatures and pressures, octahedra are formed. These, too, grow layer by layer, but on the octahedral faces. The layers in this case are of triangular form. If the temperature is maintained, the crystal grows to a certain point and then begins to dissolve. The surfaces become etched with small pits, which are triangular on octahedral faces. The pitting is similar to that produced by etching natural or synthetic crystals in molten potassium nitrate. Octahedral faces, however, being more perfect crystallographically, are more resistant to attack than other faces such as cubic and dodecahedral.

Dodecahedral crystals rarely occur in synthetic production although forms of them are common in nature. The reason is thought to be that dodecahedra are formed by part dissolving of another form of crystal. The many variations of natural dodecahedra may occur because crystals have been submitted for millions of years to attrition by natural forces. On the other hand, synthetics made with nickel and some chromium as a catalyst tend to be cubic or cube-octahedral, and other catalysts, including niobium and copper, result in a high proportion of octahedral crystals.

Rate of Growth

Diamond crystals grow rapidly when produced by the belt method. A rate of about a third of a millimeter a second has been calculated. Growth at lower temperatures is slower and at higher ones much more rapid so that masses of small crystals are formed. The latter conditions will produce the synthetic equivalent of carbonado, a porous mass of variously orientated tiny crystals.

The slower the growth, the better quality the crystal.

Twinning occurs in synthetic crystals as it does in natural ones, and macles can be grown in different thicknesses and lengths.

Research is concentrated on producing crystals large enough to be used in tools and drill crowns. There are also many possible applications in electronics for pure gem crystals.

Colour of Synthetics

Colour is, of course, of major importance in gem diamonds but not of direct significance in industrial ones. It has been found that variations in temperature and pressure during manufacture affect the colour of synthetics. As might be expected, black is common at the lower temperatures of diamond formation. As the temperature is raised, so the colour 'improves' through shades of green and yellow towards weaker colours.

The colour is also affected by interstitial nitrogen. The colours mentioned are not the only ones that can be produced to order. Shades of grey and blue, as well as of yellow and green are possible. Larger crystals can be made nearly opaque with the intensity of coloration.

Inclusions and Substitution Atoms

Inclusions occur frequently, especially when the crystals are rapidly grown. When growth is slower, inclusions tend to take up positions related to crystal

Fig. 19.6. *Synthetic industrial diamond on the pole of a magnet.*

axes. Nickel can be found up to 10 per cent and garnet has also been identified. Synthetic diamonds usually include dispersed nitrogen and are therefore Type Ib and are paramagnetic (Fig. 19.6).

Surface Features

There are differences in the surfaces of natural and synthetic diamonds that have practical uses, one of which is in identification. Tolansky has carried out extensive research on this subject. He says that the chief differences are that although trigons are very common on natural octahedral faces, they are very rare on synthetic ones. Pits are found on some octahedral faces of De Beers synthetic diamonds and are oppositely orientated to trigons, i.e. their edges are parallel to the triangular octahedral face. On the cube faces of synthetics, spiral growth patterns are sometimes seen. There is no known instance of a spiral growth on a natural cube face. One of the most striking differences is that cube faces are smooth on synthetics and always, as far as is known, very rough on natural stones.

Very occasionally a surface skin appears on G.E. synthetics. Many cleavages are found amongst synthetics. A.S.E.A. synthetics are often internally fractured in non-cleavage directions.

Types of Synthesis

G.E. scientists divide systems of diamond synthesis into five main groups:

  1. Direct transition from graphite to diamond.

330

2. Systems which involve carbon and oxygen.
3. Systems that involve carbon as salt-like carbides.
4. Miscellaneous chemical reductions.
5. Systems involving carbon dissolved in molten metals.

The first would seem to require exceedingly high temperatures and pressures – about 4,000° C at about 200,000 atmospheres. The second and third are attractive but not very successful. The third includes Hannay's method, which has not been reproduced, and the fifth has been the most successful, although it has turned out to be the most complicated.

Synthetic diamonds are now made in many countries other than those mentioned, including Holland, Japan, the U.S.S.R., and China. The Russians and Americans are experimenting with methods of growing diamonds in threads or whiskers in a gas containing carbon at under atmospheric pressures, similar to the carbon fibres developed in the U.K.

Fraudulent Coloration

Probably throughout the history of marketing there have been attempts to improve the appearance of gem diamonds, particularly of their colour. The most effective method depends upon the fact that mixing light of complementary colours produces white light. Thus the yellowish tinge of a Silver Cape stone may be partly neutralized by applying the complementary colour of violet. Even blue will effect an improvement. For the method to be effective, a painted stone must be yellowish to start with. Painting a grey stone will not be successful.

One of the earliest methods of the fakers was to use an indelible pencil or violet ink and to apply the colour to the culet, girdle, or pavilion of the stone. The girdle was marked by the moistened pencil, or the pavilion or part of it was dipped in the ink of coloured solution. The girdle, having a matt surface, is much easier to mark. Various dyes have also been used.

Such coatings can usually be seen with a $10 \times$ lens because they tend to be streaky. They may be removed by water, alcohol, or a commercial jewellery cleaner.

After the Second World War, attempts were made to improve diamonds by coating them by the same methods as used for improving the light transmission of camera lenses, by vacuum sputtering of fluorides. Stones so treated are easily detected because of the purplish bloom, as seen on lenses. The coatings are durable and have to be removed by hot acid.

In the 1940s, extra thin coatings that were resistant and almost invisible were developed for making transistors. Someone thought of applying them to off-colour diamonds and by 1950 it was possible to send diamonds, like any suitable materials for electronic uses, to a treatment laboratory in the U.S.A.

The Gemological Institute of America was shown a ring with a coated stone on which it was not possible to detect the coating. Permission to unmount the stone was refused, but the whole ring was boiled in concentrated sulphuric acid, which removed the coating from the stone and revealed its true yellowish body colour. The coatings are only a fraction of a wavelength in thickness and are applied in a small area only, often concealed by the mount.

By 1962, several specialist coaters were in business in the U.S.A., and traffic in fraudulently coloured stones – almost invariably larger ones of five carats and over – had become a menace in New York particularly. Coating lifted the price by 25 per cent and more. No easy method of detection was discovered. Chemical and X-ray methods were not effective, which left the standard technique of searching the surface of the diamond in reflected light under a microscope for local areas of coating. It has been found also that a skilled sorter cannot assign a precise colour grade to a coated stone of this type, which is a rather refined clue. No doubt some of these stones were brought to Europe and have remained undetected so far.

Detected coatings, which are often near the girdle on smaller stones are seen to be spotty, granular or splodgy, with tiny craters or burst bubbles.

Artificial Coloration

The colour of diamonds has been altered in the course of scientific experiment and as a result it is possible to have stones treated commercially to make them green, dark yellow, golden brown, or blue, by irradiation and if necessary by subsequent heat-treatment. The practice of treating decorative and gem materials has been accepted for centuries. Huge quantities of agate are dyed; all blue and golden zircons are heat-treated; and most citrine is purple amethyst that has been turned yellow by heat treatment. It is not reprehensible to colour a diamond artificially, but it is fraudulent to sell it without disclosing the fact.

First to colour diamond by irradiation was Sir William Crookes, in experiments with radium carried out from 1904. The green tint he produced is quite attractive unless it is too dark, when it is similar to the blackish tourmaline green. It is different from the apple-green of the very rare natural green stones. According to R. Webster, a score or so radium-treated stones are known to be on the market in the U.K. They can be detected immediately by a Geiger counter or, without one, by leaving the stone overnight in contact with a photographic plate in a light-tight box and developing the plate, which will show an image of the stone (an auto-radiograph) (Fig. 19.7). The amount of radioactivity is not harmful.

Development of nuclear reactors, particle accelerating machines, and other means of irradiation has made treatment of stones easier and also increased the research into the mechanism of colour change. Only a limited range of changes is possible. It is caused by damage to the crystal lattice of the diamond which alters the light absorption and therefore the visible colour. Partial annealing of the lattice by heat-treatment can change, but not destroy the colour.

It has not been found possible to remove natural colour from a stone, i.e. to change a yellowish one to a white one. The colour is additive. The 'improvement' comes from treating, say, a Cape stone and turning it into a fancy colour.

The main techniques are as follows, but only 1 and 3 are normally employed. (1) Neutron bombardment; (2) Proton, deuteron, or alpha-particle bombardment; (3) Electron bombardment; (4) Gamma irradiation.

Treatment normally turns stones green, the depth of colour depending on the length of time of treatment, which itself depends on the intensity of radiation and the weight of the stone. Time of treatment is inversely proportional to the cube root of the weight of the stone. The colour varies from a pale green to a bottle green and finally to opaque black if treatment is too prolonged.

Heat-treatment

Subsequent heat-treatment for some hours at about 500° to 900° C of green irradiated diamonds changes the colour of most stones to yellow or cinnamon brown, which is generally thought to be more attractive than the green. The yellow or brown colour is not lighter than the previous green. In other words, it is still additive. It is not possible to turn a yellow stone to green, then heat-treat it to make it a lighter yellow.

Certain diamonds treated in an electron accelerator, such as a Van de Graaff

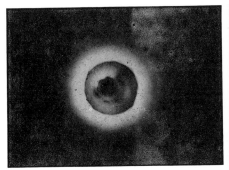

Fig. 19.7. *Autoradiograph of a radium-treated diamond.*

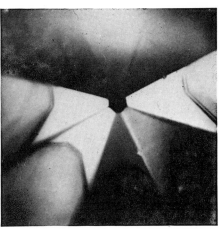

Fig. 19.8. *'Umbrella' seen around the culet of some cyclotron-treated diamonds.*

generator, are changed to an attractive pale aquamarine colour or to a greenish-blue. Gamma irradiation will produce a bluish-green colour, but is rarely employed. The colour in both cases does not penetrate the stone and can be polished off.

In the U.S.A., commercial services for the coloration of diamonds are available. Some fine colours have been achieved, not only excellent blues, but reds and purples. The most common commercial demand is for greens and golden browns because these are cheaper to produce. Only a very small number of natural diamonds can be changed to blue, red, or purple. In the U.K. the Atomic Energy Authority will treat diamonds to change the colour, but the service is of more value to scientific workers than the trade, as it is more experimental than commercial, and the higher energy machines now installed result in less critical irradiation.

The behaviour of stones under treatment depends largely on their type. All tend to turn green after neutron bombardment. Subsequent heat-treatment changes Type Ia stones yellow to amber and Type IIa to brown with intermediate shades for intermediate types. The rare Type IIb stones will become red to purple.

Electron bombardment has the same effect on Type Ia stones, but Ib and IIa stones become blue to greenish blue. Subsequent heat-treatment has the same effect again on Type Ia stones, but those of Type Ib become red to purple and IIa become brown. These comments are only a guide since it is difficult or impossible to predict colour changes with any degree of accuracy.

A stone that is neutron bombarded (by treatment in an atomic pile) is at first intensely radioactive, but the activity soon dies out. The colour goes right through the stone, because the neutrons are uncharged particles. As far as is known, it is permanent.

Diamonds treated in a cyclotron by protons, deutrons, or alpha-particles, also lose their radioactivity soon after treatment. The colour is only skin-deep because the charged particles cannot penetrate deeply. It can be polished off, but is permanent, as far as is known.

Identification

If the diamond has been cyclotron-treated through the table, a dark ring will be seen on looking down on the pavilion. If it has been treated through the pavilion, a shape like an opened umbrella will be seen on looking down through the table (Fig. 19.8).

Pile-treated stones, and those treated through the side in a cyclotron, show no particular markings, but the unnatural colour of green is an indication. The most conclusive test for stones that have been heat-treated to turn them amber or brown is a line at 5940 Å in the spectrum. Bands centred on 5040 will be induced because of the new colour, but the original 4155 system will still be evident if the stone was originally of Cape colour.

There are, however, still problems of identification of some artificially coloured stones without elaborate and expensive equipment for measuring electron spin.

A natural blue diamond is Type IIb, which is a semi-conductor of electricity. An artificially-coloured blue diamond will not be Type IIb and therefore will be an insulator. An obvious test therefore is to attempt to pass a current through the stone. A simple circuit, suggested by R. Webster, is to attempt to pass an a.c. current through the stone with a meter in series. A meter-reading indicates that

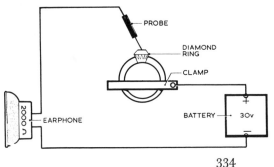

Fig. 19.9. *Circuit with earphones which will crackle if the diamond is conductive, i.e. Type II b.*

the blue diamond is natural. Alternatively the stone may be touched with a neon-indicating screwdriver while current is applied to it. Other tests are to measure the resistance with an ohmmeter, or to use a battery and earphone in a circuit and to listen for scratching when using a probe on a Type IIb stone (Fig. 19.9).

CHAPTER TWENTY

Identification of Diamond

Examination by eye

People who handle diamond crystals regularly and frequently can recognize them on sight. Those who handle polished diamonds as often can also recognize them without difficulty and are certain enough to pay extremely high prices without even considering an identification test. Nevertheless, there are times when even an experienced jeweller can make a mistake, especially when the stone is set.

Bad light conditions, an expensive setting for a fine simulant, a new simulant to the jeweller, having to make a judgement in a hurry or under unfavourable conditions, all can cause a temporary loss of skill in identification. A clever confidence trickster can be responsible for creating such conditions. Even without the atmosphere, the rare diamond doublet may deceive even a wary jeweller.

What are the characteristics that make a diamond recognizable by eye? First is its adamantine lustre. On no other material can such a high surface finish be produced. This polish, the high reflectivity and the exceptional flatness of facets produce surfaces in which undistorted reflections may be seen. By tilting a stone, a good reflection of, say, an electric light bulb or window frame, will appear in the table.

The low critical angle of diamond – 24·5° – means that a brilliant-cut stone reflects back most of the light entering from the front. It is therefore impossible to look right through a properly fashioned *modern* brilliant-cut diamond from the top and see what is below it. Only through the culet, if large enough, would anything be visible. If a loose brilliant-cut diamond is held up to the light in a pair of tongs and looked at with the naked eye from the crown side, the stone will appear black except a pinpoint of light through the culet. The less accurate the brilliant-cut, the more likely there are to be windows or areas of light, so this is also a rough check for accuracy of cut.

It is, of course, possible to look *into* a diamond. Whether the stone is set or loose, it will be noticed that it appears shallower than in fact it is, when the back facet edges are examined through the table. The cause is the high refractive index. Simulants with lower refractive indices, particularly colourless quartz, paste (glass), topaz, synthetic spinel, and white sapphire (synthetic or natural) do not foreshorten to such a marked degree.

Transparency

The greater apparent transparency of stones other than diamond, is a strong clue to their nature when examined unset, but more care must be taken when they are set. For example, it is possible to see newsprint through a loose colourless synthetic spinel placed on a newspaper table down, but not through a diamond, as shown in Fig. 20.1. But to disguise the transparency of synthetic spinels they are often backed with a reflecting surface, which may not be apparent after they are set, so that it is impossible to see through them. The expression 'apparent transparency' is used because diamond is in fact an exceptionally transparent material as may be noted when examining a portrait stone, which is thin with parallel faces. The transparency can be deceiving.

Confusion is also possible with old cuts of diamond in which full advantage of the low critical angle was not taken in cutting. Someone who has handled only

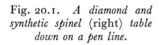

Fig. 20.1. *A diamond and synthetic spinel* (right) *table down on a pen line.*

modern brilliant-cut stones may be puzzled by some old mine stones, which, when set in antique jewellery, look like old or poor paste at first sight because of their low brilliance, apparent lack of fire, and generally 'dirty' appearance. Others which have not suffered from wear and have their original sharp edges, and which were well polished originally, will appear to be unnaturally clear or transparent for diamonds. The large culet and the facet edges will be immediately apparent to the naked eye through the table. This results from the larger angle of the pavilion facets which allows light to escape through the back of the stone. When unset, such a stone held up to the light will let much through.

Windows are not uncommonly left by cutters wishing to preserve the weight of emerald and square-cut diamonds, so the cut stones have lower brilliance and fire and more apparent transparency. However, the lustre and other features detectable by eye will reveal them as diamonds.

All diamond graders become familiar with the varying degrees of brilliance. In a top-quality diamond of fine make, the brilliance takes on what might be described as a 'blackness'. The phenomenon has also been noted with highly polished steel.

Heat Conductivity
Diamond has much higher thermal conductivity than any other gems so that it is colder to the touch and also becomes warm more quickly, when worn. If therefore a loose stone or diamond jewellery is left to attain room temperature and then touched, it will feel quite cold. Loose stones may be picked up with tongs, also at room temperature, or the jewellery by hand, and the stone touched on the lip or other sensitive parts of the face. Paste will feel relatively warm.

Surface Tension

If the top surface of a diamond is thoroughly clean and free of grease, a drop of water on the table will remain as a globule for a long time whereas on the tables of other stones the globule will spread in a relatively short time, which depends on the mineral. Diamond has an affinity for grease, a fact used in recovery and also responsible for grease from the skin adhering to the back of stones set in rings. This grease should be removed by a detergent or a diamond cleaner to avoid loss of light through the back of the stone.

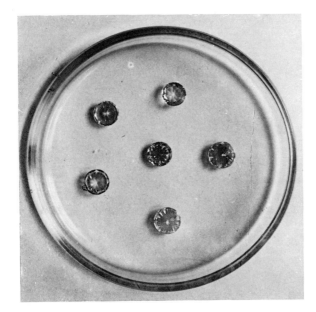

Fig. 20.2. *Stones in a cell, with diamond in the centre and, from 12 o'clock, strontium titanate (Fabulite), synthetic rutile, zircon, synthetic white spinel, and paste.*

Fig. 20.3. *The cell above filled with monobromonaphthalene (RI 1.66). The synthetic white spinel and paste have almost disappeared and the zircon is more transparent. The diamond in the centre, as well as the strontium titanate at the top and the zircon next to it are still clearly visible. Synthetic white sapphires also tend to disappear.*

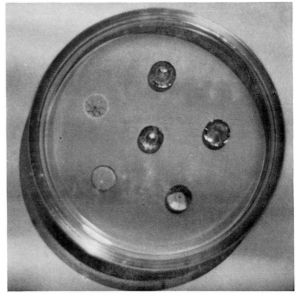

Refractive Index

If a diamond, mounted or unmounted, is put in a white cup containing a highly refractive liquid, its outline will still be visible, whereas *some* stones used to simulate diamond tend to become less visible. This simple test will only prove that a stone is *not* diamond. The safest method is to place a known diamond in the liquid with the stone being examined and to compare them (Fig. 20.2 and 20.3).

Suitable liquids are monobromonaphthalene (R.I. 1·66) commonly used in microscope work, and the standard heavy liquids methylene iodide (1·74), and bromoform (1·59). Benzene (1·50) can be used also, although lower in R.I. than the others.

If a suspect stone is immersed in a white porcelain cell, or a glass one standing on white paper, the diamonds will stand out in high relief while stones of lower R.I. will tend to disappear (Fig. 20.3). It must be noted, however, that certain substitutes including sphene, zircon, strontium titanate, yttrium aluminium garnet, and rutile have high refractive indices and will also stand out in bold relief.

B. W. Anderson, has refined this test of immersion contrast by introducing a photographic technique particularly useful for unset stones, which are immersed in a liquid of known refractive index in a glass cell. The cell is placed on hard photographic bromide paper in a dark room and illuminated from above. The best method is to use light from an enlarger. The exposure has usually to be found by trial and error. The paper is afterwards developed in the usual way.

The more light that has passed through a stone, the darker will be the area of the photographic print underneath it. When the stones are of higher R.I. than the liquid, as with diamond in the test already described, the borders will be white and the facet edges dark. Stones with lower R.I.s than the liquid will show on the print with dark borders and white facet edges.

Hardness and Wear

Even after many years of constant wear, cut diamonds will preserve their sharp edges and corners when most other stones will have become worn and chipped. Under a hand-lens, the edges of diamond facets will be clean and sharp. Most simulants after a few years of wear will have rolled (rounded) edges between facets.

Fractures in the edges and corners of substitutes which have been in wear some time in jewellery are quite common. Fractures can and do occur in diamonds, but are usually on the culet or perhaps near the girdle, caused by a knock or careless setting. The nature of the fracture will indicate diamond. Typical abraded edges of diamond after many years of use are shown in Fig. 20.4.

Unfortunately it is not easy to test a suspected diamond for hardness without damage to the stone if it is not diamond. Flat polished pieces of synthetic ruby or sapphire (corundum) are available for use as hardness test plates. The girdle of the supposed diamond is rubbed firmly on the surface of the corundum. If it scratches and the mark cannot be removed by rubbing it with a moistened finger, the stone is a diamond. Any suitable piece of ruby or sapphire, natural or synthetic, will do of course. No other gem material will scratch them. Scratching glass is no test for diamonds, as many other materials will also scratch glass.

Nevertheless, a hardness test is not recommended for a diamond, especially if a fine one, as damage may ensue. For the same reason, in no circumstances

Fig. 20.4.   *Abraded facet edges of a diamond.*

should hardness pencils, files, or other hard materials be used to attempt scratching the facets, edges or any part of the surface of a polished stone believed to be a diamond. From time to time some ignorant or stupid person will test a diamond by trying to scratch some hard material with the pointed culet of the stone, or by using a file on the point of the culet. This is almost always fatal to the culet because of fracture through cleavage.

These injunctions do not apply to diamond crystals. A reasonably well-formed crystal is easy for anyone to identify with some experience and practice but industrial diamond crystals in particular not infrequently appear to be anything but diamond. Some industrials could easily be mistaken for small pieces of coke. Using it to attempt to scratch a piece of synthetic ruby or sapphire is simple and effective, useful as a field test to prospectors without immediate access to a laboratory.

Accuracy of Cut

Because of its nature and value, diamond is usually cut much more accurately than other gemstones and the accurate meeting of the facet corners is one indication that the stone is a diamond. Similarly, polishing lines and scratches may be seen even on the best simulants but not on the best diamonds which they imitate.

Surface Features

Look on the polished surfaces for straight ridges or lines (Fig. 13.28) which are caused by twinning in the crystal resulting in differences of hardness and cannot be polished out. They occur only on diamond. There may also be irregularly shaped areas which appear to be slightly higher than the general surface, like shallow plateaux. They, too, occur only on diamond and are caused by naats (knots) or changes in crystal direction, and therefore hardness (Fig. 13.29).

The girdle of a brilliant-cut diamond is different in appearance from that of other stones. It has a matt, waxy appearance, caused by the fracturing process of bruting. It is not dull like ground glass, but has the shiny lustre of wax. Sometimes the girdle is bearded, having fine 'whiskers' – actually fractures – extending from it into the stone (Fig. 13.30). Such a flaw, caused by bruting too rapidly can occur only in diamond. Occasionally the girdle of a brilliant-cut diamond is polished or faceted. Girdles of most other cuts of diamond are polished.

A natural on the girdle or near it is an indication of diamond. A natural is part of the orginal crystal surface and usually looks much brighter than the girdle (Fig. 13.31). Trigons may sometimes be seen on naturals, when they are part of an original octahedral face. Lines across a natural indicate it was part of a dodecahedral face. Both indications are good proof by eye that the stone is a diamond, but there is one simulant, yttrium aluminium garnet, in which similar naturals are also occasionally left.

Internal Features

With a hand lens or microscope, certain internal features are diagnostic for diamond, particularly cleavage. Internal cleavages are quite common. No diamond simulants except topaz show cleavage and topaz can be eliminated for other reasons, such as its low brilliancy and lack of fire.

A cleavage (Fig. 17.36) is a split within the crystal which appears as a line edge-on and an irregular patch seen flat-on, and is often called a feather. Larger feathers are seen easily with a hand lens, but a higher powered microscope will be needed to examine smaller ones. Multiple ones are like butterflies, which is what they are called.

Fluorescence and X-ray Tests

Relative density is not easy to check unless the specimen can be tested in heavy liquids. There is only one gem similar to diamond that is near it also in specific gravity. This is sphene at 3·53 against 3·515 for diamond.

A spectroscope will give positive identification of diamond if the characteristic band at 4155 Å in the violet is seen. More details are given in Chapter Seventeen.

Although so variable, diamond fluorescence is a useful pointer in testing. On the other hand, the variance can be an advantage when testing a piece of jewellery set with many diamonds. If the jewellery is examined under either short or long wave ultra-violet light, no fluorescence or very even fluorescence indicates that the stones are not diamond. Uneven fluorescence as shown in Fig. 18.17 is an indication that the stones are diamond. A stone that fluoresces blue and phosphoresces yellow is definitely a diamond.

Diamonds have bluish fluorescence under X-rays—a reliable test.

A more sophisticated test for diamond is to use its transparency to X-rays compared with substitutes, owing to the low atomic weight of carbon. If a known diamond and the suspected stone are placed on a photographic plate and exposed

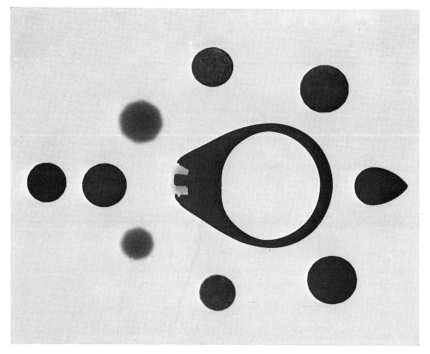

Fig. 20.5. *X-ray photograph by R. Webster showing* (left) *Paste (RI 1.62), synthetic white scheelite (at 9 o'clock, then clockwise), synthetic white spinel, white zircon, yttrium aluminium garnet, lithium niobate (Linobate – pear shaped), strontium titanite (Fabulite), synthetic rutile, and synthetic white sapphire, compared with a diamond ring in the centre.*

for a short time to X-rays, stones other than diamond will show black against the faint shadow of the diamond (Fig. 20.5). If the exposure is too long, the diamond will not show at all on the plate. Yttrium aluminium garnet, strontium titanate, paste, and zircon are all opaque. The test is often used for court evidence. Better contrast can be obtained by burying the stones in plasticine before X-raying them.

X-ray tests are used to establish the proportion of diamond to graphite and amorphous carbon and other materials in carbonado.

Double Refraction

The refractive index of diamond is too high at 2·42 to be checked on a normal refractometer, which is limited by its contact liquid to a top reading of 1·81. (There is also a real danger of scratching the soft glass table of the instrument.) Taking a refraction reading with more elaborate instruments is not within the scope of normal testing. Refractometer tests of stones which are within the range of the instrument will, of course, separate them from diamond.

Diamond is isotropic and therefore does not cause doubling. Looking through the table with a hand lens, the edges of the back facets and the culet should appear undistorted. Some simulants, including zircon and synthetic rutile are doubly-refracting. Light rays passing through the stone are split into two, so the back facet edges doubled as shown in Fig. 20.6. It may be necessary to

342

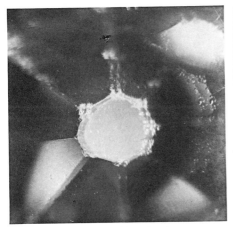 

Fig. 20.6. *Doubling in zircon.*　　　Fig. 20.7. *False doubling in diamond.*

turn the stone through different angles and look through bezel facets instead of the table to discover doubling of the back facets because there are directions of single refraction in doubly-refracting minerals.

It is not always possible to see doubling in a doubly-refracting mineral, usually because the double refraction is too small. Use of a polarizing microscope, or polariscope will quickly reveal a stone that is doubly-refracting. Diamond does invariably exhibit anomalous double refraction, however.

Diamonds never show doubling of the back facets. It does happen rarely, however, that bad cutting of a brilliant-cut stone will cause an effect known as false doubling. An example is shown in Fig. 20.7. False doubling can quickly be recognized if its nature is appreciated. It is a series of reflections which cause an image of the culet edges, *around* another image of the same edges. True doubing is a second image which is *displaced* so that it overlaps the first one. The second effect is similar to double vision.

Another diagnostic feature of diamond of modern cut is immediately apparent to the eye – the degree of fire or play of spectrum colours. Moving a brilliant-cut diamond will result in a display of flashes of pure spectrum colours from the smaller facets around the table.

Paste

Paste, that is, lead glass, is the most common substitute for diamond and can be surprisingly like diamond when well cut and mounted and seen in wear. The fire can be very similar. Dispersion of a typical lead glass is 0·041 compared with 0·044 for diamond.

The surface polish usually gives a clue at once to the material. As most paste is softer than the particles of quartz in dust, the facets may have become dulled or scratched and wear may show on facet edges and corners. A lens will often reveal small air bubbles and sometimes swirl clouds of bubbles in the glass.

Glass is singly refracting, so this offers no evidence in relation to diamond, but the refractive index does because, although it can vary considerably, it is usually between 1·52 and 1·68.

Paste was not considered a simulant for diamond in the eighteenth century and was worn in the highest circles set in fine jewellery, so the quality of the setting is not a guide. There are more comments on this on page 350. Pastes were often cut in shapes not seen or even possible with diamond.

Yttrium Aluminium Garnet (Diamonair)

A diamond substitute that appeared in 1969 is cut from manufactured crystals of a material known as yttrium aluminium garnet that has no counterpart in nature. Known by gemmologists as YAG, it has been given the trade name of Diamonair and became well known when Richard Burton bought an 69·42 carat pear-shaped diamond for his wife, Elizabeth Taylor, and had a duplicate of it cut in YAG.

YAG is extremely transparent, nearly always free from inclusions and relatively hard ($8\frac{1}{2}$ on Mohs' scale). It is singly refracting and the refractive index at 1·83 is below that of diamond, as is the dispersion, at 0·028. The first stones cut from the material were not particularly successful, but after the ideal angles were calculated by the Gemological Institute of America Laboratory in New York, YAG was found to have considerable potential as a diamond simulant, and many cut stones have been sold in jewellery.

A very good polish, with a lustre approaching adamantine, can be obtained and the fire, although low, is enough to imitate diamond. The brilliance is less if the table is looked at from an angle and compared with the brilliance direct on, which may provide the first clue that the stone is not a diamond, especially in subdued light.

Diamonair is cut from pulled boules and to retain maximum weight, cutters occasionally leave a small part of the skin on the girdle which has a remarkable similarity to a natural on a diamond girdle.

The lower refractive index will distinguish it from diamond in a refractive liquid. Occasionally, curved lines similar to those in synthetic ruby, may be seen under a low-powered microscope and when inclusions do occur they are sometimes extended bubbles.

If a stone that looks like a particularly fine white diamond is loose, it can be weighed and, if it is much heavier than a diamond of its size should be, it could be YAG, or strontium titanate. A possible procedure would be to make an accurate estimate of the weight if it were diamond using a Leveridge gauge, and then to obtain the actual weight on diamond scales. If the stone were gauged at a carat, it would be within a few points of this, if a diamond, on the scales. If YAG, it would weigh about 1·28 carat and if strontium titanate, about 1·46 carat (Fig. 20.21).

Strontium Titanate (Fabulite)

Another successful simulant of diamond, strontium titanate, is also entirely a product of man's ingenuity since it does not occur naturally. It has been given many trade names, the best known of which are probably Fabulite and Starilian, since it was introduced in 1953. Its main disadvantage is its relatively low hardness (6 on Mohs' scale), which results after a period of wear in rolled or blunted edges to the facets and particularly blunting of the sharp points where the facet corners meet. The low hardness also means that it will not take a really fine polish and under a hand lens it does not have the adamantine lustre of diamond, being almost greasy in appearance. In fact, the material is so difficult to cut that many stones are produced with flaws and many without the full fifty-eight facets of the brilliant-cut.

Nevertheless, brilliant-cut strontium titanate has almost the same refractive index and is nearer in appearance to high-quality diamond than yttrium aluminium garnet. It has often deceived those who do not know it or have never seen it. To anyone who handles polished diamonds, the first impression of a strontium titanate is that it is too good to be true. This arises from the dispersion, which can be quite spectacular. It is 0·200 compared with diamond's 0·044. Strontium titanate, being single-refracting, gives no doubling of the back facets, and is identical to diamond in this, but is much heavier (Fig. 20.8).

Under a low-powered microscope, strontium titanate immersed in a highly refractive liquid will often show inclusions reminiscent of the rungs of a ladder. Similar markings may sometimes be seen on the surface under a lens. (Fig. 20.9). A. E. Farn suggests that the 'ladders' are a surface effect, not inclusions, as he has induced them by pressure with a pin. Strontium titanate does not fluoresce under ultra-violet light.

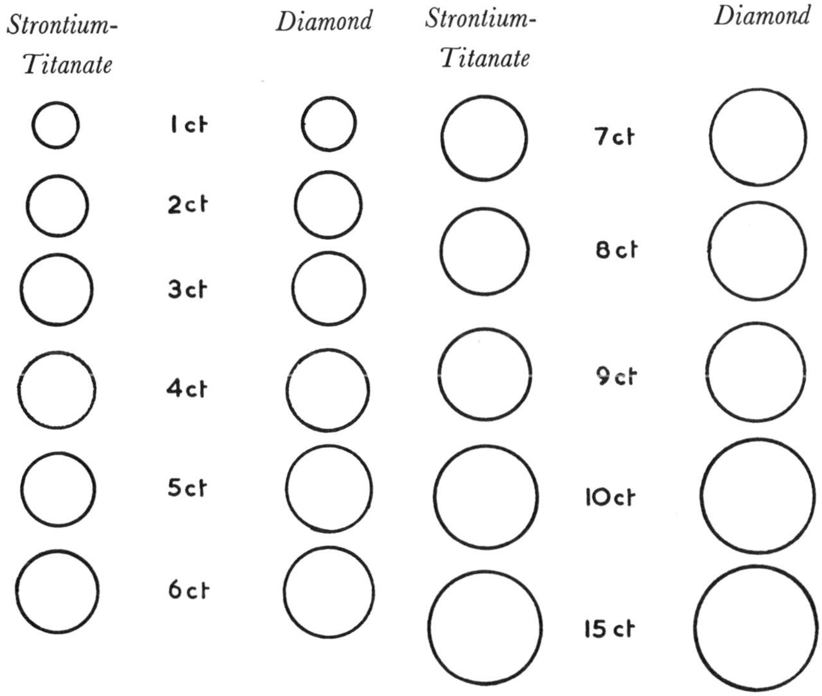

Fig. 20.8. *Comparison of diameters of diamonds and strontium titanates of the same weight.*

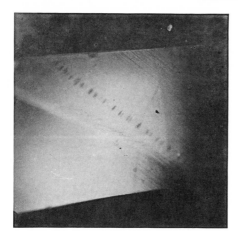

Fig. 20.9. *Ladder inclusion in strontium titanite.*

Synthetic Rutile

Another titanium compound, synthetic rutile, was first produced in 1948 and soon cut and sold under many different trade names, one of which was Titania, as a diamond simulant. It could be taken for a diamond of poor colour. It has a high refractive index – at 0·280 – six and a half times the dispersion of diamond, which gives it quite an exceptional display of fire. It is never without a yellowish tinge of body colour, however. The two effects produce an opalescence that might be described as a faintly 'baleful' appearance, recognizable after some experience.

Very occasionally synthetic rutile has been bloomed by a cathodic sputtering method, like camera lenses. The bluish tinge is intended to improve the colour, but the yellowness remains. Synthetic rutile has extremely high double refraction which usually can be seen by doubling of the back facets, an easy test.

Synthetic Spinel and Synthetic Sapphire

Synthetic white spinel is commonly used as a diamond substitute in cheaper jewellery without intent to deceive when it is sold. The same is true of synthetic white sapphire. Both are commonly used in brilliant-cut form as small stones surrounding larger coloured stones in rings. A refractometer test will immediately establish the identity of each substitute if the table facets are unobstructed.

An immersion test (page 339) is particularly useful when a number of stones that could be diamond but are more likely to be synthetic spinel or sapphire are to be tested, particularly if they are too small, numerous, or awkward to get at because of the setting, for other tests. It is particularly useful for the numbers of small transparent colourless synthetic stones often set around a large stone in a ring, for example, to imitate diamond 'chips' of Swiss and other cuts. In older jewellery which has been repaired, it is possible that a lost diamond has been replaced by synthetic spinels or sapphires, and quick identification by the same method is valuable.

Spinel is singly refracting like diamond, but sapphire is doubly refracting and will show four extinction positions when rotated between crossed polarizers, as in a Rayner or Rutland polariscope. The doubling is often difficult to see with a hand lens. Colourless white sapphires of natural origin can be identified in the same way.

Other Synthetics

Colourless synthetic scheelite is cut in brilliant style and could be mistaken for diamond. So is lithium niobate which is marketed under the name of Linobate. The constants of both materials are given in the table at the end of this chapter and will suggest tests on lines already described.

Zircon

A common substitute for diamond is colourless zircon, which is hard, has a high refractive index and wide dispersion, and is usually cut in brilliant or similar style. Its fire is less than that of diamond, but is sufficient to trap the laymen into thinking it diamond.

The visual test for zircon is simple because of its considerable double refraction. Viewing a back facet through the table with a lens the edges of the facet will usually be seen doubled as in Fig. 20.6. Zircon has a slightly steely appearance that is a quick indication to those who recognize it.

Topaz

Colourless white topaz may occasionally be found in jewellery, particularly that originating in the East or near East. Again a refractometer test is the easiest if it is possible. Visually, there is much less brilliance and particularly fire in both topaz and sapphire than in diamond, and natural colourless sapphire sometimes has a very slightly milky appearance.

Topaz, with a refractive index of 1·62 – 1·63, is doubly refracting which can be discovered by rotating it between the crossed 'nicols' of a polariscope because the doubling is not enough to be seen with a hand lens. The immersion contrast method will separate topaz from diamond as the relief in the refractive liquids mentioned is lower even than spinel.

Rock Crystal

Much the same remarks are true of colourless quartz (rock crystal). Both topaz and quartz have such low brilliance that they should not be mistaken for diamond. Quartz has a different 'feel' from most other stones. With practice, a slight tackiness can be noticed to the fingertips or the eyelid or lip.

Doublets

Diamond doublets are uncommon, and can be deceiving. The top of the stone in invariably diamond and the pavilion may be synthetic colourless sapphire, quartz, or paste, cemented on. One would normally encounter such a stone mounted, not loose (Fig. 20.11). The quality always appears poor. A lens or microscope will usually show up bubbles in the cement layer, and immersion in methylene iodide will immediately make visible the two parts of the doublet.

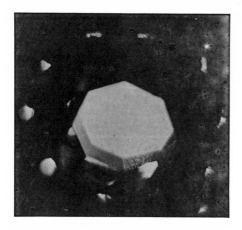

Fig. 20.10.   *Reflection in the table of a diamond doublet.*

Fig. 20.11. (top right)   *Diamond doublets are always close set.*

Fig. 20.12.   *A diamond doublet out of its setting. The crown is diamond and the pavilion another material.*

If the stone is moved while looking through the table facet with the naked eye, it is possible usually to see a reflection of the octagonal table in the cement layer (Fig. 20.10).

Another, but inferior, doublet that may deceive the unwary, is the garnet-topped version with a base of colourless glass. The garnet is a thin slice cemented to the base to become the table. Although the garnet is coloured, the doublet faces up colourless. The easy test is to immerse the stone in a white cup containing water. If viewed sideways, whether loose or mounted, the top will show up clearly.

Coloured Diamond Substitutes

It is more likely that a fancy-coloured diamond will be mistaken for another stone than that a coloured stone will be mistaken for a diamond. Fancy colours in diamond, except for browns and yellows, are rare.

B. W. Anderson says that natural scheelite should not be overlooked when identifying a stone as diamond. Although it is soft, it is very near diamond in appearance when set and brilliant-cut. It may be colourless, yellow, orange, or brown, all diamond colours. Testing on the girdle with a needle point will reveal its softness, and a lens should reveal doubling of the back facets, unless the stone is small. The specific gravity is even higher than that of strontium titanate, so a loose stone would be much too heavy for its weight if it were thought to be a diamond.

Blende can occur in transparent yellow as well as brown and orange and is cut as a specimen, although much too soft to be cut commercially as a gem for jewellery. It has a refractive index near that of diamond and is singly refracting, which gives it a diamond-like appearance. It is also called sphalerite.

The yellowish to leaf-green variety of andradite garnet known as demantoid could be mistaken for fancy diamond because of its high refractive index and its dispersion, which is more than that of diamond. Under a microscope the internal features are quite different. 'Horse tails' of fibrous material are a characteristic of demantoid.

Blue and golden zircon could possibly be mistaken for fancy diamonds, but are so characteristic in their colours that when seen a few times they should be readily recognized again. It is more likely that a diamond that has been artificially coloured blue by electron bombardment might be mistaken for a zircon or an aquamarine, if the blue is deep in colour.

Blue and yellow synthetic rutile is made and cut in Japan, but should not be mistaken for diamond if the precaution of looking for doubling is taken. Blue rutile is highly electro-conductive and could be mistaken for blue Type IIb diamond if this test is applied.

Artificially coloured diamonds and their identification are dealt with in Chapter Nineteen.

Diamonds and Simulants in Jewellery

As a very general principle, diamonds are not set in cheaply-made twentieth-century gold jewellery or even in well-made twentieth-century silver jewellery, so the quality of the setting is a quick indication of whether the stone is a diamond or a simulant. On the other hand, simulants are not infrequently set in good-quality modern jewellery, so the converse is not a good guide.

With older jewellery this rule of thumb does not hold good. From early days to the twentieth century, diamonds were very commonly set in silver and during the time that paste was popular, from about 1700 to 1865, this too was set mainly in silver jewellery, often of the highest quality. In the eighteenth century, paste was not regarded as counterfeit or a simulant but was worn in the highest court circles, by such as Madame de Pompadour and the Empress Eugenie.

From Renaissance times, stones were set in several ways: the closed setting was a rim to hold the stone closely with the base enclosed; the open setting was a similar rim without a bottom; the claw setting was a circlet of claws, which may still have a closed back, to hold the stone; and the pavé (pavement) was where many small stones were set close to each other by drilling holes in the metal to fit the pavilions of the stones and raising small grains of metal around each indentation to hold the stone set in it.

Diamonds were set in open and closed settings but after about mid-sixteenth century, the claw setting came into fashion. In the eighteenth century, claw and pavé settings were most common, the first for larger and more important stones and the second for groups of smaller ones. In the nineteenth century many small diamonds were set in a form known as millegrain, in which the metal used to hold the diamonds was crenelated by drawing a hardened steel wheel round the metal. Another setting is called illusion. A small diamond is set in a larger serrated and polished plate soldered in the claws of the setting.

Paste, on the other hand, was almost invariably close-set during the eighteenth century, the edges of the setting being tightly moulded to the edges of the stones to make them airtight. The reason was to prevent tarnishing of the reflecting foil behind the stone.

Before the eighteenth century most stones, including diamonds, were close-set and foiled at the back to improve their brilliance or deepen their colours. Foiling during the Renaissance was as important an art as cutting is today. Foils of yellow, blue, red or green, were used for tinting diamonds. Another practice was to cover the back of the diamond with lamp black or coloured paint or to set the stone in a bezel painted inside and with a reflector of crystal glass cut in a square behind the stone, according to Cellini.

In reproduction jewellery, crumpling of the foil may sometimes be seen through the stone, but in well-made eighteenth-century paste jewellery, the foil is rarely visible and still remains untarnished today, so that the paste is brilliant enough to be deceiving.

The modern equivalent of foiling, commonly employed for synthetic white spinels or sapphires, is to make the back facets into true mirrors which are then given a protective coating of gilt paint and set in jewellery so that the backs are hidden.

In much early diamond jewellery, the stones have a spot of black paint or pitch applied to the culet, which appears as a black spot when viewed through the table. The black spot also appears on the pastes in the best pieces of eighteenth-century paste jewellery, so is no guide in identification. A few modern diamonds also have the culets blackened (Fig. 20.13). The best guide is the great variety of shapes to which pastes were commonly cut. The finer paste jewellery frequently contains no circular cut stones.

Fig. 20.13. *A modern diamond, the culet of which was blackened by the cutters.*

Platinum became the accepted setting for diamonds at the end of the nineteenth century and a special trade of diamond mounter came into being. However, the rising price of platinum from about mid-twentieth century reduced its use considerably in favour of white gold. Silver persisted as a setting for diamonds in a few pieces of jewellery until the early twentieth century. Gold settings of natural colour for diamonds of good colour degrade the whiteness of the stones but have become popular in modern times when fashion can be more influential than logic. The most satisfactory compromise for diamond rings is a white gold or platinum mount on a yellow gold shank if the whiteness of the stone is to be preserved in yellow gold.

Comparison Constants

The table that follows gives the main constants and other identification features to compare when examining diamond and its substitutes and simulants.

REFERENCES

Gem Testing, by B. W. Anderson, B.Sc., F.G.A. 7th edition (London, 1964).
Gems: Their Sources, Descriptions and Identification, by Robert Webster, F.G.A. 2nd edition (London, 1970).
'Diamonair: A new Diamond Substitute', by Robert Crowingshield. *Jewelers' Circular Keystone* (December, 1969).
Four Centuries of European Jewellery, by Ernle Bradford (London, 1967).
Antique Paste Jewellery, by M. D. S. Lewis (London, 1970).

DIAMOND AND SUBSTITUTES IN APPROXIMATE ORDER OF NEARNESS IN APPEARANCE

	Hardness	Specific Gravity	Refractive Index	Double Refraction	Dispersion	Fluorescence	Transparency to X-rays
Diamond	10	3·52	2·417	none	0·044	usually dull violet to light blue l.u.v.	transparent
Strontium titanate (Fabulite)	5½	5·13	2·41	none	0·200	none	opaque
Paste (typical)	5	3·74	1·63	none	0·031	usually weak bluish or inert l.u.v., stronger blue s.u.v.	opaque
Yttrium aluminium garnet (Diamonair)	8	4·55	1·833	none	0·028	yellow l.u.v. weaker s.u.v.	opaque
Lithium niobate (Linobate)	5	4·64	1·21 – 2·30	0·090	0·120	none	opaque
Rutile (synthetic)	6½	4·25	2·610 – 2·900	0·287	0·300	none	opaque
Zircon	7½	4·69	1·926 – 1·985	0·59	0·039	yellow (mustard) l.u.v., weaker s.u.v.	opaque
Blende	3½	4·09	2·37	none	0·156	none	opaque
Scheelite (inc. synthetic)	5	6·0	1·920 – 1·937	0·017	0·026	none, l.u.v., bright blue s.u.v.	opaque
Spinel (synthetic)	8	3·63	1·727	none	0·020	none, l.u.v., greenish to bluish white s.u.v.	translucent
Sapphire (natural or synthetic)	9	3·99	1·760 – 1·768	0·008	0·018	none – sometimes bluish white s.u.v.	translucent
Topaz	8	3·56	1·612 – 1·622	0·010	0·014	weak yellowish or greenish l.u.v.	translucent
Quartz	7	2·65	1·544 – 1·553	0·009	0·013	none	translucent

l.u.v.: long wave ultra-violet rays. s.u.v.: short wave ultra-violet rays.

Figures in the first five columns are taken with permission from B. W. Anderson's *Gem Testing* (Heywood, London, 1964). The information in the last two columns was kindly provided by Robert Webster.

FOLDING A DIAMOND PAPER

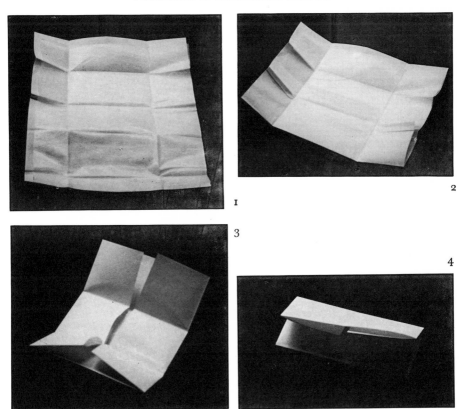

Sequence of folding a diamond parcel paper, the traditional method of carrying polished diamonds. This paper has a white lining paper. It is best to place larger diamonds in a folded piece of lint inside the paper.

APPENDIX 2

THE WORLD'S LARGEST ROUGH DIAMONDS

(more than 324 carats)

Rank	Carats	Name	Discovery Date	Place	Cut into
1.	3,106·00	Cullinan	1905	South Africa	Cullinans I–IX; 96 others
2.	995·20	Excelsior	1893	South Africa	21 gems (largest 69·80)
3.	793·00	Great Mogul	1650	India	Great Mogul (280)
4.	770·00	Woyie River	1945	Sierra Leone	30 gems (largest 31·35)
5.	726·60	Vargas	1938	Brazil	Vargas (48·26) and 22 others
6.	726·00	Jonker	1934	South Africa	Jonker (125·65 and 11 others
7.	650·25	Reitz	1895	South Africa	Jubilee (245·35) and one other
8.	609·25	Baumgold Rough	1923	South Africa	14 gems (sizes unknown)
9.	601·25	Lesotho	1967	Lesotho	17 gems (largest 70)
10.	600·00	Goyaz	1906	Brazil	80-carat gem from one fragment
11.	511·25	Venter	1951	South Africa	32 gems (largest 18)
12.	503·00	Kimberley Rough	1900?	South Africa	Unknown
13.	469·00	Victoria 1884	1884	South Africa	Victoria 1884 (185·00)
14.	455·00	Darcy Vargas	1939	Brazil	Unknown
15.	440·00	Nizam	1835	India	Nizam (277·00)
16.	434·00	Light of Peace	1969	West Africa	To be cut in 1970
17.	428·50	Victoria 1880	1880	South Africa	Victoria 1880 (228·50)
18.	428·50	De Beers	1888	South Africa	De Beers (234·50)
19.	426·50	Ice Queen	1954	South Africa	Niarchos (128·25) and two others
20.	416·25	Berglen	1924	South Africa	Unknown

354

21.	412·50	Broderick	1928	South Africa	Unknown
22.	410·00	Pitt	1701	India	Regent (140·50)
23.	409·00	Presidente Dutra	1946	Brazil	46 gems (largest 9·06)
24.	400·65	Corondel IV	1941	Brazil	Unknown
25.	381·00	Arc	1921	South Africa	Unknown
26.	375·00	Red Cross	1910?	South Africa	Red Cross (205)
27.	354·00	Tiros I	1938	Brazil	Unknown
28.	350·00	Black Diamond of Bahia	1850?	Brazil	Unknown
29.	337·00	Bob Grove	1908	South Africa	Unknown
30.	328·34	Victoria	1943	Brazil	44 gems (largest 30·39)
31.	324·00	Patos	1937	Brazil	Unknown

List by courtesy of N. W. Ayer & Son Inc. New York

355

THE WORLD'S LARGEST POLISHED DIAMONDS

Rank	Carats	Name	Colour	Shape	Present owner or location
1.	530·20	Cullinan I	white	pear	British Crown Jewels – Tower of London
2.	312·40	Cullinan II	white	cushion	British Crown Jewels – Tower of London
3.	280·00	Great Mogul	white	rose cut	Disappeared after 1747
4.	277·00	Nizam	white	dome	Nizam of Hyderabad – 1934
5.	245·35	Jubilee	white	cushion	Paul-Louis Weiller – Paris
6.	234·50	De Beers	yellow	(unknown)	Indian prince – about 1890
7.	228·50	Victoria 1880	yellow	brilliant	Indian prince – about 1882
8.	205·00	Red Cross	yellow	square	Unknown – auctioned in London, 1918
9.	199·60	Orloff	white	rose-cut	Russian Diamond Treasury – Kremlin, Moscow
10.	185·00	Darya-i-Nûr (Iran)	pink	table-cut	Iranian Treasury – Teheran
10.	185·00	Victoria 1884	white	oval	Nizam of Hyderabad – about 1885
12.	183·00	Moon	yellow	brilliant	Unknown – auctioned in London, 1942
13.	152·16	Iranian Yellow A	yellow	cushion	Iranian Treasury – Teheran
14.	150·00	Darya-i-Nûr (Dacca)	white	cushion	Nawab of Dacca – India – 1959
15.	140·50	Regent	white	cushion	The Louvre – Paris
16.	137·27	Florentine	yellow	double rose	Disappeared after World War I
17.	136·50	Queen of Holland	blue	cushion	Indian maharajah – about 1927
18.	135·45	Iranian Yellow B	yellow	cushion	Iranian Treasury – Teheran
19.	128·80	Star of the South	white	oval	Rustomjee Jamsetjee – Bombay – about 1939
20.	128·51	Tiffany	canary	cushion	Tiffany & Co. – New York

No.	Name	Carats	Cut	Colour	Location / History
21.	Niarchos	128·25	pear	white	Stavros P. Niarchos – Greece
22.	Portuguese	127·00	emerald	white	Smithsonian Institution – Washington
23.	Jonker	125·65	emerald	white	Royal Family of Nepal – 1959
24.	Iranian Yellow C	123·93	cushion	yellow	Iranian Treasury – Teheran
25.	Stewart	123·00	brilliant	white	Unknown – cut about 1875
26.	Julius Pam	123·00	(unknown)	white	Unknown – cut about 1890
27.	Iranian Yellow D	121·90	octahedron	yellow	Iranian Treasury – Teheran
28.	Moon of the Mountains	120·00	cushion	white	Disappeared after 1900
29.	Taj-e-Mah	115·06	rose-cut	white	Iranian Treasury – Teheran
30.	Iranian Yellow E	114·28	cushion	yellow	Iranian Treasury – Teheran
31.	Earth Star	111·59	pear	brown	Baumgold Bros. – New York
32.	Cross of Asia	109·26	table-cut	champagne	Unknown – exhibited about 1935
33.	Koh-i-Nûr	108·93	oval	white	British Crown Jewels – Tower of London
34.	Rojtman	107·00	cushion	yellow	Mrs. Marc Rojtman – New York – 1966
35.	Star of Egypt	106·75	emerald	white	Unknown – shown in London Office after 1850
36.	Deepdene	104·88	cushion	yellow	Private owner – 1954
37.	Great Chrysanthemum	104·15	pear	bronze	Julius Cohen – New York
38.	Ashberg	102·00	cushion	yellow	Unknown – sold about 1960
39.	Hastings	101·00	unknown	unknown	Unknown since presentation to George III, 1786
40.	Jacob	100·00	unknown	white	Bank of India – 1956
41.	Star of the East	100·00	pear	white	Unknown since abdication of King Farouk, 1952
42.	Shah of Persia	99·52	cushion	yellow	Private owner – 1965
43.	Cullinan III	94·40	pear	white	British Crown Jewels – Tower of London
44.	Shah	88·70	bar	white	Russian Diamond Treasury – Kremlin, Moscow
45.	Star of Persia	88·00	cushion	yellow	Private owner – 1965
46.	Spoonmaker's	84·00	pear	white	Topkapi Museum – Istanbul
47.	Jahangir	83·00	(unknown)	white	C. Patel – India – 1957
48.	Nepal	79·41	pear	white	Private owner – 1960
49.	Archduke Joseph	78·54	cushion	white	Private owner – 1951
50.	English Dresden	76·50	pear	white	Cursetjee Fardoonji – India – about 1939

THE WORLD'S LARGEST POLISHED DIAMONDS—*continued*

Rank	Carats	Name	Colour	Shape	Present owner or location
51.	72·00	Nepal Pink	pink	cushion	Reported in Nepal, 1959
52.	71·70	Akbar Shah	white	drop	Gaekwar of Baroda – 1867
53.	70·20	Idol's Eye	white	cushion	Harry Levinson – Chicago
54.	70·00	(from Lesotho)	white	emerald	Harry Winston – New York
55.	69·80	(from Excelsior)	white	pear	Unknown – sold by Tiffany, 1903
56.	69·42	Taylor-Burton	white	pear	Elizabeth Taylor (Mrs. Richard Burton)
57.	68·00	Tennant	yellow	(unknown)	James Tennant – 1873
58.	67·89	Transvaal	champagne	pear	Baumgold Bros. – New York
59.	67·50	Black Orloff	gun metal	cushion	Charles F. Winson – New York
60.	64·00	Golden Pelican	yellow	emerald	E. Severy and M. Ginsberg – Antwerp – 1958
61.	63·60	Cullinan IV	white	square	British Crown Jewels – Tower of London
62.	62·50	Jagersfontein	white	pear	Private owner – 1954
63.	61·50	Golden Dawn	yellow	brilliant	Aga Khan – 1926
64.	60·40	Sancy (Patiala)	white	pear	Maharajah of Patiala – 1944
65.	60·25	Prince Edward of York	white	pear	Private owner – 1901
66.	60·00	Nūr-ul-Ain	pink	table-cut	Iranian Treasury – Teheran
67.	56·60	Pam	white	brilliant	Unknown after being shown to Queen Victoria, 1892
	56·60	Porter-Rhodes	white	emerald	Private owner – 1939
69.	55·09	Kimberley	champagne	emerald	Baumgold Bros. – New York
70.	55·00	Baumgold-Brilliant	white	brilliant	Private owner – 1966
	55·00	Sancy (Astor)	white	pear	Viscount Astor – England – 1966
72.	51·00	Eugenie	white	oval	Mrs. N. J. Dady – Bombay – about 1935
73.	50·28	La Favorite	white	(unknown)	Private Owner – 1934
74.	50·00	Cleveland	white	cushion	Unknown – cut in New York, 1884
	50·00	Grand Condé	pink	pear	Condé Museum – Chantilly

List by courtesy of N. W. Ayer & Son Inc. New York

APPENDIX 4

ESTIMATED WORLD PRODUCTION OF DIAMOND 1968
(metric carats)

Country	Gem	Industrial	Total
AFRICA			
Angola	1,250,000	417,000	1,667,187
Central African Republic[e]	183,000	426,000	609,000
Congo (Brazzaville)[e 1 2]	400,000	6,100,000	6,500,000
Congo (Kinshasa)	250,000	12,162,000	12,411,919
Ghana	612,000	1,835,000	2,447,000
Guinea[e]	25,000	75,000	100,000
Ivory Coast	75,000	112,000	187,000
Liberia[1 4]	300,000	450,000	750,166
Lesotho	6,000	6,000	12,000
Sierra Leone	609,000	913,000	1,522,000
South-West Africa[4]	1,636,000	86,000	1,722,259
Tanzania	351,000	351,000	702,423
South Africa, Republic of			
Premier	486,000	1,946,000	2,431,618
De Beers Group[3]	2,307,000	1,888,000	4,194,608
Other	403,000	404,000	807,092
TOTAL AFRICA	8,893,000	27,171,000	36,064,000
OTHER COUNTRIES			
Brazil[e]	175,000	175,000	350,000
Guyana	32,000	33,000	64,569
India	7,000	2,000	9,000
Indonesia	14,000	6,000	20,000
U.S.S.R.[e]	1,600,000	6,400,000	8,000,000
Venezuela	57,000	57,000	114,000
TOTAL OTHER COUNTRIES	1,885,000	6,673,000	8,558,000
GRAND TOTAL	10,778,000	33,844,000	44,622,000

[e] Estimate
[1] Exports
[2] Probable origin Congo (Kinshasa)
[3] Includes 493,908 carats from De Beers alluvial properties in Namaqualand
[4] Probable source Sierra Leone

Figures compiled for *Jewelers Circular–Keystone* by Dr George Switzer, Smithsonian Institution, Washington, DC.

Estimated synthetic diamond grit production in 1969 was 40,000,000 carats.

INDEX